CHANTICLEER
A Study of the French Muse

CHANTICLEER

A Study of the French Muse

BY

J. G. LEGGE

KENNIKAT PRESS, INC./PORT WASHINGTON, N. Y.

CHANTICLEER

First published 1935
Reissued 1969 by Kennikat Press

Library of Congress Catalog Card No: 68-26298
Manufactured in the United States of America

TO THE MEMORY OF
A. D. C.
LOVED OF HIS FRIENDS
LOVED BETTER OF THE GODS

PREFACE

THERE are many in our country who have a fair knowledge of French, but the number of those who can appreciate French poetry, and who can, and do, read it with enjoyment is comparatively small. This book is the effort of one who has derived throughout his life intense enjoyment from this source to enlarge that circle by spreading the knowledge of the form and content, with all its varied charm, of French poetry as it pursues its course through ten centuries of European life and thought. The translation or paraphrase of French verse has attracted English poets and scholars all through the ages, and a collection of delightful poems in English, medieval, Elizabethan, Jacobean, Georgian, and modern, might be got together with which few of the versions in this book, except perhaps for literalness, might hope to compete.

But such an anthology would lack unity of purpose, while any anthology of translations from a foreign language must strike as somewhat cold and lifeless an Englishman ill-versed in the history of the country concerned, knowing little of its climate and natural conditions, its politics, its intellectual development, the changes in its social life, the sort of human beings these foreign poets were and are, and all the action and reaction between one influence and another that go to determine why a particular language took the form it has, and how its literature acquired the substance and shape it presents to a reader of alien origin. An elaborate introduction, if read, with an apparatus of notes and appendices, again if read, can do something, but not enough, to give the book warmth and colour.

When the present author, with this thought in his head, was gloomily contemplating some years ago a selection of his translations from the French, which had occupied him since undergraduate days, with long and lucid intervals during which he attended to his proper business, the idea occurred to him that he might do a useful piece of work if he made his translations, which he had taken infinite pains to keep close to the originals not only in meaning but also in pattern, illustrations in the text of a succinct account of French poetry, chiefly lyrical, from its beginnings to the close of the nineteenth century. Such an account might, he thought, provide the necessary background for the English reader, especially if no opportunity was neglected of bringing into relation with one another the history and the social life of England and France, and of saying a word about each poet himself, so as to give, as it were, to each poem some sort of personality.

He little realized at the time how ambitious was his aim, and how difficult the task he had set himself. After wide and discursive reading for many years, with no set purpose to guide one, and no systematic taking of notes, one finds on sitting down to write how scanty is the supply of exact knowledge stored in one's head. However, he persevered, turned again to his books, and pursued his task for five long years, still working over his translations, with the result that he has produced a little book which he fondly hopes will not fail utterly of its purpose.

He has read much of French criticism, as subtle and as well-informed within its sphere as any in the world; and in committing himself to a judgment upon any author he has been shy of expressing any opinion for which he could find no French warrant. He has also read much of English criticism, and has hesitated before running counter to the views of its great masters. But a man must be permitted to exercise a certain independence. One generation of critics follows another, and too often ignores or sneers at its predecessor. We may safely hope to be excused from deferring too much to the last comer, for he may be regarded in a few years as no better than a Wild Ass stamping o'er some great hunter's head. The accepted critic of every age brings some contribution worth the appreciation of his successors.

The book is not intended as a school book. Nevertheless, as the author carries his mind back to his own later schooldays, he wishes that such a book as this, or such a book as he has tried to make this, had been placed in his hands when his mind was beginning actively to develop, so that he might have ranged over the whole field of a foreign literature and found perhaps some corner of it where he might like to browse on his own. What fun he would have had in fitting the translations into the originals, and how much this pleasant pastime would have taught him in relief from continually plodding through set books with the help of a dictionary!

The author hopes that in the course of his book full acknowledgment is made of the debt he owes to others who have ranged over the fields he has been traversing, and on whom he has drawn. He is, like all Englishmen of his time, enormously indebted to Professor Saintsbury, and it gladdens him to remember that in his youth Walter Pater treated him as a friend. His first French guide in the way of books was *Les Poètes français*, published under the direction of M. Eugène Crépet as far back as 1861, a great work in its day. He was helped when he began specially to study the later poets of last century by Professor Yvon Eccles's *A Century of French Poets*. The *Oxford Book of French Verse* has been his constant companion since its publication in 1907, and the feel of two full and most scholarly French anthologies of French verse is very familiar to him, viz.: Ad. Van Bever and Paul Léautaud's *Poètes d'aujourd'hui*, and G. Walch's *Poètes français contemporains*.

He has from time to time consulted kind friends in Oxford, and among these he would like to mention Sir Edmund Chambers, Professor Ewert, Monsieur Berthon, and Mr. L. F. Powell. But above all he owes three special debts. The first is to Mr. E. A. Preece of the Alsop High School, Liverpool, and sometime of the universities of Bristol, Lille, and Strasbourg, who went through a draft of the book, queried this point or that, indicated gaps that had to be filled, and gave references to authorities that ought to be consulted, several of which proved to be invaluable. Then he has gained much from the opportunities afforded by that hive of modern language studies, the Taylorian Institution at Oxford. Finally, he shares with many others the incalculable debt owed to the Literary Supplement to *The Times*, which has now for over thirty years kept English readers in touch with what is new and important in the literature and literary criticism of the world outside our island.

A word must be added about the Appendix. This forms in itself a select little French anthology, for it is designed to contain the originals of all the poems translated. The author hopes that where copyright exists he has in all cases obtained the necessary authorization; any unintentional omission he will much regret.

The following list indicates the copyright poems, and the owners who have kindly given permission for reprinting them:

The *Mercure de France* for poems by Villiers de l'Isle-Adam, Henri de Régnier, Arthur Rimbaud, Albert Samain, Jean Moréas, Charles Guérin, Jules Laforgue, François Jammes, and Grégoire le Roy. The last-named poet has sent a cordial letter, expressing in too generous terms his appreciation of the translation of his poem which appears on p. 270.
The Librairie Alphonse Lemerre for poems by Leconte de Lisle, Sully Prudhomme, J.-M. de Heredia, and Théodore de Banville.
The Librairie Albert Messein for poems by Paul Verlaine and Tristan Corbière.
The Librairie Delagrave for poems by Victor Hugo.
The Librairie Hachette and the University of Lille for the poem by Auguste Angellier.
The *Nouvelle Revue Française*, and the poet's heirs, for the poems by Stéphane Mallarmé.

To conclude, the author has to thank (i) the Delegates of the Oxford University Press for permission to avail himself of a number of texts appearing in the *Oxford Book of French Verse*, and other works published by them; (ii) the Publishers' Reader, his own wife and one daughter for their great assistance in correcting proofs, and another daughter for the drawing of Chanticleer on the title-page.

J. G. LEGGE.

17th August 1935.

CONTENTS

CHAPTER I

No modern literature possesses a poetic literature so vast in extent, so high in general quality, as French. Since the eleventh century its stream has flowed unceasingly until to-day. We may rightly boast the supremacy of our own poetic literature, with Chaucer, Shakespeare, Spenser, Milton, Pope, Wordsworth, Shelley, and Keats to represent us on the heights of Parnassus, not to mention a host of others only less distinguished than they. Italy has the great name of Dante towering above all names save that of Shakespeare, and in the last century and a half Germany may boast in Goethe a name above all modern names. But we have to remember that France had the start of us all, was supreme from the eleventh to near the end of the thirteenth century, and that, as Professor Saintsbury has asserted, 'for something like three hundred years England, Germany, Italy, and, more doubtfully and to a smaller extent, Spain were content for the most part to borrow the matter and the manner of their literary work from France.'

Moreover, if we claim in poetry the absolute supremacy for our own country, he would be a bold critic who claimed for the body of our prose literature superiority over, or even equality with, that of France. If, again, we take the Arts, and concede to Italy or to Holland the palm in painting, and to Germany in music, let it not be forgotten, as it too often is, that in what many regard as the greatest art of all, viz. architecture, France is supreme. Such monuments in stone as the French reared in their countless cathedrals, churches, and castles, from the eleventh even to the sixteenth century, with their enrichment in sculpture and coloured glass, are prodigies of human achievement which have, and have had, no rivals in the world.

The French language, like Italian and Spanish, is a daughter of Latin. But though any one with a fair knowledge of Latin can learn in a few weeks of close application to read both Italian and Spanish without great diff.culty, this is far from the case with French. France indeed was Romanized with comparative ease, both in language and in political and social institutions. The transformation was gradually accomplished from the south, and Aquitaine in the south-west, to north: the earlier penetration of Roman influence was naturally in the south, and there the ground was in a measure prepared for it by the yet earlier colonization of the Mediterranean coast, with Marseilles as the centre, by Greek settlers. The great Provençal poet of modern days, the handsome Frédéric Mistral, used laughingly to boast that he, like his comely neighbours, the people of Arles, owed his good looks to the fact that he came of Greek stock.

But however easily the Romanization of southern France took place, and though the vocabulary and grammatical structure of French may be almost entirely Latin, the perfervid genius of the Celt, backed by the practical sense of a keen-witted trading and farming community in the south and south-west, so modified by well-recognized rules of linguistic development the words and grammatical forms of the mother-tongue as to make quite a new garment out of old materials. In the fifth century the decomposition of Latin was accelerated by the Germanic invasions that followed on the failure of Rome to maintain her hold over her vast empire. Nevertheless it took nearly a thousand years for the rustic Latin in popular use to develop into the language we call French.

The first stage was the formation of a Romance language, with actual Latin words and Latin features, but with an unmistakable French twist in it that points on to the language into which it was to develop. That this Romance language was firmly established in the seventh century is clearly shown by the appointment in that century of a bishop of Noyon expressly chosen because of his knowledge of it. But it should not be forgotten that, while a new language was in process of unconscious growth, the importance of literary culture asserted itself among courtiers and ecclesiastics and efforts were made to maintain the standard of Latin as the literary language, and to save it from the corruption of the colloquial language now gaining ground day by day.

In the eighth century a notable effort was made in this direction by one so august as Charlemagne himself, and the chief of his instruments was Alcuin, an Englishman born and educated at York, to whom the emperor put himself and his family, his court, and indeed his empire, to school. Charlemagne had met him at Parma in 780, was impressed by him, and persuaded him to come to his court. In France he remained, though with two visits to his own country, until, as Abbot of St. Gregory of Tours, he died in 804. Alcuin did more for Charlemagne than act as his right hand in the revival of learning. He was more than a scholar and a theologian, he was a poet as well, as witness the lyrics by him quoted by Miss Waddell in her *Medieval Latin Lyrics*. And he did more as a poet than write lyrics, he did much to found the great legend that grew up round the name of Charlemagne; for, as M. Pauphilet has said: 'When Alcuin in the poems that he dedicates to Charles calls him David . . . he traces already the plan of the future legend . . . he indicates forever the two aspects under which the figure of Charlemagne will always be idealized: Biblical King and Roman Emperor.'

The Romance language had many dialectal variations, but the two main divisions of it were into what are called the *langue d'oc* in the south, and the *langue d'oïl* in the north. It would naturally be supposed that the first and main development of poetry, certainly of lyric poetry, would be in Provence, and the soft, luxurious, earlier civilized south, the home of the troubadours. As regards lyric poetry, though not epic verse, this was certainly the case. Each of the gay little courts of Provence was the centre of a pleasure-loving, highly cultivated society of women, as well as of men. The high position held by women helped indeed to develop the theory of *amour courtois*, or courtly love, the fine flower of Provençal invention which spread through civilized Europe, and did something to soften the manners of an age of feudalism. This courtly love was a theory of the ennobling virtue of a love so refined that it might even be regarded as incompatible with marriage, which constituted a science and a code of love, and gave to woman a dominating position.

Princes and knights and others of high degree vied with one another in the composition of the most elaborate songs of courtly love, in which they poured out their devotion to the lady of their ideal love. These songs of admirable art, and the theory of courtly love, captivated poets in Italy and the minnesingers of Germany, and spread to Spain and Portugal, northern France, and through northern France to the English court. The most signal tribute to the importance of Provençal literature and its influence is paid by Dante, who quotes freely in his *De vulgari eloquentia*, the treatise by which he sought to establish Italian as a literary language, from the Provençal poets as exemplars, and among them from Bertrand de Born, Gérard de Borneil, Thibaut, Count of Champagne and King of Navarre, and Arnaut Daniel, whom Petrarch, following Dante, styled *gran maestro d'amor*. More than this, the relations of Dante to his Beatrice, and Petrarch to his Laura, are among the outstanding examples of the influence of the Provençal cult of courtly love.

Nevertheless, despite the brilliant success at the outset of the *langue d'oc* of Provence, it was the *langue d'oïl* of the hardy north, and particularly that dialect of it associated with the Île de Fance, the cradle of the kings of France, that ultimately prevailed. This could not be otherwise, for it was when, in 987, the French-speaking, French-thinking peers of France, brushing aside the claims of the last representative of the worn-out race of the great German emperor, Charlemagne, elected as their king Hugh Capet, Count of Paris and Duke of the Franks, that French history really began. Hugh Capet's small domain, a broad strip running from Orleans and Sens in the south to Abbeville in the north, was in the fullness of time by force of arms, by diplomacy and intrigue, and by profitable marriages, to absorb all the feudal possessions of his brother princes and create the France we know.

As for the south, the final blow that destroyed at once its political importance and its characteristic literary and social culture was dealt at the beginning of the thirteenth century by Pope Innocent III, when our English barons were in arms to wrest Magna Charta from King John. Against the heresies of the Albigenses the princes of the north were called on crusade—their leader Simon de Montfort, father of our own Simon de Montfort, who played his heroic part in the reign of Henry III. The crusade crushed the heretics, destroyed the independence of Toulouse, the seat of what was left of the earliest civilization in France, that of Aquitaine, and, as Braunschvig dryly remarks, 'the victorious invaders established the Inquisition in the south: and that was the end of a meridional civilization.'

One of the few examples that survive of the Romance language in real literary form is the charming poem known as the *Song of St. Eulalie*, which dates from about 880. St. Eulalie, born at Barcelona in 289, was martyred at Rome in 303, where she had dared to insult the pagan deities in the presence of the Roman praetor himself. The song was probably composed soon after the supposed discovery of the martyr's bones at Barcelona in 878. Here is an English version of it:

(1)
THE SONG OF ST. EULALIE

A damsel virtuous was Eulalie,
And fair of form, fairer in mind was she.
   The enemies of God would vanquish her,
Would make her choose the devil, him to serve.
   These evil counsellors she did despise,
Would have her God renounce who dwells on high;
   Not gold or silver, and not jewels rare,
No royal threat of king, or urgent prayer,
   Nothing could ever bend her to their will,
The child who needs must love God's service still.
   And so before Maximian was she haled,
Who ruled the pagan people in those days.
   He bade her do what she could not endure,
To wit, the name of Christian to abjure.
   She summoned all her elemental strength;
Through tortures manifold she meekly went,
   That she might keep her soul and body pure.
So died she honest and of good repute.
   They cast her in the fire, soon to consume,
But being without sin she could not burn.
   The pagan king this sign could not convert;
He bade them with a sword strike off her head.
   Her cruel fate the maid did not resist;
Content to quit this world, she called on Christ.
   In likeness of a dove to heaven she flew.
Now pray that she may deign to pray for us,
   That to us all Christ may be merciful,
And after death receive us in his house,
   As for his mercy's sake!

In this version it will be noted that all the couplets are not strictly in rhyme; but all are in assonance, i.e. the final syllables of each couplet may or may not be in actual rhyme, but they always play upon the same vowel sound or some modification of it. Rhyme proper did not establish itself in French poetry for many a long year yet.

By the eleventh century France had at last a fully developed and separate literary language of its own. In that century began a vast output of epic and narrative verse that lasted for three hundred years, much of which, despite the continuous efforts of societies in which distinguished French scholars have enrolled themselves, remains still in manuscript. The mass of this epic literature will be briefly indicated by a list of the main divisions into which it may be classified, on the authority of the thirteenth-century poet of Arras, Jean Bodel:

> Ne sont que trois matières à nul homme entendant,
> De France, de Bretagne et de Rome la grant.

I. The *Chansons de Geste*, epic poems recounting the exploits of Charlemagne and other French heroes. Of these the earliest and most famous is the *Song of Roland*; and it is in connection with this that we shall discuss the very interesting question of origins.

II. The Breton Romances, recounting the legends largely derived from Cornwall and Wales of King Arthur and his knights. Of these, which show the strength of the Celtic influence in France, the most authentic as in the epic vein are versions of the story of Tristan and Yseult by two Norman or Anglo-Norman poets, Béroul (1150) and Thomas (1170), both poems unfortunately incomplete. Of Thomas's poem translations into several European languages were made, and the German one by Gottfrid of Strasburg was a source drawn on by Wagner for his famous music-drama *Tristan und Isolde*. In a more artificial vein the easy, fluent, graceful Chrétien de Troyes, most admired of twelfth-century poets, did much to popularize these Celtic legends, and of his *Charette* we shall have a word to say later. In his *De vulgari eloquentia* Dante refers to the 'exquisite legends of King Arthur,' and twice in his great poem he touches on the love of Lancelot and Guenevere.

III. Romances of Antiquity, covered by Jean Bodel's *matière de Rome la grant*. Of these the outstanding ones are (i) the *Romance of Alexander*, which extends to 20,000 lines of twelve syllables each (whence the name of the most characteristic French line, the Alexandrine), and (ii) the *Romance of Troy*, with about 30,000 lines in eight-syllable verse.

Out of all this mass of epic and narrative verse let us dwell for a few moments on the first and greatest of them all, the *Song of Roland*. The author of it is unknown, but he was almost without doubt a Norman, and the precise date of it is unknown, though it is to be accepted as a work of the eleventh century, and probably of the last quarter of it. The earliest manuscript of it, generally accepted as the most reliable text that exists, was written by an Anglo-Norman scribe in the twelfth century, and is one of the treasures of the Bodleian Library at Oxford.

The poem, which extends to over 4,000 lines, and is written in stanzas of ten-syllable verse, each stanza in assonance, gives a long account of the catastrophe which occurred during a supposed crusade of Charlemagne against the Saracens of Spain, viz. the tragic end of the heroic defence by Charlemagne's rearguard under the command of his nephew, Roland, of the Pass or Roncevaux, perhaps the most romantic name in all legendary history. Roland, with all his peers, his friend Oliver, the fighting Archbishop Turpin and the rest, perished in the desperate struggle against overwhelming odds; but Roland himself, the last survivor, when mortally wounded, spent his last breath in blowing such a blast on his ivory horn to recall Charlemagne from his onward march, as put the Saracens to flight, and brought down on their heads the dire vengeance of the king, and on the traitor Ganelon, who laid the trap for Roland, his well-merited end.

The *Song of Roland* is no work of the high poetic quality of Homer's *Iliad*, that swells and subsides like the ocean itself, or of Virgil's *Aeneid*, with its easy flowing grace and vigour, high solemnity, and mingled notes of great endeavour, manly courage, and the passion and the pathos at the heart of human life. But its rude stanzas, almost childlike simplicity, sledge-hammer blows of direct appeal to the emotions, with here and there a picturesque touch or a note of wild lament, give it a real greatness of its own. The debates both among the Saracen emirs and between Charles and his peers are dramatic enough, the characters of the great king and Roland and Oliver, Archbishop Turpin, and the traitor Ganelon are finely drawn. Wonderfully true to life is the description of the quarrel between Roland and Oliver, pathetic the death scenes, strange and terrible the account of the end of Ganelon, whom most of the peers of France are for pardoning, since Roland is dead, and neither gold nor vengeance on the repentant traitor will buy back his life. But after the ordeal of combat between two of them, in which Ganelon's sponsor is killed, his death is determined upon. Bound hands and feet to four horses he is torn in pieces, and his thirty hostages are hanged on a tree. No horror of the awful scene is spared; indeed, the anatomical details of all the death scenes in the poem are a feature of it.

But the poem is not so bleak and bare as sometimes described. Picturesque touches abound, and the poet revels in the sunlight. Here is the romantic description of the Saracen emir's fleet at sea:

En sum cez maz e en cez haltes vernes
Asez i ad carbuncles e lanternes;
La sus amunt pargetent tel luiserne
Par la noit la mer en est plus bele,
E cum il vienent en Espaigne la tere,
Tut li païs en reluist e esclairet.

At the mast-head and on the prows on high
Hang lanterns and carbuncles [1] plenteously;
Which from above cast forward such a light
As makes the sea more beautiful by night,
And when against the Spanish coast they ride
The country all around is clear and bright.

When Roland gazes on Durendal, his sword, he exclaims:

E! Durendal, cum es bele e clere e blanche!
Cuntre soleill si luises e reflambes!

Ah, Durendal, how burnisht, white and fair!
Against the sun how dost thou flash and flame!

[1] The carbuncle, garnet, or ruby was supposed to glow in the dark.

The rising sun strikes the army:

> Esclargiz est li vespres e li jurz.
> Cuntre le soleil reluisent cil adub,
> Osbercs e helmes i getent grant flabur,
> E cil escuz, ki ben sunt peinz a flurs,
> E cil espiez, cil oret gunfanun.

> Night clears away, clearer the daylight grows.
> Against the sun flash weapons all arow,
> Flames on the hauberks and the helmets glow,
> On shields with all their painted flowers, also,
> On lances and on pennons gay with gold.

But the next stanza opens sombrely:

> Halt sunt li pui e tenebrus e grant,
> Li val parfunt e les ewes curant.

> Massive the mountains, shadowy and high,
> Deep are the valleys, and the torrents swift.

When the great archbishop, after prodigies of valour, yields up his life, the poet exclaims:

> Par granz batailles e par mult bels sermons
> Cuntre paiens fut tuz tens campiuns.

> By doughty deeds and sermons eloquent
> Against the pagans champion aye was he.

And Roland cries:

> E! gentilz hom, chevaler de bon aire,
> Hoi te cumant al Glorius celeste.
> Jamais n'ert hume plus volenters le serve.
> Dès les apostles ne fut hom tel prophete
> Pur lei tenir e pur humes atraire.

> Ah, gentleman, knight of a noble line,
> I yield thee to the Glorious One on high.
> Never will man serve Him more cheerfully.
> Since the apostles has no prophet risen
> So strong in faith, so apt men's hearts to win.

*B

The following versions of two of the best-known passages in the poem will give a fuller indication of its character. The first is taken from the long-drawn-out agony of Roland's death:

(2)

THE DEATH OF ROLAND

When Roland feels his sight is going fast,
He rises to his feet as best he can;
His face has lost the colour that it had.
A stone of colour brown before him lay.
Thereat he strikes ten blows in grief and rage;
The steel grates, but it breaks not, nor is scarred.
'Ah!' cries the count, 'St. Mary to mine aid!
Ah! my good Durendal, on you 'tis hard;
Now that I die, for you I 've no more care.
Through you how many battles have I gained,
And what great kingdoms in the dust have laid,
That Charles, he of the long white beard, now sways!
May no man claim you with a coward's heart!
Ne'er will there be your like in holy France.'

Count Roland feels that death has got him now:
From head unto the heart death creepeth down.
Then underneath a pine apace he goes,
And on the turf face forward lays him down;
Neath him he places sword and ivory horn.
He turns his head to face the pagan folk:
This has he done because his will was strong
That Charles may say, and with him all his host,
He died, the gentle count, with victory won.
Feebly and oft he doth his faults recount,
And for his sins holds out his glove to God.

There lies Count Roland underneath a pine;
Spain-ward to turn his face has been his will.
Of many things the memory comes to him,
Of all the realms he won, like conquering king,
Of his sweet France, of all his kith and kin,
Of Charlemagne, his lord, who nurtured him.

At thought of these he can but weep and sigh.
But of himself he must take reckoning,
And, praying God for grace, recounts his sins:
'Father of truth, the One who never lies,
Who from the dead bade Lazarus arise,
And Daniel in the lions' den bestrid,
Save Thou my soul from fearful penalties
For sins I have committed in my life!'
His right-hand glove to God he lifteth high,
Which from his hand St. Gabriel receives.
Upon his arm he holds his head inclined,
And with hands joined is gone his end to win.
God sends to him his angel Cherubin,
[St. Raphael] and St. Michael du Péril;
St. Gabriel, to join them, comes thereby.
They bear the count's soul up to Paradise.

The second is the brief, naïve, and yet touching account of the
death of Aude, Roland's betrothed, and sister of Oliver, his
friend, when Charlemagne returns to France after avenging the
hero, and tells her of his death:

(3)

The Death of Aude

The emperor is home again from Spain,
And comes to Aix his fairest seat in France.
He mounts the palace steps, enters the hall.
There comes before him Aude, that lady fair.
'Where's Roland, the great captain?' so she says,
'That he would take me for his wife he sware.'
Thereat was Charles beset with grief and pain;
His eyes shed tears, he grips his long white beard:
'Sister, dear friend, of one now dead you ask.
For him I'll give to you noble exchange:
Louis it is, nor better can I name.
He is my son, and will my marches have.'
Aude answers: 'What you say to me is strange.
God grant not, nor his angels, nor his saints,
That after Roland living I remain!'

Her colour flies, at Charles's feet she falls,
And straightway dies.   May Christ receive her saul!
For her they weep and mourn, the peers of France.

So Aude the fair unto her end has gone.
The king imagines that she has but swooned;
He pities her and weeps, the emperor.
He takes her hands to raise her from the ground;
Back on her shoulders, see, her head sinks down.
When Charles is ware she 's dead whom now he holds
Straightway four countesses he summons forth:
Unto a nunnery her body 's borne;
All night they watch by her until the morn.
Fair burial by an altar they bestow.
To her the king much and great honour showed.

Now, the slender historical basis for this great national epic
is the massacre in 778 of the rearguard of Charlemagne's army
by the Basques on his return from an expedition of doubtful
success into Spain, an expedition undertaken possibly on the
invitation of one of two rival Saracen factions in Spain.   Legend
must have been at work to provide the poet of the *Song of Roland*
with the rich detail of his poem, which makes the catastrophe an
episode in a Holy War or crusade, converts the Basques into
Saracens, makes a venerable figure, with a beard like Aaron's,
of Charlemagne aged but thirty-six in 778, and describes as
living in that year Ogier already dead, Ganelon and Girard de
Roussillon, who belong to the ninth century, and Joffroy d'Anjou
and Richard of Normandy who belong to the tenth century, and
even includes among Roland's conquests with the help of his
trusty sword, Durendal, England, Scotland, Ireland, and Wales!
How the legend arose is still the subject of debate.   The
original theory was that the poem was strung together, much like
the *Iliad* on the Wolfian hypothesis, out of the popular songs or
lays recited by minstrels and embodying legends of Germanic
origin, dating back possibly to the mists of antiquity.   But
another theory has been widely popular since it was developed
with infinite skill and research, and most eloquently expounded
by that artist in scholarship, M. J. Bédier.
The period during which the national epics were incubated,

and towards the end of which they made their appearance, viz. the tenth and eleventh centuries, was one of great political and religious movement, the end of the Carolingian empire, the great age of church-building, and of pilgrimages to famous shrines, furnished with sacred relics calling for adoration, pilgrimages culminating at the close of the eleventh century in the first crusade. The pilgrim routes were punctuated with sanctuaries, each with its complement of clerics anxious to co-operate with the *jongleurs*, or minstrels, who enlivened the pilgrims on their way by exploiting the sanctity, and the treasures of each particular shrine. And so, according to M. Bédier's ingenious and well-worked-out scheme, each shrine became the seed-bed of legend, or, in other words, the shrine preceded the legend.

Roncevaux was on the route to one of the most famous of all shrines, that of St. James of Compostella at Santiago, and so Roncevaux and the stages approaching it became the centres of legend about the great battle of 15th August 778, and the majestic figure of Charlemange and his supposed nephew, Roland, the hero of the disastrous day.

Recently, however, more than one scholar,[1] reverting in a measure to the first theory, has taken the view that legend long preceded the shrine, and has adduced arguments, not less cogent than those of M. Bédier, for believing that the poet of the *Chanson de Roland* worked upon songs, ballads, or earlier and ruder experiments in epic, whether orally transmitted or recorded in lost Latin or Romance script, all connected with the vast legend that grew up round Charlemagne. The poet, selecting or only interested in the episode of Roland, built up out of these earlier materials his masterpiece. Of these primitive sources none remain, but, if we may believe William of Malmesbury and Wace, verses from among them were chanted before the battle of Hastings, nigh three hundred years after Roncevaux, to hearten the knighthood of Normandy. As to origins, therefore, the doctors disagree, and the debate will still go on.

The *Song of Roland* and the other great national epics were composed no doubt for the delectation of castle and hall, but early appeared imitations or travesties of them, evidently designed

---

[1] See M. R. Fawtier's *La Chanson de Roland*, 1933; also M. A. Pauphilet in *Romania*, 234, April 1933. The author owes these two references to his daughter, Miss M. D. Legge.

to reach a popular audience. The *Song of Roland* was followed by a short epic, the *Pilgrimage of Charlemagne*, recounting his fantastic adventures and grotesque diversions on his way to Jerusalem, and on his return by way of Constantinople, neither of which places he ever visited. Both Gaston Paris and Bédier see in this poem a vein of parody, which show that a jovial and prosperous middle class was now to be catered for by way of literary entertainment, as well as princes, nobles, knights, their womenkind, and their retinues. The *Pilgrimage* was undoubtedly the joint invention of clerics and minstrels, composed to tickle the fancy of the vast crowds who flocked to the great summer fair at Saint-Denis, whose abbey was a treasure-house of relics.

Similarly it is difficult, in connection with the Breton romances, not to detect a note of comedy in Chrétien de Troyes's *Le Chevalier à la Charette*. It is true that Chrétien began this poem at the instance of Marie de Champagne, like her mother, Eleanor of Aquitaine, a great upholder of the cult of courtly love. But here we have vividly displayed the extravagances of that artificial cult. We are told how Lancelot placed himself in such absolute subjection to his lady-love that he was ready not only to face any danger, but also to submit to any indignity in her behalf. When Guenevere is carried off, and Lancelot in pursuit of her loses his horse, he defies all laws of chivalry, mounts a cart driven by a dwarf to continue his journey, and endures the scoffs and sneers of all who see him installed in what was for one of his high degree a travelling pillory. And he is made to suffer even worse indignities for his lady's sake until he finally rescues her.

All this must have amused a wider circle than that immediately surrounding Marie de Champagne and her noble friends. A wider circle too than the immediate court of Henry II and Eleanor in England must have welcomed with enthusiasm the poems of Marie de France, a contemporary of Chrétien de Troyes and his rival in popularity. This Frenchwoman domiciled in England dedicated [1] her versions of Breton legend, whether derived from Brittany, Cornwall, or Wales, to Eleanor's husband, Henry II, as, in all probability, she did the Fables she also wrote to William, Earl of Salisbury, Henry's son by Fair Rosamund.

Space fails to do justice to the charm and importance of her

[1] See M. J. Bédier in *Revue des Deux Mondes*, October 1891.

poetry. Suffice it to say that in her simple style she wrote her poems to be *read* by the closely watched, high-born ladies of her time, immured within their castle walls, and wearing out as best they could their time in the absence of their lords by the indulgence of their amorous fancies; for the love that was the burden of her lays was not the courtly love of the knightly troubadours with all its artifice and etiquette, but the passionate love that throbs through the great Provençal *alba,* to be quoted later, a love that absolves from all moral and conventional restraint those well enough born, and handsome, brave, or beautiful enough to claim its privileges, a love which, however apparently illicit, however crude, however cruel in its manifestations, is condoned by a Church that could only exist in fairyland. It was in the Breton tales that she found and gave out to the world of her time the element of the fairy tale with fairy women, nightingales, goshawks, swans, white hinds, and were-wolves, weird and mysterious, now terrifying, now enchanting, which has ever since afforded one of the resources of idyllic poetry.

Here are ten lovely lines from her *Lai du Chievrefoil,* where she tells how Tristram, hiding in a wood on the way to Tintagel, schemes to guide Yseult to him by placing in her path a branch of hazel split in two with his name carved on either face. Thus he tells his parable of the Woodbine and the Hazel:

> Cume del chievrefoil esteit
> Ki a la coldre se perneit:
> Quant il est si laciez e pris
> E tuz entur le fust s'est mis,
> Ensemble poeent bien durer;
> Mes ki puis les vuelt desevrer,
> La coldre muert hastivement
> E li chievrefoilz ensement.
> 'Bele amie, si est de nus:
> Ne vus sanz mei ne jeo sanz vus!'

> As with the woodbine must it be
> That reaches for the hazel-tree:
> When as the tree is close embraced
> And round a branch the flower enlaced,
> Long may they flourish, two in one.

But, torn apart, they 're soon fordone,
The hazel fadeth soon away
The woodbine dies the self-same day;
Even so, fair friend, lost should we be,
Thou without me, I without thee.

It is not extravagant to claim that since Marie de France no poet has told his tale with more economy and with more simple, unaffected grace. And worth noting, as a sign of her widespread and well-merited popularity, is the fact that early in the fourteenth century appeared a Middle English translation of one of her poems, *Le Fraisne*, or *The Ash-tree*, which tells the story of twin sisters, one of whom is married by the Archbishop of Dol to some noble lord, who for years has been living with her sister in ignorance of their relationship. The discovery is made on the night of the wedding, and next day the complacent archbishop dissolves the first marriage, and unites in a second marriage the rightful pair.

As education spread a mass of popular literature soon made its appearance, some of it supposedly instructive, some moralizing, some satirical, and some with an element of coarse humour. There are the *Bestiaries*, moralizing treatises on beasts. There are the *Romances of Reynard the Fox*, examples of that form of literature which has persisted throughout the ages, the fable with animal characters. Famous has always been the cunning of the fox, to which the finest tribute was paid in the eighteenth century by the greatest of all German poets, Goethe himself, in his *Reineke Fuchs*, which it is worth while learning German in order to read. There are the *Fabliaux*, depicting most realistically racy scenes in the life of the ordinary folk of the time; they are spicy enough, and the frequency with which a priest is the butt shows, like the later portion of the *Romance of the Rose*, of which we speak in the next chapter, that all was not simple piety in what has been called the age of faith.

It has not been possible in discussing, however briefly, the origins of French poetry, and its sources from northern as well as southern France, to leave out of account the great mass of epic and narrative verse. But the way is now clear to approach what comes more closely within the proper compass of this book, viz. a brief study of the lyrical and other verse that make up the *corpus* of the shorter poems of France. French lyric poetry makes its appearance in the twelfth century, and becomes fairly plentiful in the thirteenth. How far back this takes us in the history of our own country will be realized if we recall the fact that these two centuries cover the period between the accession of Henry I almost to the close of the reign of Edward I.

A personage of peculiar interest in connection with the poetical development of the period was Eleanor of Aquitaine, who, after her divorce from Louis VII of France, became the wife of our Henry II. Henry already possessed Anjou, Touraine, Maine, and Normandy, and his marriage with Eleanor added Poitou and Guienne to the vast French domains of the English king. Eleanor, as Gaston Paris tells us, was a lady of lively and poetic temperament, and she nursed the cult of *l'amour courtois*, courtly love, and the poetry which embodied it in the courts of France and England, as did her daughters in their smaller circles at Rheims and Blois. We have already described this theory of courtly love, and indicated its place of origin in Provence, the home of the troubadours. But, thanks to Eleanor's interest, the torch was soon handed by the troubadours of the south to the trouvères of the north, and many of the examples of early lyric that have survived come from the more northerly portion of what we now know as France.

This early literature lay neglected for centuries, and indeed it was not until well on in the nineteenth century that scholars began to show some interest in the mass of rare old manuscripts buried in continental libraries, public or private. Germans were early at work, e.g. Karl Bartsch of Heidelberg; and the most distinguished of French pioneers, Gaston Paris, roundly reproached his fellow-countrymen for their neglect of the treasures of their own literary past, a neglect he was himself, with a crowd of scholarly followers, prominent among them Mario Roques, nobly to redeem. The result has been that the patient work of the last seventy or eighty years has opened out a fascinating new field to lovers of poetry, and the most attractive introduction to it known to the present writer is to be found in Sir E. K. Chambers's essay [1] on *Some Aspects of Medieval Literature*, included in Chambers and Sidgwick's *Early English Lyrics*, published by A. H. Bullen in 1907.

[1] Reprinted in his *Sir Thomas Wyatt and Other Studies*, 1934.

During the last few years an added impetus has been given to this comparatively new study by the enchanting works of Miss Helen Waddell, *Medieval Latin Lyrics* and *The Wandering Scholars*. In the former book she gives one cause to realize how much the early French lyric owed to medieval Latin lyric, and carries the source of the latter back even beyond Ausonius, the silver Latin poet, whose verse at times has the modern feeling commonly called 'romantic' as opposed to 'classic,' to the classical age itself. Those who care to follow their exploration of sources a few centuries further back will not do amiss to read a fine, old-fashioned, early Victorian piece of scholarship, now forgotten by most, Macaulay's introduction to his *Lays of Ancient Rome*. In *The Wandering Scholars* Miss Waddell tells the story of how these *vagantes*, despite the ecclesiastical training of most of them, carried on, and spread abroad in their wanderings, the passionate and secular and very human tradition of pagan times. Versions of a few examples of these early French lyrics will be found later in this chapter. But those who wish to roam more at large among them may be invited to turn to the fine translations in Mr. Abbott's *Early French Medieval Lyrics*, recently published by Constable, a book which has much of the charm of Miss Waddell's *Medieval Latin Lyrics*. In French the pleasant guides to seek are M. A. Jeanroy's *Origines de la Poésie lyrique en France au moyen âge*, and his two recently published volumes, *La Poésie lyrique des Troubadours*.

Admittedly the *chansons courtois*, among whose authors were not only nobles and knights, but even anointed kings, such as our Richard I and Thibaut, King of Navarre, were not written for a popular audience; but for very restricted and courtly circles, by authors well skilled in the arts of writing and composition. A favourite pastime at the Provençal courts and the courts of Queen Eleanor and the feudal nobility of her time was the writing of love songs of the most highly sophisticated kind and most intricate form, where Love's humble vassal, nobleman, knight, squire, or page, pours out his praises of the liege lady to whose service he is vowed, from whom he can hope for no favour in return, and yet to whom he must maintain a plaintive, tearful loyalty to the end. This *fine amour* or *amour courtois*, though the origin of the romantic love that has permeated literature up to the present century, must have soon become in itself little more than a literary convention, co-existing, as in Petrarch's case, with a physical love of a more robust nature. Queen Eleanor herself can have been no prude, and how pitiless she was, according to legend, to her second husband's light-of-love, fair Rosamund!

It has to be confessed that many of the *chansons courtois* are stilted and artificial to a degree. But here is the version of one by Richart de Semilli of Paris, a poet of the twelfth century, with a real lilt to it, and no more exaggeration of sentiment than was admitted to nineteenth-century verse. The version, though written in a simpler metre than the original, endeavours to preserve its pattern:

(4)

A Song

'Tis love will set me singing,
　My fair one's praise to tell,
I 'm off in all abandon
　To serve and love her well.
Much has she made me suffer,
　No gleam of hope will show,
'Tis only scorn she offers;
　Alas, I 've loved her so!
　Lady, how happy will it be,
　The day your love is given to me.

I 've never loved another
　Save her for whom I sing,
And, well I know, none other
　Such love again will bring.
Sweet one I prize so dearly,
　You know that, for your part,
Soon as your heart it pleases
　Will cease my bitter smart.
　Lady, long since I 've urged my plea;
　When will your love be given to me?

My lady, richly dowered,
　A word within your ear:
Though high may be your value,
　Of pride God keep you clear!

Accost with kindly greeting
　　All men both great and small;
You will not always find us
　　So instant in our call.
　　Lady, who holds my heart in fee,
　　When will your love be given to me?

If you have years in plenty,
　　For you will come a day
When old age lies in waiting,
　　And all will hear you say:
'Alas, how I was foolish,
　　Who loved not in my prime
When many lovers sought me,—
　　The scorn of all in time!'
　　Lady, loved in all loyalty,
　　When will your love be given to me?

Go, song, and to that beauty,
　　The radiant-featured, fly,
And bear to her this message:
　　For love of her I die.
Since I can bear no longer
　　The grief that loads my breath,
Nor can I hope for healing
　　While she approves my death.
　　Lady I love whole-heartedly,
　　When will your love be given to me?

But the *chansons courtois* are far from exhausting the resources of early French lyric. Many of the troubadours, and of the most highly placed, wrote also satirical verses with a political trend, and even lampoons of a personal character. There is besides much poetry of a more popular character, some indeed which seems to have the dew of the morning upon it. Nevertheless we have to be careful in claiming close contact with folk-song. Professor Ker, in his invaluable introduction to the study of our own early literature,[1] has pointed out that 'the distinction between popular and cultivated lyric is not always easy to make

[1] *English Literature: Mediæval*, Home University Library.

out, as any one may recognize who thinks of the songs of Burns and attempts to distinguish what is popular in them from what is consciously artistic.' The classic instance in English is the famous lyric with which the *Oxford Book of English Verse* opens:

> Sumer is icumen in,
>   Lhude sing cuccu!
> Groweth sed, and bloweth med,
> And springth the wude nu—
>   Sing cuccu!

Nothing could sound more like the spontaneous outburst of a simple, native poet. But the original manuscript shows that the song was written to music, and the music is given—music regarded by musicians as very learned music indeed. Latin words as well as English are given, and the careful directions laid down for singing the music are in Latin. The song is therefore one of studied art, and the general conclusion reached by Professor Ker is that perhaps 'all popular poetry in Europe, at any rate for the last thousand years, is derived from poetry more or less learned in character, or, like the cuckoo song, from more or less learned music.'

Professor Ker goes on to suggest that 'the first popular songs of the modern world were the hymns of St. Ambrose, and the oldest fashion of popular tunes is derived from the music of the Church.' But Gaston Paris rightly points out that the Roman Church in its most ancient hymns must have imitated the old popular songs of Italy, of which Macaulay, as already indicated, was aware, and he finds at least a parallel source for French lyric, and one even more ancient, in the *carole*, a combination of song and dance performed by bands of girls, divided into leader and chorus, which was the most popular feature of country festivals in celebration of the coming of May. These festivals dated back very probably to pagan times and, so far from being religious, were often accompanied by so much hard drinking and loose love-making as to constitute them a scandal to the Church.

Few of the *caroles* dating from early in the twelfth century survive in their entirety, though their refrains are often incorporated in poetry of later date. Limousin and Poitou appear to be their first home, and Gaston Paris makes the quite reasonable suggestion that they form an original stock which spread rapidly throughout Provence and the south, and out of which came the *chansons populaires* that developed by various gradations into the *chanson courtois* of a sophisticated society. Here is a version of one of these *caroles*, sung by dancing girls at spring merry-makings in Poitou:

(5)

Carole

When the skies begin to clear, eya,
For to show that joy is near, eya,
And in jealous hearts strike fear, eya,
Eager will our queen appear,
Proud to show she is not coy.
   Jealous one, away, away!
   Leave us, leave us to our play,
   Dancing to a roundelay.

She has sent a summons clear, eya,
Far as ocean one can hear, eya,
Lads and lassies there and here, eya,
Never a one but must appear,
Dancing in our dance of joy.

From afar the king draws near, eya,
With the dance to interfere, eya,
For he lives in mortal fear, eya,
Some gallant may prove too dear,
And our April queen decoy.

But, how hard he persevere, eya,
No old man will she have near; eya,
Some gay spark will win her ear, eya,
Who knows well the way to cheer,
One whose kisses never cloy.

Who has seen her dancing here, eya,
Seen her lissom body veer, eya,
He can cry with lips sincere, eya,
In the world is not the peer

Of our queen, the queen of joy.
Jealous one away, away!
Leave us, leave us to our play,
Dancing to a roundelay.

Professor Ker quotes from Giraldus Cambrensis, a Welshman
writing in the twelfth century, an amusing story which not only
illustrates the levity of the *carole*, but also shows how soon a
French custom was acclimatized in England. Somewhere in
the diocese of Worcester a wake was carried on all night in a
churchyard, and the refrain constantly repeated by the dancers
was so dinned into the priest's ears that he could not get it out
of his head, but said at Mass instead of *Dominus vobiscum* 'Sweet
Heart, have pity!' or 'Swete lemman, thin are.' If in the
twelfth century much of the English countryside was as gay as
Worcestershire, one can understand the epigram of Richard de
Cluny, quoted by Ascoli [1]:

Anglia, plena jocis; gens libera, nata jocari,
    Tota jocosa, velim dicere tota jocus;
Quae nihil a Gallis, sed Gallia mutuat inde
    Quidquid laetitiae, quidquid amoris habet.

Perhaps too we can understand how French minstrels to England
in the twelfth century, after enjoying the freedom of a few of
these wakes, might bring back stories that made proverbial the
beauty of English women:

Qui veut belle dame acquerre
Prenne visage d'Angleterre.

More elaborate are the *reverdies* and *aubes*, among which are
to be found the loveliest of these early lyrics. The *reverdies*,
hymns to spring, are instinct with the call of mating birds, the
fresh green of the tender grass, the soft hues of blossoming trees;
in short, the young life of all growing things; and the note of the
reverdie runs through many an early lyric. The *aubes* represent
the lyrical outcry of lovers forced to part at dawn, of which the
supreme example is the balcony scene in *Romeo and Juliet*. And
there are the laments: the lament of the ill-married wife, sometimes with a touch in it of the old *fabliau*, the lament of the girl

---

[1] *La Grande-Bretagne devant l'opinion française.*

who has lost her lover, of her who has not got one, and of the
nun, immured in the cloister, who is denied one. Here are
versions of a *reverdie* and of an *aube*, or *alba*, to give a Provençal
poem its proper Provençal name, the latter perhaps the most
famous of its kind:

(6)

REVERDIE

In the sweet spring-time, in May
When with green the fields are gay,
A nightingale upon a spray
Heard I singing loud and clear.
 Ta-lirra ta-tweet!
 'Tis so sweet
Sleeping by the greenwood here.

Falling in a reverie,
Down I sat beside a tree:
Slumber light came over me,
So the bird's sweet song to hear.
 Ta-lirra ta-tweet!
 'Tis so sweet
Sleeping by the greenwood here.

When I found myself awake
Thanks I bade the song-bird take
Who made merry for my sake:
New delight my heart will cheer.
 Ta-lirra ta-tweet!
 'Tis so sweet
Sleeping by the greenwood here.

And when to my feet I spring,
Take my lute and pluck a string,
How the bird began to sing
By me in the meadow near!
 Ta-lirra ta-tweet!
 'Tis so sweet
Sleeping by the greenwood here.

The nightingale I heard complain:
Wellnigh mad with stress and strain
How it gave him bitter pain
That a clown his song should hear.
    Ta-lirra ta-tweet!
    'Tis so sweet
Sleeping by the greenwood here.

(7)

ALBA

Within a garth neath hawthorn-boughs they hide:
The lady clasps her lover to her side,
Until the watchman's voice the dawn has cried.
Ah God, ah God, the dawn!   How soon it comes!

'O would to God that night might last for aye,
Nor far from me my lover ever stray,
Nor ever watchman see or dawn or day!
Ah God, ah God, the dawn!   How soon it comes!

Sweet lover, thou and I, come kiss and cling
Down in the meadows where the sweet birds sing;
Risk all, nor fear what jealousy may bring.
Ah God, ah God, the dawn!   How soon it comes!

Sweet lover, once again love's fortunes try,
Here in the close where birds make melody,
Until the watchman winds his horn on high.
Ah God, ah God, the dawn!   How soon it comes!

How sweet the radiant air that comes my way
From my tall lover, courteous and gay;
His breath thrills through me like a sweet sun-ray:
Ah God, ah God, the dawn!   How soon it comes!'

Lovely the lady is and rich in grace;
So beautiful, men crowd to see her face,
And her true heart in love finds still its place.
Ah God, ah God, the dawn!   How soon it comes!

With still more of conscious art in them are the *chansons d'histoire*, so called because they tell some sort of a story. A popular class of these were the *chansons de toile*, or songs sung by ladies over their needlework. One of the earliest and best-known of these is *Belle Érembor*, and of this we venture to offer a version, in assonance as with the original:

(8)

Fair Érembor

When comes the month called May whose days are long,
And home the peers of France return from court,
Renaud returns, and marches in the front;
He passed before the house of Érembor
But did not deign to turn his head aloft.
   Ah, me! Renaud, my love!

Beside the window sits fair Érembor,
Upon her knees gay broidery she holds.
She sees the peers of France return from court,
She sees Renaud, who marches in the front.
Raising her voice, she cries her plaint aloud:
   'Ah, me! Renaud, my love!

'My love, Renaud, well have I known the day,
Passing my father's tower upon thy way
Thou wouldst have grieved, had I no word to say.'
'Thine, daughter of an emperor, the blame!
Thou 'st loved another, let my memory fade.'
   Ah, me! Renaud, my love!

'Lord Renaud, by the saints my name I 'll clear;
A hundred virgins shall my oath receive,
And thirty matrons I will bring with me,
That I have loved no other man than thee.
Believe me, and a kiss shall be thy fee.
   Ah, me! Renaud, my love!'

Count Renaud climbed the steps from the courtyard.
Of shoulders broad, but slim at the waist-band,
His yellow hair curling in ringlets small,

Never, nowhere was bachelor so tall.
Érembor sees him, and her tears lets fall.
        Ah, me!   Renaud, my love!

Count Renaud now has entered in the tower;
He seats him on a bed broidered with flowers,
And there beside him sits fair Érembor.
Then recommence their raptures as of yore.
        Ah, me!   Renaud, my love!

Another and very remarkable example of the *chanson de toile* is
Bele Doette, which seemed in the translator's mind naturally to
take a form suggested by the old Scots ballad.   He ventures to
dedicate his version to Professor Boillot of Bristol, at whose
instance it was undertaken.

(9)

FAIR DOUSIE

Fair Dousie by the window sat,
    A buik lay idle on her knee;
She thocht her of her ain true luve,
    Was jousting gaen ayont the sea.
        O wae is me!

A horseman lit at the ha' door,
    And aff his saddle-bags he drew;
Fair Dousie 's loupen down the step;
    O' tidings ill nae fear she knew.
        O wae is me!

Fair Dousie askit him aff-hand:
    'Where is my lord, sae lang frae sicht?'
Sair grieved, the page let fa' a tear.
    Fair Dousie stert, and swooned for fricht.
        O wae is me!

Fair Dousie rose and held her straight,
    And brawly faced him, standing there;
Her heart was torn wi' teen and dole
    For the guid lord she 'll see nae mair.
        O wae is me!

Fair Dousie hastit for to ask:
  'Where is my lord I luve sae weel?'
'Fore God I darena hide the news:
  My lord is deid: at joust he fell.'
    O wae is me!

Fair Dousie groaned, and syne she moaned:
  'Ill chance was thine, gentil lord Doon!
For luve of thee a leathern shift,
  Nae robe of fur, shall hap me roun'.
    O wae is me!
I 'll tae St. Poulis kirk, and tak the vaile for thee.

'For thee will I an abbey build,
  Shall for the feast-day ready be;
And nae fause luve may enter there,
  Nane such shall haud the richtfu' key.
    O wae is me!
I 'll tae St. Poulis kirk, and tak the vaile for thee.'

Fair Dousie hastit for to build;
  Stately the kirk, shall rise amain,
And welcum a' gudeman, gudewife,
  Who tholed for luve baith grief and pain.
    O wae is me!
I 'll tae St. Poulis kirk, and tak the vaile for thee.

More sophisticated still are the *pastourelles*, many examples of which have survived. It cannot be denied that the reading of a series of these induces a feeling of tedium. The pattern of them is much the same. A knight or squire riding through the countryside encounters a charming shepherdess by the way; he dismounts and makes love to her, and is sometimes snubbed for his pains, though at other times the meeting leads to a *dénouement* more agreeable, as Mr. Abbott suggests, to the Wife of Bath. The pastoral setting of this artificial form is proof in itself of its affinity, in the last resort, to the folk-song. Very striking is the vogue of this pastoral note; in one form or another the pastoral persists in literature and art throughout the ages. It is to be found in the poetry of the Pleiad; Molière makes good fun of it

near the beginning of his *Bourgeois Gentilhomme*; Watteau adapted
it to his art; and an embodiment of it late in the eighteenth
century was the *fermerie* with its little rustic settlement attached to
the Petit Trianon at Versailles for the amusement of Marie
Antoinette. Here is an attempt to render one of the thirteenth-
century *pastourelles* in a form closely corresponding to the original:

(10)

PASTOURELLE

From St. Quentin to Cambrai
  As of late I ambled on,
In a wood beside my way
  Such a lass I chanced upon!
      There she shone
Fresh as is a rose in May;
      Heart as gay,
    For I heard her say,
    Singing merrily:
'In God's name, I 've one at call
      Handsome and tall,
    Nutbrown though I be.'

To my shepherdess I went,
  Whom I 'd seen in her retreat;
Courteously my head I bent,
  Said: 'May God thee kindly greet,
      'Tis but meet!
Maid I 've found here, rest content;
      Love once lent
    Claims ready assent.'
    With a smile said she:
'In God's name, I 've one at call
      Handsome and tall,
    Nutbrown though I be.'

Then I sat me by her side,
  And I begged a kiss of her.
'Love like yours I 'll ne'er abide,'
  So she said, 'for I prefer
      Robin, sir,

And I 'll be a shepherd's bride.
He 's my pride;
Of my lover tried
Sing I cheerfully:
In God's name, I 've one at call
Handsome and tall,
Nutbrown though I be.'

To end this brief review of early lyrical verse in France we have still to find room for that strange and beautiful combination of prose and verse, the tale of Aucassin and Nicolette. This *chantefable* or song-story, which may be the only survivor of several of its kind, has been claimed to be a mime, or dramatic monologue, animated by gesture and modulation of voice, breaking periodically into song; for the music to accompany the verse passages is given, as with the cuckoo song, in the original manuscript. It tells the story, in alternate passages of prose and lyrical seven-syllable verse, of two lovers, Aucassin, son of the Lord of Beaucaire, and Nicolette, a Saracen slave in the household of one of the count's vassals. Such a *mésalliance* as a marriage between them was not to be thought of, and they were forcibly separated. Nicolette was imprisoned in a tower, from which she escaped, and fled across fields and through the forest. Aucassin set off to find her, and succeeded in tracking her down. But after a series of romantic adventures the lovers are captured by a company of Saracen pirates, and carried off in different ships across the sea.

A storm scatters the ships, and Aucassin is wrecked near Beaucaire, his home, where his father now being dead he is hailed as rightful lord. Nicolette is carried off to Carthage, where it is discovered that she is the daughter of the King of Carthage, from whom she had been stolen as a child. At Carthage they sought to marry her to a Paynim king, but her heart is set on Aucassin; she disguises herself and escapes as a wandering gipsy minstrel, ceasing not in her wanderings over sea and land until she finds herself again in Beaucaire. There, with the help of her old mistress, she artfully discovers herself to her lover, overjoyed. Next day Aucassin, Lord of Beaucaire, is married to Nicolette, daughter of the King of Carthage, and they live together happily ever afterwards.

This wonderful little story did not become well known to the literary world until the nineteenth century. In England, in late Victorian days its fame was spread abroad by the successive translations of F. W. Bourdillon and Andrew Lang. It was not merely the exquisite passages in verse, charged with the love that Robert Browning in an inspired line speaks of—'O lyric love, half angel and half bird!'—that captivated the modern world, but also the daring of one of the prose passages that is worth quoting. When Aucassin is told that to marry Nicolette, a Saracen slave, is impossible, and that if he carries her off to be his mistress his soul will lie in hell, and he can never enter heaven, he replies: 'What have I to do in Paradise? I seek not to enter there, so that I have Nicolette my most sweet friend. For to Paradise . . . go old priests, old cripples, and maimed wretches who grovel all day and night before altars, and in mouldy crypts, those clad in threadbare cloaks and in rags and tatters . . . who die of hunger and thirst and cold and miseries. These go to Paradise; with these I have naught to do. But to Hell will I go. For to Hell go goodly clerks and goodly knights, who have died in tourneys and great wars, and good soldier-men and free-born men: with them will I go. And there go those fair and gracious ladies who have lovers two or three, beside their rightful lords . . . with them will I go, so that I have with me Nicolette, my most sweet friend.' This in the age of faith, in one of the great centuries of the building of churches and cathedrals, sculptured bibles in stone! Here was a new light on the Middle Ages.

However, read now the song of Nicolette in prison, rendered not, as in the original, in assonance, but in rhyme, in the attempt to give a modern reader more nearly the charm of it:

(11)

NICOLETTE IN PRISON

Nicole must in prison lie
In a vaulted chamber high,
Built with art most curious,
Dight with paintings marvellous.
Gainst the marble window she,
She so young leaned wearily.
Blonde the hair upon her head,

And well-arched her eyebrows' spread,
Oval was her face and bright;
Ne'er saw man a prettier sight.
Gazing on the close below
There she saw the roses blow,
Heard the birds make music wild,
And thus wailed that orphan child:
'Woe is me, poor captive me!
Wherefore should I prisoned be?
Young Lord Aucassin, give ear;
Long it is you 've loved me dear;
You can feel no hate for me,
Though for you I prisoned be
In this vaulted chamber high,
Where I live in misery.
But, by God, whom Mary bore,
Soon my durance will be o'er,
⠀⠀⠀⠀If I succeed.'

Next follows Aucassin's song when searching for Nicolette:

(12)

AUCASSIN'S SONG

Little star, whom now I see
By the moon that wooeth thee,
Nicolette is with thee there,
My mignonne, the blonde of hair.
Doubtless God would have her light
To adorn the queen of night,
That she may be lovelier still.
If it pleased his sovran will,
Mignonne who so far dost hide,
Now to raise me to thy side,
Though I fall to earth again,
How to kiss thee I would strain!
If a king's son I be born,
Well wouldst thou my rank adorn,
⠀⠀⠀⠀Sweet sister mine.

Finally, here is a version of the happy ending, when at the

last one of his court ladies, Nicolette's old mistress, takes him
to the arms of his lost love:

(13)

The Happy Ending

So when Aucassin heard now
That his love of radiant brow
In the land was, as of yore,
Joyful was he, never more!
With the dame he went apace,
Till he reached her resting-place;
To the chamber soon they get
Where sits waiting Nicolette.
When she saw him at the door,
Joyful was she, never more,
Sprang, to face him, on her feet.
And when he her eyes could meet,
Both his arms he opened wide,
Softly folded her inside,
Kissed her both on cheek and eye.
So they let the night go by,
Till at dawn in morning light
Aucassin his troth could plight,
Make her lady of Beaucaire.
Life for many a day they share
Mid delights that ne'er grow less.
Aucassin has happiness,
Nicolette the like has won:
Song and story now are done,
No more 's to tell!

As one dwells on the exquisite charm of early French lyric
one is tempted to regret that the eyes and ears of the Romantics
at the beginning of the nineteenth century, caught by the beauties
of the poetry of the Pleiad, had not yet revealed to them the
light and music of a native lyric of far earlier date, to bewitch
their brooding fancy.

c

CHAPTER II

THE most conspicuous link between the early and later medieval period, and between courtly and popular poetry, is to be found in that remarkable poem, completed in the last quarter of the thirteenth century, the *Romance of the Rose*,[1] the most influential of all early French poems on the course of European literature. The history of the poem is peculiar. It was begun about 1225 by Guillaume de Lorris, a young scholar who, inspired by Ovid, desired to give his countrymen in a long and intricate allegory a complete Art of Love. His work ended abruptly at his early death, when he had written between four and five thousand lines. Nearly fifty years later another poet, Jean Clopinel of Meung-sur-Loire, took up the unfinished work, and added another 18,000 lines to it, quite changing the character of the poem as a whole.

Whereas the first part was full of exquisite poetry, a charmingly graceful production, designed for courtly readers, many passages in it recalling to an English reader the fluent, dreamy charm of the best of William Morris's *Earthly Paradise*, the second part of it is the work of one less graceful, but more vigorous, a man with a satirical turn, and one who had followed closely the political, social, and religious movements of the day; who poured his learning and philosophy into his work, with the result that the poem becomes a treasury of the life and thought of the period. The vogue of this great poem is attested by the existence of over two hundred manuscripts of it, and by the fact that Chaucer, well on in the fourteenth century, occupied himself by translating at least portions of it. Early French printers issued edition after edition of it, and in the sixteenth century it is one of the distinctions of Clément Marot that he took in hand the re-editing of it.

But the work of Jean de Meung, in which realism was so marked a feature, did not stand alone. Realism and individuality had

[1] A very great achievement is Mr. F. S. Ellis's verse translation of this poem, published by J. M. Dent & Sons.

appeared in the poetry of northern France even before the end
of the twelfth century in Arras, the great centre of a teeming,
prosperous, quarrelsome, social life in Picardy. The earliest
of this new type of trouvère, very different from the Provençal
singer of nightingales and blossoming trees, of warm summer
nights and passionate love, was Jean Bodel, a most versatile
poet, who wrote besides *pastourelles* and other poems a decadent
chanson de geste or *roman d'aventures* on Charlemagne's conquest of
the Saxons, and struck out for himself a new line in the seculari-
zation of the mystery or miracle-play by introducing into his
Jeu de St. Nicolas a vein of broad, human comedy, suitable for
the cabaret or the tavern. Smitten by leprosy and forced to
leave Arras, he wrote a pathetic poem of farewell.

After him came Adam de la Halle, who was also forced to leave
Arras, driven out by internal dissensions, and he too wrote a
touching but dignified farewell. He prospered in exile, and
has the distinction of having written, perhaps fired by the success
of Bodel's *Jeu de St. Nicolas*, the first two purely secular plays in
France, in *Le Jeu de la Feuillée* a comedy, and in *Robin et Marion*
what may almost be called an *opéra comique*.

A third well-known trouvère was Colin Muset, of whose work
but few examples survive, some of them light-hearted pieces with
more than a touch of the *reverdie* and the *pastourelle* about them,
and often a naïve personal note; but one of his poems is a precious
document for the period, in that it gives a vivid picture of the
varying fortunes of the professional minstrel's vagabond existence.
Here is a version of this poem which attempts, while reproducing
the form of the original so far as the translator's capacity could
serve him, to give all its picturesque detail:

(14)

The Minstrel's Life

My lord, within thy halls I 've stayed,
And on my lute before thee played,
But naught for wages hast thou paid
To one who plied for thee his trade.
     'Tis villeiny!
Now, by my faith in Saint Marie,

No more thy follower I 'll be.
An ill-found satchel here 's to see,
And a purse lean through poverty.

My lord, come, let thy heart persuade
Thy will to grant to me some aid,
For, sire, a gift that 's freely made,
A generous gift not long delayed,
            Marks high degree.
Trust me, I purpose verily
To travel home to my country.
If I return with purse empty,
My wife will have no smile for me.

In words like these hear her upbraid:
Sir Starveling, where can you have stayed,
Who not a penny-piece have made?
Too long about some town you 've strayed
            In revelry.
Limp saddlebags you bring to me,
For stuffed with naught but wind they be.
Oh, what a shameless wretch is he
Who 'ld travel in your company!

But when I 'm home, and undismayed
My wife has all my load surveyed,
Fat saddlebags behind me laid
And me in good grey cloth arrayed,
            Such finery,
She flings her distaff down in glee;
She cannot hide her ecstasy,
But laughs at me for jollity
And round my neck clings lovingly.

For joy her work is not delayed,
Straps are unloosed, my stuff displayed;
My man has watered well my jade,
And rubbed her down, ere word was said;
Two capons from the yard my maid
Has killed and cooked, and ready laid
            So savoury;

My daughter out of courtesy
Has brought in hand a comb for me.
So I'm at home His Majesty
In undisturbed felicity;
Say, can a man so happy be?

More important, however, than any of the Picard group was a man of humble origin, Rutebeuf, who, possibly born in Burgundy, lived out his penurious existence in Paris. He was a contemporary of Jean de Meung, and his poems give a picture of his time as valuable as the second part of the *Romance of the Rose*. The two poets must have known one another, or their work, and have reacted on one another. He was always poor, and he tells us much of the miseries of his life, particularly of his second marriage, in 1261, to a plain and elderly wife as poor as himself, of the worries of a fast-growing family, of the loss of his right eye, 'the one with which he saw the best,' of cold and hunger, and, with a veracity like Villon's, he makes no concealment of his haunting taverns and cabarets, and his passion for gambling, a passion he bitterly deplores. He wrote for money eulogies and elegies, and also sacred poems, including a play, his *Miracle de Théophile*, in the writing of which, despite the irregularities of his life, he was, like Villon, and Verlaine in certain moods, sincere.

But he was most himself in his satires, in his *fabliaux*, some of them coarse enough, and his monologues written for his own pleasure and that of his kind. A pamphleteer, he sang of most questions that agitated public opinion in his time, the time of St. Louis and Philip III. He shot at all who made a business of religion, pietists, hypocrites, religious orders, old and new, the mendicant orders, who, said he, under the protection of the king nourished themselves at the expense of the country. He took an active part, on the side of the secular clergy, in the violent quarrel that arose between the University of Paris and the Dominicans, and he rallied prelates, the nobility, and the rich on their lukewarmness in support of the Crusades. In this connection one of the best-known and most characteristic of his serious poems is a long dialogue between two knights, one of whom strives, and successfully, to convert the other to join a Crusade.

It has to be admitted that there is none of the glamour and music and sweeping rhythm of Villon's poetry about Rutebeuf's work. But he is forceful, epigrammatic at times, fond of a play upon words, and always tingling with verve. No love-song has he left. As illustrations of his work we offer, first, an example of the vigour of his attack on any, even religious, movement that struck him as among the abuses of his time. The *Béguines* against whom this skit was directed were women who lived in communities, without renouncing the world, for their vows were temporary only. The very picturesque *Béguinage* at Bruges will be familiar to visitors to that charming old city.

(15)

THE LAY-SISTERS

Whatever a lay-sister says
Is good, and merits only praise;
Whatever in her life you see
Bears the impress of sanctity.
She speaks as speaks a prophetess,
Her smile reveals her friendliness;
Her tears religious zeal attest,
Asleep, she communes with the blest;
Her dreams are visions from on high.
Ignore it, should she tell a lie.

If a lay-sister turn to bride,
'Tis but to show her social side;
Her vows, her calling, do not bind
Unto her death one of her kind.
There's time for tears, and time for prayer,
And time a wedding-ring to wear;
Martha or Mary, as she warms
To cloister, or a husband's arms.
Of such an one never speak ill:
Such is our good king's sovereign will.

Then comes a version of his appeal to St. Louis, where he gives a poignant picture of the poverty of a poet, and incidentally reveals one of the seamy sides of the Crusades, in robbing the country of the rich and powerful, who might have spent their money and their energy ᾿ profitably on their tenants and clients, and their property at home.   In his version the translator has failed to reproduce precisely the rhyme-scheme of the original:

(16)

THE POET'S POVERTY

Where to begin I do not know;
Such are the stores of grief that grow
As I recount my misery.
True King of France, in God's name give
The wherewithal a man may live;
So wilt thou show great charity.
I 've lived on gifts of other men,
Loans that they thought I 'd pay again.
At last no credit have I left,
All know I 'm poor and deep in debt;
And since abroad thy course is set,
Of my sole hope I 'm now bereft.

Hard times and this my family—
Of healthy appetite they be—
Leave naught on which to raise a loan.
Before me people shut the door,
In art of giving scant their lore,
Though all well-schooled to guard their own.
Death has made havoc of my friends,
And thou, good king, for pious ends,
Hast swept my patrons far from me
In two crusades to distant lands,
Where Tunis, savage waste of sands,
Rears an ill brood in heresy.

Great king, if I should fail with thee,
I 've failed with all, no fault in me!
Food fails me, and for food I fail.
None grips my hand, I 've nought to pawn;
From cold I cough, from hunger yawn,
Both ills my tortured frame assail.

I 've neither coverlet nor bed,
Far as Senlis none so ill-fed ;
Sire, I know not what way to go.
How the hard straw my sides doth gall !
A bed of straw 's no bed at all,
And I 've for bed but straw to strow.

Sire, take to heart what I have said,
I 've nothing left to buy me bread :
Round me in Paris men have all,
But naught is mine to cheer my soul.
Paulatim comes some meagre dole,
Which makes me think more of St. Paul
Than all the other saintly powers.
Our Father ! ay, but is he ours,
When these hard times have ruined me,
And have my lodging so bereft
I 've neither creed nor credit left?
I 've nothing but what you can see.

Of the importance of Rutebeuf in those critical days of
the later thirteenth century when the knell of feudalism had
been sounded, and the power of the Roman Church begun to
suffer some eclipse, a reader can satisfy himself by studying the
references to him in Lavisse's *History of France.* And to show the
contrast between the tone and temper of the early French lyric
of the true southern type, whether written by troubadours or
trouvères, and the specimens given of Colin Muset's and Rutebeuf's
work, it will not be amiss, before passing on to the fourteenth
century, to revert to that halycon period, and to quote two
delightful verses from writers of *chansons courtois* but little earlier
in date. Here is a verse from the farewell of the Châtelain de
Coucy to his lady-love, whether the poetess known as the Lady
of Faël, or some other, before starting on crusade :

Je m'en vois, dame ; a Dieu le creator
Comant vo cors, en quel lieu que je soie ;
Ne sai se ja verrez mais mon retor :
Aventure est que ja mais vos revoie.

Por Dieu vos pri, quel part que li cors traie,
Que voz convenz tenez, vieigne o demor,
Et je pri Dieu qu'ensi me doinst onor
Com je vos ai esté amis verais.

Lady, I go; to God our Sire's embrace
I do commend thee, wheresoe'er I be;
I know not if once more thou 'lt see my face:
'Tis but a chance if I return to thee.
God grant that thou mayst still be true to me,
If I return or no, whate'er my place,
And I pray God to grant me of his grace
So long as I too keep my fealty.

Here, too, a pretty fancy from a poem by Gace Brulé, friend of
Thibaut de Champagne:

Les oisillons de mon païs
   Ai oïz en Bretaigne;
A lor chant m'est il bien a vis
   Qu'en la douce Champaigne
      Les oï jadis,
      Se n'i ai mespris.
Il m'ont en si dous penser mis
Qu'a chançon fere me sui pris
   Tant que je parataigne
Ce qu'Amours m'a lonc tens promis.

The song-birds of mine own countrie,
   I 've heard them in Bretayne;
And as they sang it seemed to me
   I heard at home again
      Their melody.
      O phantasy!
They lulled me to a reverie
So sweet, it set me singing free
   That so I might attain
To what long since Love promised me.

But the day of the troubadours was over.   Who was to succeed
them?
      * c

It must be admitted that the later medieval period which covers the fourteenth and fifteenth centuries did not at first fulfil the promise of the earlier, whose last years indicated the possibilities of some great, new departure. It might well have been imagined that the vigour of satire, thought, and speech shown by Rutebeuf and Jean de Meung in the second part of the *Romance of the Rose*, and the graphic touches in their work that suggest the growth of a keen, questioning middle class, quick in the uptake, and enjoying life for all its stress and strain, for all its injustices, its hardships, and its petty annoyances and cares, would have been followed by a great development of realism in literary art.

Such was not the case. A mass of poetry was indeed produced in the two centuries under review, but, as will be learned as we proceed, most of it was poetry artificial in form, with no great depth of thought or profundity of feeling. And yet the period produced at its close one of the greatest of French poets, François Villon, perhaps the one poet in all modern literature who, measured by the bulk of his verse, ranks as a minor poet, though by the quality of it he ranks with the very greatest.

No doubt the explanation of the comparative barrenness of the period lies in the terrible conditions that prevailed throughout France, and particularly in northern France, during the Hundred Years' War, when towns and countryside were devastated not only by the invading armies of the English, but also by the roving forces set in motion by the internecine strife between the Burgundians and the adherents of the kings of France, struggling to maintain their insecure sovereignty at the heart of France, and to extend it over the nation as a whole.

The Hundred Years' War was mainly the result first of inevitable disputes arising in connection with the French possessions of the English kings, in respect of which they were reluctant vassals of the kings of France, and then of the claim of Edward III to the throne of France itself. The glories of the battles won against heavy odds, Crécy won by Edward III in 1346, Poitiers by Edward the Black Prince in 1356, and Agincourt by Henry V in 1415, have obscured the hopeless character of the English kings' efforts to conquer France. No series of expeditionary forces, even if composed of the finest fighting men in Europe, and led by the greatest captains of the day, could hope to conquer an alien country larger than England itself, where no indigenous rising came to the support of the invaders. And when, through the heroic exertions of Joan of Arc, the maid-warrior of all time, the tide of victory turned in favour of France, and we were driven by a united nation out of the country, our own civil Wars of the Roses were preoccupation enough to cause us to abandon the struggle.

Dismal as were conditions in town and country during this devastating period, court life still went on, and a number of poets flourished, pouring out elegant poetry in the most artificial forms, ballades, rondels, rondeaux, chants royaux, virelais, and so forth. These are often graceful enough and of astonishing ingenuity; they are marked by an intricacy of pattern that resulted from playing on a mere handful of rhymes and the enforced repetition of the same refrain.

Readers of the lyrics of the early medieval period cannot fail to note that most of them, *chansons courtois* and the rest, have elaborate rhyme schemes, and many, from the *caroles* onwards, have a burden or refrain recurring at regular intervals. As the substance of a poem grew in content, and as the burden or refrain was also elaborated, while the two were knit together by an intricate nexus of rhyme, we find here the origin of the complicated artificial forms of the later medieval period. But the tendency, already noticeable in the more stilted of the *chansons courtois*, for song to pass into a metrical exercise becomes marked as we pass into the fourteenth century, and no one can be more severe on its poetry than Gustave Lanson, the most popular historian of French literature, who stigmatizes it as poetic form without poetry, or mere rhetoric, where all is technique and all technique the surmounting of difficulty.

Nevertheless it is well to remember that an intricate form of verse of early date, which the Pleid borrowed from Italy and established in France, viz. the sonnet, has survived through the ages, and no great poet has been trammelled by the elaboration of its form in the use of it for the expression of deep passion or high thought. This is worth recalling when we are faced with the marvellous ease with which Villon handled his ballades and rondeaux, and the tremendous force he put into them.

We may appropriately commence our illustrations of the poets of this period by an example from one of the earliest of them, Guillaume de Machault (*c.* 1290–1377), whom Lanson calls the initiator of the rhetoric he denounces, with his *rimes serpentines, équivoques, léonines, croisées* or *rétrogrades, sonnantes* or *consonantes.* He was one who moved in high circles, and indeed was at one time secretary to the blind King John of Bohemia, who was killed at the battle of Crécy. Of his great output of 80,000 lines we offer but one little poem, a rondeau, which, one feels, might fitly be inscribed on vellum in the style of the illuminators of his time:

(17)

Fair as a lily, redder than the rose,
And like an orient ruby shining bright,
While in mine eyes your matchless beauty glows,
Fair as a lily, redder than the rose,
My rapt desires no other goal disclose
Save, for your sake, to live as in Love's sight,
Fair as a lily, redder than the rose,
And like an orient ruby shining bright.

Next we offer versions of two rondeaux by Jean Froissart (1337–1410), who well holds his own with his brother poets, though far more famous as a prose-writer than as a poet. His glorious Chronicles unfold the story of the wars between England and France like one of the brilliant tapestries of early date, and still captivate their reader with the vigour and picturesqueness of their style. The first of these rondeaux is akin in sentiment to that of Machault, but the second strikes a simpler and more domestic note:

(18)

Scent of the rose fills all my heart with glee,
Sight of my mistress is my heart's delight;
Which of the two should win the mastery?
Scent of the rose fills all my heart with glee.
Now, by my soul, this must the answer be:
Harmless the scent, I dare not trust my sight.
Scent of the rose fills all my heart with glee,
Sight of my mistress is my heart's delight.

(19)

Come back, my friend, too long dost thou delay;
Trouble and grief thine absence makes for me.
My spirit calls for thee the livelong day.
Come back, my friend, too long dost thou delay;
For there is none, save thee, can make me gay,
Nor shall, till home again I welcome thee.
Come back, my friend, too long dost thou delay;
Trouble and grief thine absence makes for me.

But now we come to Eustache Deschamps (*c.* 1340–1410), a native of Champagne, of humble birth though he rose to important office under King Charles V, surnamed 'the Wise,' and Charles VI. He must be accounted the most important poet of his time, and deserves more indulgent treatment than he receives from Lanson. His output, certainly, was prodigious, for we have over 1,500 ballades by him, not to speak of lais, rondeaux, virelais, etc. There is realism and moral fervour in his work, he had complaints of his own to air, and he wrote much on the vices and miseries of his time, and in hatred of the English, to whose invasions so much of the suffering of his country was due.

Among his ballades are two of special interest, one on the death of Bertrand du Guesclin, the first French fighting-man, who as a leader of the Italian *condottiere* type, but a patriot, proved a match for any English general, the refrain of the ballade running

Lament, lament the flower of chivalry,

and the other a tribute to our own Geoffrey Chaucer, whose achievement in the translation of French he celebrates in the refrain:

Grant translateur, noble Geffroy Chaucier.

One of Deschamps's virelais, unfortunately quite untranslatable into English of anything like its delightful pattern, is as gay, as enticing a poem as will be found in all French literature. The first and twelfth of thirteen stanzas, with the *introit*, run as follows:

Sui je, sui je, sui je belle?
Il me semble, a mon avis,
Que j'ay beau front et doulz viz

Et la bouche vermeillette;
Dittes moi se je suis belle.

C'est un mondains paradiz
Que d'avoir dame toudis,
Ainsi fresche, ainsi nouvelle;
Sui je, sui je, sui je belle?

To represent Deschamps in English versions here we must
confine ourselves to a rondeau by him, and a rondel, the latter
of which shows that the fear of death was never far from the
poets of those days:

(20)

Rondeau

In summer is the time to go to war,
Or in the spring, when grass grows thick and green,
When days are warm, and winter quits the scene:

Horses have what they love in ample store,
And snug the quarters that so cold have been.

In summer is the time to go to war,
Or in the spring, when grass grows thick and green:

Deep buried, snow and hail are here no more,
Down every street one hears men sing serene;
Fight then; in winter lie the sheets between.

In summer is the time to go to war,
Or in the spring, when grass grows thick and green,
When days are warm, and winter quits the scene.

(21)

Rondel

Hasten to my jubilee:
I have passed my fiftieth year:

Gone my days of jollity:
Hasten to my jubilee.

Fare ye well!   Remember me!
All my body quakes with fear.
Hasten to my jubilee:
I have passed my fiftieth year.

After the middle of the fourteenth century there came, in
1364, to the throne the remarkable king, Charles V, surnamed
'the Wise.' He was a delicate, sickly creature, and of poor
appearance; but he had just the qualities required to cope with
the English king, Edward III, viz. shrewdness and tenacity.
He did much to improve the finance of the country by reforming
its coinage, and after his experience, as dauphin, on the field of
Poitiers, from which he escaped by flight, he realized that the
right policy was to avoid pitched battles and wear down the
English by delay. And if no soldier himself, he found in Du
Guesclin, the son of a Breton gentleman, the well-forged instrument to reform French warfare, as he had himself reformed the
French coinage. A picture of Charles's simple, ordered life, as
well as of his unscrupulousness, is given in one of the writings of
Christine de Pisan, the most remarkable woman of her time, of
whom we have now to speak.

Christine de Pisan (*c.* 1363–1430), one of the select company of
eminent women poets, was a pupil of Deschamps. She was the
daughter of one Thomas de Pisan, an Italian, who became
astrologer at the court of Charles V. Losing early both father
and husband, she had to devote herself to letters as a means of
livelihood for herself and her three children. She wrote much
in prose as well as verse, and, as indicated above, her works are
among the contemporary sources for the history of the reign of
Charles V and for a knowledge of the social life and the manners
and domestic life of her time.

As a champion of her sex she was among the earliest, and she
wrote a spirited defence of women against the satirical attacks
of Jean de Meung in the *Romance of the Rose*. It is interesting to
note that a woman of her quality was much sought after, and she
was tempted by offers to make her home at the courts both of
England and Milan, but she remained faithful to her adopted
country, France. How graceful her poetry could be may perhaps
be gauged from the following versions of three of her rondeaux,
all of which have a suggestion of that feminine touch of which

more will be said when we come to deal with Louise Labé and
Madame Desbordes-Valmore:

(22)

Gay, flashing eyes, who have my heart confined
Within your glances' love-encircling net,
To you I yield me with no fond regret,
Rejoicing to be caught by lure so kind.

So rich the virtues in your light enshrined,
None can compute the price thereon to set,
Gay, flashing eyes, who have my heart confined.

Sweetness, charm, courtesy are so combined,
There 's not the man, whatever cares may fret,
Who will not, if but one sweet glance he get,
Feel comfort steal into his troubled mind,
Gay, flashing eyes, who have my heart confined.

(23)

If frequently to mass I go,
My beauty there I fain would see;
Fresh as a new-blown rose is she.

Men waste their time who gossip so;
Why should they talk maliciously,
If frequently to mass I go?

Nor road nor path my footsteps know,
Save one that leads where she may be.
How foolish he who fool calls me,
If frequently to mass I go.

(24)

How hard a thing it is to bear,
When the heart weeps and the mouth sings.

When even lament one has to spare,
How hard a thing it is to bear.

Such is her lot if one should dare
To face what slanders envy flings;
How hard a thing it is to bear!

Next in order of date among the leading poets of the period
comes Alain Chartier (*c.* 1386–1444), a scholar of the University
of Paris, who rose to court office. He was attached as secretary
to Charles VII, whose throne was saved for him by Joan of Arc,
and who was crowned King of France at Rheims in 1429, with
the heroine standing by his side. During Charles's troubled
reign, though English invasion, thanks to Joan of Arc, became
less and less effective, there was still much misery abroad, and
of this, as of the vices of the nobility and clergy, Alain Chartier
has much to say in his prose works.

It is of him that the charming story is told, how Margaret of
Scotland, Queen of France, finding him asleep one day, kissed
the precious lips 'from which had fallen so many good sayings
and virtuous words.' The story is probably quite mythical, for
dates do not favour it, but what a tribute is the story to the high
estimation in which a famous poet was held! The example to
be given here of his poetry differs from those so far given of others
of his period, which are of lighter import. Of Alain Chartier
we offer a version of his fine ballade on the folly of mankind,
written in high moral vein, a piece more worthily representing
the serious poetry of the period than anything we have offered
from the great output of his predecessors:

(25)
O Fool of Fools!

O fool of fools, fool that is mortal man,
Who trusts so much in gifts by Fortune strown,
Upon this earth, the prospect where you scan,
What can you find to call your very own?
Nothing is yours, save what by way of loan
Nature with gracious hand to grant may deign.
If Fortune's smile should chance at last to wane,
And you are left of what you had forlorn,
She robs you not, but both are quits again,
For you had naught the day when you were born.

Neglect not sleeping all the hours you can
Upon your bed when dark the night is grown,
To pile up wealth in heaps you scarce can span;
Nor covet anything beneath the moon,
From Paris even as far as Pampelune,
Save what poor human creatures must obtain,
Such food and drink as will your frame sustain;
Suffice it that brave deeds your life adorn,
And that your sepulchre some honour gain:
For you had naught the day when you were born.

The trees' delicious fruits when time began
And everything as common good was known,
Sweet honey, swelling grain, by nature's plan
For food to man and wife sufficed alone.
No ground for quarrel then, no cause to moan.
Sore tried by heat or cold never complain,
But take as fair what Fortune may ordain.
Under your losses grumble not, nor mourn
Beyond due measure where the limit's plain,
For you had naught the day when you were born.

If Fortune deals a blow to give you pain,
Hers is the right, and yours no cause for scorn,
E'en though she strip you bare against the rain;
For you had naught the day when you were born.

And now we break loose for a moment from the artificial
literary atmosphere of a period when the art and science of
rhetoric flourished so luxuriantly, to drink in a breath of the
popular poetry which did exist at the same time. In 1875
Gaston Paris published for the Society of Ancient French Texts,
as its first volume, a fine old manuscript in the National Library,
probably written at the beginning of the sixteenth century. The
manuscript contained also the old music to accompany the songs,
and this too was transcribed by a skilled hand. These poems
are not of the high lyric quality of the songs of the troubadours
and the trouvères, but they are marked by a delightful simplicity; some have more grace than others, and they vary in the
delicacy of pure poetic quality. They reflect the manners and

the sentiment of days long past, and here and there is a touch impressed by some great event of the time.

As examples we offer first a version of the well-known song on the death of Olivier Basselin, adopting the text of Gaston Paris's manuscript, according to which Bachelin is the proper spelling of the name. Basselin was a fuller (whence his 'white livery'), born in the Val de Vire in Normandy. His drinking-songs became famous under the name of *vaux de vire*, whence is derived the modern term 'vaudeville.' He is supposed to have been killed about the middle of the century in the English wars:

(26)

LAMENT FOR OLIVIER BASSELIN

Alas! Olivier Basselin,
Shall we have further news of you?
Or have the English done you in?

Your heart was wont in song to soar,
You lived a life of jollity,
And the white livery you wore
Through all the land of Normandy.

Far as Saint-Gilles in Coutentin,
In any pilgrim company
Was none made such a merry din.

The Englishmen have made a hell
For the good folks of Val de Vire:
No more the lads who sang so well
Will sing the songs we used to hear.

Pray God, whose good heart hateth sin,
And the sweet Virgin Mary too,
An ill end may the English win!

Next take this charming piece, a popular lament for some knight slain in the Breton wars, possibly, as Gaston Paris suggests, at the battle of St. Aubin in 1488:

(27)

Lament

Brave gentlemen of France,
  Whom bound for war I see,
I beg you, of your grace,
  To greet my love for me.

'How can I greet your love,
  Whom I know not by sight?'
'Easy is he to know,
  Clad all in armour white;

'A white-cross knight is he,
  Golden the spurs he wears,
And silver-gilt the tip
  That on his lance he bears.'

'Cease weeping, lady fair,
  For he is dead, I know:
In Brittany he fell,
  The Bretons laid him low.

'I saw men dig his grave
  On a green meadow's rim,
And heard four friars sing
  The last, sad mass for him.'

As a pendant to the lament for the fate of Olivier Basselin it may not be amiss to quote a verse from a French poem,[1] expressing pity for the misery of some English prisoner during the Hundred Years' War, who can only vent his grief in his own language:

De son grand mal pitié avais,
Et aussi mon cœur se doutait
Que un jour avoir eu pourrais
Autant, qui me déconfortait.
Et quand a lui on demandait:
'Hélas, qu'avez-vous, mon ami?'
  Autre chose ne répondait:
'God and Ourl Lady, help my!'

[1] Quoted by Ascoli. See note, p. 23.

Lastly we offer a little love-song, not because of its poetic merit, which is small, but because of the extreme simplicity and modernity of it:

(28)

The Post

And I 've had letters, sooth to say,
    Sent by my love to me;
Ah, how I 'll guard them night and day!
    I live in ecstasy.

For on my troth I love him so,
    I 've nought can ease provide
Or make my heart contentment know,
    Like living by his side.

Other delights are as the wind,
    Whatever meets the eye;
To have near by one's lover kind,
    Can there be joy so high?

Reverting now to the literary poetry of the fifteenth century, we end our account of this later medieval period by introducing the distinguished name of Charles d'Orléans (1391–1465), and the far greater name of Villon. Charles d'Orléans, grandson of Charles the Wise, and father of Louis XII, is remarkable as one of the greatest of the select company of royal poets. He had Italian blood in him, for his mother was daughter of Gian Galeazzo, Duke of Milan.

As a youth he married for his first wife his cousin, the young widow of our Richard II. At the age of twenty-five he was captured by Henry V at Agincourt, and carried off to England. A prisoner whose person was so near to the throne of France was not lightly to be parted with, and his captivity, far from a rigorous one, lasted for twenty-five years, and it may be that the enforced leisure he enjoyed gave the incentive as well as the opportunity to indulge his poetical bent. He learnt English, and indeed wrote poems in our language. But his best work probably dates from his fiftieth year, when he was finally ransomed and returned to France. There he took little part in politics, but during the long autumn of his life kept court at Blois, where he gathered round him poets of the day, and held as it were literary tournaments, in which his guests could prove their skill. Among those he thus entertained—and this is one of his titles to fame—was Villon himself, whose high repute as a poet and, no doubt, brilliance in talk and jest quite outweighed in the eyes of his gifted host his unattractive exterior and unsavoury character.

As a poet Charles d'Orléans shows little depth of thought or strength of passion, but in delicate grace and a languid charm he surpassed all his contemporaries, and in these qualities has not been excelled by any poet of his race. And there is a note of spring in his verse and of wistfulness, and a mild melancholy, all of which are among the characteristics of Ronsard and his school in the halcyon days of the French Renaissance. As examples of his work we venture to give versions of two of his exquisite rondeaux, which will find a place in French anthologies for all time:

TWO RONDEAUX

(29)

The year his winter cloak lets fall;
Wind, snow, and rain, he lays them by,
And dons the shining broidery
Of lucid sunlight, gilding all.
The birds and beasts, both great and small,
Do in their jargon sing or cry:
The year his winter cloak lets fall;
Wind, snow, and rain, he lays them by.
River and brook and waterfall
Wear, for a sparkling livery,
Their gold and silver jewelry;
All deck them for high festival.
The year his winter cloak lets fall.

(30)

O God, how good she is to see,
My gracious lady, kind and fair!
For the great virtues to her share
All mortals in her praise agree.

Who could find stale her company?
Fresh beauties still are budding there.
O God, how good she is to see,
My gracious lady, kind and fair!
Or here, or there, across the sea,
Matron or maid I find nowhere
With her perfection can compare;
Dream-like she comes in thought to me.
O God, how good she is to see!

The reader may find it interesting to compare with these modern renderings one written in English contemporary, or almost contemporary, with the original French. In 1827 Dr. Watson Taylor published for the Roxburghe Club, from a manuscript in the British Museum, an English translation of a mass of Charles d'Orléans's poetry, and of a number of poems by other authors; he claimed these English renderings for the duke himself. This is hardly believable, and such English, French, and German critical opinion as has occupied itself with the matter is dead against the claim. The question remains, what English (or French) poet of the time was accomplished enough to write them, many of them so admirably done. Here is the early rendering, not too adequate, of the second of the two rondeaux given above:

(30A)

O God how that she lokith verry fayre
The goodly swete my very hertis blis
That for the grace the which that in hir is
To everi wight hir prays doth newe repayre
Who is it he that kouthe hit loo contrayre
For hir bewte renewith ay y wis
    O God how that she lokith verry fayre
    The goodly swete my very hertis bliss
She hath no peere she lyvith wt-outen eyre
Of alle the fayre y except noon as this
For in hir loo ther nys oon poynt amys
Tis a dere hert worth a thousand payre
    O God how that she lokith verry fayre
    The goodly swete my very hertis bliss.

Finally let us set against this early English translation a short English poem that is probably an authentic piece by Charles himself:

> My hertly love is in your governauns,
> And ever shall whil that I live may.
> I pray to God that I may see that day
> That we be knyt with trouthfull alyauns.
> Ye shall not fynd feyning or variauns
> As in my part; that will I trewly say:
> My hertly love is in your governauns.

Grim beside the figure of Charles d'Orléans is that of Villon,[1] which now confronts us. He was born in Paris in 1431; whether his real name was Montcorbier or Des Loges is still a matter of dispute, but, his mother living in great poverty, he was taken charge of by a kindly benefactor, Guillaume de Villon, chaplain of the collegiate church of St. Benoît, who received him into his house, and saw him through his university course. From this good friend he took the name by which he is universally known. The facts of his life are derived from an intensive study by French scholars of his works, in themselves largely autobiographical, and also of the criminal records of his time.

In his early boyhood English soldiers with their Burgundian allies still haunted the taverns of the city, and roamed through its alleys; and though the Hundred Years' War was soon at an end, and the kingdom of France established, the narrow ill-lighted streets of the capital must long have swarmed with a wild population always bred in a long period of misery. It is not, therefore, surprising that the young Villon, an attractive figure for his recklessness, his brilliance, and his wit, though not indeed for his good looks, soon fell among evil companions. Two of these, Roger de Montigny, of good family, and Colin de Cayeulx, son of a locksmith, and so a useful member in any company of thieves, ultimately came to bad ends, the former being hanged, and the latter broken on the wheel. A contemporary was that amazing figure of her time, the notorious Huguette du Hamel, Abbess of Port-Royal, a very different representative of the Church from the benign Guillaume de Villon, but whose licen-

[1] For a full and vivid account of Villon's life and works see D. B. Wyndham Lewis's *François Villon*, Peter Davies, London.

tious life shows what was possible in unbridled vice in Paris of the fifteenth century.

The first of Villon's serious escapades occurred when he was nearly twenty-five years of age. On the evening of the 5th June 1455, the day of the popular festival of the Fête-Dieu, Villon was seated on a bench near St. Benoît's with a girl named Isabeau and Gilles, a priest, when up came another priest named Sermoise and Jean le Hardi, a master of arts of the university. An altercation followed, ending in a scuffle. Gilles and Isabeau made themselves scarce, and Villon had to defend himself against the two aggressors. Sermoise drew first blood, but received a dagger thrust in return, and a blow from a stone in the face. He died of his wounds, and Villon fled from Paris. In his absence he was sentenced to banishment. But in six months' time the sentence was remitted, and Villon returned to his old haunts.

His pardon on this occasion, and the leniency shown again and again in his short life, seem to indicate that if his brilliant qualities gained him the fatal friendship of the ruffians and outcast women who were his boon companions, they won for him also the interest of men of good standing and of influence. Anyhow, within a year he was in trouble again, and hastily left Paris for Angers. In his *Lesser Testament* he accounts for his flight by the resentment he felt after the humiliation of a thrashing he received under the very eyes of one, Catherine de Vaucelles, to whom he was paying his addresses, and who treated him like a heartless coquette : he sought to shake off the shackles of his love. But he had other good reasons for disappearing. He had recently been engaged with the gang of thieves he had formed, or joined, in more than one great robbery in Paris, including one at his old seminary, the Collège de Navarre ; and Angers, where an uncle of his was living as a monk, was worth surveying as a field for further operations. Ultimately, through the indiscreet revelations made in his cups by one of his confederates, Guy Taberie by name, the authors of the burglary at the Collège de Navarre were discovered.

Thus two years after he had left Paris Villon was arrested, tried, and sentenced to death. Again it is probable that influential friends intervened in his behalf, for the death penalty in his case, though not in Guy Taberie's, was commuted to perpetual banishment from Paris. Probably it was in the interval between the death sentence and the commuting of it that he wrote his tremendous ballade in expectation of being hanged.

There was nothing for him now but a wandering life, and it was in the course of this that he must have found his way to the court of Charles d'Orléans at Blois, where he took part in one of the duke's poetic tournaments. It is indeed conceivable that Charles, steeped in poetry himself, and realizing in Villon the poet behind the rogue, was one who, when appealed to for help in dire distress, did not turn a deaf ear. But once more Villon's evil fate dogged him, for in 1461 he was again arrested, apparently for sacrilege, and imprisoned by the Bishop of Orleans in a sort of dungeon in the Castle of Meung, the birthplace of the poet who completed the *Romance of the Rose*. Of the miseries and the tortures he endured during his incarceration there we have a full account in his *Greater Testament*. He obtained pardon and release late in the year on the accession of Louis XI, whether as the result of a general gaol-delivery or out of special favour is unknown.

The important fact is that on his immediate return to Paris he took in hand the composition of his monumental poem, the *Greater Testament*, the work that has immortalized him. He was only thirty years of age, but there can be no reasonable doubt that his short life of crime, debauchery, and privation, with the constant prickings of a tortured conscience and the terrors of a hunted animal, had made a wreck of him, and he was conscious that the hand of death was on him. However, there was to be no peace for him. A year later he was once more in serious trouble. He had been present at an affray, again near St. Benoît's, in which a well-known notary and his clerks had been grossly assaulted, and the notary himself wounded with a dagger. It would appear that Villon himself took no part in the scuffle. Nevertheless he was sentenced to death a second time. He appealed, and the order issued by the Parliament of Paris, dated 5th January 1463, which commuted the sentence of death to one of banishment gives us the last authentic news we have of him. Out into banishment he went and, this time, out into the void.

Such, in brief outline, is what is known of Villon's life and character. The poetry which has given him his high rank among the great poets, not merely of a nation, but of the world, is small in quantity. It consists in the main of two poems, the *Lesser Testament* of forty stanzas, and the *Greater Testament*, a longer poem with some twenty ballades and rondeaux of matchless quality interspersed. The kind of poem known as a Testament was a recognized type in medieval France. The author in the guise of testator disposes of his real and imaginary belongings among his boon companions and friends, his enemies and oppressors alike, and the scope afforded for the expression of wit, humour, irony, satire, and even invective on the one hand, and gratitude, admiration, and affection on the other, as well as, in the case of one of Villon's temperament and course of life, of bitter regret and remorse, will readily be recognized.

The *Lesser Testament* was written after his second flight from Paris, which he accounted for as a move to escape from the heartless Catherine de Vaucelles, though as suggested above there were probably other reasons as well; but the *Greater Testament* was, we repeat, written with the shadow of death hanging over him, after he had got release from the Bishop of Orleans's prison at Meung, and returned to Paris a broken man. An intensely personal note is struck throughout the poem; it is nothing less than an *apologia pro vita sua*, and never has one more poignant been written by man. It is haunted by remorse for an ill-spent youth, the horror of old age, and the fear of death, the certain end that awaits all mankind, prince and pauper, beauty born in high degree, and the wanton of the streets, saint and outcast. But for all this fear of death, he is frank throughout, does not disguise how low in debauchery he sank, nay, avows his enjoyment at the time of the sensual man's good things in life, rich food, good wine, and love, chuckles over success in crime, makes no pretence of suffering for others' guilt. It is this utter absence of hypocrisy, the frank avowal of his shame as of his repentance, and his blank dismay in the face of death that have atoned in just men's eyes for much that would otherwise arouse but disgust and reprobation, and given him a moral standing of his own.

He is not to be envied who can rise from a study of Villon without that pity for the man which is akin to love, as well as an exultant admiration of his genius. As a poet he handled the complicated verse-forms of his day with an ease and mastery that make their content as plain and straightforward as anything written in less sophisticated form. Indeed it may be argued that the very restraint imposed by form on one of his tumultuous power has given his poems the greatness that they have. They display wit, humour, grace, tenderness, and pathos, strength, biting satire, and fierce invective, and in none of these qualities has he been surpassed. With a single word, a short incisive phrase, a touch of sheer realism, a haunting refrain, he can raise one to romantic heights, or hurl one into the depths. A fine tribute to him will be found in the eloquent introduction to John Payne's great translation [1] of his poems, which made Villon known in this country as never before. Let us quote a fragment from it: 'He rejects nothing as common or unclean . . . his wit and pathos are like the sun which shines with equal and impartial light upon the evil and the good.'

The compelling charm of Villon's poetry has drawn many translators to the attempt to give some indication of its quality to English readers. Most of them have realized that in Villon's case no mere paraphrase will do; a real effort must be made to give as far as possible the form as well as the substance of the original. That has been the present writer's purpose, and if to some degree he has achieved it, without sacrificing all the magic of the master's verse; if, in other words, his versions do recall to those who know the originals the faintest suggestion of their peculiar charm, the labour he has expended will not have been in vain. Let us begin by giving a version of the stanza in the *Greater Testament* in which he speaks of his humble origin:

(31)

GRANT TESTAMENT, XXXV

Poor was I ever since a lad,
Of poor and humble stock I came;
No wealth at all my father had,
Nor his forbear, Horace by name;
Poverty dogs us, aye the same.
And where my ancestors are laid
(Whose souls God in his bounty claim!),
No crown or sceptre is displayed.

---

[1] A later, and very accomplished, translation is Mr. J. H. Lepper's *The Testaments of François Villon*, 1924, Casanova Society.

Then may follow the poignant expression of his regret for a wasted youth:

(32)

GRANT TESTAMENT, XXVI—XXIX

Ah, God! if in my foolish youth
My books at school I'd duly read,
And followed honesty and truth,
A home were mine, and feather-bed.
But no! away from school I fled,
As naughty little boys will do.
As I set down what I have said,
My heart is like to break in two.

The Preacher's word too lightly won
My will, and brought but wretchedness,
Who said: 'Enjoy thyself, my son,
Whiles thou art young.' Nevertheless
Another truth he doth impress
Elsewhere, and so he says again—
These are his words, nor more or less—
'Youth and the prime of life are vain.'

My days, says Job, away are fled,
Like threads before the burning tow,
Which o'er the cloth before him spread
The weaver passes to and fro;
If one loose thread its end should show
He burns it in a flash away.
So now I fear nor threat nor blow;
Death will at last all pain allay.

Where are the lads so gay and tall
Whom I forgathered with of old,
In speech and song so ready all,
In word and deed so frank and bold?
Some of them now are stiff and cold,
No vestige of them will you find:
May Paradise their souls enfold,
And God save him who lags behind!

A page or two after this cry of regret we are confronted with the first and most beautiful of all his ballades, one of the loveliest poems in the world, the *Ballade of Ladies of Old Time*. The version which follows the translator offers with many apologies. Mr. Paul Hookham's rendering of it in his *Ballades of François Villon interpreted into English Verse*, a little volume published by Messrs. Blackwell, and as delightful to handle and to look at as to read, had long seemed to him the one which had more of the tang of the original than any other. It had so sunk into his consciousness that he found himself quite unable to produce an original version of his own. For more than one reason he was unable to borrow it and print it as it stood. But the ballade would not let him be, and in desperation he set himself to work on Mr. Hookham's version. If he has done what he ought not to have done he craves indulgence, and hopes he may be forgiven, provided that he has not ruined both the original and the poetic quality of Mr. Hookham's rendering, in his passionate desire to give in his book some version of these haunting lines:

(33)

LADIES OF OLD TIME

Tell me where, in what country is
Flora, the beautiful Romane;
Archipiada, and Thais,
Who cousin was to her germane;
Echo, whose accents still retain
The call that sounds o'er stream and mere,
Who beauty had more than humane?
Say where the snows of a past year!

Where is the all-wise Heloise,
For whom, unmanned, did monk remain
Pierre Esbaillart at Saint-Denys?
His love it was cost him that pain.
And where the queen who did ordain
That Buridan, once loved too dear,
Sewn in a sack should drown in Seine?
Say where the snows of a past year!

Queen Blanche, as fair as fleur-de-lys,
Who sang with siren-voice her strain;
And big-foot Berte, Bietris, Allys;
Harembourges, mistress over Maine;
And Jeanne, that good soul from Lorraine,
By English burnt at Rouen here;
Where are they, Virgin Soveraine?
Say where the snows of a past year!

Prince, where they are, ask not again
This week, this year, in hope to hear;
Live haunted still by this refrain:
Say where the snows of a past year!

Who were these dead ladies whose names Villon has immortalized? Flora was the name borne by many a well-known Roman courtesan; Archipiada, or Archipiades, stands for one of her Greek compeers, though the name is a corruption of that of Alcibiades, legends of whose beauty and licentious life led by some strange chance to his being mistaken in the Middle Ages for a woman. Echo is the nymph changed by Narcissus into a rock. Of Heloise and Abelard the story is well known. An expanded version of the legend of Buridan and Margaret of Burgundy, unfaithful wife of the quarrelsome Louis X, will be found in Dumas's thrilling cloak-and-dagger drama, *La Tour de Nesle*, of which a good translation by A. L. Gowans has been published by Gowans and Gray. Queen Blanche was Blanche of Castile, mother of St. Louis. Thuasne has pointed out that Berte, Bietris, and Allys are the three great ladies who figure in the Lotharingian epic, *Hervi de Metz*. Aelis, daughter of Pierre, Duke of Lorraine, married a courtier of her father's. Their son, Hervi, married Bietris, whose brother was Flores, father of Berte, the mother of Charlemagne. Thus Berte was the niece of Bietris, daughter-in-law of Aelis. Harembourges, or Haremburgis, heiress of Maine, is probably the lady who married Fulke V of Anjou; Madame Duclaux has made the enticing conjecture that she may stand for the fair Érembor of the old *chanson de toile*. Joan of Arc we know.

The address of this ballade to a certain *prince* recalls a feature of the poetical life of medieval times, viz. the verse-contests, such as the famous *Jeux floraux* of Toulouse. These were presided over by a president, styled prince, and naturally the *envoi* to many ballades was addressed to him. Often enough in Provence, and later, as at Charles d'Orléans's court at Blois, the president may have been a prince in very fact.

Next we give the stanzas from the *Greater Testament* leading up to the fine ballade he composed for his mother's sake, followed by a version of the ballade itself.

(34)

GRANT TESTAMENT, LXXV—LXXIX

First, give I this poor soul of mine
Unto the blessed Trinity,
And to Our Lady's grace resign,
Who harbour'd our Divinity;
Beseeching all the charity
Of the nine Angel Orders fair,
That they may bear the gift on high
Before the throne so rich and rare.

Item, I give my body here
To mother earth, who all men bore;
Small fat thereon the worms will cheer,
Hunger has ravaged it so sore.
Quickly my flesh to her restore;
From earth it came, seeks earth again.
All things, unless I err the more,
Gladly their proper place regain.

To Master Guillaume de Villon,
Who more than father was to me,
Kinder than mother to her son,
The child from swaddling bands set free:
He saved me after many a spree,
And therefrom got scant happiness;
Wherefore I pray on bended knee
Some joy at last his soul may bless.

Item, I give my library,
And *Legend of the Stolen Mascot*,
The which Master Guy Tabarie

Wrote out, the man who lieth not;
Under a table lies the lot
In quires, and though but rudely writ,
Its theme so great a fame has got
As makes up for the form of it.

Item, on my poor mother I
Bestow this prayer to Our Mistress;
She wept for me full bitterly,
And had, God knows, cause for distress:
No other stronghold or fortress
Than Her above can I provide
For soul and body in sore stress,
Nor elsewhere my poor mother hide.

Of the nine orders of Angels referred to in the first stanza Milton's famous line names five:

Thrones, Dominations, Princedoms, Virtues, Powers.

The remaining four are the two highest orders, Seraphim and Cherubim, and, to complete the list, Archangels and Angels. There is a useful note of Butler's on these angelic hierarchies; see l. 98, Canto XXVIII, of his edition of Dante's *Paradiso*. The third stanza contains Villon's tribute to his great benefactor, Guillaume de Villon, whose name he took. In the fourth stanza we have ventured to translate *Le Rommant du Pet au Deable* by *The Legend of the Stolen Mascot*. The *Pet au Deable* was a boundary stone in front of the Hôtel du Pet au Deable, the residence of one of the great Parisian families in the service of the court. A band of riotous undergraduates, including Villon, uprooted it, carried it off, and set it up in the university quarter, where they danced and sang ribald songs round it. The attempt of the civic authorities to recover it led to tumult and even to bloodshed, and Parliament had to intervene. The translation offered was suggested by the struggles that arise from time to time between the Faculties in some of our provincial universities for the possession of some treasured mascot. That at Liverpool is known as 'Sister Jane,' and the fight for her possession a few years ago waxed so hot that it threatened to embroil civic and university authorities, though trouble was nipped in the bud by the intervention of a dignified city councillor.

D

The Merseyside university produced no poet capable of celebrating this notable event in fitting verse, but with the loss of Villon's romance of the *Pet au Deable* has disappeared what must have been the finest example ever written of undergraduate wit, humour, grim irony, and licentious language. Characteristic in this same stanza is Villon's sardonic reference to Guy Taberie's truthfulness, for, as told above, it was the latter's outspokenness in his cups that led to the discovery of Villon as one of the authors of the notorious burglary at the Collège de Navarre.

(35)

BALLADE THAT VILLON MADE ON THE REQUEST OF HIS MOTHER FOR A PRAYER TO OUR LADY

Lady of Heaven, Regent on earth below,
And Empress of Inferno's marshy plain,
Take me, who humbly pay my Christian vow,
That I may count with those whom you ordain,
Though by no merit I thereto attain.
Your virtues, O my Queen and my Mistress,
Are greater far than is my wickedness,
And without them no soul can reach the sky;
So I aver, being no false prophetess.
  In the which faith I fain would live and die.

That I am His, give Him your Son to know;
May He blot out my sins, and grace again
As on the Egyptian, so on me bestow,
Like clerk Theophilus, that priest profane,
Whom you set free, cleared of his guilty stain,
Though faith in Satan he did once profess.
Guard me, lest I like him should e'er transgress,
Virgin intact, who bore in purity
The Host raised high at Mass our souls to bless—
  In the which faith I fain would live and die.

A poor old woman I, and well I trow
No wit is mine; to read were labour vain;
But in my parish, when to church I go,
There Heaven, with harps and lutes, is painted plain,

And Hell, with damned souls in boiling pain;
This gives me fear, that joy and cheerfulness.
Give me such joy to have, high-born Goddess,
To whom should sinners all for refuge fly,
Faithful, sincere, quit of all slothfulness,
    In the which faith I fain would live and die.

Envoi

Virgin, whom we revere, you bore, Princess,
Iesus the King, whose name shall ne'er grow less.
Lord of all might, He endured our feebleness,
Left Heaven, and found for us the remedy,
Offering to Death His dear young loveliness.
None else our Lord, and Him I so confess.
    In the which faith I fain would live and die.

The second verse of this prayer to Our Lady contains reference to St. Mary of Egypt, who turned saint from courtesan, and Theophilus, the monk who, like Faust, sold himself to Satan, in order to win promotion in his holy calling. These legends were the subject of two of the most remarkable of Rutebeuf's works, probably familiar to Villon, and were favourite subjects for the decoration of Romanesque and Gothic churches, either in sculpture or in the coloured glass of windows. The story of Theophilus figures twice in stone at Notre-Dame, in glass at Laon, and in one or the other elsewhere; but the most remarkable presentation of his legend is perhaps that on a bas-relief at Souillac in the Dordogne. Of St. Mary the Egyptian there is a naïve statue at St. Germain l'Auxerrois in Paris, and also a representation of her legend in a window.

Of the ballades which Villon wrote without incorporating them in his *Greater Testament* the outstanding one is that which he composed in expectation of being hanged. By common consent he attained in this the very pinnacle of his art, and no poet has written lines more sombre, more human, more moving, and more powerful—lines that must have been written by one who had plumbed the depths of vice and misery, and who, in a moment of intensity, was yet capable of soaring into the empyrean. Here is a version of it which has at least the merit of keeping close to the original:

(36)

Ballade that Villon made in Expectation of being Hanged with his Companions

O brother men, who live when we are dead,
Keep not your hearts against us hardened so,
For, if on our poor souls a tear you shed,
Sooner will God His grace on you bestow.
You see us, five or six, hanged in a row;
As for our flesh, once fed luxuriously,
'Tis long devoured and rotted, as you see,
And we, mere bones, in dust and ashes fall.
Let no one mock us in our misery;
    But pray to God that He forgive us all!

And if we call you, brothers, be it not said
That, since from Justice came the fatal blow,
You scorn us. Sure, there 's not in each man's head
Store of sound sense to guide him; this ye know.
Plead for us, since we 're gone where dead men go,
With Him, the Virgin Mary's Son, that He
May keep for us His mercy flowing free,
And save us, whom the fires of Hell appal.
Harry us not: we 're dead! So let us be,
    But pray to God that He forgive us all!

The rain has soaked and washed us, every shred,
The sun has dried and blackened us enow,
The crows have dug our eyes from out their bed,
From beard and eyebrows pluckt the hairs also.
No rest is ours, no rest; but to and fro,
Worse pitted than a tailor's thimble, we,
The pecked of birds, swing here continually,
As shifting winds hither and thither call.
For the which cause join not our company,
    But pray to God that He forgive us all!

Envoi

Prince Jesus, who dost hold the world in fee,
Grant not that Hell win o'er us mastery;

With Hell, O Lord, be our account but small.
Men, this is not a time for mockery;
 But pray to God that He forgive us all!

By way of relief from this grim utterance let us revert to the
Greater Testament, and read the versions of two poignant and
beautiful rondeaux that appear in it:

(37)

Death, I denounce thy cruel dart;
Thou hast my mistress snatched from me,
And showest still no clemency
Except I languish in my smart:
Since when my force and strength depart;
But how could she in life hurt thee,
  Death?

Twain were we and had but one heart;
If that be dead, so must I be,
Or lifeless live like saints we see
In choirs, carved by the mason's art,
  Death!

(38)

When I return from durance vile,
Where I have left my life well nigh,
If Fortune looks at me awry,
Judge how she vents on me her bile!
It seems to me she well might smile
Whom reason's plea should satisfy,
  When I return.

But if she still be full of guile
And wills that I die utterly,
God grant that in His house on high
My soul be quit of her aye-while,
  When I return!

Finally, here is a version of the epitaph, terminating in a
rondeau, which fitly finds its place near the end of the poem:

(39)

Epitaph

Here lies and sleeps in garret low
One whom love's dart has stricken dead,
A poor, wee scholar years ago,
One François Villon, be it said.
Off land of his he never fed.
He gave you all he had, ye know,
His tables, benches, baskets, bread:
Gay lads, sing this for him now sped:

Repose eternal give to him,
Lord God, and light perpetual,
Who never had the wherewithal
Fills bowl and platter to the brim.
As men a turnip peel or trim,
Shorn was he, head, beard, eyebrows all.
    Repose eternal give to him.
Exiled he was by judges grim;
They kicked his rump and garr'd him fall
Though 'I appeal' was aye his call,
In language plain, no pedant's whim.
    Repose eternal give to him.

CHAPTER III

THE passage from the fifteenth to the sixteenth century in French literature is like the change from winter to spring. The chill and gloom and blackness of the times in which Villon lived, like the dead winter season of which he writes:

> When upon wind the wolves are fed,
> And for the rigour of the time
> One hugs the hearth from none to prime,[1]

are in strange contrast to the atmosphere of warmth and radiance that enveloped Ronsard, the next great poet of France, by the middle of the sixteenth century. Even the thought of death, never absent from the heart of French poetry, which to Villon was the last agony of man in all its horror, induced but a mild melancholy, typified by the fading of a flower, in the minds of Ronsard and his school. And French poetry, frozen so long in artificial moulds, burst out and flowered into new and luxuriant forms, with a range of expression, which in fullness, in grace, and in music, has rarely been equalled.

For the prime cause of this new and prodigious development we have to go back to the middle of the fifteenth century and the epoch-making invention of printing. This was soon followed by the capture of Constantinople by the Turks and the break-up of the Byzantine Empire, with the great diffusion of classical learning, and particularly of the literature of Greece, that naturally followed. Books were rapidly multiplied, the number of men who read for themselves increased, and the number of those who thought for themselves, with the result that much of the scholasticism and superstition of the Middle Ages was shaken off like a cloak. The sombre challenge, *memento mori*, yielded place with many to the exhilarating call, *memento vivere*. Italy, both at Rome and in its flourishing city-states, was the first to reap the harvest of the new learning. But France was soon to

---

[1] J. Payne's translation.

71

catch the enthusiasm of what then seemed a golden prime, and to drink long draughts of the beauty and the wisdom and the poetry of a pre-Christian world. And the pioneer was not to be a poet, but the great Rabelais himself, born at Chinon near the end of the fifteenth century, and whose prose epics of *Gargantua* and *Pantagruel* mirror the France of his time. He was a man of immense learning, successively monk, priest, wandering scholar, physician, lecturer, priest again, and, above all, author of works, which for all their coarseness and even buffoonery are such prodigies of humour and learning, and instinct with such a gusto for the good things of life, as to stand out among the everlasting triumphs of French genius.

As the Crusades had been intellectually fruitful in bringing together men of all European cultures, so did the Renaissance, and more markedly, provide a common ground for all humanists and scholars whatever their origin. In the sixteenth century contacts between Great Britain and France were close, and if we were still heavily in France's debt we were beginning in a small measure to repay our debts. Of English humanists the most conspicuous in French eyes was the great figure of Sir Thomas More, of whom Rabelais borrowed freely; and from the general attitude of Frenchmen to More, it is quite impossible to believe, as some would have it, that he was the 'great English scholar' ridiculed by Rabelais in his second book under the name of Thaumastes.

Second only to More comes Thomas Linacre of Oxford, equally famous as physician and scholar. Linacre himself had studied Greek under that dazzling Italian scholar, Politian, and to him in turn came More and Erasmus for instruction in the language. Of his Latin textbooks edition after edition was published in France, where it is odd to discover a treatise on arithmetic of English origin a popular textbook, for, in speaking of Gargantua's education, Rabelais in Book I, Chapter XXIII, names Tunstal, Bishop of Durham, its author. Rabelais pays Linacre himself an equivocal compliment in one of his coarser passages, when he tells the wholly apocryphal story of a visit of Villon to our Edward V, in the course of which, addressing the king, he refers to Linacre as 'your learned physician.'

But a more widespread influence on France from our side of the Channel came later than Linacre or More in the person of

George Buchanan, the greatest of Scottish humanists, and among the best of late Latin poets. Buchanan indeed for many years of his life became a real Frenchman by adoption. Lecturer at the Collège de Guienne at Bordeaux, rector of the Collège de Boncour, tutor in the household of the Marshal de Brissac, a traveller welcomed wherever he set foot, he became a warm friend of a host of Frenchmen of high rank, and of poets and scholars, including the great J. C. Scaliger. His poetry was admired by the poets of the Pleiad, of whom Du Bellay dedicated a sonnet to him; while Montaigne, prince of essayists, claims, in his essay on 'Education', Buchanan, whom he calls 'the great poet of Scotland,' among his tutors, and boasts that he played with success the chief parts in his Latin plays at the Collège de Guienne.

But notwithstanding these contacts between England and France in the early days of the Renaissance, which certainly had their influence on Rabelais, English poetry was still of small account in France. Chaucer, indeed, in his day, was regarded as a promising offshoot from a French stem, *grant translateur*, as Deschamps called him; and Clément Marot, an exact contemporary of Rabelais, and the chief French poet of the first half of the sixteenth century, who must be regarded as the link between Villon and Ronsard, was less directly influenced by the new learning than Rabelais. Naturally, for as a poet he was steeped in the *Romance of the Rose* and Villon, in the old learning rather than the new, and yet he could not fail to drink in draughts of the new atmosphere in which he moved. Marot, of Norman ancestry, was born in 1497, and lived through the reigns of the weak but kindly Louis XII, son of the poet, Charles d'Orléans, and the brilliant but reckless Francis I, whose name is always associated with our Henry VIII through the magnificence of their friendly meeting on the Field of the Cloth of Gold.

It is curious to reflect how the kings of France, so soon after the end of the terrible Hundred Years' War, and when the subtle brain and masterful though spider-like policy of Louis XI, the halting, sombre, superstitious figure that dominates the scene in Scott's *Quentin Durward*, seemed to have abolished the reign of feudalism, and to have established the kingdom of France on a basis of absolutism, repeated the blunder of their English rivals. Just as our English kings instead of fostering their own dominions at home wasted our manhood and wealth in the vain effort to

*D

maintain their shadowy claim to the throne of France, so did Louis XII and Francis I, with a rich and glorious kingdom of their own, now in the sixteenth century, invite disaster in the foolhardy enterprise of gaining a firm foothold in Italy.

In 1524 Clément Marot, who had early obtained a position at court, accompanied Francis on the fatal expedition into Italy where the poet was wounded and captured in the defeat at Pavia. He soon returned to France, and thenceforward devoted himself to poetry. He was, no doubt, well read in Latin, and he was also influenced by Italian, but his chief claim to scholarship lies in his knowledge of the earlier poetry of his own country; and he is greatly to be honoured for the editions he published both of the *Romance of the Rose* and of Villon's works. A most facile versifier on his own account, he poured out a stream of verse which, without neglecting medieval forms altogether, was more free, more elastic, and more varied than any poetry yet known. His vast output of occasional verse contained much in the way of licentious epigram, but he developed a strong religious side, and his translations of the Psalms, some of which are quite excellent, brought him under suspicion of heresy, and he had to flee the country, first to Geneva, not a congenial atmosphere for him, and then to the north of Italy, where he died in 1544.

A striking illustration of the varieties of thought and religious opinion which existed during the intellectual turmoil of the early Renaissance may be found in Dean Kitchin's assertion that it is not improbable that in 1528 Loyola, Rabelais, and Calvin were in Paris together.

As a specimen of Clément Marot's work at its most graceful we may offer a version of one of his songs:

(40)

SONG

Who seeks the happiness
    That one kind glance can give
Must meet with my mistress—
    God grant her long to live!
Such is her tender grace,
    That even the sight of her
A thousand griefs would chase,
    Or more, if more there were.

Marvellous to mine eyes
  My fair one's virtues seem;
When thoughts of her arise
  My heart stirs in a dream.
Her beauty sovereign
  Would make me swoon to death,
Did not her bounty deign
  To guard my fleeting breath.

And here is an artful epigram on himself:

(41)
Epigram on Himself

I cannot as I was abide,
  And never again shall I be young;
My lovely spring and summertide
  Are through an open window sprung.
O Love, my master here on earth,
  Fore other gods I 've done thy will;
Could I but have a second birth,
  How I would serve thee better still!

On the sterner side he may be illustrated by his epigram on the execution of Samblançay, superintendent of finances under Francis I, who had been falsely accused of embezzlement:

(42)
The Judge and the Condemned

When Maillart, judge of Hell, led Samblançay
  Up to Montfalcon's gibbet, there to die,
Which of the two in your opinion, pray,
  Looked best his part?   To help you let me try.
  'Twas Maillart seemed the man whom death was nigh,
While Samblançay appeared so stout of heart,
  You might feel sure his hand the noose would tie
That on Montfalcon's height should hang Maillart.

The most direct influence of Marot is to be detected in a school of poetry that before the middle of the century grew up in the wealthy city of Lyons which, as a half-way house between Italy and Paris, had early developed a cultured society. One of the younger poets of that school, and the most famous, was a woman, Louise Labé, born in 1526, whom some critics claim to be the greatest poetess France has produced. Certainly she was a very remarkable personality. Known as *La Belle Cordière*, she was the daughter of one rich ropemaker and the wife of another. In her romantic youth she donned armour, like another Joan of Arc, and rode in the suite of the Dauphin to the siege of Perpignan.

Her poetical output was not large, and consists of elegies and a number of sonnets. Some of these sonnets are of astonishing excellence; indeed a peculiarly Shakespearian quality has been claimed for them. However this may be, the poems of this young woman, almost an exact contemporary of Ronsard, have a passionately human touch, a personal, modern thrill, which you will not match in all the sonnets of either Ronsard or his friend, Du Bellay. Thus in her confession of a woman's hopes and disappointments and passion addressed to the ladies of Lyons she ends with a call to Love:

> Mais si tu veus que j'ayme jusqu'au bout,
> Fay que celui que j'estime mon tout,
> Qui seul me peut faire plorer et rire,
> Et pour lequel si souvent je soupire,
> Sente en ses os, en son sang, en son ame,
> Ou plus ardente, ou bien egale flame.
> Alors ton faix plus aisé me sera,
> Quand avec moy quelcun le portera.

> If I must nurse a love beyond recall
> Grant thou that he whom I account my all,
> He who alone can make me laugh or cry,
> For whom, alas, so oftentimes I sigh,
> Feel in his bones, and blood, and soul, a fire
> Ardent as mine, or burning even higher.
> Then easier shall I find thy load to bear
> When by my side stands one its weight to share.

Those who are familiar with Christina Rossetti's famous sonnet entitled *Remember* will find a kinship with it in the two sonnets of Louise Labé, versions of which follow, the inspiration of them

being perhaps her love for Olivier de Magny, one of Ronsard's
protégés. The feminine note rings through Louise Labé's
sonnets as through that of Christina Rossetti—the feminine note
to appreciate which you have only to listen to the prouder, less
unselfish, less resigned, masculine note to be heard in Shakespeare's sonnet lxxi.

(43)

So soon as I have laid me wearily
On my soft bed to find my longed-for rest,
My troubled spirit steals from out my breast
And flies incontinent where you may be.

Ah! then it seems that I hold close to me,
On my soft bosom what I love the best,
What I have hoped for, sighed for, so distrest
I 've thought my heart would break for agony.

O gentle sleep, and night my comforter!
O sweet repose, that smooths away all care,
Nightly this dream to my closed eyes admit;

And if true happiness may never stir
In waking hours the poor fond heart I bear,
Now let me clasp at least its counterfeit.

(44)

While from my streaming eyes the tears can fall,
In fond regret, for moments spent with thee;
And o'er my sobs I can win mastery
And make thee hear a voice however small;

While I can bid my hand thy charm recall
And from my little lute pluck melody;
While in my heart I can contented be
With but one wish, to know thee all in all;

I have no weak desire that I may die:
But when of tears I feel mine eyes run dry,
My voice grow feeble, and my fingers tire,

And when my heart, pent in this house of clay,
Can show no glimmer more of passion's fire,
I 'll pray that Death may cloud my brightest day.

When we come to Ronsard we are launched on the full tide of
the Renaissance in French literature. It is difficult to recall a
name that signifies more in the way of achievement. One of the
most fascinating, most illuminating studies of any period is
Mr. Hilaire Belloc's on the poetry of the French Renaissance,
with its happy title *Avril*, which conveys in a single word all the
gaiety, the light, the colour, and the scent of spring. When he
comes to treat of Ronsard himself he leads off with a passage so
fine and so true that one may be excused for appropriating it.
'If it be true,' he says, 'that words create for themselves a special
atmosphere, and that their mere sound calls up vague outer
things beyond their strict meaning, so it is true that the names
of the great poets by their mere sound, by something more than
the recollection of their work, produce an atmosphere corresponding to the quality of each; and the name of Ronsard throws
about itself like an aureole the characters of fecundity, of leader-
ship, and of fame.'

Prince of Poets, as he was called, Ronsard was born on the
banks of the Loire, near Vendôme, in 1524. He came of good
family, and entered court life at the age of ten. When Made-
leine of France, daughter of Francis I, married in 1537 James V
of Scotland, Ronsard, then a boy of twelve, went in her train to
Scotland, and spent two years in Edinburgh, where a Scottish
gentleman initiated him in the study of Virgil and Horace.
Clearly his interest in classical learning must have begun early.
In later youth he accompanied French ambassadors to England,
Flanders, Holland, and Germany. But when about twenty he
was attacked by serious illness, and though he recovered he
was left with a permanent deafness which unfitted him for the
active life for which he was destined. Hence he turned his
thoughts to literature, and devoted himself for years under
Daurat, a distinguished scholar of the day, to the study of the
classics, the new learning that had so lately dawned on the world.
Among his fellow-students were Du Bellay, Belleau, Baïf, and
others.

The enthusiastic band of young scholars formed a coterie of

seven, to which was given the name of the Pleiad, after an Alexandrian constellation of seven tragic poets, who flourished in the third century B.C. They set themselves by the ardent study of Greek and Latin to reform the French language, and found on classical models a literature which might rival those of Greece and Rome. They were saved from pedantry, and the dull industry of the copyist, by the intellectual excitement that fired them, and the deep affection they felt for their own language, and their pride in the possibilities of a new culture of which it should be the mouthpiece. They were kept fresh by their passionate love for natural beauty, which made them revel in the joys of the countryside, each in that particularly of his own native soil.

In 1549 Du Bellay published their manifesto in the shape of a *Défense et Illustration de la Langue française*, a work which, though largely modelled on an Italian original, set out fully their aims in relation to French. These were largely realized; they did succeed in enriching their language, not only with words and expressions derived from Greek and Latin, but also from the picturesque speech of the countryside and of the arts and crafts, while they developed not only new metres but new rhythms as well, and a smooth fluency which involved no loss of dignity. Indeed, they made French the language that we know, and to realize fully what their achievement was we have only to compare the French they wrote with that of Clément Marot and Rabelais, with both of whom they were younger contemporaries. One verse-form of an artificial character they did affect, viz. the sonnet, and of this they produced several long sequences, among which Ronsard's *Sonnets pour Hélène* [1] and Du Bellay's *Antiquités de Rome*, for all its borrowings from Latin, old and new, stand out pre-eminent. Du Bellay's *Antiquités de Rome*, indeed, is admitted into the select company of the great sonnet sequences of literature, while of single sonnets it may be claimed that the most famous and best-loved of all ever written is Ronsard's *Quand vous serez bien vieille*, in the series to Helen, of which a version will presently be given.

But we should be doing Ronsard as man and poet an injustice if we confined ourselves too closely to the strict limits of this book

[1] A free translation of the whole of this series has recently been published by Mr. Humbert Wolfe.

and confined ourselves to the illustration of his sonnets, odes, and lyrical verse by which he is best known. He wrote as well a great quantity of poetry of more serious intention. His epic, the *Franciade*, written in glorification of a French royalty of mythical Trojan ancestry, is by general consent a failure, a dull exercise in rhetoric rather than poetry, written in cramped, decasyllabic verse instead of the alexandrines of which he was so easy a master. But when he threw himself into the controversies aroused by the wars of religion that broke out in his time he shows himself the grand poet that he was. He was strongly on the side of the Catholics against the Huguenots, for he conceived the struggle to be between authority, based upon reason and tradition, against what he terms 'opinion.'

His series of *Discours des Misères de ce temps*, though they are sometimes, like all controversial writing when read after the occasion for them has passed, of tedious length and at times positively choked with passion, contain passages of burning eloquence, almost irresistible argument, fine feeling, and urgent prayer for peace. For his picture of 'opinion' he draws on all the resources of his recollections of the descriptions by classic authors of Fama and Bellona; he attacks fiercely Wyclif and John Huss, Luther, Zwingli, Bucer, and, of course, Calvin; but he is fair-minded enough to realize how much of the trouble has been occasioned and is aggravated by abuses within the Church of Rome itself. Thus in the elegy he wrote following the tragedy of Amboise he appeals to the preachings of St. Paul, and cries:

> Que diroit-il de voir l'Église à Jésus-Christ,
> Qui fut jadis fondée en humblesse d'esprit,
> En toute patience, en toute obéissance,
> Sans argent, sans crédit, sans force, ny puissance,
> Pauvre, nue, exilée, ayant jusques aux os
> Les coups des fouets sanglans imprimez sur le dos;
> Et la voir aujourd'huy riche, grasse et hautaine,
> Toute pleine d'écus, de rente et de domaine?
> Ses ministres enflez, et ses Papes encor
> Pompeusement vestus de soye et de drap d'or?

> What would he say, to see the Church of Christ,
> Founded of old in humbleness of heart,
> Patient always, always obedient,

No silver, credit, strength, nor force of arms,
Poor, naked, exiled, bleeding to the bone
From lash of whip imprinted on the back;
To see her as to-day, rich, fat, and proud,
Bulging with coin, with revenues and land?
Her ministers puffed up, ay, and her Popes
Arrayed in pomp of silk and cloth of gold.

Indeed, there are outbursts in Ronsard's *Discours* that cannot be surpassed by anything in the *Tragiques* of Agrippa d'Aubigné, the great Huguenot poet, in whom M. Dorchain sees the precursor of the Hugo of the *Châtiments* and *L'Année terrible*.

Ronsard lived for over sixty years, and his production was immense. In his lifetime fame and popularity were his in profusion. But as in the case of many another great poet who wrote much, the bulk of his work cannot be read now without some feeling of weariness. Nevertheless, in almost everything he wrote one is thrilled now and again by the inimitable Ronsardian touch. Of such of his work as lives to-day in all its grace and charm, and can never die, we give but few examples, two of them the most familiar of his poems, of either of which it is perhaps a presumption to offer a rendering. But we may perhaps be permitted, first, to give in the original French one of the most exquisite of his little poems, based on Hadrian's dying address to his soul:

> Animula, vagula, blandula,
> Hospes comesque corporis,
> Quae nunc abibis in loca
> Pallidula, rigida, nudula;
> Nec, ut soles, dabis jocos?

The jewel-like quality of this poem of Ronsard's makes it irresistible, but its free use of charming French diminutives, for which no fair equivalent can be found in English, renders it, like Eustache Deschamps's *Sui je, sui je, sui je belle*, quite untranslatable:

A Son Ame

> Amelette Ronsardelette,
> Mignonnelette, doucelette,
> Tres-chere hostesse de mon corps,

Tu descens là bas foiblelette,
Pasle, maigrelette, seulette,
Dans le froid royaume des mors;

Toutefois simple, sans remors
De meurtre, poison, et rancune,
Mesprisant faveurs et tresors

Tant enviez par la commune.
Passant, j'ai dit: suy ta fortune,
Ne trouble mon repos: je dors.

We now offer a version of that most famous of his sonnets to
which allusion has already been made, and for this version
perhaps this much may be claimed, viz. that it does keep close
to the original:

(45)

When you are old and near the hearth's warm blaze
You wind and spin by candle-light at eve,
Singing my songs you 'll say, and scarce believe:
Ronsard once loved to hymn my beauty's praise.

No maid that hears the words her mistress says,
Though half asleep the toilsome thread she weave,
But, starting at my name, will cease to grieve,
Blessing your name now crowned with deathless bays.

I shall be underground; a formless ghost,
Mid myrtle shades I 'll keep my quiet post:
You 'll crouch in eld and watch the fire-light play,

My love regretting and your cruel scorn.
Live now, I charge you, wait not for the morn:
Gather Life's roses while 'tis yet to-day.

There follows a version of an ode scarcely less well known than
the foregoing sonnet:

(46)

Mignonne, come let us seek the rose
In morning light we saw disclose
Her robe of crimson to the sun;

Has she not lost at eventide
Her robe's smooth folds in crimson dyed,
    And the soft bloom like yours she won?

Ah, see within how short a space,
Mignonne, she falleth from her place,
    Alas, her beauties disarrayed!
O cruel step-dame, Nature, why
Should flower so fair so early die,
    Unfold at dawn, at even fade?

Then, if you trust me fair, Mignonne,
While youth's gay flourish still is on
    And thrills you with the green of spring,
Enjoy, enjoy your girlhood's prime!
As with this flower, old age in time
    Will ruin on your beauty bring.

Finally, here is a version of another of his loveliest sonnets which well illustrates the point raised earlier, how the thought of death which to Villon was man's last agony seemed but to affect Ronsard and his school with the mild melancholy occasioned by the fading of a flower:

(47)

Lo, on her slender branch, the rose of May,
In lovely youth, in her first blossoming hour!
The sky grows jealous of the glowing flower
That tearful dawn waters at break of day.

Grace nestles in her cup, with love to stay,
Perfuming garden-plot and shady bower:
But dashed by rain, or the fell dog-star's power,
Languishing leaf by leaf she fades away.

And so with thee: in thy young loveliness,
When earth and sky alike thy beauty bless,
Struck down by fate must thou in dust repose.

For obsequies receive my tears like showers,
This bowl of milk, this basket full of flowers,
That, quick or dead, thy body rest a rose.

Joachim du Bellay, born in 1525, undoubtedly the second in rank of the Pleiad, came like Ronsard of good family, and from the same rich countryside, the watershed of the Loire with its wide, open, sunny spaces drained by the most leisurely and luxurious of the great French rivers. It was at an inn near Poitiers that in 1547 he first met Ronsard, and thenceforward they worked together like brothers in their patriotic efforts for the glory of their country's literature. Two of Du Bellay's kinsmen, Guillaume du Bellay and his younger brother Jean, the cardinal, were men of high distinction, indeed the ablest diplomats in the service of Francis I. Guillaume du Bellay was a patron of Rabelais, who twice speaks of him in terms of reverence, and gives a moving account of his death of which he may have been an eye-witness. In 1553 the cardinal took his young kinsman, the poet, in his train to Rome. There Joachim spent over four years, though he was not happy in the life he led. The papal throne was occupied for the first half of his stay in Rome by the notorious Julius III, of whom Olivier de Magny, a brother poet of the Pleiad, wrote the bitter lines:

Il laisse à son trespas d'un chacun en tous lieux
Sans complaintes la bouche et sans larmes les yeux,
Tant a esté sa vie à chacun détestable
Et tant est ceste mort à chacun profitable.

No one on all this earth was left when he lay dead
With either voice to mourn, or eyes a tear to shed,
So loathed he was by all as long as he drew breath,
And such advantages all purchased by his death.

As secretary to the cardinal the poet saw too much of the detestable intrigue that then enveloped the papal court, and as manager of the cardinal's household he was plagued by the worries of finding money to meet his master's heavy expenditure. And there was a trouble of his own, his love for a Roman lady, married to an old and jealous husband, the lady who figures as Faustine in the Latin poems in which the poet spoke more frankly of his love than in his own language. On his return to France he published two series of sonnets composed or thought out in Rome; in his *Regrets* he reveals the torment of homesickness that came over him abroad, and there, as in the masterly series in which he dilates on the fallen glories of Rome, he gives expression to the deepest note of melancholy to be found in all the poetry of his school. That great scholar and critic, George Saintsbury, has been charged with falling at times into a slovenliness of style, but at his highest he rises to a pitch as high as any of his confrères have ever reached, as when, e.g., he speaks of 'that inebriating wine of poetical melancholy which the Renaissance had the secret of pressing from the eternal vineyard,' and continues : 'Of this Melancholia—the real Tenth Muse, and one of the greatest inspirers of poetry—Du Bellay is perhaps the high priest in French.'

Even on his return to France Du Bellay was not altogether happy; he gradually lost his distinguished kinsman's favour, ill health dogged him, deafness afflicted him, as it did both Ronsard and Belleau, and in 1560, at the early age of thirty-five, he died—when Edmund Spenser, his great English admirer, who was to translate his Roman sonnets, was yet a child.

Du Bellay's career was thus cut short, and his figure does not loom as large as Ronsard's, but, even if others cannot attain to what we have ventured to call the inimitable Ronsardian touch, Du Bellay for sustained and dignified excellence probably ranks in the eyes of posterity quite as his equal. Would that it had been possible to give here examples from his *Jeux rustiques* of his poems in lighter vein! His epitaphs on two of his domestic pets, Peloton, a little dog, and Belaud, his cat, have certainly no superior among all exercises in a fascinating, delicate art. We offer, first, the version of a sonnet from the sequence *In Praise of Olive*, generally said to be the anagram of the name of a certain Mlle de Viole, but more probably his cousin, and early love, Olive de Sévigné. It may be interesting to compare it with the last quoted sonnet of Ronsard's, for the nominal subject of both is the rose, in poetry the undisputed queen of flowers, and by no poets more worshipped than by those of the Pleiad :

(48)

THE ROSE OF DAWN

Whoe'er has seen the rose at dawn of day
Steeped in the honeyed liquor of the sky,
When shimmering red and white together vie
Within the flower poised on her artless spray;

He will have seen how all things own her sway
And favour her; the trampling foot goes by;
No violating hand has yet drawn nigh;
And even the oxen dare not come her way.

But ravished from the stem on which she grew,
Faded the freshness of her lovely hue,
She 's scorned by men on earth and gods sublime.

Alas, one seeketh now my rose to mar,
And what can I but worship her afar,
Though vain my verse, in cunning-simple rhyme?

Those who are curious to trace the classical or Italian originals that suggested this or that turn of thought or expression to the receptive minds of the poets of the French Renaissance will find how much this sonnet owes to the most glorious of all Catullus's poems, lines 40–7 of the *Hymen o Hymenaee !* or to Ariosto's lovely paraphrase of the passage in the *Orlando Furioso*, i. 42–3.

Next we give a version of Du Bellay's most famous poem, the little ode of the *Winnower to the Winds*. Despite the danger of attempting any rendering in English of a work of art so exquisitely light and airy, we are tempted to make the effort because no better example can be given of the spirit and method of much of the Pleiad's work. We have stated how Ronsard and his school founded themselves on the study of Greek and Latin. Though the Pleiad did much in the way of actual translation, Du Bellay claimed that what was wanted was not merely translations, but poems in the French language and in French rhythms in imitation of classical models, conveying the atmosphere, the sentiment, and the feel of the originals rather than the letter and the form. The original of this ode of Du Bellay's is to be found in the following lines of Navagero, one of the graceful neo-Latin poets who flourished in Italy:

Aurae quae levibus percurritis aera pennis,
    Et strepitis blando per nemora alta sono;
Serta dat haec vobis, vobis haec rusticus Idmon
    Spargit odorato plena canistra croco.
Vos lenite aestum, et paleas sejungite inanes,
    Dum medio fruges ventilat ille die.

And here is our version of what Du Bellay has made of them:

(49)

The Winnower to the Winds

To you, troop of the air,
Who round the wide world fare
  On wing so fugitive,
And to the shady trees,
Stirred by your lightest breeze,
  A lisping murmur give,

I offer violets,
Lilies and these flowerets,
  And roses gathered near,
Roses of vermeil hue,
Scarce blown when fell the dew,
  And these carnations here.

With your sweet breath all day
Sweep through this house, I pray,
  Sweep o'er these fields of wheat;
While on the winnowing floor
I toil, and pant so sore
  In the fierce noon-tide heat.

Walter Pater, who in the seventies of the last century preached, as no one else, the gospel of the high Renaissance, said of this poem of Du Bellay's: 'Du Bellay has almost been the poet of one poem; and this one poem of his is an Italian thing transplanted into that green country of Anjou; out of the Latin verses of Andrea Navagero, into French; . . . and the form of the poem as it stands, written in old French, is all Du Bellay's own. . . .' And he goes on to say that the poem 'has in the highest degree the qualities, the value, of the whole Pleiad school of poetry, of the whole phase of taste from which that school derives, a certain silvery grace of fancy, nearly all the pleasure of which is in the surprise at the happy and dexterous way in which a thing slight in itself is handled.' That is finely said, but the truth of it is far from the whole truth. There is a deeper note in Du Bellay, and indeed in others of his school.

No one to-day would dare to suggest that Du Bellay was the poet of one poem. Take the following three sonnets from the *Antiquities of Rome*. The translations we offer call for no apology. They are by our own Edmund Spenser, and afford a happy illustration of how at this period just as the French borrowed from the Italian, so our Elizabethans borrowed from French and Italian alike. For it is one of the glories of the Renaissance that it brought about in Europe an inter-communion of poets, artists, and scholars, with no sentimental twang of internationalism about it, such as to-day the League of Nations' Committee for Intellectual Co-operation may well envy.

(50) [1]

Thou stranger, which for Rome in Rome here seekest,
And nought of Rome in Rome perceiv'st at all,
These same olde walls, olde arches, which thou seest,
Olde palaces, is that which Rome men call.
Beholde what wreake, what ruine, and what wast,
And how that she, which with her mightie powre
Tam'd all the world, hath tam'd herselfe at last;
The pray of Time, which all things doth devowre!
Rome now of Rome is th' onely funerall,
And onely Rome of Rome hath victorie;
Ne ought save Tyber hastning to his fall
Remaines of all: O worlds inconstancie!
    That which is firme doth flit and fall away,
    And that is flitting doth abide and stay.

(51) [2]

Such as the Berecynthian Goddesse bright,
In her swifte charret with high turrets crownde,
Proud that so manie Gods she brought to light;
Such was this Citie in her good daies fownd:
This Citie, more than that great Phrygian mother

---

[1] Du Bellay's sonnet is itself virtually a translation from an Italian late-Latin original.

[2] See Virgil's *Aeneid*, vi. 784:

            . . . qualis Berecynthia mater
Invehitur curru Phrygias turrita per urbes,
Laeta deum partu, centum complexa nepotes,
Omnes caelicolas, omnes supera alta tenentes.

Renowm'd for fruite of famous progenie,
Whose greatnes by the greatnes of none other,
But by her selfe, her equall match could see:
Rome onely might to Rome compared bee,
And onely Rome could make great Rome to tremble:
So did the Gods by heavenly doome decree,
That other earthlie power should not resemble
  Her that did match the whole earths puissaunce,
  And did her courage to the heavens advaunce.

(52)

He that hath seene a great Oke drie and dead
Yet clad with reliques of some Trophees olde,
Lifting to heaven her aged hoarie head,
Whose foote in ground hath left but feeble holde,
But halfe disbowel'd lies above the ground,
Shewing her wreathed rootes, and naked armes,
And on her trunke all rotten and unsound
Onely supports herselfe for meate of wormes;
And though she owe her fall to the first winde,
Yet of the devout people is ador'd,
And manie yong plants spring out of her rinde;
Who such an Oke hath seene, let him record
  That such this Cities honour was of yore,
  And mongst all Cities florished much more.

Of the remaining poets of the Renaissance the two outstanding
ones are Remi Belleau and J. A. de Baïf, probably the two most
distinguished scholars of the Pleiad. Remi Belleau was born in
1528, at Nogent-le-Rotrou, a small town some forty miles south-
west of Chartres, and thus like Ronsard and Du Bellay breathed
in youth, though more remotely, the atmosphere of the rich
watershed of the Loire; and, curiously enough, like them he
became a victim to deafness. In the train of René de Lorraine,
Marquis d'Elbeuf, he saw military service in an expedition to
Naples. But on his return from Naples the marquis appointed
him tutor to his son, Charles, whom Belleau educated so well as to
make him a real patron of art and letters, with the result that in the
household of this illustrious family he lived until his death in 1577,
in undisturbed enjoyment of leisure for his studies and his poetry.

In these circumstances it is not surprising that the volume of his work is immense. His translation of Anacreon was the first to appear in France, and in the line of translation or adaptation he wrote also paraphrases of Ecclesiastes and of the Song of Solomon. Among his original work, some of it under Italian influence, one comedy, *La Reconnue*, a souvenir of Terence, stands to his credit. But his two great works were his *Amours et Nouveaux Échanges des pierres précieuses*, and *La Bergerie*. The former is well worth study, for it is full of exquisite poetry. Now you get a perfect little ode addressed to a particular jewel, such as the diamond or pearl, now you get a princess or some loved woman hymned in guise of a jewel, now a fable or legend, such as that of the nymph Améthyste changed into a stone by Diana to save her from Bacchus and his troop, and then by the god in his grief baptized, not with his tears, but with the juice of the purple grape; or the loves of Iris and Opalle, shepherd of Neptune's flock, whom Juno's messenger, when her wrathful mistress turns her lover into stone, tinges with the iridescent colours of her tears. *La Bergerie* is an immense compilation in mingled prose and verse, and cast in a pastoral form which becomes, it must be confessed, more strained and artificial as it proceeds. Some idea of its bulk and its variety may be gleaned from the fact that it contains eighteen songs, forty-six sonnets of a general character, forty-eight love sonnets, nine prayers, six eclogues, three odes, three epithalamia, three laments, two epitaphs, with twelve other poems, some of them of considerable length.

It is not perhaps surprising that Belleau's fecundity, facility, and brilliance have tempted some to claim for him the rank of first poet of the Pleiad, but greater qualities than those are to be found in the human touch vouchsafed to Ronsard and Du Bellay that made them great poets not of a time, but of all time. While he lived it was his *Pierres précieuses* that made Belleau most famous, and this work is enshrined in the wonderful epitaph Ronsard wrote for him, and which was carved on his tomb:

> Ne taillez, mains industrieuses,
> Des pierres pour couvrir Belleau :
> Lui mesme a basti son tombeau
> Dedans ses *Pierres précieuses*.

Of the mass of his poetry one single poem survives to win a

place in all anthologies, his famous *Song to April*, to be found near the beginning of *La Bergerie*, before the pastoral setting wears too thin. To attempt to give a translation of it within the compass of the original metre is to court failure; so many of the exquisite turns in the original are bound to be slurred over. But a really fine paraphrase of it is to be found in the reprint of Cary's *Early French Poets*, published in 1923 by A. M. Philpot Ltd., as No. II of the Campion reprints. T. Earle Welby's intro-duction does full justice to this pioneering work of Cary, one of the greatest of English translators, whose paraphrase of Belleau's poem certainly scores point after point of exact equivalence with the choicest expressions in the original, and gives us a poem with something of the flavour of Keats in it. But hardly inferior to the April ode, is the one to May which follows it, and whose comparative neglect may be due to the intrusion in it of five stanzas, which convert a song to May, full of delicious touches that indicate a wider and closer observation of nature than was common among the poets of the Pleiad, into a complimentary ode addressed to a brother-poet. Of this *Ode to May* we venture to offer a version, which omits the five extraneous stanzas:

(53)

ODE TO MAY

While in a course that never ends
May to the old year vigour lends,
   And in the seasons takes her place;
While man and earth and atmosphere
Are thrilled again with right good cheer
   Beneath the sky's fresh youthful face:

And while the springtide's kindly spell
Makes earth's fruit-bearing bosom swell
   In these most beautiful of days,
And earth herself with flowers imprest,
And by all balmy odours blest,
   Her features with new charms arrays:

While little swallows praises sing,
Their little throats a-twittering,
   To May, the one all months among,

And with that little tool, their beak,
At work like little masons seek
   To build the cup that holds their young:

This month sweet Venus comes again,
Young Love and all the sacred train
   Of Graces, Laughter and of Dance,
To set alight within our veins
The burning heat of amorous pains
   Eyes kindle in us with a glance.

What time in youth the slender vine,
Nursing in secret her design
   To rear the grape in clusters green,
Sends little feelers to embrace,
And clinging tendrils to enlace
   A neighbour elm with her soft sheen:

And while the blunt-nosed little lambs
Nibble the grass beside their dams,
   And, dancing on his feet, the kid
Rubs hard his horn and leaps in air
Before his mother, browsing there
   On the young shoots by boulders hid:

While perched upon the hawthorn-tree
The nightingale sings silvery,
   Trilling a hundred melodies:
And on her quivering winglets light
The busy bee directs her flight
   Heath-ward where her pavilion lies:

While in the soil, watered again
With dewy drip of cool soft rain,
   Earth's seedlings germinate and grow,
And winds light as a Zephyr's lisp
Caress the ships' white sails and crisp
   The surface of the sea below:

What time the tender turtle-dove,
Pigeons and other birds of Love,
   Mate in this month fair as a dream,

And, with their little beaks' twin tips
Taking by turns quick, little sips,
  Skim o'er the surface of a stream:

While Ceres' yellowing tresses, kist
By slants of wind that curl and twist,
  With rippling lights are sunnied o'er,
As when the billow's watery cave
Breaking advances wave on wave
  At gallop on the sandy shore:

In short, while sea and land like one,
This nether world's great torch, the sun,
  All take their pleasures in their turn,
While birds in air make revelry,
And even the fishes in the sea
  In pairs caught by Love's ardours burn:

Remember how the rose, our pride,
That blooms from dawn to eventide,
  Loses her colour and her scent
How thievish time will rend and soil
What sweets the spring has left to spoil,
  Leaves, flower, and fruit, till all are spent.

Remember how old age will come,
To bend our backs, our strength to numb,
  And make us totter on our way;
And how grey hairs, and eyes sunk in,
And wrinkled cheeks, and shrivelled skin,
  Will dog us all to our last day.

    J. A. de Baïf, born at Venice in 1532, was the natural son of
Lazare de Baïf, a man of culture and learning, and the ambassador
of France, by a Venetian lady of good family. As Lazare de Baïf
was in orders marriage was impossible, but he acknowledged his
son, and took infinite pains over his education, placing him under
some of the most eminent scholars of the day. It has been
stated that the precocious boy of eleven helped Ronsard, eight
years older, in his early Greek studies. In later life he wrote freely

Latin poems, published numerous translations both from Greek and Latin, and produced several plays, including versions of Sophocles's *Antigone* and two comedies based on originals by Plautus and Terence. And, like Clément Marot and others, he indulged himself in translating the Psalms.

In Paris he enjoyed richly the royal favour, and founding in 1567 an Academy of Music and of Poetry, which some have claimed to be the prototype of the French Academy and the Paris Conservatoire, his house became a centre for the lovers of the two arts. He lived on to 1589, and, as in the case of Ronsard and Belleau, the mass of his French poetry is enormous. There is much variety in it, but the bulk of it is tedious to a degree, including his laborious and not unscholarly attempts to apply rules of quantity, as in classical metres, to French versification. But at his best he well deserves his place as one of the four chief poets of his age; witness these charming stanzas, from his *Amours de Méline*:

(54)

So Sweet a Rose

Did ever so sweet a rose
In the light of morning fair
So fresh a blossom disclose?
No gillyflower can compare
With the living crimson there,
On thy lips that put to shame
All colours the flowers may claim.

There 's no one has tasted yet
A liquor so sweet to sup,
By Dawn's rosy fingers set
In the tender petalled cup,
While still the green sap mounts up
In the scented spring divine,
As thy honeyed lips on mine.

I 've tasted the sugar'd flower
Of the honeysuckle wild,
And the store that hour by hour

The provident bee has piled,
But thy peerless kiss, my child,
The honeysuckle will shade
And the honey's savour fade.

Baïf had another side to him, a sense of humour and a gift for satire. Of this some slight indication will be found in his *Epitaph on Rabelais*:

(55)

O Pluto, welcome Rabelais,
And mid the crowd that owns thy sway,
None of whom ever laughs at all,
Find one with laughter at his call.

Ronsard died in 1585, satiated, as he said himself, with fame. But the great work of the Pleiad was soon to be half undone. It may be that the temperamental outlook of the whole nation was changed as a result of the cruel series of civil wars, known as the Wars of Religion, which broke out in 1562 between Huguenots and Catholics. They were savagely conducted on both sides, though the horror which stands out in the memory of mankind is the massacre of St. Bartholomew in 1572; and they were not ended until several years after the accession in 1589 of Henry IV, Macaulay's 'King Henry of Navarre,' the hero of the battle of Ivry, whose final acceptance of Catholicism gave hopes at last of a united kingdom. 'Paris is well worth a mass,' said he.

But, in any case, the very success of the Pleiad was bound to provoke a reaction towards formalism; no poet, or school of poets, whatever the final verdict of history, is in the ascendant for more than one generation; in the third they are often either forgotten or denounced. Philippe Desportes (1546–1606), a follower of Ronsard, despite his elegance and ingenuity well illustrates the gradual failure of the Ronsardian tradition. Boileau's bitter lines in denunciation of Ronsard, which show a good, sound, common-sense critic at his worst, run as follows:

Ronsard qui le suivit, par une autre méthode
Réglant tout, brouilla tout, fit un art à sa mode,
Et toutefois longtemps eut un heureux destin.
Mais sa muse en Français parlant Grec et Latin

Vit dans l'âge suivant, par un retour grotesque,
Tomber de ses grands mots le faste pédantesque.
Ce poète orgueilleux, trébuché de si haut,
Rendit plus retenus Desportes et Bertaut.

But it was certainly not because he was shocked by what
Boileau calls Ronsard's 'pompous pedantry' that Desportes
became more *retenu*; the causes were self-indulgence and lack
of power. He may be regarded as the court poet of Henry III,
the king concerned in two great crimes, the massacre of St.
Bartholomew and the assassination of the Duc de Guise. The
king heaped benefice after benefice on his favourite, a cleric
merely by profession, who thought to make the best of both
worlds. He was much admired by several of our Elizabethans,
and A. H. Bullen, to whose fine taste and scholarship we owe so
many discoveries in Elizabethan lyric, gives in his *Lyrics from
Elizabethan Romances*, *etc.*, a translation by Thomas Lodge of one
of his sonnets, which may be compared with those of Spenser
from Du Bellay's *Antiquities of Rome*:

(56)

If so I seek the shades I suddenly do see
The god of love forsake his bow and sit me by;
If that I think to write, his Muses pliant be,
If so I plain my grief the wanton boy will cry.

If I lament his pride he doth increase my pain;
If tears my cheeks attaint, his cheeks are moist with moan;
If I disclose the wounds the which my heart have slain,
He takes his fascia off and wipes them dry anon.

If so I walk the woods, the woods are his delight;
If I myself torment, he bathes him in my blood;
He will my soldier be if once I want to fight;

If seas delight, he steers my bark amid the flood:
In brief the cruel god doth never from me go,
But makes my lasting love eternal with my woe.

Desportes himself translated freely from the Italian without acknowledgment, and Lodge says nothing about this poem of his being a translation from Desportes. Furthermore this same sonnet gave Lodge the hint for his poem beginning:

> Turn I my looks unto the skies,
> Love with his arrows wounds mine eyes;
> If so I gaze upon the ground,
> Love then in every flower is found;
> Search I the shade to fly my pain,
> He meets me in the shade again.

Similarly he modelled on the opening stanzas of a poem by Desportes,

> La terre naguère glacée
> Est ores de vert tapissée,
> Son sein est embelli de fleurs,
> L'air est encore amoureux d'elle,
> Le ciel rit de la voir si belle,
> Et moi j'en augmente mes pleurs,

his poem in *Scylla's Metamorphosis*, beginning:

> The earth late choked with showers
>   Is now arrayed in green;
> Her bosom springs with flowers,
>   The air dissolves her teen:
> The heavens laugh at her glory,
> Yet bide I sad and sorry.

Bullen goes on to give examples of borrowings from Desportes by Nicholas Breton and Edward de Vere, Earl of Oxford, and claims with justice that Lodge and others greatly improved upon their models. To drive this point home it is only necessary to give two more illustrations. Contrast Desportes's

> On verra défaillir tous les astres aux cieux
> .   .   .   .   .   .
> Plutôt que la fureur des rapports envieux
> Efface en mon visage un trait de votre image,

with Lodge's

> First shall the heavens want starry light
> .   .   .   .   .   .
>   Before I false my faith to thee.

How Lodge carries one's thoughts on to Burns and his *O my Luve 's like a red, red rose*! Still more striking yet is the contrast between Desportes's

> O Nuit, jalouse Nuit, contre moi conjurée,
>   Qui renflammes le ciel de nouvelle clarté,
> T'ai-je donc aujourd'hui tant de fois désirée
>   Pour être si contraire à ma félicité,

and the passionate cry of an anonymous poet in *The Phoenix Nest*, beginning:

> O Night, O jealous Night, repugnant to my measures!
>   O Night so long desired, yet cross to my content!
> There 's none but only thou that can perform my pleasures,
>   And none but only thou that hindereth my intent.

So faded the wreath that for so long encircled Ronsard's brow. As we shall see in the next chapter, to quote Walter Pater's words, 'the poetry of Malherbe came with its sustained style and weighty sentiment, but with nothing that set people singing; and the lovers of such poetry saw in the poetry of the Pleiad only the latest trumpery of the Middle Age.' But the lyrical sweetness of the Renaissance, not to win popular favour again until its rediscovery in the nineteenth century, did persist into the seventeenth century, and we may close this chapter with two examples. First take a version of the most graceful of the idylls written by Vauquelin de la Fresnaye, lawyer, poet, and critic, who lived on to the year 1606:

(57)

An Idyll

> Where flowers, where lilies vigil kept,
> My Phillis like an infant slept,
>   And all about her visage fair
> The little Loves, in childish glee,
> Frolicked and danced triumphantly,
>   Gazing on heaven's bright image there.
>
> And as I watched my wonder grew,
> She was so fair, my heart so true;
>   But Reason whispered in my ear:

'Thou fool! when such a moment's lost,
Time and again we rue the cost;
    A marvel, did it reappear!'

Admonished thus I bent me low,
And, creeping silently and slow,
    I kissed her lips incarnadine.
Tasting such bliss my spirit cries:
'These are the joys of Paradise
    Reserved for souls we call divine.'

Then read the smooth-flowing epitaph composed for himself
by a nephew of Desportes, Mathurin Regnier, most famous as a
satirist, who lived on to 1613:

(58)

Epitaph on Himself

I 've lived my life in careless ease,
And come and gone as best might please,
    Obeying nature's harmless call;
I wonder what the cause may be
That Death should turn her thoughts on me,
    Who never thought of her at all.

CHAPTER IV

THE AUGUSTAN AGE

DURING the sixteenth century the social and political condition of France had been marvellously changed. From a poor and struggling kingdom in 1500, fighting for consolidation against rival forces within its borders, it bade fair early in the seventeenth century, despite the check occasioned by the Wars of Religion, to become the wealthiest and most powerful kingdom in Europe. The revenue of Louis XII, son of Charles d'Orléans, the poet, was at the beginning of the century about two million crowns. The reckless Francis I squeezed some five millions out of his people. His son, Henry II, father-in-law of Mary Queen of Scots, and, by the irony of events, killed in a joust by the Scottish knight, Montgomery, had six and a half millions, and was forced to contract loan after loan. It is no wonder that his son again, Henry III, whose mother was Catherine de Médicis, whose reign was distracted by the Wars of Religion, who assassinated the Duc de Guise and was himself assassinated by a fanatical priest, was loaded with debt though his revenue had risen to nine millions.

Taxation grew to a pitch that was unendurable, and the situation was aggravated through wholesale plundering by tax-collectors. It was estimated that when the Duc de Sully, the great minister of Henry IV, took the finances in hand at the end of the century, not half the nominal sum arising from taxes found its way into the treasury. Sully it was who not only initiated measures of reform, but carried them through. Though not enlightened enough to encourage industry and commerce, he increased the productivity of the country by fostering agriculture, but perhaps his most effective line of action lay in the ruthless stamping out of peculation. His work was continued, after a lull during the reign of Louis XIII, by that trusty servant of Louis XIV, Colbert, the first real financier France had produced. He began on Sully's lines by stamping under foot the notorious

Fouquet, peculator in chief, of whom the best that can be said is that he lavished some of his ill-gotten gains on the patronage of letters, and in befriending La Fontaine in particular. Colbert was a man of far greater insight than Sully, for he promoted industry and commerce, and not merely agriculture, and he built up for France not only a navy, but also a mercantile marine. The immense wealth with which he furnished Louis XIV was squandered by *le Roi Soleil*, the Sun King, on foreign adventures, and works of luxury such as Versailles, in the effort to fulfil with due splendour the destiny prepared for him by Richelieu in the lifetime of his father, Louis XIII.

Of the four great statesmen produced in France during the seventeenth century, Sully, Richelieu, Colbert, and Mazarin, who created for France the absolute monarchy that crashed before the end of the eighteenth century in the French Revolution, the greatest as a political figure is Cardinal Richelieu, who ruled the country during the nominal kingship of Louis XIII. No one can ever forget the towering figure of Richelieu and his haughty air, who has read Dumas's *Three Musketeers* or Vigny's darkly-drawn *Cinq Mars*, or seen the gorgeous portrait of him by Philippe de Champaigne, in full robes, surmounted by the narrow head, keen, crafty face, cold, searching eyes, and pointed beard.

It was the heyday of absolutism in France that covered the Augustan age, and the approach to it during the early part of the seventeenth century was a period of transition from the gaiety, alternating with a mild melancholy, and the graceful charm of Ronsard and his school, with its music suggesting now an air of Mozart's, now an idyllic murmur as soft as one of Debussy's, to the measured pomp and circumstance of the reign of Louis XIV. The age was that which produced four of the outstanding figures in French literature, Corneille, Racine, Molière, and La Fontaine; so eminent indeed are they that the claim made for them that theirs was the classic age of French literature is not extravagant. The age has also been called the age of the Alexandrine, so entirely does that metre dominate it. But we must not forget that the establishment of the Alexandrine as the characteristic metre in French poetry was the work of the Pleiad, and the movement initiated during the early half of the seventeenth century was towards the standardizing of it by rules almost as strict as those of Latin prosody, and the provision of a content full and dignified enough to be carried on its long and measured beat.

We may be allowed during the lull in the production of lyric poetry which marks the age of the Alexandrine, to be greatly daring, and to say a word in favour of it. We have not been fair in this country to the Alexandrine. Matthew Arnold said of it: 'It seems to me that . . . the Alexandrine is inadequate; that as a vehicle for high poetry it is greatly inferior to the hexameter or to the iambics of Greece (for example) or to the blank verse of England. Therefore the man of genius who uses it is at a disadvantage as compared with the man of genius who has for conveying his thoughts a more adequate vehicle, metrical or not. Racine is at a disadvantage as compared with Sophocles or Shakespeare. . . .'

He begs the question. The man of supreme genius is not the slave of his instrument. Villon was not the slave of the artificial verse-forms of his age. Matthew Arnold would not have dared to suggest that Dante with his *terza rima* was at a disadvantage as compared with Milton and his blank verse. Had a Dante and a Milton arisen in France, would the Alexandrine have cribbed, cabined, and confined them? Devastating examples of ill-informed and even grotesque misrepresentations of the Alexandrine on the part of English critics of high repute are given by Émile Legouis in his *Défense de la Poésie française*, a book which ought to be in the hands of every English student of the language. Three points are to be borne in mind if an English reader desires to realize the full value of the Alexandrine as a vehicle of poetic expression.

Firstly, the Alexandrine is not merely a line of six feet, but one of four stressed accents as well—some modern prosodists would say *three* stressed accents at times — the stressed accents varying in position in one line as compared with another and, furthermore, between the stressed accents one syllable may be emphasized more than another. To show what variety this introduces into the Alexandrine as a Frenchman reads it aloud or in his mind, Legouis gives as an example six lines taken not from one of the great classic French poets, nor from Victor Hugo or one of the other emancipators of the nineteenth century, but from Boileau, the so-called 'Lawgiver of Parnassus' in the seventeenth century, who in his *Art poétique*, one of the most remarkable

critical poems ever written, codified as it were the principles of
Malherbe. In reading the following passage note that the four
stressed accents of each line have the *plus* sign over them, while
any syllable between them calling for some emphasis is marked
by the *long* sign:

Le commandeur voulait la scène plus exacte;

Le vicomte indigné sortait au second acte;

L'un, défenseur zélé des bigots mis en jeu,

Pour prix de ses bons mots le condamnait au feu;

L'autre, fougueux marquis, lui déclarait la guerre,

Voulait venger la cour immolée au parterre.

English blank verse read as if one were scanning it ruthlessly
would be as intolerable as the Alexandrine so treated. Compare,
e.g.:

All night the dreadless angel unpursued,

with:

Où sont-ils, les marins sombrés dans les nuits noires?

And yet nine out of ten Englishmen when denouncing the Alexandrine thus thump it out.

Secondly, let us not forget that the French speak faster than
the English, and also, as that great dramatic critic, William
Archer, spent years in trying to drive home to us, French actors
have studied the art of diction, the clear enunciation of words
and the phrasing of sentences as carried across the footlights,
more assiduously than we have. The long speeches of Racine
have wearied many an English reader, as compared with one of
Shakespeare's longest efforts, precisely because he takes them at
the deliberate pace at which, in accordance with the English
tradition, blank verse is delivered on the stage.

But if an Englishman has heard at the Odéon in Paris a good
French actor declaim one of Racine's great speeches, written in
long sinewy Alexandrines, beginning deliberately, then increasing
the pace as his audience warms to the spoken word, and almost
chanting the more rhythmical passages, until the climax of the

speech is reached, and the final words are poured out in a veritable torrent of eloquence, he is once and for all shaken out of
his insular misconception and misunderstanding. He may still
prefer his English blank verse deliberately spoken to the impassioned delivery of the French Alexandrine. But he cannot
say that a hundred Alexandrines spoken by a French actor take
longer than a hundred lines of blank verse as rendered on the
English stage. The rhythm of the Alexandrine is like the rhythm
of a racing eight, a long, sweeping rhythm with every now and
then a change in the rate of striking. What boating man but
knows the thrill that runs through a well-trained crew, still full
of rowing, when stroke sets himself, as the expression goes, to
give them ten?

Thirdly, we must recognize what resonance is given to French
by the richness of its nasal tones. These are as difficult for some
Englishmen to appreciate, and to almost all Englishmen to render,
as to indicate the value of the mute *e*. If you doubt it ask an
English friend, and after him a French friend, to pronounce
the simple French words *non* and *pain*, and then the more
subtle place-name, *Laon*. It is almost incredible that Landor,
a distinguished man of letters, and one of wide culture, should
have sunk so low in abuse of the resonance of French as this:
'Your nasal twang, the most disagreeable and disgusting of
sounds, being produced by the same means as we reject a stink,
and thus reminding us of one.' Let Landor speak for himself,
and, to forget him, invite some Frenchman of your acquaintance
to read to you the sestet of Heredia's superb sonnet on the death
of the eagle that rashly dared the lightning:

> Avec un cri sinistre, il tournoie, emporté
> Par la trombe, et, crispé, buvant d'un trait sublime
> La flamme éparse, il plonge au fulgurant abîme.
> Heureux qui pour la Gloire ou pour la Liberté,
> Dans l'orgueil de la force et l'ivresse du rêve,
> Meurt ainsi, d'une mort éblouissante et brève!

Note in this passage not only the nasal sounds, but also the variety
of the long and short vowel sounds. In what language can you
find six lines more rhythmical and more resonant?

But let us return now to Malherbe, who constituted himself
the reformer of French poetry from the Pleiad's florid luxuriance

and freedom in phraseology and metre.   To a new age, when the
fount of lyrical inspiration was running dry, their handling of
the Muse seemed a sort of trifling with what should be regarded
as a very dignified, statuesque figure.   Malherbe was born at
Caen and as far back in the sixteenth century as 1555.   But it
was not until after its close, when he was nearly fifty years of age,
that he rose to prominence, and as a favourite at the court of
Henry IV became the dominant poet of his time.   His self-
imposed mission was, to quote a summary of Mr. Saintsbury's,
to foster a tendency 'towards the restriction of vocabulary and
rhythm, the avoidance of original and daring metaphor and
suggestion, the perfecting of a few metres (with the Alexandrine
at their head) into a delicate but monotonous harmony, and the
rejection of individual licence in favour of rigid rule.'   His work
was ably seconded by Boileau, who took up his mantle in the
latter half of the seventeenth century and, as we have already
said, in his brilliant *Art poétique* codified his principles.

Malherbe's own poetry, small in amount, as perhaps is only
to be expected in the case of one who was as critical of himself
as of others, does not invite translation, so finished is it and so
restrained in its chill perfection.   The most delightful and
famous of his lines, which occur in an elegy on the death of a
friend's daughter:

> Et rose elle a vécu ce que vivent les roses,
>   L'espace d'un matin,

are an echo of the Ronsard whose influence he set himself to
destroy.   But here is a version of the fine sonnet he wrote on
the death of his son, killed in a duel, which, despite what the
father says in his grief, is generally allowed to have been quite
fairly fought:

(59)

ON THE DEATH OF HIS SON

That my son should have cast mortality,
That son so brave, and whom I loved so sore,
I write not this against ill-fortune's score,
Since in the course of nature man must die.

But that two rogues, by sudden treachery,
Should deal the tragic death I now deplore,

* E

Therein my grief can find no comfort more,
And all my feelings throb in harmony.

My God, my Saviour, since through law of thought,
There being no medicine for a soul distraught,
The vow of vengeance is by sanction strong,

Stand Thou beside me to avenge my loss;
Thy justice pleads, and those who did the wrong
Are sons to those who nailed Thee on the cross.

And here is a version of his short poem on the death in infancy
of Mlle de Conty, which shows how high within his range was
Malherbe's poetic sense, and how the union of grace, finesse, and
tact makes a French compliment the most exquisite in the world:

(60)

This little child do not compare
With goddesses however fair
Who lived, we 're told, in days of yore;
These are but fancies woven in space.
Say this, and you need say no more:
She has her mother's lovely face.

Malherbe did not have it all his own solemn way in the work
of reform. A popular poet contemporary with him, though
much younger, was Vincent Voiture, born in 1598, who enjoyed
himself in exercises on the model of artificial forms of a far earlier
date. Indeed, he went back for inspiration, as Théodore de
Banville has insisted, past Ronsard to Clément Marot. He was
a great favourite with the ladies of the *salon* held in the Hôtel
Rambouillet, whose provincial cousins were satirized by Molière
in *Les Précieuses ridicules*, the most sparkling of his comedies.
Here are versions of the best known of his sonnets, and of his
rondeaux:

(61)

SONNET TO URANIE

I 'll have to end my days in love of Uranie:
Absence nor lapse of time avails to cure my pain,
And I see nothing left that can my life sustain,
Or bring me back again, once lost, my liberty.

For many a day I 've known how strict her scruples be,
But thinking of the charms that now my death ordain,
I bless my martyrdom, and even to die am fain;
I dare not breathe a word against her tyranny.

Reason from time to time a shy approach has made,
Telling me to revolt and promising her aid;
But when in sore distress I 've sought for solace there,

After I 've struggled hard, and love in vain withstood,
She says that Uranie alone is sweet and fair,
And ties me up more tight than all my senses could.

(62)

RONDEAU

My God, 'tis done with me: for Isabeau
Has called on me to write her a rondeau,
And my embarrassment thereat 's extreme.
What! thirteen lines, eight rhyming *owe*, five *eam*!
I 'd just as soon build her a boat to row.
But there you have a heap of five or so,
Let 's make them eight, enlisting friend Brodeau,
And adding one more by some clever scheme:
      My God, 'tis done!
If I could rack my brain and safely stow
Yet five lines more, well would my cargo show.
But now I 'm in the eleventh, it would seem,
And here 's the twelfth, a fact I 'll swear, no dream;
Lo and behold, thirteen in even flow!
      My God, 'tis done!

And here is an amusing epitaph by François Maynard, diplo-
matist and lawyer, born at Toulouse in 1582. Though he was
an avowed pupil of Malherbe, he did not always write in his
master's vein:

(63)

EPITAPH ON A HARD DRINKER

Here lieth Paul who dropped his eyes
When sober people came his way,
And without ceasing prayed the skies
For three Octobers to one May.

Stout pillar of the public-house,
His rule was: well your herring souse,
To flavour bottles numberless.
Stranger, who happen here to call,
His soul's one wish you 'll lightly guess—
To drink your health, the wherewithal!

The Augustan Age may be said to begin with Corneille, in the
first portion of the seventeenth century, during the reign of
Louis XIII, and under the commanding influence of Richelieu.
The passion and splendour of Corneille's earlier tragedies, which
dominated the French stage for twenty years, stamp him as
possibly the greatest poet of the seventeenth century. Modern
taste and criticism may confer that title on his younger rival,
Racine, whose perfection of form and the deeper psychological
insight claimed for him seem to have won favour now for many
years. These two great poets must be regarded as dramatic
poets pure and simple, for they wrote little that even approximates
to lyric verse, and cannot therefore be regarded as coming
strictly within the scope of this book. But even if there was not
in either of them, as there was in the case of Shakespeare, a rich
lyrical vein to force them now and again to some outburst of
lyrical song, how is it possible in any study of French poetry to
leave entirely out of account two of the three or four greatest of
French poets? Let us venture, then, to say something of them
and their work, leaving those who wish to enjoy a fuller account
of the riches to be found in them, as also of the treasury of
Molière's wit, to read what Mr. Lytton Strachey says of them in
the third and fourth chapters of his incomparable introduction
to French literature, *Landmarks in French Literature*, published in
the Home University Library, and, in English, the masterpiece
of its kind.

Pierre Corneille (1606–84) was born at Rouen, and was the
son of a lawyer of some standing. He was educated by the
Jesuits, well grounded by them in Latin, and began life in the
practice of the law. Soon, however, he turned his attention to
the writing of plays. He began with comedies, and met with no
small success, and it is possible to see in them the first glimmer
of what was later to ripen in Molière's brain into the full glory
of a Comic Muse that has dominated the world ever since.

Corneille did collaborate with Molière in *Psyché*, and it may be regretted that the latter did not take over and complete Corneille's fine figure of fun, the Falstaffian Matamore, who redeems his clumsy play within a play, *L'Illusion comique*. Later on when in the full tide of success as a tragedian he wrote a comedy, *Le Menteur*, which held the stage.

But his fame rests on six or eight masterpieces in a whole series of plays written during a long life that lasted to 1684. The play that placed him on a pinnacle of fame in 1636 was that most romantic of all classical dramas, *Le Cid*, the scene of which is laid in Spain, always to the French a country of romance, and this was followed by *Horace*, *Cinna*, *Polyeucte*, *Pompée*, and *Rodogune*, all of them great examples of his art. But in 1664, Corneille's fifty-ninth year, was produced *La Thébaïde*, the first great play of his rival, Racine, and thenceforward as the fame of Racine grew that of Corneille declined.

Jean Racine (1639–99) was born at La Ferté-Milon, near Soissons, where his father held some official position. He lost both father and mother in infancy, but his grandparents looked well after his education, which ended with three years at the celebrated school at Port-Royal, where he learned Greek as well as Latin, and a year at the Collège d'Harcourt in Paris. His success with *La Thébaïde* naturally led him to concentrate on the writing of plays, and during the next thirteen years he produced in regular succession eight plays of the finest quality, including a comedy, *Les Plaideurs*. In 1677 appeared *Phèdre*, by general consent a greater play than any of its predecessors, but its prospects of success were ruined by a court intrigue, in which no less a personage than the Duchesse de Bouillon, a niece of Mazarin, was concerned. This reverse mortified Racine so deeply that for twelve years he wrote no more plays.

But he was a born courtier, and as a favourite of Louis XIV he did not fare too ill. Certainly his later years were not tormented as were Corneille's by poverty and neglect. In 1689 and 1691, twelve and fourteen years after *Phèdre*, he produced, to please Madame de Maintenon, and very probably at her request, two biblical plays, *Esther* and *Athalie*, the latter admittedly the one rival to *Phèdre* for pre-eminence among all his plays, surely an achievement hard to parallel after so long a period of silence.

Fate has ordered it, that in life and death these two great

poets and dramatists should be regarded as rivals, and that not only in their own country, but also abroad. At one period Corneille has been acclaimed as the master, at another Racine. To trace the history of the controversy is beside our purpose. But it may be claimed that Mr. Lytton Strachey in his passionate advocacy of Racine's claims has indulged in a good deal of special pleading. Let it not be forgotten that Corneille *made* the great French drama of the Augustan Age—Racine, thirty years his junior, founded himself on the achievement of his predecessor. Here is a summary of what can be said, and has been said, in reviewing the comparative merits of the two poets.

The difference in mood and temperament of the two men accounts for differences in the style and quality of their work. Corneille's was a wholly masculine temperament, in Racine's there was a feminine element. In Corneille's plays a man is generally the dominant figure, in Racine's it is as often a woman. There is a rhetorical splendour about Corneille's verse which stars his plays with gorgeous lines; at times he overstrains himself until his speech offends by excess of emphasis. Fine lines, great lines, are not rare in Racine, e.g. the much quoted:

C'est Vénus toute entière à sa proie attachée,

but they are not so numerous, and generally his versification is smoother and more level, and his effects of emphasis obtained by subtler means; but he tends to monotony, and if Corneille's failing at times is bombast, Racine's is insipidity.

Racine had the advantage of studying Greek at Port-Royal, and Euripides gave the inspiration for his *Phèdre*, a greater figure perhaps than any conceived by Corneille, and one that has kinship with the sombre figure of Lady Macbeth herself. But for Shakespearian pomp and majesty in speech or scene the one play that stands out among all that either of them wrote is Corneille's *Pompée*. The pity is that its end provides no worthy conclusion, like the four superb lines that end *Le Cid*, when Don Fernand, King of Castile, resolves on a hopeful note the tangle in which the sorely tried hero, Don Rodrigue, finds himself enwound:

Espère en ton courage, espère en ma promesse;
Et, possédant déjà la cœur de ta maîtresse,
Pour vaincre un point d'honneur qui combat contre toi,
Laisse faire le temps, ta vaillance et ton roi.

The will of a strong man dominates Corneille's interest, and the complexities of love, and honour, and patriotism, that may stand in the way of the smooth exercise of that will introduce the complications that make up the stuff of tragedy. The love interest dominates Racine, love not as a mere emotion, but as an absorbing passion, the power of which is bound to work havoc with the other interests of life. And yet there is something of Racine in Corneille's *Polyeucte*, and a good deal of Corneille in Racine's *Athalie*. It is claimed that Racine was the subtler psychologist of the two, and this perhaps has to be conceded, but psychology is, like rhetoric, a much-abused term, and the advantage is not as overwhelmingly on Racine's side as Mr. Strachey would have us believe. The fact is both dramatists dealt mainly in types, though they differentiated the individuals of a type fairly well; only Racine created in *Phèdre* the subtlest figure of them all. Racine adapts himself easily to the requirements of the three unities; Corneille chafes under them at times, and with him, as in the case of *Le Cid*, the conventions now and again wear thin.

Finally, just as we have claimed that the temperaments of the two poets determined the qualities of their work, so we may claim that the temperaments of their critics will determine their attitude. If your critic is of a fine intellectual cast, who likes to settle down in his arm-chair and read without emotional disturbance a smoothly written work of the highest literary distinction, let him choose Racine. But if he is one who likes to stiffen in his chair at times, and even to shout out aloud a verse that rouses him, then Corneille is his man.

An English reader finds difficulty in appraising the work of Corneille and Racine for two reasons. First he is at a loss, as we have already pointed out, to appreciate the rhythm of rhymed Alexandrine verse, on which a Frenchman can play as on a musical instrument. Secondly, he cannot help contrasting the freedom and luxuriance and variety of the Elizabethan dramatists, Shakespeare in chief, with the concentration and constraint imposed on French drama of the Augustan period by the three classic unities of time, place, and action, which required that a play should centre on one single point of interest, *none* of the action in relation to the subject taking place on the stage, that the scene right through the play should not be changed and, finally, that the whole action of the play should be concluded within a limited time.

French critics have pointed out that it was a sense of realism that confirmed a tendency to the observance of the unities. Means of lighting and staging were limited, and confinement of the action as far as possible to one adequate set scene necessarily limited both time and action as well. However this may be, there is one important fact that confronts those who still denounce the unities whole-heartedly. The art of the theatre in modern times has tended to relinquish the picturesque luxuriance of Elizabethan days, and to conform to certain limitations that approximate to those imposed by the principles underlying the three classic unities. Indeed, the modern three-act play without change of scene, not uncommon on the London stage to-day, is almost a complete return to the classic tradition.

To illustrate the work of these two great poets we propose to give renderings in blank verse of one scene from a play of each of them, and we make bold to think that those who know well their characteristics will recognize each as a fair example of its author, and such an one as could not have been conceived or written by the other. The renderings are in the blank verse familiar to us, for even were it possible to make a translation of these passages in rhymed English Alexandrines, their rhythm could not hope to represent the dramatic force and vigour of the French originals. It may be pointed out that such a master of translation as M. Derocquigny of Lille has been forced in his remarkable translations [1] into French verse of Shakespeare's great tragedies to adopt *unrhymed* Alexandrines.

Let us begin with Corneille and, before producing our chief example of his work, indulge ourselves with a fine specimen of the rhetoric of which his plays are full. This is the outburst in Act I. Scene 5 of *Le Cid*, when the aged veteran, Don Diègue, who has been singled out for distinction by his king, is struck in the face by a jealous and a younger rival, the Count de Gormas —an insult which at his age he is powerless to avenge:

(64)

Wrath and despair! Old age, mine enemy!
Have I then lived so long but to be shamed?
Have I grown grey in warlike exercise
To see my laurels blasted in a day?

[1] See the bi-lingual *Collection Shakespeare* published in Paris by J. M. Dent & Sons.

Mine arm, the admiration of all Spain,
Mine arm that has so oft this empire saved,
So oft upborne its monarch's royal throne,
Does it now fail my need, do nought for me?
O cruel memory of glories past!
Work of so many days effaced in one!
New dignity fatal to my content!
Sheer precipice whence crashes my renown!
Must I behold the count out-soar my fame,
And die without revenge or live despised?

The play from which our main example is to be taken is
Horace. The legend that furnishes the plot of the play runs as
follows. Alba Longa is still Rome's rival for supremacy. The
Alban army is besieging Rome, and by agreement it is decided
that in order to save bloodshed the issue shall be decided by
combat between chosen champions of either side. The three
brothers Horatius are selected to represent Rome, the three
brothers Curiatius Alba. But both armies are shocked when it
is realized how closely bound are the two families by ties of
relationship. Sabina, wife of the eldest Horatius, is a sister of
the Curiatii; while Camilla, sister of the Horatii, is affianced to
the eldest Curiatius. The matter is therefore adjourned that
the gods may be consulted. Alas! the decision of the gods is
that the combat must proceed. At the first clash two of the
Horatii are slain, and all three Curiatii wounded. The eldest
Horatius, unwounded, feigns flight, and then turns on his
wounded pursuers and kills them one after another. Horatius
returning in triumph meets his sister, and calls on her to con-
gratulate him. Instead, she reviles him; whereat in wrath and
indignation he slays her. After trial he is, not without much
heart-searching on the king's part, acquitted of her murder.

Worth hearing is Sabine's speech, in behalf of Camille and
herself, when told by her father-in-law of the gods' decision that
the combat must proceed; it affords an illustration of the fine
irony of which Corneille is a master:

(65)

I may admit your news is strange to me:
For in the godhead I had thought to find
Much less injustice and far more good will.

Console us not; 'gainst such a weight of ill
Pity but speaks in vain, and reason palls.
We have it in our power to end our griefs;
Who can face death, fears no calamity.
Easy were it for us while you are here
To make a specious calm of our despair.
But when one can be weak without disgrace,
To make an outward show is cowardly;
The practice of such arts we leave to men,
And only seek to pass for what we are.
We ask not that a courage great as yours
Should stoop, like us, to murmur against fate.
Meet without flinching mortal shocks like these.
Watch our tears flow, nor mix with them your own,
And for a crowning grace, in such a coil
Be constant still in mind, but let us weep.

The speeches of both Sabine and Camille, as indeed of Horace
and Curiace, are worth study, for they show the psychological
insight displayed by Corneille in the differentiation of one
character from another.

But the way is now clear for us to approach the great scene,
Horace, IV. 5:

(66)

HORACE

Sister, behold the avenger of our brothers,
The arm that stemmed the course of adverse fate,
That makes us Alba's master; even the arm
That rules alone two nations' destinies;
Behold these trophies, witness to my fame,
And pay thy due to my triumphant hour.

CAMILLE

Take then my tears; they are the debt I owe.

HORACE

Rome wants not tears after exploits like these,
And our twain brothers' deaths, mischance of war,
Are too well paid in blood to call for tears:
Nothing is lost, when the loss is avenged.

CAMILLE

Since they are satisfied with blood outpoured
I 'll wear no more for them my mourning weeds,
And I 'll forget their deaths thou hast avenged.
But who 'll avenge for me my lover's death,
To make me suddenly forget his loss?

HORACE

What sayst thou, wretch?

CAMILLE

O Curiace, my love!

HORACE

Unworthy sister, past all bearing bold!
Of one whom I 've laid low, Rome's enemy,
Thy lips protest the name, thy heart the love!
Thy guilty ardour panteth for revenge!
This is thy cry, thy very heart-beat this!
Yield less to impulse, tighter curb thy will,
And make me blush no more to hear thy sighs;
Stifle thy flaming passions from henceforth;
Banish them from thy mind; brood o'er my triumphs.
Let these henceforward be thy sole concern.

CAMILLE

Give me then, savage one, a heart like thine;
And if thou wishest me to speak my mind,
Give back my Curiace, or let me love;
My joy, my grief were bound up with his fate;
I loved him living, and I mourn him dead.
Seek not to find thy sister as she was;
Thou seest but an injured lover now,
Who, like a fury clinging to thy heels,
Will never cease to blame thee for his death.
Tiger, athirst for blood, who bann'st my tears,
Who bidst me in his death find something fine,
And, to the sky extolling thy exploits,

Wouldst have me kill him yet a second time!
May such misfortunes dog thee through thy life,
That thou mayst sink until thou envy me!
Mayst thou ere long by some base deed befoul
The fame so dear to thy brutality!

HORACE

Heavens! who has ever seen frenzy like this!
Dost thou believe that outrage leaves me cold,
And that I 'll bear this dark stain on my race?
Commend, commend a death that 's well for us,
And to the memory of a man prefer
The debt thy birth entails, the good of Rome.

CAMILLE

Rome, the one hate of my indignant soul,
Rome, to whom thou hast sacrificed my lover,
Rome, whom thy heart adores, where thou wast born,
Rome, whom I loathe because she honours thee!
May all her neighbours, sworn confederates,
Sap her foundations still not firmly laid!
And if all Italy is not enough,
To combat her may East combine with West,
From the world's ends nations a hundred come,
And cross, for her destruction, mountains and seas!
On her may she herself pull down her walls,
Tear out her entrails with her proper hands,
And may the wrath of Heaven, lit by my prayers,
Rain down on her a cataract of fire!
To see with mine own eyes the lightning fall,
Houses in ashes, thy laurel-wreaths in dust,
See the last Roman at his latest gasp,
I the sole cause, and then to die for joy!

HORACE [*sword in hand pursuing his sister, who flies off stage*]

Too much, my patience must to reason yield;
Go down to Hell and mourn thy lover there!

CAMILLE [*wounded behind the scene*]
Ah, traitor!

HORACE [*reappearing*]
So may sudden doom await
All who dare mourn an enemy of Rome!

Now let us turn to Racine. The play of his from which we make bold to present the translation of a scene is *Phèdre*, generally regarded as his masterpiece. Phaedra, or Phèdre, as we shall always designate that famous figure, whose mother was Pasiphae, daughter of Helios, the Sun, and whose father was Minos, a son of Zeus, is married to Theseus, King of Athens. She conceives a passion for her stepson, Hippolytus, who himself is in love with Aricia, daughter of a rival to the throne of Athens, whom Theseus had slain. Hippolytus repulses her, and reveals his love for Aricia. Frantic with jealousy Phèdre, through her confidante, Oenone, accuses Hippolytus to his father of an incestuous love for her. While the unhappy king is torn with doubt and horror, news is brought to him that his son, in flight, has been hurled from his chariot by his maddened steeds and killed. Oenone drowns herself, and sudden and terrible remorse comes over Phèdre, and in the last act she poisons herself, and makes full confession of her guilt to Theseus.

It is to be noted that while in Euripides's treatment of the legend the centre of interest is Hippolytus, Racine transfers it to the woman, Phèdre.

In Act IV there occurs the most wonderful of all Phèdre's speeches, in which she expresses her despair over the horror of the position in which she finds herself involved:

(67)

What is my purpose? Whither stray my wits?
Consumed with jealousy, Theseus I call
To help me, him, my husband who still lives,
While I love—whom? Whose heart commands my will?
Each word I speak makes my hair stand on end.
Swollen beyond all measure are my crimes;
Deceit and incest taint the air I breathe;
My homicidal hands itch for revenge,
Steeped though they be in blood of innocence.

Can wretch like me still live, and gaze upon
This blessed sun who is my ancestor?
The sire of gods, their lord, is my forbear;
All heaven and earth are full of my forbears.
Where hide me?   Shall I seek eternal night?
Ah, no! my sire there clasps the fatal urn,
That fate, men say, has placed in his strict hands,
Minos, the judge in hell of ghostly men.
How his dark form will tremble there, aghast,
When he beholds his daughter face to face
Forced to avow so many divers sins,
And crimes perhaps unknown as yet in hell!
Father, what wilt thou say at this dread sight?
Methinks I see the urn fall from thy hands;
Methinks I see thee search out some new way
With thine own hands to execute thy child.
Pardon!   Some cruel god has doomed thy race;
See in thy daughter's madness his revenge.
Alas! my sad heart never reaped the fruit
Of those dread crimes whose shame pursues me still.
Dogged by misfortune to my latest breath,
In torment I yield up my wretched life.

Now we may proceed to the last scene of the great tragedy:

(68)

Theseus

Ah, well! the triumph 's yours; my son is dead.
What ground have I for fear!   What cruel doubt,
Though heart forgives him, rightly startles me!
But, madam, he is dead; cling to your prey;
Joy in his death, whether deserved or no.
I 'm ready that mine eyes be aye abused;
I hold him guilty, since you bring the charge.
His death affords me food enough for tears,
Without my seeking odious evidence,
That cannot bring him back to my just grief,
And might perchance but add to my distress.
Let me escape, far from these shores and you,
The bleeding image of my mangled son.

Haunted, confused by tragic memories
I 'd banish me from the whole universe.
All seems to rise against my injustice.
My very fame augments my suffering:
Less known of men, the easier might I hide.
I hate the high gods' gracious care of me;
I 'll plead with them for some death-dealing gift,
And plague them now no more with useless prayers.
Whate'er their tragic kindness does for me
Cannot repay what they have robbed me of.

Phèdre

No, Theseus! an ill silence must I break,
And give back to your son his innocence:
He was not guilty.

Theseus

   Hapless father, I!
It was upon your word that I condemned him.
Ah, cruel one, think you excuse enough——

Phèdre

My moments now are precious; hear me, Theseus:
'Twas I who on thy son, modest and chaste,
Dared cast an eye profane, incestuous.
Heaven kindled in my breast a fatal flame:
Detestable Oenone did the rest.
Fearing Hippolytus, my madness known,
Might noise abroad the passion that he loathed,
The traitress, using my extremity,
Hastened to meet you, and with her own lips
Charged him.   Her forfeit 's paid.   Fearing my wrath,
She found beneath the waves a doom too kind.
Already had a dagger slit my life,
Were injured innocence not left to mourn:
By thus confessing my remorse, I 've sought
A gentler path to lead me down to death.
What I have drunk runs through my burning veins
A poison that Medea brought to Athens.

Already has the venom reached my heart,
And on that dying heart strikes strangely cold.
E'en now I see but through a mist the sky,
And him, my husband, whom my presence wounds:
And death has robbed the brightness of mine eyes,
To render pure the daylight they have stained.

PANOPE [*a lady-in-waiting*]

She's dying, sire!

THESEUS

            Would that the memory
Of such a deed, so black, might die with her!
Mine error too well known, let us shed tears
To mingle with the blood of my poor son!
Let us embrace what's left of that dear son,
To expiate a curse that I abhor.
Pay him the honours he has earned too well.
And, better to appease his angry ghost,
Despite the plottings of a hostile house
His lover now shall hold a daughter's place.

Among Corneille's few shorter poems there is one that cannot
be omitted, for it constitutes one of the chief ornaments of this
book. The name of writers of good sonnets, of fine sonnets, is
legion, but Corneille joined the select company of those who
have written great sonnets when he composed his epitaph on
Élisabeth Ranquet, of which a version follows:

(69)

EPITAPH ON ÉLISABETH RANQUET

O stranger, shed no tears upon this tomb near by;
This woman's funeral bed is one of precious worth.
Her body was all-pure, here her pure ashes lie,
But her heart's zeal loves on, here where she rests in earth.

Ere yet the debt was paid owed by all nature's kind,
Her soul, mounting beyond the compass of her eyes,
In her Creator's hands His creature had resigned;
And while she walked on earth her life was in the skies.

The poor, more than herself, held count of all her wealth;
Patience in suffering served her for joy in health.
It was for love she sought with her last breath to pray.

Stranger, thus fired by her, strive to attain her bliss,
And, far from pitying her now she has lost our day,
Believe one never dies who dies a death like this.

And we may well work into our scheme a version of one of
Racine's hymns, still sung in Protestant churches in France,
which illustrates the religious side he displayed, if not in early
manhood, in his later years:

(70)

Hymn

My God, what wars my bosom fill!
  I find two different men in me:
  One would that, out of love for Thee,
My heart to Thee were faithful still;
The other, rebel to Thy will,
  Would make me scorn Thy law's decree.

The one, a soul of heavenly birth,
  Would have me choose my mansion there,
  To things eternal give a care,
And count all else as nothing worth.
The other bends my head to earth
  By weight of gloom I cannot bear.

Alas, within I strive and strain!
  Where can I hope to find my rest?
  I would—but idle is the quest;
I would—but, O the bitter pain,
The good I love I seek in vain,
  And do the evil I detest.

O Grace, O Light that shines to save,
  The strife within me pacify!
  And win him over tenderly,
This man that dares Thy will to brave,
And make of him Thy willing slave,
  Who, else, a slave to Death must die.

Nothing suitable for our purpose is to be found in Molière, born in 1622, the undisputed prince of comedy, whose name is probably better known, more welcome to the world at large than that of any other French writer. To illustrate the shorter poems of the Augustan Age we have to fall back on the fourth of the outstanding poets of the period, La Fontaine, in whom we find perfection of form as in Racine, and wit, humour, ar. l worldly wisdom as in Molière. Moreover, he reached with his more popular appeal a wider circle than either Corneille and Racine, whose dramas were the glory of a splendid court and an aristocratic society, or even than Molière, whose delightful *Le Bourgeois Gentilhomme* was written for the amusement of the court, and first performed in one of the halls of Chambord, still standing to-day, and though now no more than a shell, the most magnificent of all the gorgeous châteaux of Touraine.

La Fontaine, though one of the darlings of high society, was no more than his great contemporaries of gentle birth. He was born at Château-Thierry in Champagne in 1621, and lived on to the year 1695. His father was ranger of the neighbouring forests, and to that post he succeeded. But his literary bent and his vague and desultory disposition made him little suited for the practical business of life, and even, it would seem, for household affairs; since eventually he sold his office, effected what was apparently a friendly separation from his wife, and made his way to Paris. There he was admitted to the literary household of Fouquet, Louis XIV's magnificent but unscrupulous Superintendent of Finance, and when he, like Wolsey, fell, La Fontaine found a constant succession of influential patrons until the end of his life. His high standing in the literary world of his time may be gauged by the fact that he became one of a little coterie with Boileau, Molière, and Racine, who met once a week for dinner at a tavern in the rue Vieux-Colombier, a site whose literary associations were illuminated in this twentieth century by Copeau's theatre of the name, which rivalled for some years the *Comédie française* itself.

Of La Fontaine's works the outstanding one, on which rests his fame, is the *Fables*. His *Fables* have survived even the rude test of their use as a school-book by those too young to appreciate their merits, and the final word on their author was said by that distinguished Frenchman, poet, critic, scholar, and greatest of

all literary *causeurs*, Sainte-Beuve. 'To speak of La Fontaine,'
he says, 'is never tedious, even when one is quite certain that one
has nothing new to add. It is to speak of experience itself, of
the moral lessons taught by life, of good common sense, subtle
and profound, general and particular, lit up by wit and humour,
animated with charm and imagination, corrected too and em-
bellished by man's higher sentiments, and, above all, fraught with
the consolations of a friend. In short, it is to speak of all those
things that one never realizes better than when we have grown
ripe ourselves. This La Fontaine, who is given to children to
read, is never relished so well as after one's fortieth year; his is
that old wine of which Voltaire speaks, and to which he has
compared the poetry of Horace; he improves with age, and just as
each of us appreciates La Fontaine better as we grow older, even
so French literature, as it goes on and prolongs its life, seems to
accord him a higher place and to recognize in him a greater figure.'

Critics have vied in extolling La Fontaine's work, not only for
perfection of form, but also for richness of content. The stories
enshrined in his fables are models of short narrative, only to be
surpassed perhaps in this line by the parables to be found in the
Gospels, and the moral of each fable is often such a marvel of
compression as to constitute an epigram in itself. The moral is
always a sound one; there is no toying with paradox, no touch of
mere malice, no suggestion of political or sentimental propaganda. Then come the flexibility of his phrasing, and his
aptitude for hitting on just the right word wanted, either noun
or adjective or verb. His vocabulary is enriched, like the
Pleiad's, with words drawn from the technical terms of the arts
and crafts, or from the rustic speech of the countryside. Thus
his descriptions of living creatures, of natural scenes, of the beauty
of parkland, woodland, and running streams have a certainty
that impress them on his readers with a sudden sense of familiarity.
And then there are the rich stores of his wide knowledge of
human nature to vivify and humanize the whole.

Sainte-Beuve has likened the charms of La Fontaine to those
of old wine; playing on this idea, we can apply to him the fine
phrase of one of our own great critics, Hazlitt, who said of
William Godwin: 'You perceive by your host's talk as by the
taste of seasoned wine that he has a *cellarage* in his understanding.'

In the following versions of poems by La Fontaine a sedulous effort has been made to preserve the actual form of the original. In the preface stress has been laid on the importance in the translation of a poem of preserving its *pattern*. In no case is this more important than with La Fontaine, where the changes in length of line give his poems the distinctive charm of a curving grace as form winds in and out to suit the content of the fable. And this bestows on his rhythm a fine athletic quality, for the smooth transition from long line to short gives one at times the same sort of thrill as is to be had from watching the sudden, easy swerve of a fast three-quarter-back in full career.

Here, then, are versions of four of La Fontaine's *Fables*:

(71)
THE HAUGHTY MULE

A bishop's mule laid claim to old nobility,
    And talked all day and everywhere
    Of nothing but his dam, the mare,
    Of whose exploits he boasted high:
How here or there she 'd been; how this or that she 'd done.
    He thought that as he was her son
    His fame a chronicler should find.
Ne'er had he deigned to serve a humble doctor's will.
But, growing old, he found his destiny—a mill!
And then at last his sire, the ass, came back to mind.

    If of misfortune this be said,
    It puts some sense in a fool's head,
    Surely the proposition 's true:
    Misfortune has its uses too.

(72)
THE WOLF AND THE DOG

A wolf there was, a thing of skin and bone,
    So well the dogs their part had played.
The wolf met with a hound, stalwart and handsome grown,
And sleek and fat, who there by some mischance had strayed.
    To spring, and tear him limb from limb,
    Had been Sir Wolf's first sudden whim;
    But he must fight for such a prize,
    And our mastiff was of a size

In self-defence to make some show.
The wolf, then, neared him, bowing low;
And soon the compliments began to flow,
How he admired one quite so stout!
'Good sir, it 's surely your look-out
If you are not as fat as me,' the dog replied.
'Best quit the forest where you hide:
What miseries your kind appal!
Poor, stupid, starveling devils all,
Whose sad condition is to pine for food and die.
Just think, nothing assured! no mouthful at your will!
Your only food, what you can kill!
Come, follow me and find a better destiny.'
The wolf replied: 'What tasks will come my way?'
'But few,' exclaimed the dog: 'beggars and rogues to chase,
Who flaunt a stick before your face;
To make the household smile, your master's will obey:
If this you do, you 'll have for pay
Great heaps of dainty scraps of every mortal kind;
Chickens' and pigeons' bones you 'll find,
Not mentioning pat and caress.'
The wolf already dreamt of such celestial fare
As made him weep for tenderness.
While they walked on he saw the dog's neck rubbed and bare.
'What 's this?' he asked.   'Nothing.'   'What, nothing!'
So to me!'
'But yet, what is it?'   'Well, the collar that I wear,
By which I 'm chained, may be the cause of what you see.'
'Chained!' said the wolf, 'why, then, you can't be free to run
At your sweet will!'   'Not always: but why fret?'
'Such cause have I to fret, that of your meals not one
I 'll share, whatever feasts you get;
To buy a treasure at your price suits not my will.'
So said, good Master Wolf ran off; he 's running still.

(73)

THE FOOL AND THE WISE MAN

A certain fool pursued with showers of stones a sage;
The wise man, turning round, hailed him: 'Friend, take
your due,

Bravely you 've done your bit, here 's half a crown for you;
You 've tired yourself enough to earn a larger wage.
The labourer, 'tis said, is worthy of his hire;
Look at that passer-by, he 's rich, if you inquire;
Pass on your gifts to him, and earn your proper pay.'
Lured by the hope of gain the fool ran off to play
      His pranks upon the wealthy one.
But not in silver now was paid the price of fun;
Bailiffs came running up; one caught him such a thwack
      He stunned him and half broke his back.

At courts of kings such fools their arts disclose;
At your expense they make their masters roar.
To stop their chattering tongues do you propose
To knock them down? Of strength you may need more
Than you possess. Best tempt them to assail
Another who can safely wield the flail.

(74)
The Cobbler and the Financier

There was a cobbler sang from morning until night:
      He was a marvel to the sight,
A marvel to the ear; he trilled and trilled again,
      More happy than the seven wise men.
Not such his neighbour's lot; though laced with gold his
        dress,
      He sang but little, slept still less:
      A broker he, with funds to spare.
If at the break of day sleep sometimes got the best,
The cobbler with his songs was sure to break his rest;
      Bitter the plaint he then addrest,
      That Providence for all its care
Had not arranged the sale on any market-stall
      Of sleep, as well as food and drink.
      Therefore he bade the singer call
At his fine house, and said: 'Come, friend, just let me
        think—
What do you earn a year?' 'A year, sir, 'pon my word!'
      Said, smiling at the thought absurd,

Our cobbler blithe and gay, 'in no such way do I
Make up accounts; I 've scarce a penny to put by
   From day to day: and when the year is dead
      If both ends meet I 'm satisfied;
      Each day provides my daily bread.'
'Tut, tut! What do you earn a day?' the broker cried.
'Sometimes more, sometimes less: the worst is that always
(And but for that we 'd think our earnings good enough)—
The worst is, every year brings many holidays,
   When one can't work; these fêtes eat up our stuff;
A feast day spoils the next; and parson up his sleeve
Has always some new saint to make the church bell ring.'
The broker smiled to find a man quite so naïve
And said: 'To-day I mean to make of you a king.
Here are a hundred pounds, keep them; if you take heed
      You 'll find their use in time of need.'
The cobbler thought that all the gold before him glowed
     Man in a hundred years could find
     To meet the wants of humankind.
He hurried home, and there, safe in the cellar, stowed
     The gold, his joy too, side by side.
     He sang no more: his tongue was tied
The moment that he won the source of all our woes.
     Sleep never entered at his door:
     Care was his constant visitor,
     Suspicions vain, fantastic foes.
Throughout the day he kept a watchful eye; at night
     A noisy cat gave him a fright;
The cat was after gold! At last, and fit to weep,
He ran to him whom now he could awake no more:
'Give back to me my songs,' he cried, 'give back my sleep;
     Your hundred pounds let me restore.'

As a final example of La Fontaine we venture to offer the version of a charming poem not cast in the form of a fable, his *Invocation to Delight*. Here it must be confessed that the pattern of the original has so far been departed from as to substitute for the Alexandrines, where they occur, lines of five feet into which the subject‑matter seemed easily and naturally to run:

(75)

INVOCATION

O sweet Delight, from childhood without thee
Alike to humankind were life and death,
Lodestar of every creature drawing breath,
To draw us on how fierce thine energy!
 'Tis thou dost move all here below.
  For thee through strife and pain we go,
  For thee and for those charms of thine:
  No captain, private of the line,
Subject or prince, or minister of state,
  But follows thee alone like fate.
We too, thy nurslings, were our toil in vain,
With no delicious music for refrain,
No trancing sound that tingling ears rehearse,
  Should we compose a single verse?
What men call glory, using splendid names,
What served for prize in the Olympic games,
Is nought but thee, thyself, divine Delight.
And joy of sense, is that of value slight?
  For what are Flora's gifts displayed,
  The sky at dawn and eve arrayed,
  These dainties from Pomona's hoard,
  Bacchus, to animate the board,
  The woods, the meadows, and the streams,
  Kind mothers all of tranquil dreams?
And why the fine arts, dandled in thine arms?
Ah, why these Chloes with triumphant charms,
  Except to give us touch with thee?
In innocence I mean: the heart's desire,
  Repressed with rigour though it be,
  Still warms us with a pleasant fire.

Delight, Delight, his mistress long ago,
  Who was the wisest Greece could show,
Disdain me not, but make this breast thy home,
  Not there in idleness to roam:
Gaming and love, music and books are dear,
Country and town, I love them all; nay more
  As sovereign good I 'd fain adore;

To sombre joy even melancholy's near.
Come then, O sweet Delight; and wouldst thou guess
The proper term I claim for such a boon?
Assume a hundred years I need—no less;
    An end at thirty were too soon!

Yes, La Fontaine is a delightful poet to read and to savour;
and yet one cannot but feel that others have something that he
lacks, if it be only a *personal* touch that thrills the reader as it has
thrilled the poet, and that there are others who soar higher.
But tastes differ.   The writer well remembers meeting at dinner
in Paris, soon after the war, one of the most eminent of professors
of French literature in France.   Overbold, he ventured in the
course of conversation to suggest to the professor that in England
there were many lovers and students of French poetry who held
that as pure poet Villon was greater than La Fontaine.   The
professor's indignation overpowered him, and, fortunately for
the Englishman, it rendered an eloquent Frenchman almost
speechless.   No doubt from his very tenable point of view he
was right.
    Rarely do we find in the seventeenth century the simple and
direct, but tragic, personal note that touches the deepest chord
in our nature; but we get it in the poignant epitaph composed
for himself by Paul Scarron, 1610–60, whose name is so strangely
bound up with that of Madame de Maintenon.   Scarron, a
popular man of letters of his period, and a dramatist, but best
known as the author of *Le Roman comique,* a picaresque novel,
married in 1652, when himself deformed and hopelessly crippled by
the tortures of some rheumatic affection, the charming but penniless
granddaughter of Agrippa d'Aubigné, Henry IV's friend, and
distinguished soldier and poet.   She nursed him to the day of
his death, and then got some sort of footing at court as governess
to Louis XIV's children by Madame de Montespan.   Madame
de Maintenon, as she was now called, without loss of her own or
others' esteem, gradually won the affection of the king who, on
the death of his queen, actually married her in the winter of
1685–6.   The ceremony was a private one, and she never
assumed in public any royal prerogatives, but she made the king
as good a wife as she had proved to Scarron.   Here is a version
of the epitaph Scarron, her first husband, wrote for himself:

F

(76)

Epitaph on Himself

He who lies here, and sleeps at last,
Pity, not envy, justified;
Through all the pangs of death he passed
A thousand times before he died.
O thou that passest by, tread light,
Lest, at a sound, his slumber cease
On this, the first and only night
Poor Scarron found to sleep in peace.

It is worthy of note that during this Augustan Age there are signs that men of culture indulged themselves in practising the old verse-forms of the medieval period. Ménage, a distinguished scholar of the period, and one of the tutors of the celebrated Madame de Sévigné, was the subject of a satirical epitaph by La Monnoye, a rival of his:

(77)

On Monsieur Ménage

Come, leave in peace Monsieur Ménage
A very worthy personage,
    Whose friendship all who had would keep;
Now let him in his turn repose,
Whose poetry, whose works in prose
    Have often sent us sound asleep.

Ménage may have been a dull fellow, but he it was who gave the title of 'King of Triolets' to the following little poem, written in that metre by Jacques Ranchin, a legal luminary of the time, which is certainly difficult to match among triolets ancient or modern for its subtlety and completeness as a work of miniature art:

(78)

The King of Triolets

The first day in the month of May
Counts for the happiest in my life.
How fair a plan I formed that day,
The first day in the month of May!
I saw you and I loved straightway;
And if my plan pleased you, my wife,
The first day in the month of May
Counts for the happiest in my life.

CHAPTER V

THE EIGHTEENTH CENTURY

Louis XIV's reign dragged on into the new century, until 1715, but his last years were gloomy in the extreme. The Duke of Marlborough delivered, one after another, smashing blows at his once victorious armies, Blenheim, Ramillies, Oudenarde. Colbert's work was undone, for the country was wellnigh ruined by the Sun King's wars, the extravagance of his passion for display, and his personal expenditure, including that involved in his craze for magnificent buildings, parks, terraces, and fountains, of which Versailles is the standing monument. Of his family his son and his grandson were dead, and his heir, a great-grandson, was a sickly child of five. Even Madame de Maintenon, for all her force of character and her patience, was so tired of her royal consort that she could not endure the penance of keeping watch by his deathbed.

The sickly child, under indifferent guardianship, grew up into the licentious and degenerate Louis XV, whose reign over a distracted country lasted until 1774 without any effective effort on his part to restore its greatness, or even to arrest its decadence. During the earlier portion of his reign the administration of Cardinal Fleury was fairly successful, but from 1735 onwards foreign affairs became involved, the cardinal's age rendered him less capable of coping with difficulties abroad as well as at home, and after his death, at the age of ninety, in 1743, there was no strong hand to guide the policy of the realm. The king's capable mistress, La Pompadour, was no wise counsellor. He had, indeed, subordinates who, however exasperated by superannuated institutions, and by the privileges of the nobility and the Church in matters of taxation, did their best to find remedies for abuses that threatened the stability of their country. But the intellectual ferment of the time was too much for them, and the king's attitude may be gauged from the remark attributed to him, and, if not well founded, well foisted on him: 'Things will last my time,' to which La Pompadour is supposed to have rejoined : 'And after us the Deluge.'

It is not then to be wondered at that during his disastrous reign the French colonies in both Canada and India passed into the hands of England, and that the result of the Seven Years' War (1756–63), when France in alliance with Austria was hopelessly defeated by the combination of Frederick the Great and England, was that the hegemony in Europe was transferred from France to England.

Such a period was certainly not one favourable to any outburst of lyrical song after the long and splendid reign of the Alexandrine in the Augustan Age. A Juvenal might have found free scope, had a Juvenal appeared. But the eighteenth century was one of feverish intellectual effort, and produced a galaxy of great writers in prose, whose object was not merely to interest and amuse, but also to make people think, and to instruct them.

Prominent among these was that dignified relic of the seventeenth century, Fénelon, Archbishop of Cambrai, who lived on until 1715. He was tutor to Louis XIV's very promising, but short-lived, grandson, the Duke of Burgundy, and impressed on his pupil the doctrine that a prince exists for his subjects, not his subjects for their prince. Fénelon was one of the first to voice the feeling now growing rife in all classes against the doctrine of absolutism. There was Montesquieu, who made laws and constitutions the subject not of mild acceptance or of violent prejudice, but of critical examination and of political judgment. There was Diderot, most versatile and fertile of thinkers, who rallied round him a great company of publicists, scholars, and philosophers to produce his monumental encyclopaedia, a compendium of knowledge well calculated to feed the intellectual curiosity of the age. And there was Voltaire, one of the most dazzling figures in all French literature.

Of the brilliance and the range of Voltaire's writings in prose, tales, including of course *Candide*, by general consent the masterpiece of ironic narrative, histories, criticism, and philosophy, with countless political and other pamphlets, and letters innumerable, it is outside the scope of this book to speak. Of two complete editions of his works one contains forty-eight and the other fifty-two volumes, and the reader if he wishes to form some idea of their quality may be referred, as in the case of the great figures of the Augustan Age, to what Mr. Lytton Strachey says of their author in his *Landmarks in French Literature*.   His energy was tireless throughout a life which lasted from 1694 to 1778, and it may fairly be said that intellectually he dominated the reign of Louis XV.   His incisive attacks on all authority, on men, and on institutions, and on things of his day, his irritability and vanity, even his readiness to rouse himself in the defence of the persecuted, all made him enemies enough.   He was twice imprisoned in the Bastille, and much of his life had to be spent on the frontier, whence escape abroad was easy, and even for a time across the frontier, in Switzerland itself.

Interludes in his life were an early visit of three years to England, which did much to enlarge his knowledge of the world, and a much later visit, again of nearly three years, to the Court of Frederick the Great at Potsdam.   Frederick had long endeavoured to secure the residence at his court of the most distinguished of living Frenchmen, whose name throughout the civilized world was in every mouth; but when he did succeed in getting him he found him far too prickly an object to make a domestic pet of.   They quarrelled, and the circumstances of their final parting entailed a scandal which has not yet died down.

Vast as was the volume of his work in prose, Voltaire wrote much poetry as well, and was regarded as easily the greatest poet of his time.   Despite the command he had over the mechanism of verse his reputation as a great poet has not survived. His plays, some of which were most successful in his lifetime, are not now accepted as rivalling the drama of the Augustan Age. But he could write verse of exquisite grace, and use it too as a vehicle for the expression of his supreme gift of bitter irony and savage wit, in which he has never been surpassed.   These qualities are notably to be found in his epigrams, and versions of a few of them will suffice to establish the claim that in this art, practised by so many distinguished poets, he stands without a rival.

Here is an inscription for a garden statue of Love, possibly in the garden of his friend, Madame du Châtelet, in whose frontier château at Cirey he lived for so long; and this is followed by a motto composed for the lady herself:

(79)

On a Garden Statue of Love

Whoe'er thou be, thy master see;
He is, he was, or has to be.

(80)

Motto for Madame du Châtelet

Rest, a few trifles, reverie,
    A book or two, no bore or dun,
A friend to keep one company;
    Such is my lot, a happy one.

Next, here are two of his bitterest epigrams, and they are probably not to be equalled for keen, incisive, cruel wit in all literature. The first is an example of the attacks he indulged in against the Church and its ministers. The second indicates his intolerant contempt for authors he fell foul of; Le Jay, a publisher, had produced a title-page with his portrait between those of two of his pet aversions, Fréron, a leading critic and an estimable man, and La Beaumelle, an old teacher of Voltaire:

(81)

On a Figure of Christ in the Jesuit Habit

Consider, pray, the artfulness
    Industrious monks like these can show.
My God, they 've clothed Thee in their dress,
    Lest men should love Thee here below!

(82)

On the Placing of his Portrait between two Others

'Twixt Fréron and La Beaumelle me!
    What can Le Jay by this have meant?
It were indeed a Calvary,
    Had either thief been penitent.

Here is yet another epigram on Fréron, based on an ancient model, most pleasantly developed by Goldsmith in his *Elegy on the Death of a Mad Dog*:

(83)

THE SNAKE THAT BIT FRÉRON

One day, down in the vale below,
A snake bit Fréron on the toe.
And what ensued, I ask you? Why,
It was the snake that had to die.

Then read this gibe at J.-J. Lefranc, Marquis de Pompignan, whom he had once flattered, but whose metrical renderings of passages from Holy Writ excited his derision:

(84)

ON LEFRANC'S TRANSLATIONS FROM JEREMIAH

Can you suggest why Jeremy
Wept all his life so copiously?
Prophet, he saw a prospect grim:
Lefranc one day would murder him.

Finally here is an epigram of high moral import:

(85)

AN EPITAPH

He who lies here one law did own:
To live but for himself alone.
No heed to his example give,
Or men may scrawl on thy headstone:
Here lies one with no right to live.

It is a curious but not perhaps a very profitable undertaking to speculate on what an author might have achieved had he written in another age, under social and political conditions more congenial, less irritating, less apt to turn a man from poetry to prose, to drive him into pamphleteering, however brilliant and incisive. But of this we may be sure, that had one of Voltaire's prodigious energy and intellectual power been contemporary with Corneille, Racine, and Molière, either the serious drama of the Augustan Age would have been the work of a triumvirate, or an Aristophanes would have taken his stand by Molière. How

fine a poet there was in Voltaire may in some degree be realized
from the following version of a poem he addressed to Madame
Lullin when he was over eighty years old:

(86)

To Madame Lullin

Ah, then you feel astonishment
   That though with eighty winters hoar
My aged muse, her vigour spent,
   Should hum a simple song once more.

Sometimes a few small shoots of green
   Gleam through the frosts that bind the clay:
Nature rejoices at the scene,
   But early nipt it dies away.

We still can hear the note of bird,
   When skies no more are blue above;
But tender tones no more are heard;
   He sings no longer of his love.

And so I pluck again the strings,
   Though rebel to my hand the lyre;
Still try my voice, though while it sings
   Its trembling accents must expire.

'I would that when I say good-bye,'
   Such was Tibullus' fond demand,
'I fixed thee, Julia, eye to eye,
   And touched thee with my dying hand.'

But when we 're sure that now 's the end,
   And soul with life must fly away,
Have we the eyes to see our friend
   Or hands the last caress to pay?

At that dread moment we forget
   All that we did in sanity;
What mortal man with joy has met
   Eyes called to watch his agony?

Delia in turn that fate must share,
　And pass into eternal night,
Forgetting that she once was fair,
　And that she lived for love's delight.

We 're born, we live, my shepherdess,
　We die, but wherefore is not clear.
All of us sprang from nothingness:
　But whither bound? . . . God knows, my dear.

On his serious side read the following version of a fine passage from his poem on the earthquake at Lisbon in 1755, which cost the lives of over 30,000 people, and the horror of which sent a shock throughout the whole civilized world. Here we have a good example of that *saeva indignatio* in the expression of which Voltaire is one of the greatest masters. He combats here the cold-blooded indifference of some, the foolish optimism of others who claim that somehow all is well despite a disaster in one corner of the world, the cant of those who look upon such a disaster as a judgment for sin, and in uncompromising terms raises the whole problem of evil:

(87)

On the Earthquake at Lisbon

O miserable men! O sorrow-laden world!
O concourse full of dread, where meets all humankind,
Where we discuss our griefs always without avail!
Philosophers befooled who tell us: 'All is well,'
Hither, and contemplate with awe these ruined walls,
These rubbish heaps, these rags, these ashes of the doomed,
Women and children, one upon another piled,
These human limbs dispersed neath shattered monuments;
Thousands of hapless ones whom yawning earth devours,
Who, bleeding, gashed, and torn, and palpitating still,
Buried beneath their roofs, end without hope of aid
In torment and despair their lamentable days!
Hearing the cries half-formed that dying voices hiss,
Before this ghastly sight, burnt bodies smoking yet,
Dare you say: ''Tis the effect of sempiternal laws,
That God, who 's free to choose and good, must set in force'?
　*F

Dare you say, when you see these victims heaped on
    high:
'God is avenged; their death is the price of their sins'?
Was Lisbon, now no more, a fouler haunt of vice
Than London, Paris are, both steeped in luxury?
Lisbon is swallowed up; at Paris people dance.
O tranquil lookers-on, whose hearts are undismayed,
Who contemplate unmoved your shipwrecked brothers
    drown,
You can discuss in peace the causes of a storm!
But when you feel the blows of hostile destiny,
Grown human then at last, you 'll weep as we do now.
Trust me, now that the earth opens its gulfs profound,
My plea is innocent, my protests justified.
Surrounded on all sides by cruelty of fate,
Fury of wicked men, the gins and snares of death,
Buffeted by the shocks of all the elements,
Companions in distress, dismiss not my complaint. . . .

    Thus the whole universe in all its members groans;
For torment all are born, and one by one they die;
And you would have us build, where tragic chaos reigns,
Of each man's separate griefs a general happiness.
What happiness, O man, weak, mortal, in despair?
You tell us: 'All is well,' in a voice full of tears;
The world gives you the lie, and even your proper hearts
Prove false a hundred times the errors of your brain.
The elements, brute beasts, and men are all at war.
We must admit the fact; *evil* is in the world:
Its secret principle is quite unknown to us.
Has evil come from Him, the author of all good? . . .

    But how conceive a God, goodness in very self,
Prodigal of His gifts to children that He loves,
Who yet has poured on them evils with lavish hands?
What eye can penetrate the depth of His designs?
Evil cannot be born of the all-perfect One;
Cannot come from elsewhere, since God sole master is.
And yet it does exist.   O lamentable truth!
O blend astonishing of contrarieties!

Voltaire was the tragedian of the eighteenth century, but a claim of that century which demands recognition is the part it played in the development of comedy, often in spite of the jealousy and active hostility of the *Théâtre française*. The most distinguished of the writers of comedies and vaudevilles were Lesage, best known as the author of *Gil Blas*, and Beaumarchais, author of the *Barbier de Seville* and the *Mariage de Figaro*; but among them were also Marivaux and Piron, one of the liveliest of them all as a writer of light verse. Piron's name will live for ever, if only for one of the most brilliant epigrams written in this age of epigrams, his ironic epitaph for himself:

> Ci-gît Piron, qui ne fut rien,
> Pas même Académicien.

> Here Piron lies; worth nothing he,
> Not even to grace the Academy.

A popular poet in the latter part of the eighteenth century was a great-nephew of Voltaire, Florian (1755–94) by name, whose fame is still kept alive by the success of his *Fables*, graceful imitations of those of the supreme master in this art, La Fontaine. Of the high quality of his work the following version of one of his fables, *The Phoenix*, may give some idea:

(88)

THE PHOENIX

> The Phoenix, flown from Araby,
> Came to our woods one summer's day:
> What chirping mid the birds!   In one great flock they fly
> To their fine guest, due court to pay.
> They watch him; on his charms refine:
> His plumage and his voice, his gift of melody,
> All, all is beauty, grace divine,
> All gives delight to ear and eye.
> For the first time on earth one sees envy depart
> Before the call to praise and love one's conqueror.
> The nightingale declared: 'Of sweetness such a store
> Has never thrilled my ravished heart.'

'Never,' the peacock said, 'colours more rich in hue
          Have had the glow that pleases me:
They fill my dazzled eyes and will not let them be.'
The other birds said much in praise, but nothing new.
          His privilege they voted good:
How he alone, bird-king, offspring of heaven on high,
When old 's laid on a pyre of scented cedar-wood
And, self-consumed, reborn to immortality.
While all this talk went on, only the turtle-dove,
          Without a word, breathed forth a sigh.
          Her mate just touched her wing in love,
          And, pressing closer, asked her why
          Such gloomy thoughts possessed her mind:
'Like him, that happy bird, to live, is this your whim?'
          'Ah no, friend!   How I pity him,
          The solitary of his kind!'

Florian is in the tradition of the seventeenth century, and it is perhaps in the early poetry of Évariste de Parny, born on the island of Bourbon in 1753, and thus a Creole like more than one of the leading French poets of the nineteenth century, that we get the earliest premonition of the sort of poetry France was yet to produce. The ease, simplicity, and sweetness of his early, and mostly erotic, verse are very remarkable, but his later poems, dull from their very length, contain among other extravagances obscene attacks on Christianity, and ill-natured, ill-founded diatribes against our own country. Among his early poems is to be found one that will give him immortality, for no French anthology will ever be complete without it. This is his *Elegy on the Death of a Young Girl*, which might have been written by that charming but unhappy poet, Gérard de Nerval, in the nineteenth century. Here is a version of it:

(89)

An Elegy

Her age was just past infancy,
Like innocence her gaiety,
And lent by Love himself her charm.
A few more months, a few more days,
In her pure heart that knew no harm

Had dawned child-love's first rosy rays.
But Heaven, prescribing soon her doom,
Vowed her young beauties to the tomb.
She gave her breath back to the skies,
And quietly she closed her eyes,
Complaining not of Heaven's decrees.
Even so a smile may fade in air,
So die, nor leave an echo there,
A bird's note, mid the woodland trees.

Florian and Parny may both be called charming, fluent, and easy poets, but of another cast were three other eighteenth-century poets who deserve mention: Saint-Lambert, Léonard, and Gilbert. Saint-Lambert (1717–1803), no great poet indeed, was highly praised by Voltaire, and he in turn spoke thus of Voltaire, placing him above Corneille and Racine:

Vainqueur des deux rivaux qui règnent sur la scène.

His special interest to us is that he came strongly under English influence, and in 1769 published his principal work, an imitation of James Thomson's *Seasons*. His *Saisons* is by no means the equal of its original. Saint-Lambert is obsessed with the idea that he is bound on every possible occasion to draw a moral from the course of nature, and he is hampered by the consciousness that he is ploughing a lonely furrow. He frankly declares that while Thomson wrote for an audience that knew nature, and loved it, he is writing for one that knows it not, and regards it with indifference.

Léonard (1744–93), born at Guadeloupe, and thus a Creole like Parny, settled early in France. He began his poetic career unsuccessfully with a series of exercises in religion and philosophy. In idyllic, elegiac, and pastoral poetry, however, to which he turned, he won some popularity. But how strained, how anaemic, how insipid this sort of poetry tended to become in the latter half of the eighteenth century may be gauged from an example of his poems which still catches some readers' eyes:

(90)

The Two Streams

Daphnis, who lost his lover dear,
Told this sad tale to win a tear
From those who blamed his loud lament:

Two streams in one their course enwound,
And through a meadow flower-besprent
Flowed gently on in peace profound.
E'en from their source, a bare hill-side,
The same slope made their waters blend,
And their one wish was so to end,
Lost in the ocean's swelling tide.
Ah, why should fate, devoid of grace,
Oppose itself to love so sweet?
These rippling streams are doomed to meet
A rock that severs their embrace.
One of them, lost in loneliness,
Hurls itself madly on the beach,
And all the valley's echoes stress
An answer to its plain ive speech.
A passer-by in anger said:
'Why flow not with a murmur mild
Within your smooth and sandy bed?
The noise you make, it drives me wild.'
'Do you not hear,' the streamlet cried,
'There, on this hillock's other side,
My other self its lot bemoan?
O stranger, on your way depart,
And pray the gods that your fond heart
May never lose what was its own.'

If Léonard's original poetry does not attract us, he has, like Saint-Lambert, a special interest for us in that he too came under the influence of English poetry and in his *Village détruit* produced a version of Goldsmith's *Deserted Village*. A French critic, M. Pierre Malitourne, has claimed that he conquered this for French poetry by the personal accent he gave to it, while remaining true to the spirit of the original. What Léonard did was to reduce the length of Goldsmith's poem by about two-thirds, and in the course of this process the political implications of the original, which a French writer might not appreciate, have mostly disappeared, while his success in preserving the epigrammatic force of so many of the English lines, which has incorporated them in our current speech, has been small. Here are two brief specimens of Léonard's work, the first the beginning of his

description of the village schoolmaster, the second the passage
leading up to the exiles' departure:

Ici du magister la demeure bruyante
A fait place aux buissons qui bordent le chemin
 De leur muraille verdoyante.
 Dès qu'il paraissait le matin,
Les enfants, à sa voix paisible ou menaçante,
 Étaient instruits de leur destin.
Quand parfois un bon mot s'échappait de sa bouche,
Son front épanoui brillait d'un ris flatteur;
 Mais il inspirait la terreur
Sitôt qu'il reprenait son air dur et farouche.

Qu'ils ont maudit le jour, où loin de leur patrie,
 Ils fuyaient sous un nouveau ciel!
Que de pleurs, en quittant leur cabane chérie!
Comme ils tournaient leurs yeux vers ce toit paternel,
 En proie à la flamme ennemie!
L'adieu qu'ils lui disaient devait être éternel.
Près de s'en séparer, leur troupe fugitive
Y retournait, pleurait, baisait encor la rive.
Hélas! s'écriaient-ils dans leurs sanglots amers,
Sur des bords inconnus nous trouverons peut-être
Un asyle semblable au lieu qui nous vit naître:
Mais comment traverser ces effroyables mers?

More important than either Saint-Lambert or Léonard is
Nicolas-Laurent-Joseph Gilbert, who was born in Lorraine in
1751, and educated at the Collège de l'Arc, but must have settled
early in Paris. He became well known in his short life as a
satirist of real power, and in his satire on the eighteenth century
among the signs of decadence which provoked shrewd thrusts
from him were the activities of Voltaire and of the Encyclopae-
dists, thus:

Trop fortuné celui qui peut avec adresse
Flatter tous les partis que gagne sa souplesse;
De peur d'être blâmé, ne blâme jamais rien;
Dit Voltaire un Virgile, et même un peu chrétien.

 . . . . .

Mais qu'on n'ose prôner de sophistes pesans,
Apostats effrontés du goût et de bon sens:
Saint-Lambert, noble auteur dont la muse pédante
Fait des vers fort vantés par Voltaire qu'il vante . . .
Et ce lourd Diderot, docteur en style dur,
Qui passe pour sublime, à force d'être obscur . . .
Et ce froid d'Alembert, chancellier du Parnasse,
Qui se croit un grand homme et fit une préface. . . .[1]

But Gilbert is best remembered for a touching poem he wrote, in a moment of sadness, and which still survives in anthologies. Here is a version of it:

(91)

FAREWELL TO LIFE

I 've shown my heart to God, the God of innocence;
    He 's seen my contrite tears from far,
Heals me of my remorse, arms me with constancy:
    For all who grieve His children are.

My scornful enemies have cried out in their wrath:
    'Die, and thy glory die with thee!'
But, father-like, the Lord says to the heart He soothes:
    'Their hate thy sure safeguard will be.

'Thy dearest friends have caught their enmity from them.
    All play on thy simplicity:
He whom thy hand has fed will sell thine image pure,
    Blackened by some foul calumny.

'But God has heard thy groans, God to whom thou art bound
    By true remorse born of a tear,
God who is ready still to pardon all mankind
    For weakness shown in mortal fear.

'I will awake for thee pity, and justice too,
    That time, which cannot err, holds fast;
Thy foes themselves will clear, by arts too finely spun,
    Thine honour which they hoped to blast.'

[1] His preface to the Encyclopaedia.

All praises be to God, who deigns to give me back
      Innocence, with a noble pride;
To Him who wills to keep my ashes undisturbed
      And watch and wait my bier beside!

To life's great banquet I, a guest unfortunate,
      Once found my way, and I must die;
Must die, and on the tomb, where slowly I arrive,
      To shed a tear none will come by.

Farewell, fields that I loved! and you, fresh foliage green!
      Ye woods, where happy exiles dwell!
Ye heavens, man's tented roof, thou nature we adore,
      Farewell, for the last time farewell!

Ah! may they live to see your sacred beauty long,
      Those friends, deaf when my farewells rose!
May they die full of days, may mourners mourn their death
      And friendly hands their eyelids close.

The impression left by this poem, coupled with his early death
in 1780, before he was thirty years of age, seems to have given
rise to a legend, nursed by Charles Nodier among others, that
Gilbert was a sort of French Chatterton, who died in poverty
and neglect. There is probably no foundation for any such
supposition. His hostility to Voltaire and the philosophers
commended him to the Court and the Church, and from
both he received pensions. His death was occasioned by a fall
from his horse; after the accident he was carried to a public
hospital, quite probably because it was the best place for
one who needed a serious operation, on the faint chance of
saving his life.
    The last quarter of the eighteenth century did have the
fleeting vision of a great poet, André Chénier, born in 1762, and
guillotined in 1794. His fate was sadder than that of either
Keats or Shelley; for tragic as was the early death of both of
them, his was more tragic still, done to death as he was in the
savage excesses of the Reign of Terror. The French Revolution
was the awful but inevitable sequel to the Sun King's selfish
splendour and extravagance, and the callous licentiousness of

the court of his degenerate great-grandson. There is a famous portrait by Boucher, fit artist to adorn such a reign, which represents Louis XV's notorious mistress, La Pompadour, in all her beauty of face and form, and all the preposterous magnificence of her attire. Art has here, as often, enshrined the vice of luxury. But with that vision of her in mind, contrast it with the vision of the viragos of the Revolution, who shrieked in frenzy around the guillotine, and would have torn her in pieces had she lived to encounter their fury. Her successor, indeed, the beautiful Madame du Barry, was guillotined in 1793.

André Chénier was perhaps the most to be lamented of all the victims of the Reign of Terror. He was of gentle birth; his father was consul-general at Constantinople, and his mother a Greek. For four years, 1787 onwards, he was attached to the French Embassy in London; on his return to Paris he was a moderate in politics, and did little to deserve his cruel fate, guillotined simply as a matter of the revolutionary routine. It is said that as his sentence was pronounced he touched his head and said: 'And yet there was something there!'

His early poems, idylls, eclogues, elegies, and the like, were steeped in the spirit of Greek literature of the Alexandrian Age, and though much of his work was left in a fragmentary condition there are passages to be found in it as lovely as many of Keats's poems. The *Iambes*, poems he wrote in the prison of Saint-Lazare while awaiting his execution, and which he had to leave unfinished, unpolished, and unrefined, are sterner stuff. Blazing with anger and indignation at his own fate, and the fate of many of his own friends, they hiss and stab like bullets, as Thomas Seccombe has said. Only two or three of his poems were published in his lifetime, or indeed in the eighteenth century at all, and it was not until 1819 that anything like a collected edition of his works appeared. He was thus in no sense a precursor of the Romantic revival, but the last and most harmonious, most colourful poet of the classical tradition. We know not, alas, what he might have become had he lived on, and caught the enthusiasm of the France renewed by Napoleon Bonaparte.

As examples of his poetry we offer first the version of a charming reminiscence of his father, entitled *La Flûte*, a version not in Alexandrines, but in ten-syllable verse, which seemed readily and smoothly to contain the poem:

(92)

THE FLUTE

The day comes back to me in tender thought
When first the flute close to my mouth he brought,
And, with a smile, lifting me near his heart
Called me his rival, more than counterpart.
He trained my prentice lips, still so unsure,
To breathe a note harmonious and pure,
In cunning hands took my young finger-tips
Raised them and lowered, with half a hundred slips,
And taught them thus, however small and weak,
To close the stops, and make the wood-wind speak.

Next comes a version of one of his shorter classical elegies, *Clytie*:

(93)

CLYTIE

To Clytie thus my ghost: 'Farewell, Clytie, farewell!
Art thou the one whose step has deigned hereby to dwell?
Speak, Clytie, is it thou, or must I wait alway?
Ah! if thou com'st not here alone at break of day,
To think how short the time that I have lived for thee,
To see thy lover's shade and speak a word to me,
Elysium's peace will bring my heart but bitterness,
Nor lightly, as before, earth on my bones will press.
Whenever in this place cool airs at dawn's behest
Come to caress thy lips, and flutter on thy breast,
Weep, weep, 'tis I! O weep, adored one of my heart!
It is my soul that dares from her high home depart,
And on those lips of thine still loves to rest in bliss.
Weep, open wide thine arms, and give her kiss for kiss.'

Then we offer a version of a lovely elegy on the death of a child:

(94)

ON A CHILD'S DEATH

A victim innocent, in this her home on earth,
She only saw the spring, the one that gave her birth.
Nothing is left of her save name and mystery,
A memory, a dream, a form one cannot see.

Farewell, thou tender child our arms have clasped in vain;
Farewell, in thy new home whence none returns again.
We shall not see thee more, when clothed with ripening
    wheat
The summer countryside empties the village street;
We shall not see thee more round the paternal nest,
Where once thy hands and feet and limbs half bare caressed
The grasses and the flowers wherewith the nymphs of Seine
Engarland year by year the hillsides of Lucienne;
Thy little carriage-wheels, a toy for thy delight,
Guided by faithful hands that tend thee day and night,
No more will leave their track by stream, or through the mead.
Thy gaze, thy babbling tune, sweet language hard to read,
No more to busy us will some new care invent.
No more we'll hail with joy and cries of wonderment
Efforts thy rosy mouth with stammering tongue may make
To give again the sounds thine ears, too young, mistake.
Farewell in thy far home where we shall follow thee,
Whither thy mother's eyes e'en now turn jealously.

    Finally comes an attempt to render one of his *Iambes*, written
in prison, rude at times because unrevised, and almost inarticulate here and there through the rage that consumes the poet:

(95)

SAINT-LAZARE

As a last ray of light, last waft of zephyr's wings,
    Brighten a lovely day's decline,
Even on the scaffold's step I'll seek to tune my strings;
    Perchance the next turn will be mine.
Perchance before Time's self, who marches round and round,
    On the smooth dial's face has set,
Within the sixty steps whereby his course is bound,
    His foot that strikes the hour when met,
The slumbers of the tomb will weigh my eyelids down.
    Ere from my lips imperfect falls
My song, nor end is heard the unfinished work to crown,
    Perchance within these startled walls
The messenger of death, the Shades' grim monitor,
    Escorted by his foul patrol,

Will waken with my name this long, dark corridor
    Where mid the crowd I wander sole,
And polish bright my darts to meet the face of crime,
    Frail arms the just man to assist.
Suddenly on my lips he may arrest a rhyme,
    With fetters bind me, wrist to wrist,
And drag me through the crowds who throng to watch me go,
    Sad comrades in captivity,
All of whom knew me well ere came the fatal blow,
    But who no more my face will see.

    .   .   .   .   .

Ah, well! I 've lived too long.   What pride in truth heart-
    whole,
    Of manly faith and constancy
What blest examples dear to every good man's soul,
    What gleam of fortune come near by,
What Judge to punish crime rising in majesty,
    What tears a noble grief lets fall,
Of antique benefits what loyal memory,
    What sweet exchange at true love's call,
Make worthy of regret men's habitat on earth?
    Pale fear 's their god, of aspect fell.
Despair! . . . Deceit! . . . Ah, me! cowards are we from
    birth,
    All, all.   Farewell, this earth, farewell.
Come death, come welcome death, and my deliverance give.
    Does then my heart, worsted in strife,
Sink neath its load of ill?   No, no, would I might live !
    Virtue sets store upon my life.
An honourable man, victim of hate and fear,
    In prison cell, by the grave's side,
Holds higher still his head, and speaks in tones more clear,
    Glowing with all a generous pride.
If by God's will no sword shall from its scabbard leap,
    To glitter when I deal a blow,
This other arm, the pen in ink and gall I steep,
    May help to serve man here below.
Justice and truth, if words fallen from my lips sincere,
    Thoughts I have nursed in secrecy

Have never brought a frown upon your brows severe,
  And if the march of infamy,
Atrocious laughter, or (worse insult to endure)
  Praise from a monstrous crime-stained band
Have driven in your hearts wounds that are hard to cure,
  Save me! Sustain a stout right hand
To hurl your bolts, a friend to render blood for blood.
  To die, with arrows yet unspent!
Unpierced, untrampled on, unmortared in their mud
  Those who our laws have fouled and rent,
Cadaverous worms who feed on France stretched in her gore,
  Their victim! . . . O thou treasure rare,
My pen! Malice and wrath, horror, gods I adore!
  Through you alone I breathe heaven's air,
Even as the burning pitch, hid in the torch's veins,
  When shaken wakes a dying gleam.
I suffer, but I live. Far, far from all my pains,
  Through you, hope in a rushing stream
Transports me. Without you, like poison purple-dyed
  Chagrin's sharp tooth naught can withstand,
The oppression of my friends, the lying homicide,
  Brass sceptre of success in hand,
Good men whom he condemns to loss of all, even life,
  By shameful law of lawless men,
All had dried up my life, or driven their steely knife
  Deep in my very heart. What then?
None would remain to win the heart of history
  For all these just men done to death,
Console their widows, sons, their memory;
  To check the abhorred brigands' breath
Before dark portraits drawn to show them as they stand;
  To plunge down even into hell,
To seek the triple whip, whip for the Avenger's hand,
  Now raised to serve these perverts well;
To spit upon their names, gloat o'er their suffering!
  Come, stifle now thy bitter cry;
Suffer, heart big with hate, for justice famishing.
  Thou, Virtue, weep, if I should die.

The Revolution with all its horror swept away for ever

absolutism in France; even the interludes of the first empire under the great Napoleon, of the second under his feebler great-nephew, and between them the short reigns of Louis XVIII, Charles X, and Louis Philippe, cannot conceal the fact that a nation conscious of itself was henceforward master in its own household, that the people were sovereign, and their ruler, whatever his designation, their nominee. Leading up to the Revolution was a national ferment inevitably occasioned by the oppression of the masses, and the miseries of their existence, and the restless desire for reform stirred up in the middle classes by Montesquieu's brilliant essays in political philosophy, the intellectual propaganda of Diderot and his band of collaborators, and the biting criticisms of Voltaire. But the most explosive personal force of all was Rousseau, the creator at once of romanticism and of the worship of nature, and, despite his moral weaknesses, one of the greatest of social reformers, the first chapter of whose *Social Contract* begins with the shattering sentence: 'Man is born free, but everywhere he is in chains.' It was the irony of fate that sent Rousseau to deal the final blow at absolute monarchy in France, for though this idol of the Revolution was a Swiss, born at Geneva in 1712, he was the descendant of a French ancestor who had emigrated from France in the sixteenth century.

The prodigious result to French literature, and to French poetry in particular, of the complete change in the conditions and the outlook of France brought about by the Revolution will be seen in the next chapters, treating of the nineteenth century. Nevertheless, it is important to bear in mind that it was no mere sudden shock that brought about the radical change in literature and art, as well as in social and political conditions, which made a new age of the nineteenth century.

We have said enough in this chapter of the feverish intellectuality that marked the reigns of Louis XV and Louis XVI, an intellectuality devastating in its criticism of the *ancien régime*, and not only critical but also in a measure constructive. And in the restricted sphere of poetry we have seen that the young poet, André Chénier, who perished by the guillotine, had begun to write poetry of a sort that pointed to a future he was not to see. Nor were the influences on French life and thought in the eighteenth century confined to France itself. During the later years of Louis XV's reign, and all through Louis XVI's, Paris

as the centre of fashion drew a constant stream of visitors
to it from among the English aristocracy, and as an intellectual
centre attracted many of the most prominent amateurs and
intellectuals from our side of the Channel. Such men as Horace
Walpole, Gibbon, David Hume, and Adam Smith found themselves there in an atmosphere stimulating or provocative. Also,
from across the Rhine came from time to time reverberations of
the great renaissance in philosophy, scholarship, and literature
that marked the last half of the century in Germany.

The literary relations between England and France during
the eighteenth century, previously not fully explored, have
recently been exhaustively surveyed by Professor Green of
Cambridge, in his volume entitled *Minuet : a Critical Survey of
French and English Literary Ideas in the Eighteenth Century*. The title
explains the character of a remarkable work. Professor Green
is not carried away by a desire to exalt English influence on the
development of the drama, poetry, or the novel in France, and
to prove more than the facts warrant. Influence there was.
Writers of eminence in either country were aware of what was
being produced in the other. Shakespeare was known, Pope
was known, and to others beside Voltaire Defoe was known,
Richardson was well known and widely read, Thomson's
Seasons, Goldsmith's *Deserted Village*, Young's *Night Thoughts*,
all found French poets ready to adapt them, but the fundamental
Frenchness of French literature remained, and was little affected.
To take one extreme example : Prévost may well have known of
Defoe's *Moll Flanders* before he wrote his *Manon Lescaut*, but how
grotesque to suggest that the latter was in any sense an adaptation
of the former !

Incidentally Professor Green does a great service in rendering
full justice to Voltaire's eminence as a poet, and in the precise
account he gives of Voltaire's attitude to Shakespeare, with
whose plays his stay in London had familiarized him, an attitude
not so bitterly prejudiced as has been popularly supposed. It
was not, be it remembered, until after the revolution that Shakespeare's direct influence on French drama asserted itself; and
then, as will be suggested later, on the introduction, as it were,
of Schiller.

In the nineteenth century one of the greatest of French poets
did show Shakespeare undisguised devotion, viz. Alfred de

Vigny, whose fine adaptation of *Othello* for the French stage is a noble tribute to his hero.   Of Shakespeare Vigny said: Il ne suffit pas d'entendre l'anglais pour comprendre ce grand homme, il faut entendre le Shakespeare qui est une langue aussi; le cœur de Shakespeare est une langue à part. . . . It has been suggested that the influence of Shakespeare on the Romantic drama was exercised mainly through his follower, Schiller, who gradually subdued the form of his plays to rule, and so became as it were the mediator between Shakespeare and Racine.   His dominant influence cannot be denied, and sufficient proof of this will be adduced later in this chapter.

But the attention of the present writer has been called by Mr. Preece to a very remarkable passage to be found in Chapter L of Dumas's *Impressions de Voyage*, which shows how shattering was the impact of authentic Shakespeare on Dumas, Berlioz and other young enthusiasts in the heyday of the Romantic movement in the nineteenth century.   This passage calls for a full summary.

Dumas begins by describing how on entering his bedchamber in a Swiss chalet he found on the walls portraits of Talma and Mlle Mars, the great tragedians of their day.   The sight of them recalled one of their great triumphs in a contemporary play. For three or four years, says Dumas, he had been tormented with the desire to write for the theatre; he had conscientiously studied the great French masters, and had a profound admiration for them; but he found it impossible to accomplish anything within the rules they had imposed upon themselves.   He needed a new style of drama, more pliable in form, more free in movement, more true to nature in its details, to express the passions of a new age.   He thought he saw something of what he wanted in the play in which Talma's and Mlle Mars's performance delighted him, but only such indications as the flight of birds and the seaweed floating on the waves that showed Columbus he was near land.

Six months later the English players arrived in Paris.   Three years earlier they had been greeted at the Porte-Saint-Martin theatre with hisses and a shower of apple-cores.   Now they were playing at the Odéon, and high society in Paris queued up to applaud Miss Smithson and Kemble.   Till then, he confesses with shame, he had only known Shakespeare in Ducis's imitations.

He had seen Talma play Hamlet, and tragic as the actor was in a pale copy of the great original, the piece gave him but little pleasure. Thus he had some difficulty in persuading himself to go to see Hamlet played by Kemble, an actor of less repute than the great Talma. But he went, and of the excitement that soon visited him in the theatre his own words must speak:

'Il me serait difficile de raconter ce qui se passa en moi dès la première scène: cette vérité de dialogue dont alors je ne comprenais pas un mot, il est vrai, mais dont l'accent simple des interlocuteurs me donnait la mesure; ce naturel du geste qui s'inquiétait peu d'être trivial, pourvu qu'il fût en harmonie avec la pensée; ce laisser-aller des poses qui ajoutait à l'illusion, en faisant croire que l'acteur, occupé de ses propres affaires, oubliait qu'elles se passaient devant un public. Au milieu de tout cela, la poésie, cette grande déesse qui domine toujours l'œuvre de Shakespeare, et dont Smithson était une si merveilleuse interprète, bouleversait entièrement toutes les idées acquises, et, comme au travers d'un brouillard, me laissait apercevoir la cime resplendissante des idées innées.

'Enfin, quand j'arrivai à la scène où toute la cour réunie regarde la représentation fictive de cette tragédie dont la mort du roi de Danemarck a fourni le sujet réel, quand, apres avoir vu le jeune Hamlet, dans sa feinte folie, se coucher aux pieds de sa maîtresse, jouant avec son éventail et regardant sa mère à travers les branches, je le vis, à mesure que l'intrigue infernale se déroulait, rendre progressivement à sa figure l'expression lucide et profonde d'une haute intelligence; lorsque je le vis ramper, comme un serpent, du côté droit au côté gauche de la scène, s'approcher de la reine la bouche haletante, les yeux étincelants et le cou tendu, et, au moment où, s'apercevant qu'elle ne peut plus supporter le spectacle de son propre crime, et qu'elle se trouble, et qu'elle se détourne, et qu'elle va s'évanouir, il se dresse tout-à-coup en criant: "Light! Light!" je fus prêt à me lever comme lui, et à crier comme lui: "Lumière! Lumière!"'

Of influences from Scotland as well as England on the development of the Romantic movement towards the end of the eighteenth century Ossian cannot be left out of account, for of books that are events Macpherson's compost or pastiche of Celtic

legend, published in 1765 as *The Works of Ossian,* is certainly one.
It sent a thrill through Europe, and was rapidly translated into
language after language.   Its effect on the Romantic movement
was tremendous, even greater in Germany, where Herder and
the young Goethe welcomed it with almost hysterical enthusiasm,
than in France.   As for the standing of our novel in France in
the early days of the Romantic movement it may suffice to
mention that such was the esteem for Scott that when he died
Hugo among other literary figures of the time wore mourning
in honour of his memory.

But of our poets at the close of the century it was Byron who
counted most as an influence on the Continent.   He did not leave
Lamartine or Hugo or Vigny untouched, but it was on Musset
that he left the deepest impression, and it was the Byronic strain
in Musset that provoked the violent reaction against him of
Baudelaire, and others of a younger school.   Baudelaire himself
fell under the spell of Edgar Allen Poe, who fairly dominated
him, as he did also Mallarmé for a time.   But all through the
next chapter will be found continual traces of English influence.
Chateaubriand, Lamartine, Sainte-Beuve, Vigny, Baudelaire,
Laforgue, Rimbaud, Verlaine, and Mallarmé certainly knew
English well, and four of them, Lamartine, Vigny, Laforgue,
and Mallarmé, married English wives, while Berlioz married
Henrietta Smithson, the Irish actress, who had so fascinated
Dumas with her performance in *Hamlet.*

Of German influence on the Romantic movement it is possible
to speak with certainty, and also with great definiteness, since
the publication by Professor Eggli of his monumental work,
Schiller et le Romantisme français.   No one can go through the mass
of evidence collected in its 1,310 pages without realizing how
considerable German influence on French letters had become
by the end of the eighteenth century, and how penetrating was
that of Schiller in particular.   The story is an interesting one,
and deserves telling.

Long before the Revolution a knowledge of German literature
had become familiar in cultivated circles in Paris.   The cosmopolitan and versatile F. M. Grimm, German in origin, but
French in culture, a close friend (for a time) of Rousseau, Madame
d'Épinay, Diderot, and Catherine II of Russia, wrote in January
1762 : 'German poetry and literature are becoming the fashion

in Paris, as English has been for some years.' And Condorcet, an unimpeachable Frenchman, is responsible for this statement: 'The peoples of Europe gazed with astonishment on German poetry, hitherto unknown, as offering them masterpieces worthy of rousing the jealousy of nations that had for centuries disputed among themselves the empire of letters.' Goethe's *Werther*, published in 1774, was a European portent, and the sobbing sentimentality of that tale of tragic love caught the spirit of the age. Three translations of it appeared in France within three years, and Werther's dress, blue coat, yellow vest, yellow hose, and top-boots, became a fashion and was worn even in Paris. Years later Sainte-Beuve described the book as 'the act of a conqueror and a high-priest of art.'

But from the point of view of the rise of the Romantic drama in France the epoch-making event was the performance at Mannheim in January 1782 of Schiller's *Robbers*. In 1785 an admirable French translation of it appeared in a series of German plays published in Paris, and there is no doubt that in Paris this new type of play, evidently inspired by Shakespeare, was much canvassed, and roused interest not only from the novelty of its form, ignoring as it did the unities of the old classical drama, but also from the radicalism of its ideas, for Schiller had learned much of his social philosophy from Rousseau. This is not the place to attempt a summary of Professor Eggli's massive argument, but it may be pointed out that among those touched to the quick by the *Robbers* of Schiller and other plays of his or Goethe's was Charles Nodier, to whom allusion is made in the next chapter; and it is impossible to believe that he did not from time to time hold forth to Hugo and other young Romantics gathered round him in his *cénacle* on the glories of both Goethe and Schiller.

Translations of Schiller, poems as well as plays, became almost innumerable, and borrowings from both, quite legitimate borrowings, are frequently to be detected, as, e.g., in the plays both of Hugo and Dumas. To deny as some have attempted to do, the importance of both German and English influence on the Romantic movement in France is absurd. The matter cannot be put more bluntly than it was by Dumas himself: 'The great literary shock that overturned the old edifice of our drama was administered to France by Germany and England.' As to the means we may recall Charles Nodier's fine saying: 'The true revolutionary in literature is the translator.' Finally, we must not forget the tremendous effect of the propaganda carried on during the early years of the nineteenth century by that brilliant woman, Madame de Staël, whose famous book, *De l'Allemagne*, was published in 1813.

Of the efforts to find at the end of the eighteenth century new forms and means for dramatic expression a striking example can be given in the work of the prolific poet and playwright, Népomucène Lemercier, born in 1771. A sarcastic French critic has described him as gifted by nature with a restless disposition, and by his parents with a ridiculous name, and certainly both in his poetry and his plays he was always experimenting, and when he was good he was really very good, and when he was bad he was horrid. Such was his precocity that at the age of sixteen a play of his was performed at the *Théâtre français*, partly no doubt through the influence of his godmother, the Princesse de Lamballe, high in whose service his father was. His tragedy of *Ophis*, on an Egyptian subject, attracted the notice of Bonaparte when full of his Egyptian expedition, and Lemercier was on the best of terms with him until his independence of character was shocked by the establishment of the empire. Though his work hardly suggests it, Lemercier was a man full of charm, and Talleyrand spoke of him as the best talker of his time.

He wrote plays both orthodox and unorthodox, a few successful, the others utter failures. Of those which still tended to follow tradition the best and most popular was his *Agamemnon*, and of his new departures the outstanding one was *Pinto*. This is a remarkable play, well deserving of study, both for its own interest and its importance in the history of French drama. First played in 1799, it tells how the courage and resource of the humble Pinto succeeded in freeing Portugal from Spain in the revolution of 1640, and establishing his master, the Duke of Braganza, on the throne. Here is Lemercier's own account of the aim and object of the play: 'Mon but en composant cette comédie a été de dépouiller une grande action de tout ornement poétique qui la déguise, de présenter des personnages parlant, agissant comme on le fait dans la vie, et de rejeter le prestige, quelquefois infidèle, de la tragédie et des vers. Heureux si, après m'être efforcé dans *Agamemnon* de prouver mon respect pour les lois de Melpomène, je pouvais ouvrir une route nouvelle au théâtre, où l'on suit trop souvent les ornières des chemins battus.'

Dumas himself, with all his eloquence, hardly said more in defining his purpose as a playwright; but Lemercier, though he followed up *Pinto* with his *Christophe Colomb* in 1809, which he wrote in verse and styled a *comédie Shakespirienne*, and which, quite undeservedly, was hissed off the stage, steadfastly opposed the new school. Elected to the Academy in 1810 he consistently stood out against the election of Victor Hugo, and it was by the irony of fate that after his death in 1840 Hugo stepped into his seat.

Nevertheless, when all has been said, and the effect of English and German influences on the development of the Romantic movement in France during the nineteenth century has been fully admitted, we are bound to admit as sound the French claim that all such foreign influences end by losing themselves in the great river which they as tributaries have helped to form.

CHAPTER VI

THE ROMANTIC MOVEMENT

Part I

THE first half of the nineteenth century was marked by an outburst of poetry in volume, in richness, in variety, in vigour, in
music, in sensuous charm, so remarkable as to make the whole
century, throughout which the impulse was sustained, perhaps
the golden age of French verse. At the end of the last chapter
a brief indication is given of the causes that led not only to the
political revolution at the end of the eighteenth century that
brought down the monarchy in ruin, but also to a literary
revolution that shook off the rules and the traditions that governed
the Augustan Age, reintroduced the personal note, and set the
poet free to write as he wished, on what he wished, and even to
sing. It seemed as if the Pleiad rose phoenix-like, more splendid
from its ashes.

The pioneer of the Renaissance was not a poet, but a prose-
writer, the glorious, almost Falstaffian figure of Rabelais, and so
the pioneer of the new movement at the end of the eighteenth
and beginning of the nineteenth centuries was not primarily a
poet, but the great writer of prose saturated with poetic feeling,
Chateaubriand, who dominated French literature all through the
first empire, and was himself the inheritor of much of the spirit
and style of Rousseau.

François-René, Vicomte de Chateaubriand, scion of a noble
family, was born in 1768 at St. Malo. The picturesque features
of his father's ancient château of Combourg and its immediate
surroundings, and the feel of the remote and legendary Breton
countryside, profoundly influenced, as in Renan's case long
afterwards, the early life of a sensitive boy, and left their mark on
him throughout his later years. He entered the army and, like
Chénier, was not altogether unfavourable to the cause of the
Revolution in its first stages, but its excesses soon shocked him,

and when his regiment was disbanded, he sailed to America, where the still unspoilt virgin forests, wild mountainous scenery, and what he saw, or heard, of the life of the Red Indians, stirred his romantic enthusiasm, as, in later years, did his travels in the east.

On hearing of the arrest of Louis XVI at Varennes in 1791, he returned to France, but the following year joined the band of royalist emigrants abroad. He was wounded while fighting on their side, and ultimately, after some thrilling adventures, made his way to London. There he lived in great poverty for several years, during which he made a close acquaintance with English literature. How close this was may be judged from the fact that he translated the whole of *Paradise Lost* into fine, dignified French prose, and wrote a long study of English literature, which, with all its attractive discursiveness, is well worth reading by those who enjoy the opportunity of entering into a talented foreigner's point of view.

Among his poems is an elegy in imitation of Gray's. The following extracts show how close he kept at times to the original, and where imitation amounts to translation how good it is:

Dans les airs frémissants j'entends le long murmure
De la cloche du soir qui tinte avec lenteur.
Les troupeaux en bêlant errent sur la verdure ;
Le berger se retire, et livre la nature
A la nuit solitaire, à mon penser rêveur.

.   .   .   .   .

Souvent, ô laboureurs ! Cérès mûrit pour vous
Les flottantes moissons dans les champs qu'elle dore ;
Souvent avec fracas tombèrent sous vos coups
Les pins retentissants dans la forêt sonore.
En vain l'ambition, qu'enivre ses désirs,
Méprise et vos travaux et vos simples loisirs :
Eh ! que sont les honneurs ?   l'enfant de la victoire,
Le paisible mortel qui conduit un troupeau,
Meurent également ; et les pas de la gloire,
Comme ceux du plaisir, ne mènent qu'au tombeau.

Qu'importe que pour nous de vains panégyriques
D'une voix infidèle aient enflé les accents?
Les bustes animés, les pompeux monuments
Font-ils parler des morts les muettes reliques?

.   .   .   .   .

'Souvent nous l'avons vu, dans sa marche posée,
Au souris du matin, dans l'orient vermeil,
Gravir les frais coteaux à travers la rosée,
Pour admirer au loin le lever du soleil.
Là-bas, près du ruisseau, sur la mousse légère,
A l'ombre du tilleul que baigne le courant
Immobile il rêvoit, tout le jour demeurant
Les regards attachés sur l'onde passagère.
Quelquefois dans les bois il méditoit ses vers
Au murmure plaintif du feuillage et des airs.
Un matin nos regards, sous l'arbre centenaire
Le cherchèrent en vain au repli du ruisseau;
L'aurore reparut; et l'arbre et le coteau,
Et la bruyère encor, tout étoit solitaire.
Le jour suivant, hélas! à la file allongé,
Un convoi s'avança par le chemin du temple.
Approche, voyageur! lis ces vers, et contemple
Ce triste monument que la mousse a rongé.'

ÉPITAPHE

Ici dort, à l'abri des orages du monde,
Celui qui fut longtemps jouet de leur fureur.
Des forêts il chercha la retraite profonde,
Et la mélancholie habita dans son cœur.
De l'amitié divine il adora les charmes;
Au malheureux donna tout ce qu'il eut, des larmes.
Passant, ne porte point un indiscret flambeau
Dans l'abîme où la mort le dérobe à ta vue:
Laisse-le reposer sur la rive inconnue
         De l'autre côté du tombeau.

Thus he set himself to spread the knowledge of English literature in France, a service which, as indicated in the previous
chapter, Madame de Staël, another prominent figure in the

G

literature and politics of the time, had already performed for
German life, letters, and thought. And throughout the century
we shall see again and again signs of the influence of both
England and Germany on developments in France.

Prose so eloquent as that of Chateaubriand is hard to match
in any language. What he gave to prose was not only a more
harmonious, more musical rhythm than hitherto known, but
colour as well, so that whole passages in his *Génie du Christianisme*,
his romances, the account of his travels in the East, and, above
all, his wonderful memoirs, published after his death, seem to
glow like the pictures of some great painter. The title of
those memoirs, *Mémoires d'Outre-Tombe*, is in itself an epitome
of literary Romanticism. We have in him a vague, brooding
melancholy, a passion for the picturesque in nature, a sensitive-
ness to the haunting charm of the medieval past and its ruined
monuments, a waywardness of thought and fancy, all bearing
the impress of his own Byronic personality, seen with his eyes or
fused in his brain, itself intoxicated, to adapt a well-known
phrase, with the exuberance of his own self-centred egotism.
Critic after critic has pointed out that there are few notes struck
by the great Romantic poets that are not to be found in him.

In the politics of his time Chateaubriand, despite his efforts,
failed to play a successful part. He gained the favour of Napoleon, but on the murder of the Duc d'Enghien refused to serve
him longer; and all through his later life, which did not end
until 1848, he was not quite able to reconcile his liberalism with
his legitimist sympathies. But after Napoleon's fall it was
perhaps a pamphlet of his that paved the way for the restoration
of the Bourbons.

A minor, but very useful, part was played at the outset of the
Romantic movement by Charles Nodier, born at Besançon in
1780. After sowing his wild oats as a youthful Jacobin he became
suspected of sympathy with persons who were secretly helping
royalist emigrants. His father, the Mayor of Besançon, placed
him for safety in charge of more than one distinguished scholar,
and thus he got the opportunity of becoming a considerable,
though discursive, scholar himself. Greek, English, German,
natural science, philology, and bibliography were the subjects of
his study, too wide a field for him to reach pre-eminence in any
one of them.

After a wandering life he settled in Paris, and was appointed in 1824 librarian of the Arsenal, a treasure-house of fine manuscripts and books. He made his house a centre for the young enthusiasts of the new movement, Vigny, Hugo, Sainte-Beuve, Musset, Dumas, and the rest, who were able to draw liberally on his stores of knowledge and enjoy his genial Bohemianism. As Musset gaily sang:

> Alors, dans la grande boutique
> Romantique,
> Chacun avait, maître ou garçon,
> Sa chanson.

Nodier's *Contes fantastiques*, short stories in prose, are among the best in form and content published in a century rich in brilliant examples of the kind. But he also wrote poetry, and one most charming little poem of his deserves to live as an exemplar, not only for its beauty, but also for the simplicity and modernity of it, which show very clearly how at the beginning of the nineteenth century we are in a new age, and an age that has not yet passed away:

(96)

THE YOUNG GIRL

How fair she was when plainly drest at dawn
  She conned the budding marvels on earth's breast,
  Watching her bees in their ambrosial nest,
And wandering round the flower-encircled lawn.

And fair she was amid the starry gleam
  Shed by the ball-room's lustres round her head,
  When, decked with sapphires blue or roses red,
She frolicked in the dancers' eddying stream.

Fair, too, behind the shelter of her veil,
  That fluttered as she wooed the cool night-air,
  While we, at gaze afar, stood silent there,
Happy to see her in the starlight pale.

Yes, she was fair with all the charms that glow
  When tender thought and vague, sweet hopes are met;
  Love only lacked to make her fairer yet!
But hush! . . . across the fields her mourners go.

Striking proof of Nodier's flair for what is new, and fine, in art as in literature is furnished by the fact that he was one of the very first, either at home or abroad, to recognize the greatness of Constable, the English landscape painter. He bought his 'Hay Wain,' and had it exhibited in the Paris Salon of 1823, with results on the course of French painting that are now among the commonplaces of the art historian.

There are yet two important names to be mentioned before we are launched on the high tide of Romanticism. The first is Béranger, a man of humble origin, born in Paris in 1780. In his early youth he assisted his aunt in running an inn in Péronne, and was later apprenticed to a printer. He grew up a sturdy republican, though the glamour of Bonaparte attracted him, and never lost its spell over him. With but a smattering of literary education, poor in health, and in dire poverty, he strove unsuccessfully to make a living by writing, but in 1804 was rescued from penury by the generosity of Lucien Bonaparte.

He concentrated on the writing of songs bacchanalian, amatory, satirical, and even political, and his fame among the populace spread rapidly throughout France, his songs being passed from hand to hand by one enthusiast to another. But not until 1812 did a collection of them appear in print. More than once his political songs brought on him fine and imprisonment, which he underwent with patience and even good humour. In the revolution of 1830 he took a prominent part, but, after the fall of the Bourbon dynasty, he refused to receive any favours for himself from the Orleanist, Louis Philippe, though he secured a pension for the aged and penniless Rouget de Lisle, author of the *Marseillaise*. His immense popularity grew year by year, and in 1848, after the flight of Louis Philippe, he was elected by a huge majority to a seat in the Constituent Assembly, which he could not refuse, but which he resigned as soon as he could, and though he still continued to write, and, as always, deliberately, he lived on quietly, beloved by the people and honoured by many of the great, until his death in 1857.

His character was amiability itself, his generosity unstinted, and his songs developed more and more as he went on in life an ardent sympathy with the poor and outcast, even a tragic note being struck now and again. His poetry is so personal an expression, and, though very carefully studied, so apparently artless, that to give any representation of it in English verse is quite impossible. And the reason may well be that not having had a classical education he was not, like most of the great French poets, in the classical tradition which has rendered it possible for those in the same tradition to give versions of their works with some relationship in form and expression to the original.   Here, with its rollicking refrain, is the first verse of his most famous song, the ever-memorable *Roi d'Yvetot*:

> Il était un roi d'Yvetot
>   Peu connu dans l'histoire :
> Se levant tard, se couchant tôt,
>   Dormant fort bien sans gloire,
> Et couronné par Jeanneton
> D'un simple bonnet de coton,
>   Dit-on.
> Oh, oh, oh, oh, ah, ah, ah, ah !
> Quel bon petit roi c'était là !
>   La, la.

Here is a verse from *Roger Bontemps* :

> Posséder dans sa hutte
> Une table, un vieux lit,
> Des cartes, une flûte,
> Un broc que Dieu remplit,
> Un portrait de maîtresse
> Un coffre et rien dedans ;
> Eh gai ! c'est la richesse
> Du gros Roger Bontemps.

Here is a verse from *Les Souvenirs du Peuple*, where the old grand-mother in her cottage tells her excited grandchildren how more than once she saw the great Bonaparte :

> Mes enfants, dans ce village,
> Suivi de rois, il passa ;
> Voilà bien longtemps de ça :
> Je venais d'entrer en ménage.
> A pied grimpant le coteau,
> Où pour voir je m'étais mise,
> Il avait petit chapeau
> Avec redingote grise.

Près de lui je me troublai,
Il me dit : Bonjour, ma chère,
Bonjour, ma chère.
— Il vous a parlé, grand'mère !
Il vous a parlé !

And here is a verse from his *Gipsy Song*, the final refrain of which is *Le bonheur, c'est la liberté* :

Voir c'est avoir.   Allons courir !
Vie errante
Est chose enivrante.
Voir c'est avoir.   Allons courir !
Car tout voir c'est tout conquérir.

M. Hippolyte Babou has quoted Lamartine's description of Béranger, not as a violinist, but as 'the fiddler who, whenever he drew his bow across the strings, drew it across millions of human hearts to strike a note of exaltation or of pity.' It is as a great writer of popular songs that Béranger has been jealously admitted to the canon of French poetry. In a poem published after his death he tells with characteristic modesty how he settled down to song-writing. His early ambition was to write an epic, then he thought a tragedy would take less time, and still less time an ode. Even that was too exacting a task, and so he settled on song-writing : 'J'ai rêvé d'aigle et m'éveille pinson.'

M. Jubinal, the editor of Rutebeuf's works, writing more than fifty years ago, described Rutebeuf as the Béranger of his time. The older poet was the greater poet, in range as in accomplishment, but both were popular poets, born of the people, both had something of the pamphleteer in them, and M. Jubinal's remark does serve in a measure to bridge the gulf that separates the thirteenth century, the great century of the trouvères, from a precursor of the Romantic movement in the nineteenth century. It will be suggested later in this book that one of the most brilliant of the moderns, Laforgue, will be found to strike now and again the same native note as Béranger, and catch the accent of his folk.

The other name that has to be mentioned before we take our plunge into the Romantic movement is that of Marceline Desbordes-Valmore, *la grande Marceline,* as Charles Bonnier, sometime Professor of French at Liverpool, termed her. Madame Desbordes-Valmore was born at Douai in 1786, and died in 1859. She had not an easy life; for much of it she was engaged in a hard struggle to keep her family; but she wrote poetry that has led most critics to claim for her at least equal rank with Louise Labé as the leading poetess that France has produced. There are those who have blamed her for carelessness in composition, and for writing passionately when the fit was on her, instead of waiting to transmute into poetry passion remembered in tranquillity. The truth is that, like Louise Labé in the days of the Pleiad, Madame Desbordes-Valmore was always herself, and wrote as herself. The personal note is always there, and her reward has been the tributes of the great poets of her time to her poetry precisely because of its sincerity.

What one of these has said of her is worth quoting because he, none other than Charles Baudelaire, was poles asunder from her in mind, in the form and content of his work, and in morals. Of her poetry he said: 'I like it, probably and precisely, because of the violent contradiction that my whole being finds in it.' Art may fail her at times, he agrees, but 'a sudden beauty, unexpected, that cannot be equalled, suddenly confronts you, and lo! you are irresistibly transported to the height of the poetic heaven. Never was any poet more natural; never was one less artificial. No one has been able to imitate that charm, because it is altogether original and native to her. . . . Her song keeps always the delicious accent of the woman's voice; no borrowing, no factitious ornament, nothing but "the eternal feminine."'

Here is a version of a very simple piece of hers, a poem of childlike sentiment, that has been enshrined in the *Oxford Book of French Verse*:

(97)

A Little Girl's Pillow

Dear little pillow, soft and warm beneath my head,
Filled with the nicest down, and white, and made for me!
When thunder, wind, or wolf would frighten me in bed,
Dear little pillow mine, how well I sleep on thee!

Many, many children, poor, naked, motherless,
Homeless and pillowless, have nowhere soft to sleep;

They 're always sleepy, all their lives in wretchedness!
O Mummie, dear Mummie, I think of them and weep.

And when in prayer to God these little ones I 've blest
Who have no pillow soft, I give a kiss to mine.
Drawn up close to thy feet, alone in my sweet nest,
I bless thee, Mummie dear, and from my bed touch thine.

I shall not wake again until the peep of day;
How gay it is to see through curtains blue the light!
And now I hush my voice my tenderest prayer to say,
But give me one more kiss, dear Mummie—and good-night!

 . . . . .

God of the children, hear a little girl at prayer,
Under my folded hands my heart is beating sore;
They 're always telling me of orphans without care,
In years to come, dear God, oh, make no orphans more!

Send Thy good angel down when evening comes, I pray,
And bid him speak kind words to all poor ones who weep.
Under the lost child's head, whose mother 's gone away,
A little pillow set, that he may fall asleep.

The following is an attempt to render what is perhaps her most famous poem, one that recalls both Louise Labé and Christina Rossetti:

(98)

Had he but Known

Had he but known the heart he wounded so;
 Tears from the heart, had he but seen them fall;
Oh, had that heart, in passion's overflow,
 Retained the power in words to tell him all,
He could not now have changed as he has done.
 Proud of the hopes he raised, and did disown,
He would have nursed the wealth of love he won,
  Had he but known!

Had he but known all that one can demand
　Of such a heart, pure, passionate, sincere,
He would have chosen mine to understand;
　The love that he inspired had then been clear.
My downcast eyes concealed a smouldering flame,
　And was it modesty he saw alone?
Well worth his soul the secret there to claim,
　　　Had he but known!

Had I but known the yoke that I must bear,
　When I lay captive, gazing on his eyes,
I 'd not have yearned for him like vital air;
　I might have sunned myself neath other skies.
Too late! My life no second dawn will see;
　It was my life, that fond hope overthrown!
Wilt thou not say, who took my life from me,
　　　'Had I but known!'?

Finally is offered the version of a short outburst of passion,
which is not easily to be matched in the work of any poet:

(99)

SOUVENIR

When he grew pale one eve, and when his stammering tongue
Grew silent suddenly, leaving a word half-said;
And when his searching eyes, beneath hot lids that stung,
Wounded me with the dart I thought for him was sped;
When his most moving face, illumined by the fire
　　　That cannot ever die,
Left on my inmost soul the print of live desire;
　　　Who loved? Not he, but I!

The first great representative poet of the Romantic era was
Lamartine, born in 1790. He drank deep of the cup extended
by Chateaubriand, but distilled the spirit he derived from his
master into a poetry restrained in form, spontaneous as is the
work of few other poets, and treating generally of love, religion,
and nature, all touched with a meditative sentimentality that
has led some critics to discern in him a quality akin to that to be
found in some of our English poets—a view combated vigorously

* G

by M. Legouis. The spontaneity of his poetry seems at times to amount to improvisation, and this may be ascribed to a failure to revise his work as he might profitably have done, but we have to remember that he did not put his whole strength into poetry. He wrote also much in prose, but more important was the part he played in public affairs, which occupied much of his time and energy.

Being of good family he entered the diplomatic service, and took to him an English wife. In the troubled reign of Louis Philippe, 1830–48, he interested himself more and more in politics. At the crisis in 1848 his reputation as a poet coupled with his liberal sympathies and his remarkable eloquence made him for a short time one of the most eminent of French statesmen. But he failed to make good his position; he lived on to 1869, while his reputation faded away, though his last two years were cheered by a handsome grant from the government of the third empire in recognition of his public services and his eminence as a literary figure.

Few French poems are better known in England than Lamartine's *Le Lac*, and of this more than one good translation exists. The first example we shall give is a version of that delightful little piece, *Le Papillon*:

(100)

THE BUTTERFLY

To come to life with spring, and die when dies the rose;
Borne on a zephyr's wing to float in heaven's pure height;
Dandled upon a flower, whose petals scarce unclose,
To drug himself with scents and draughts of azure light;
And shaking from his wings, still young, the powdery down,
To flutter like a breath to earth's eternal crown;
Such is the butterfly's enchanted destiny.
How like Desire he is, that rests not in its flight,
But still unsatisfied, though kissing all things bright,
Returns at last to seek its pleasure in the sky!

Next we give an extract from one of his longer poems, his *Chute d'un Ange* (*Huitième Vision*), a passage selected by Charles Bonnier to represent Lamartine in his subtle little volume, *La Lignée des poètes français au XIXème siècle*:

(101)

THE PROPHETS

(Chute d'un Ange, Huitième Vision)

Of men of woman born gentlest are those
Whose inward eye the senses cannot close,
Whose heart is deep and mobile as the sea,
Whose nerves thrill at a touch, though light it be,
Whose intellect, rapt by the sacred fire,
Vibrates beneath God's finger like a lyre,
With echoes streaming through the universe
To learn its speech, its harmonies rehearse:
Best in their limpid and transparent thought
The image of infinity is caught,
And there the Eternal's vast design gleams bright
In hues ineffable and radiant light!
These men, who shun the crowd and seek the shade,
Have with the desert secret friendship made;
When on the wave-washt shore they come and go,
Voices they hear for our dull ears too low.

. . . . .

Mark well their prayers, for these your prophets are.

Finally, here is a passage from the beginning of a cantata
written by the poet for an orphanage.   Certainly the lyric with
which it concludes is remarkable indeed for the boldness of its
imagery, which, we hope, is fairly carried over in the translation:

(102)

THE CHILD CHRIST IN THE TEMPLE

The doctors of the law, chiefs in the house of prayer,
    Were seated there in all their pride;
They hid their eyes beneath brows bent with thought or care,
Or seemed with haughty glance to wave the crowd aside;
They spoke to catechize shy children on the floor;
Their furrowed foreheads showed how vast their wisdom's
      store,
That brought from Sinai its antique majesty.

Down from their long white hair, and from each bearded
          chin,
A man might think there stole over their breast's bare skin
          A stream of light and charity,
          As from the mountains crowned with snow
Descends, O Sharon, on thy fields and gardens low
          The daylight and fertility!

A child there was, came forth before them full of grace;
The crowd, in wonderment, made way his face to see,
          Then closed their ranks behind his trace;
          It seemed he flooded all the space
With supernatural light—undazzled only he!

          Out of the shadow of his hair
          His forehead gleamed, a ray of light,
          Like one that, cleaving clouds of air,
          Reveals a grim skyline at night.

          Smooth, but presaging signs of woe,
          That brow o'erhung his eye divine,
          Like some majestic portico
          That stands before a sacred shrine.

          The heavenly radiance of his mind
          Shone softly through his tranquil eye,
          As fiery starlight glows more kind
          From out the depths of azure sky.

          He spoke: the wise men doubted sore
          The creeds they built their pride upon;
          And listening ears the columns wore,
          The columns reared by Solomon.

   Another of the most distinguished of the pioneers in the
Romantic movement was Alfred de Vigny, born at Loches in
1797, who lived on to 1863, though much of his finest poetry
was written in the first half of his life, and his later years were
spent in retirement. The last collection of his poems published
in his lifetime appeared in 1837; after that date poems, or frag-
ments of poems, found their place in the *Revue des Deux Mondes*,

and after his death these were collected and published with other now well-known poems in a volume entitled *Les Destinées*.

The bulk of his poetry is not large, nor was he a lyric poet, but he stands with Victor Hugo at the head of the Romantics. Like Victor Hugo at his best, Vigny, far less exuberant and less verbose, had consistently what Matthew Arnold happily termed the grand style, and this with his dignity of thought, and calm restraint in moments of passionate feeling, profoundly influenced later poets, and secured him a place among the highest of his fellows. Croce, indeed, the great Italian critic, rates him highest among French poets of the century, and calls attention to his rare gift of writing great gnomic lines, such as these:

Aimez ce que jamais on ne verra deux fois.

Fais énergiquement ta longue et lourde tâche.

La mort n'est que la mort, et n'est pas la vengeance.

Ne ternis plus tes pieds aux poudres du chemin.

Le vrai Dieu, le Dieu fort, est le Dieu des idées.

Vigny, who came of gentle stock, followed the family tradition and entered the army, where he served for twelve years. The fruits of his military service appeared in 1835 in his *Servitude et Grandeur militaires*, with its cold, keen analysis of Napoleon's character, and its glowing tribute to Admiral Collingwood as most humane of men, and the model of efficiency and devotion to duty. Though he held somewhat aloof from his brother poets, he did not fail to win their admiration, and Barbey d'Aurevilly termed him in a happy phrase, 'the Racine of Romanticism.' It is interesting to note that Vigny knew English well, and, like Lamartine, married an English wife. He wrote, in the vein of Walter Scott, a famous novel, *Cinq-Mars*, a tale of the days of Richelieu, and, among other plays, an original one entitled *Chatterton*, and versions of *Othello* and the *Merchant of Venice*.

In revealing one of Vigny's proclivities, a taste for English beer, a letter of Baudelaire's brings us pleasantly to earth. This letter, dated 1862, warns Vigny against any bottled ale bearing the label *Harris*; it will only make him ill. Allsopp and Bass, he says, are good brewers, but then their labels may be forged. Vigny had best have recourse to some honest dealer in Paris, and he gives him two addresses where he may be sure of getting the real stuff. One of these firms, he thinks, sells also 'old ale' which, says he, *est d'une force extrême*. This friendly regard for the creature comforts of his friends was an amiable trait in Baudelaire, for we find him in 1860 strongly recommending to Sainte-Beuve English gingerbread, *très épais, très noir, tellement serré qu'il n'a pas de trous, ni de pores*. . . . He tells him to cut it in slices as thin as roast beef, and, if he likes, to spread butter or jam on it.

The first example of Alfred de Vigny's work we shall offer is the version of a passage, again selected by Charles Bonnier as representative, from his mysterious poem, *Eloa*. The passage gives a description of Eloa herself, who, born of a tear shed by Christ at the grave of Lazarus, and become an angel of pity in heaven, seeks Satan in hell to comfort him in his suffering, seeks him—and falls. The poem is worth noting for three reasons: firstly, as showing a strong Miltonic influence; secondly, as indicating one of the sources of Romanticism in France, for in this poem the name of Ossian is invoked; and, thirdly, as being itself one of the influences on Baudelaire, with its sympathy for Satan, no less than on the development of the Symbolist school later in the century:

(103)

From 'Eloa'

Richly attired she walks, beneath Heaven's watchful eye,
To Godward, like a bride within the sanctuary,
And lily-like, so smooth, so pure and white its hue,
Her lovely brow upholds a veil of azure blue;
Her clustered locks, arrayed like sheaves of golden grain,
Blend in the vaporous air their soft and wavy train,
As one can see on high the comet's tresses bright
Melt, as it flashes past, on the dark breast of night;
No rose in the first light of early dawn can show
So virginal a flush as makes her freshness glow;

Nor can the moon that lights the deep wood's mysteries
Rival in tenderness a glance from her soft eyes.
Her wings of silver are; her robes like twilight pale
By turns her white foot show and of a sudden veil;
Her palpitating breast, that eye can scarce perceive,
Uplifts the tissue's folds that heavenly fingers weave.
She is a woman too, though angel from above,
For spirits such as these, this family of love,
Who for us, near us, pray, and watch continually,
Mingle their essence pure in love with sanctity:
The Archangel Raphaël, on his descent to earth,
Told this sweet mystery when Eden first saw birth.
But of those sister souls that God for angels found
None brought such happiness to heaven where joys abound.

In contrast with this read a fine passage on Stoic resignation from *La Mort du Loup*:

(104)

THE DEATH OF THE WOLF

Alas, so have I thought, despite Man's name so proud,
What shame I feel for us, a poor, weak, human crowd!
How to quit life and all its ills, when comes the time,
'Tis you that know this well, O animals sublime.
In face of what man is on earth, what he forgoes,
Silence alone is great; all else the weakling shows.
—Ah! well I understood, wild one, thy noble part,
And that last look of thine has pierced me to the heart!
It said: 'Strive, if thou canst, that thy soul may be brought
By studious reverie, by dint of arduous thought,
Even to that high degree of stoic strength and pride
That I, the forest-born, could reach in my first stride.
To groan, shed tears, cry out, all mark the coward soul.
Go through with energy thy long and heavy rôle,
Whatever be the part fate has on thee conferred,
And then, suffer like me and die without a word.'

We come now to the undisputed chief of the Romantic school, and, in the opinion of many, the greatest poet that France has ever produced, Victor Hugo. The bulk of his work was enormous. Quite apart from his long and often turgid novels in prose, and the long series of his plays, he poured out poem after poem, short and long, in an infinite number of metres, on an infinite variety of subjects, during a life that lasted from 1802 to 1885. During this lifetime he was acclaimed by all for the incomparable poet that he was. But the very mass of his dramatic, lyrical, and epic poetry, not to speak of his prose, has tended to obscure his essential and true greatness. Some cannot see the trees for the wood. Others are repulsed by the rodomontade, the false rhetoric, the sound and fury signifying little, the mushy sentiment that are to be found abundantly in much that he wrote.

Nevertheless, when the worst has been said there remains so much of the most simple, eloquent, dignified, musical, crystalline, colourful verse ever written as to keep his title to greatness unassailable. The best of his work, so essentially simple in statement is it, so straightforward, so charged with a rhythm inseparable from its actual words, that translation is quite impossible. In *Gastibelza* he wrote the finest of all Romantic ballads :

> Gastibelza, l'homme à la carabine,
> Chantait ainsi :
> 'Quelqu'un a-t-il connu doña Sabine?
> Quelqu'un d'ici?
> Dansez, chantez, villageois! la nuit gagne
> Le mont Falû.
> — Le vent qui vient à travers la montagne
> Me rendra fou!'

In *Le Chasseur noir* he wrote the finest of all political ballads :

> — Qu'es-tu, passant? Le bois est sombre,
> Les corbeaux volent en grand nombre,
> Il va pleuvoir.
> — Je suis celui qui va dans l'ombre,
> Le chasseur noir!

For pure lyric spontaneity, take this :

> Puisqu'ici-bas toute âme
> Donne à quelqu'un
> Sa musique, sa flamme,
> Ou son parfum;

> Puisqu'ici toute chose
> Donne toujours
> Son épine ou sa rose
> A ses amours ;
>
> .   .   .   .   .
>
> Je te donne à cette heure,
> Penché sur toi,
> La chose la meilleure
> Que j'aie en moi !
>
> .   .   .   .   .
>
> Reçois mon bien céleste
> O ma beauté !
> Mon cœur dont rien ne reste,
> L'amour ôté !

Or these stanzas from *La Chanson d'Éviradnus* :

> Si tu veux, faisons un rêve.
> Montons sur deux palefrois ;
> Tu m'emmènes, je t'enlève.
> L'oiseau chante dans les bois.
>
> Viens, sois tendre, je suis ivre.
> O les verts taillis mouillés !
> Ton souffle te fera suivre
> Des papillons réveillés.
>
> Allons-nous-en par l'Autriche !
> Nous aurons l'aube à nos fronts ;
> Je serai grand, et toi riche,
> Puisque nous nous aimerons.
>
> Tu seras dame, et moi comte ;
> Viens, mon cœur s'épanouit,
> Viens, nous conterons ce conte
> Aux étoiles de la nuit.

For wonderful rhythm take his *Oceano Nox* :

> Oh, combien de marins, combien de capitaines
> Qui sont partis joyeux pour des courses lointaines,

Dans ce morne horizon se sont évanouis !
Combien ont disparu, dure et triste fortune !
Dans une mer sans fond, par une nuit sans lune,
Sous l'aveugle océan à jamais enfouis !

In his great epic, *La Légende des Siècles,* will be found in *Booz endormi* the most perfect idyll ever written. And in the fifth book of *Les Châtiments* are to be found in *L'Expiation,* the episodes of Moscow, Waterloo, and St. Helena, a poet's summary of history in verse which it is not easy to match. None of these, nor others like them, need translation. Any one with a smattering of French can read them easily.

Victor Hugo was the son of a general who distinguished himself in the service of Napoleon, but the son, for all his radical enthusiasm in literature, became a loyalist under Louis Philippe, and indeed accepted a peerage from him. At the outbreak of the revolution of 1848 he became a republican. To Louis Napoleon, *Napoléon le Petit* as he termed him, he was furiously opposed, and had to flee his country. For nearly twenty years, during the whole of the third empire, he lived in exile. His home for most of this period was Guernsey, in a house high up on the cliff above St. Peter Port; and no one who has ever visited his study at the top of that house will forget the scene that must have been a constant source of inspiration to the poet, the rocky coast-line, the harbour, the sea of ever-changing colour with island after island breaking its smooth or stormy surface, and in the distance the shores of his native France.

Another discovery the visitor will make in Guernsey as at his home in Paris, viz. his amazing gift as a draughtsman in black and white when the fancy seized him to dash down in graphic form the imaginings of his brain. And yet, superbly as his figure stands out in literary history, one gift he lacked, a gift whose importance is often exaggerated, but which in the case of one so possessed by the consciousness of his powers, one living in a constant atmosphere of adulation, might have proved a saving grace, the gift of a sense of humour.

Too many anecdotes about Hugo seem to reflect an over-weening egotism, but here is a glorious story told by Dumas which gives the genesis of Gautier's noble poem on the anniversary of Corneille's birth, and shows the Olympian in quite another light, as a man of fine feeling and deep human sympathy, and prodigal of the gifts of his genius. A group of poets and literary men were discussing art and literature in a lady's *salon* on the 2nd June 1851. One of them, Arsène Houssaye, Director of the *Théâtre français*, remarked that in four days came the anniversary of Corneille's death, and he suggested that Gautier, who was present, should write a poem for the occasion. Gautier pretended not to hear. Houssaye repeated his demand, and Gautier then declined it peremptorily on the ground that nothing was more tiresome than to write an official encomium of a great poet.

'You're wrong, Théophile,' broke in Hugo, who was also present, 'and if I were in a position to do what Arsène asks of you, I should do it.' Gautier suggested that Hugo would pass in review all Corneille's dramas, and would make bold to speak of his comparative failures. 'No!' said Hugo, 'I should say nothing of all that.' 'Then,' retorted Gautier, 'you would not pass an encomium on Corneille; when one passes an encomium on a poet you must above all praise his bad work: what one does not praise one criticizes.' 'No!' said Hugo, 'I should not treat the subject so; I should pass no vulgar encomium. I should describe Corneille wandering in old age through the streets of Paris, with his threadbare cloak over his shoulders, forgotten by Louis XIV, less generous to him than Richelieu, who had persecuted him, had been. I should describe Corneille calling at some poor cobbler's shop to have a worn-out shoe repaired, while Louis XIV lords it at Versailles and takes a stroll with Madame de Montespan, Mademoiselle de la Vallière, and Madame Henriette in the galleries of Le Brun or the gardens of Le Nôtre. Then I should console the poet's ghost by showing posterity setting each in his place, and in proportion as days follow days, months follow months, and years follow years, making more of the poet and less of the king.'

'What are you looking for, Théophile?' asked his hostess of Gautier, who had suddenly risen. 'I'm looking for my hat,' said Gautier. 'Then you're leaving us!' said Arsène Houssaye. 'Yes, indeed, I'm off to write your lines; you shall have them to-morrow.' So Gautier went off to compose his poem, only to have it, when completed, censored by the Censor of Plays under President Louis Bonaparte.

A diffident contribution towards the study of Hugo's genius

will be found in the following versions of five of his shorter poems. The first two are attempts to render with such faithfulness as is possible in English the form and content of two of his songs:

(105)

A New Song to an Old Air

Is there a lovely garden
    That heaven keeps wet with dew,
Where every changing season
    Shines out a blossom new,
And, gathered as we please,
Bloom jasmine, lily, heartsease;
Where treads your foot by these,
    I 'll make the path for you!

Is there a kindly bosom
    With honour for a guide,
Where loyalty unyielding
    And tenderness abide;
And if for chivalry
That noble breast beat high,
There may your forehead lie
    On the pillow I provide!

Is there a dream love-laden,
    And scented with the rose,
Where some delightful pleasure
    Successive days disclose,
A dream that God hath blest
Where soul meets soul at rest;
There will I build the nest
    To give your heart repose!

(106)

Aubade

Day breaks and still thy door is fast;
My pretty one, why slumber on?
The rose awakes now night is past,
Wilt thou not bid dull sleep begone?

> Enchantress, rise
> And lend thine ear,
> Thy lover's sighs
> And song to hear!

All knock at thy blest gates for thee:
Dawn says, I am the light above;
The bird says, I am harmony;
And my heart says, Lo, I am love!
> Enchantress, rise
> And lend thine ear,
> Thy lover's sighs
> And song to hear!

O woman loved, angel adored!
God who through thee has made me whole
Has for mine eyes thy beauty stored,
And for my heart has kept thy soul.
> Enchantress, rise
> And lend thine ear,
> Thy lover's sighs
> And song to hear!

The next little piece may perhaps be taken as representative of the simple, domestic poetry of which Hugo was a master:

(107)

MOTHER AND CHILD

The child sang on; fordone, the mother on her bed
Struggled for breath, in gloom her fair face shadowing;
Shrouded in shifting mist Death hovered overhead;
I listened while she choked, I heard the infant sing.

The child was five years old, and by the window played;
Her laughter and her games made sweeter still her song;
The mother, close beside her darling little maid
Who sang so sweet by day, lay coughing all night long.

Within the churchyard wall the mother went to rest;
Gaily the little child began her song again—
For grief is like a fruit, that, by God's high behest,
Grows not on any stem too weak to bear the strain.

The following is one of his odes, somewhat artificial, no doubt, and indicating a gloomy pose rather than gloom itself, but it does show the freedom and skill with which he played with metre even within the limits of a single poem:

(108)

MORNING

Now morning o'er the hills spreads her bright canopy.
See, in yon gathering ray the ruined tower gleams white;
Already under heaven in rapt embrace unite,
  Like joy that comes with victory,
The first wild woodland note and the first beam of light.

Yes, smile upon the sun that paints the sky with gold!
If, when the morrow comes, the grave my body hold,
You 'll see as bright a sun shine down upon your gloom,
Hear the same song of birds hail morning as of old,
  Over my dark and silent tomb!

But to another sky my spirit will have fled,
Where limitless is time before the soul set free.
  So soon as dawns eternity,
  It is from life we wake when dead,
As from a sombre night or dream of agony!

Last comes a fine hymn, which might be regarded as a hymn for any Armistice Day. In the original of it, at least, will be heard notes sounded by the organ-voice of Hugo:

(109)

HYMN FOR AN ARMISTICE DAY

Those who have piously died for their fatherland
May claim that by their grave in prayer a crowd should
  stand.
Amid all glorious names theirs shine most gloriously;
Ephemeral by theirs all glories fade and fall.
  And, like a mother's tender call,
A nation's mighty voice intones their lullaby.

Hail, mother France, immortal one,
And yours who died, their duty done,
The martyrs, and the strong and tried!
Hail those whom their examples fire
To seek the temple of desire,
And who will die as they have died!

'Tis for the heroic dead, whose souls are welcome here,
The great Pantheon soars amid the clouds, to rear
High over Paris, o'er the thousand towers she sways,
Queen of our Babylons and Tyres of old renown,
    His lofty colonnaded crown,
That day by day the sun regilds with orient rays.
    Hail, mother France, immortal one,
    And yours who died, their duty done,
    The martyrs, and the strong and tried!
    Hail those whom their examples fire
    To seek the temple of desire,
    And who will die as they have died!

So when such dead as these within the tomb are laid,
Vainly oblivion's night, though mortal things she fade,
Visits their sepulchre by which we stand and pray.
Faithful to them alone, at daybreak rises bright
    Glory, perpetual source of light,
Regilds their names and keeps their memory fresh for aye.
    Hail, mother France, immortal one,
    And yours who died, their duty done,
    The martyrs, and the strong and tried!
    Hail those whom their examples fire
    To seek the temple of desire,
    And who will die as they have died!

Born at Boulogne in 1804, only two years after Hugo, Sainte-
Beuve, scholar, critic, and poet, was one whose influence on the
early Romantic movement was only next, perhaps, to that of
Hugo himself. His mother was half-English, and at Paris, where
he completed his education, he made friends with a fellow-
boarder, an Englishman named Charles Neate, a fellow of Oriel

College, Oxford, and M.P. for the city. He had thus foreign contacts to widen his intellectual sympathies. His first intention was to pursue a medical course, but he soon abandoned this in favour of literature, and literary criticism in particular, in which he reached the very highest rank. Indeed, he deserves to be regarded as the first and greatest of modern critics; his sympathies were wide, he had no code of rules by which to judge of an author's work, but studying the man and his age and environment sought to discover his object or his purpose, and recognizing that form and content react on one another found the intrinsic merit of his writings in the success with which he carried out his aim or his message.

His first important book, a collection of his articles on French poetry of the sixteenth century, was epoch-making, for it flashed on the eyes of the young enthusiasts of Romanticism the dazzling beauties of the Pleiad, and thus, as it were, built a bridge between the new Renaissance and the old. Since he poured out until his death in 1869 a constant stream of studies of French literature, his range became enormous, and his knowledge of French history, as well as literature, so profound as to justify Matthew Arnold's claim that 'as a guide to bring us to a knowledge of the French genius and literature he is unrivalled.' There are few more delightful possessions in a library than a set of his *Causeries du Lundi* or his *Nouveaux Lundis*.

But Sainte-Beuve's fame as a critic must not be allowed to extinguish altogether his reputation as a poet. In early days he was one of Charles Nodier's circle at the Arsenal, and published under the name of Joseph Delorme more than one volume of verse. His poetry, though never so widely popular as that of other poets of the time, had a great influence on his brother poets, and deserves to survive for the qualities of simple directness and sincerity that distinguish it. He strikes at times a note that carries one back to André Chénier, and it may fairly be said that though he wore the robes of Romanticism he wore them with a difference. We can offer an interesting example of his work in a sonnet he wrote on the model of one of Wordsworth's. We print first the original by Wordsworth, then Sainte-Beuve's sonnet, the sestet of which will be found to be an admirable piece of translation:

Personal Talk

I am not one who much or oft delight
To season my fireside with personal talk,—
Of friends, who live within an easy walk,
Or neighbours, daily, weekly, in my sight:

And, for my chance-acquaintance, ladies bright,
Sons, mothers, maidens withering on the stalk,
These all wear out of me, like Forms, with chalk
Painted on rich men's floors, for one feast-night.

Better than such discourse doth silence long,
Long, barren silence, square with my desire;
To sit without emotion, hope, or aim,

In the loved presence of my cottage fire,
And listen to the flapping of the flame,
Or kettle whispering its faint undersong.

Sonnet

Imité de Wordsworth

Je ne suis pas de ceux pour qui les causeries,
Au coin du feu, l'hiver, ont de grandes douceurs;
Car j'ai pour tous voisins d'intrépides chasseurs
Rêvant de chiens dressés, de meutes aguerries,

Et des fermiers causant jachères et prairies,
Et le juge de paix avec ses vieilles sœurs,
Deux revêches beautés parlant de ravisseurs,
Portraits comme on en voit sur les tapisseries.

Oh! combien je préfère à ce caquet si vain,
Tout le soir, du silence,—un silence sans fin;
Être assis san penser, sans désir, sans mémoire;

Et, seul, sur mes chenets, m'éclairant aux tisons,
Écouter le vent battre, et gémir les cloisons,
Et le fagot flamber, et chanter ma bouilloire!

CHAPTER VII

Part II

THERE remain to be discussed as conspicuous representatives of the Romantic movement in its earlier phase four distinguished poets, though perhaps only one of them, Alfred de Musset, still floats on the main stream of it. In the others, Gérard de Nerval, Théophile Gautier, and Théodore de Banville, the Benjamin of the family, wayward tendencies are to be found that point to this or that change of direction, the story of which will be told in the following chapter.

Gérard de Nerval, whose real name was Labrunie, was born at Paris in 1808. His father was an army doctor, a cultured man, who looked well after his son's education, and himself taught him the elements of Greek, Latin, and modern languages, and even a smattering of Arabic and Persian. As a schoolboy he distinguished himself at the Lycée Charlemagne, and became precociously a remarkable scholar. Indeed, the fever with which he read and studied may either have been the result of an excitable mental condition or have sown the seeds of insanity which showed itself later. At twenty years of age he published a translation of Goethe's *Faust*, Part I, as well as portions of Part II, and it was the emotion roused by the reading of this that incited Berlioz, on his own confession, to the composition of his *Damnation de Faust*. His interest in German led to a friendship with Heine, who said to him one day, half ironically, half affectionately: 'Ah, my dear Gérard, you must do as I did; I married a Frenchwoman who has taught me French, do you marry a German who will teach you German.' By the age of twenty-one his literary reputation was assured, and he was for a time associated with his friend Gautier in dramatic criticism. Leading an eccentric life, and dreaming over the occult lore of the Cabbala and of Swedenborg, he travelled in Germany and other countries as far as Constantinople, and the account he wrote of his travels had a great vogue. He wrote one or two plays, and a number of fantastic sketches and tales. Two of the latter, *Aurélia* and *Sylvie*, are in a measure autobiographical, for they are inspired by the succession of passionate and yet ineffective loves that seemed to follow him throughout his life, from Adrienne the love of his youth, who became a nun, to Aurélia, or Jenny Colon, to give her real name, the actress, whose marriage and early death seemed finally to unhinge his reason. Certainly after her death he appeared incapable of sustained effort, though in lucid and semi-lucid intervals he wrote several wonderful poems, including the sonnets, which reveal him as perhaps the first of Symbolists.   In them he anticipated in the most extraordinary way almost all the qualities that were later developed by Mallarmé and Verlaine.   There is a very remarkable essay on his claim in this regard to be found in Arthur Symons's *The Symbolist Movement in Literature,* published in 1894, and still the classic in our language on the subject.   From this we shall have to quote later.

The eccentricities that grew on Nerval took the form of sudden disappearances, the wearing of odd ornaments, or such pranks as leading round the Palais-Royal a live lobster attached to a blue ribbon.   'In what,' he asked, 'is a lobster more ridiculous than a dog?   I like lobsters, which are tranquil, serious, know the secrets of the sea, and do not bark.'   Every Sunday his devoted old father laid a place for him at his own table, saying: 'Perhaps this will bring him home.'   But he became more and more Bohemian in his habits, was frequently in distress, and in 1855 was found hanged at the bottom of the dark, narrow rue de la Vieille-Lanterne, a sewer-like alley, leading from the place du Châtelet down towards the river.

His poetry, not great in bulk, reflects the delicacy and the mysterious quality of his mind, and not even Verlaine ever dwelt more exquisitely in the wonderland that lies between poetry and music.   His rarest lyric is quite untranslatable in anything like its original form, and yet it is easy to read:

LES CYDALISES

(*The Light of Love*)

Où sont nos amoureuses?
Elles sont au tombeau!
Elles sont plus heureuses
Dans un séjour plus beau!

Elles sont près des anges
   Dans le fond du ciel bleu,
Et chantent les louanges
   De la mère de Dieu!

O blanche fiancée!
   O jeune vierge en fleur!
Amante délaissée,
   Que flétrit la douleur!

L'éternité profonde
   Souriait dans vos yeux . . .
Flambeaux éteints du monde,
   Rallumez-vous aux cieux!

And here are versions of two other charming poems of his:

(110)

AN ALLEY IN THE LUXEMBOURG

Ah, the young girl, she's come and gone,
   As quick and lively as a bird:
Her fingers held a flower that shone,
   A new song on her lips I heard.

Perhaps, she was on earth the one
   Whose heart could give response to mine,
And on a gloom too deep for sun
   Could shed one beam of light divine.

But no, my youth is gone from me.
   Farewell, thou dear rejoicing ray!
Girlhood, perfume, and harmony . . .,
   'Twas joy that passed, and fled for aye!

(111)

IN THE WOODS

In spring the bird is born and sings:
   You've heard his voice the boughs between?
How plaintive, simple, pure it rings,
   The bird's voice—in the woodland green!

In summer for a mate he 'll call,
   And once for love his feathers preen:
How peaceful, soft, and safe through all
   The bird's nest—in the woodland green!

Then misty autumn comes, and he
   Is dumb in face of winter frore.
Alas, how sweet his death must be,
   The bird's death—in the woodland hoar!

Of the sonnets referred to above, which anticipate so strikingly
the later Symbolist movement, two will be found in the *Oxford
Book of French Verse*. These, though most difficult to translate in
verse, are not difficult to paraphrase in prose, for the language
of them, and their import, are fairly straightforward. But the
most beautiful of them, entitled *Artemis*, not perhaps the Hel-
lenistic, but the more mystical Taurian Artemis, requires as much
study for its elucidation as Mallarmé's Swan sonnet. Here is an
attempt to give an English rendering of it:

(112)

ARTEMIS

The thirteenth here again . . . before the first has passed;
And always still the same,—or yet unchanged the hour:
For art thou queen, thou there! what matter first or last?
Art thou king, thou the sole or the last paramour?

Love her who has loved you from cradle to the tomb;
Her I loved, I alone, loves me still tenderly;
'Tis death, or the dead one. . . . O joy! O agony!
For rose her fingers hold a hollyhock in bloom.

Blest Neapolitan, whose hands are full of flame,
O flower of Saint Gudule, rose with the violet heart:
Hast found thy cross amid the desert of the skies?

White roses, fade and fall! You put our gods to shame:
Fall down, white ghosts, and from your burning heaven
    depart:
—The Saint of the Abyss is holier in my eyes!

The significance of the octet is plain enough. The poet writes as one to whom past, present, and future are merged into one, time being one continuous stream, or, as Bergson, one of the most popular of modern philosophers, has put it, time is to be regarded as an illusion, finite being and eternity as one. And so love is but one, for each new love is only as it were a reincarnation of the old. The idea is summed up in the vision of the hollyhock in the eighth line—the hollyhock, one flower, and yet how many flowers! In *Aurélia* there comes to Nerval the dream of a lady in a garden, nursing on her bare arm a long spray of hollyhock, and being ultimately herself transformed into the garden.

Another dream that comes to him in *Aurélia*, and is quoted by Symons, runs as follows: 'During my sleep I had a marvellous vision. It seemed to me that the goddess appeared before me, saying to me: "I am the same as Mary, the same as thy mother, the same also whom, under all forms, thou hast always loved. At each of thine ordeals I have cropped yet one more of the masks with which I veil my countenance, and soon thou shalt see me as I am."' Akin in thought is this passage from *Sylvie*, also quoted by Symons: 'This vague and hopeless love, inspired by an actress, which night by night took hold of me at the hour of the performance, leaving me only at the hour of sleep, had its germ in the recollection of Adrienne, flower of the night, unfolding under the pale rays of the moon, rosy and blonde phantom, gliding over the green grass, half bathed in white mist. . . . To love a nun under the form of an actress! . . . and if it were the very same! It is enough to drive one mad!' So much for the octet of this fascinating sonnet.

As regards the two saints referred to in the first two lines of the sestet the present writer has been unable to trace any relevant legend to explain the significance of the lines. But the drift of the whole sestet is clearly towards the yearning expressed in another of his great sonnets, entitled *Delphica*, for the pagan gods of ancient days. The cross in the third line may be a reference to the cross that greeted Dante's dazzled eyes near the close of the fourteenth canto of his *Paradiso*. So too the white roses, and the white ghosts may carry one back to the great white rose, composed of the company of saints displayed in the ineffable light of the thirty-first canto. As for the

Saint of the Abyss mentioned in the last line, need we go further to look for her than to Vigny's Eloa, whose story is told on page 174?

Alfred de Musset, born in Paris in 1810, ranks perhaps next in popular estimation to Hugo among the earlier Romantic poets, though a very different type, for he had not Hugo's tumultuous power and energy. In his *Confession d'un Enfant du Siècle*, Musset is frank in his acknowledgment of the influence of Goethe and Byron on the young writers of the time. Of the influence of *Werther* and *Faust* and *Manfred*, in particular, he suggests that they brought about a convulsion that was, as it were, 'a denial of all things in heaven or on earth, that one can call disenchantment, or, if you will, despair.' Here Musset was speaking, no doubt, more for himself than others. Certainly a Romantic element found strongly in him was the Byronic feeling of self-pity, which marks his longer poems; so that despite all the beauty to be found in them, they do not form the base of his great and enduring fame. That is founded on his exquisite lyrics, and on his prose comedies, both of them so perfect in form, and the latter so original in type and so scintillating with wit, as to give them immortal charm.

As in the case of Nerval, whom he rivalled in early fame, his life was not a happy one despite his literary success. At times he wrote carelessly, and so he lived carelessly. Like Chopin later, he became dominated by the charm and commanding personality of George Sand, the great woman-novelist of the century, and one of the most distinguished women in French literature. They went off to Venice together, and when she left him he returned to Paris a broken man. But, more fortunate than Gérard de Nerval, he had a family in good circumstances, and influential friends to look after him, so that he escaped the material miseries that dogged the steps of so many brilliant Frenchmen of the century. He died in 1857, leaving behind him, notwithstanding his desultory habits, a mass of fine work, the best of which will always keep his name alive.

To represent Nerval, we quoted the best of his lyrics in French. Let us do the same for Musset, and give in the original one of his haunting melodies, untranslatable into English in its epigrammatic form, but easy to read:

Quand on perd, par triste occurrence,
        Son espérance
        Et sa gaîté,
Le remède au mélancolique,
        C'est la musique
        Et la beauté.

Plus oblige et peut davantage
        Un beau visage
        Qu'un homme armé,
Et rien n'est meilleur que d'entendre
        Air doux et tendre
        Jadis aimé.

Here is a version of the short dirge that begins and ends his elegy, *Lucie*:

(113)

A Dirge

Friends of my heart, when I am dead,
Oh, plant a willow by my grave;
I love its leaves, like tear-drops shed;
It soothes me with its pallor suave,
And lightly will its shadow wave
Upon the earth that makes my bed!

Next we offer, greatly daring, a version of Fortunio's famous song from his comedy, *Le Chandelier*:

(114)

Fortunio's Song

If you have hopes that I may tell
        Whose love I claim,
Not for an empire would I sell
        The world her name.

Join hands, if such your fancy fond,
        A catch repeat,
How I adore a beauty blonde
        As is the wheat.

I do what any fantasy
    Makes her prefer;
And if she asked my life of me
    I 'd give it her.

The sufferings that love unconfest
    Deals cruelly,
They torture so my wounded breast
    That I could die.

But love like mine will still deny
    Whose love I claim,
And for my sweet I 'd sooner die
    Than breathe her name.

Lastly we give a version of his octosyllabic sonnet, *Tristesse*
which well expresses the vein of self-pity that was in him:

(115)

MELANCHOLY

My vigour and my life are done,
And gone my friends, my gaiety,
Gone even the pride that stirred in me
High hopes of fame by genius won.

When first I thought of Truth at all,
She seemed a friend that I could claim,
But ere full knowledge of her came
I found that Truth began to pall.

Nevertheless, she cannot die,
And if on earth we pass her by,
How vacant must our minds appear.

God speaks, and man must answer give;
My one good action that will live
Is that at times I shed a tear.

A very different poet was Théophile Gautier, born in 1811 at
Tarbes, in the Pyrenean country, and thus with southern warmth
in his blood. He made friends at school in Paris with Nerval,
but began life as a painter. Soon, however, he turned to literature, and was swept into the rush of the Romantic movement.

H

He became a leader in the band of devotees who gathered round Victor Hugo and, conspicuous in a pink doublet, and with a mass of long wavy hair, led the storm provoked by the first two representations of *Hernani*, rightly regarded as an attack on the classical stage. Conspicuous among his early poems, and indeed the longest of all his poems, was *Albertus*, a fine exercise in one of the cruder aspects of Romanticism, the melodramatic and macabre, which serves incidentally to show that he was steeped in a knowledge of painting, that he knew something of Shakespeare, of Goethe, of Hoffmann, and of Walter Scott, whose Meg Merrilies, he says, resembled his witch Véronique. Had he only known Burns's *Tam o' Shanter* the whole poem might have been recast more in the ironical vein of its conclusion.

But Gautier, always drawing on Spain for Romantic colour and suggestion, settled down to produce some of the most finely finished little poems in all French literature, objective rather than subjective, which, though not to be dismissed as merely the triumph of art for art's sake, undoubtedly pointed the way for the new departure of the Parnassians in the second half of the century. Baudelaire owed much to him, and defends him vigorously against the charge that he was devoid of sentiment, a term in which he includes both thought and feeling, and he pays this fine tribute to him as a master: 'Victor Hugo is taught and paraphrased in the universities; but every man of letters knows that the study of his resplendent poems ought to be completed by a study of Gautier's poems. Some even remark that while the majestic poet was at times carried away by enthusiasms little propitious to his art, the precious poet, more faithful, more concentrated, has never stepped out of it. Others note that he has even reinforced French poetry, that he has enlarged its repertory, and increased its vocabulary, and this without ever failing to observe the severest rules of the language that his birth obliged him to speak.'

This passage from Baudelaire is important, for it supports the contention that Gautier is a great figure as the landmark that separates the earlier from the later developments of the Romantic movement. Certainly French poetry changed in style, in rhythm, in form and direction after the publication of *Émaux et Camées*, and there must have been something protean in the genius of a man who could influence as he did poets so various as Baudelaire, Leconte de Lisle, Mallarmé, and Verlaine.

Poetry is only one title to Gautier's fame. He was equally distinguished in prose, and his long series of brilliant novels and tales, short and long, and his almost innumerable miscellaneous articles and criticisms, reach the high-water mark of the flood of such literature poured out in France during the nineteenth century. For a final example of his versatility take his knowledge of, and interest in, the ballet. According to her husband's testimony, the most famous of modern dancers, Anna Pavlova, made her first great triumph in Gautier's own ballet, *Giselle*—a delightful fantasy based on a Slavonic theme suggested by Heine. And it remained her favourite ballet.

There has been a tendency with some to belittle Gautier as merely the high-priest of Art for Art's sake. But we know Baudelaire's opinion of him, and in our own country George Saintsbury has been a jealous guardian of his fame. A study of Spoelberch de Lovenjoul's two great volumes devoted to an analytical and chronological account of all his productions leaves an overwhelming impression not only of the mass of his work, but of the consistently high quality of it. More than industry and talent was required to leave behind so vast a monument. It was genius that made it possible. Of the strain involved in constant work at high pressure there is evidence pathetic enough in a letter printed in Lovenjoul's introduction, where Gautier, a married man with a family of his own, writing from Russia, explains why he has not been able to send his sisters more money, however hard he drives himself. He died in 1872, broken-hearted by the disasters of the Franco-German war.

The examples of his poetry offered here reflect the lighter side of his accomplishment, but they are versions of three poems which fired the youthful enthusiasm of the writer, which he attempted, and failed, to translate over forty years ago, and which he has only succeeded during the last few years in rendering, even to his own satisfaction:

(116)

THE BUTTERFLIES

In swarms they flutter o'er the sea,
   The butterflies like flakes of snow;
Fair butterflies, would I were free
   By azure paths of air to go!

Now tell me, O thou peerless gem,
  My bayadère with eyes of jet,
Could I but borrow wings of them,
  Dost know which way my course I 'd set?

I 'd seek no rose for honeyed sips;
  O'er valleys deep and forests high,
I 'd hurry to thy parting lips,
  Flower of my soul, and there would die.

(117)

The Spectre of the Rose

O raise again the lids you close,
  To greet a vision virginal;
I am the spectre of a rose
  You wore last night at beauty's ball.
With silvery drops you watered me,
  And plucked me still impearled with dew,
And mid the starry lustres' glee
  Where'er you walked I went with you.

You cannot chase me from your sight,
  For you were cause why I am dead;
My rosy spectre all the night
  Will come and dance beside your bed.
But fear me not; no mass for me,
  Nor solemn *De Profundis* sing:
A guest from Paradise you see,
  My soul, this faint perfume, I bring.

Who would not envy me my fate?
  That so a man should meet his doom.
His life were not a gift too great,
  For in thy breast I make my tomb.
On alabaster I repose;
  A poet there, with kiss of love,
Has written fair: Here lies a rose
  That kings might well be jealous of.

(118)

THE NAUGHTY WORLD

The world is naughty, little one,
  With mocking smile it says of thee,
That at thy side in place of heart
  A watch is ticking steadily.
And yet thy palpitating breast
  Doth, like the ocean, rise and fall,
When, circling through thy tender frame,
  Surges life's tide at nature's call.

The world is naughty, little one,
  It says thy sparkling eyes are dead
And in their orbits stiffly move,
  Like children's toys with weights of lead.
And yet a rainbow-coloured tear
  Hangs on thine eyelids' quivering rim,
As clings a drop of pearly dew
  Still to the emptied goblet's brim.

The world is naughty, little one,
  It says thou hast but little wit,
And that the lines I read to thee
  Might just as well be in Sanscrit.
And yet upon thy rosy mouth,
  The flower that opes and shuts at will,
A smile plays, like a cunning bee,
  To sip the charm of grace or skill.

'Tis that thou lov'st me, little one,
  And hat'st them, all those gossipers.
Quit me, and soon we'll hear them say :
  Oh, what a heart, what wit are hers !

We have told how Gautier wrote the libretto for Pavlova's famous ballet, *Giselle*. The second of the above poems, *The Spectre of the Rose*, inspired the gem of Fokine's ballets, arranged for Nijinsky, and its beauty can be realized by any one who reads the account of it in the Life of Nijinsky by his wife.

We fitly end this chapter with the mention of that charming poet, and delightful personality, Théodore de Banville, the son of a naval officer, and born in 1823. With a remarkable facility in rhyme, rhythm, and metre, which was all his own, he owed much to Gautier, and much also to the poets of the Pleiad, and the medieval poets; ballades, including what is by general consent the finest of all modern ballades, the *Ballade aux Enfants perdus*, rondeaux, and triolets he reintroduced into French, and by his success fired Andrew Lang, Austin Dobson, and even the late poet laureate, Robert Bridges, to make their graceful experiments on the same lines in English verse. He wrote several comedies, some of which, like *Gringoire* and *Le Baiser*, still take the stage from time to time, many tales also, and much good criticism, but it is the gaiety of his lyrics, the genial atmosphere that envelops his work, so that even his irony is light as thistledown, and his unfailing grace that made him the power he was and have endeared him to posterity.

These qualities were only a reflection of his sunny personality. Anatole France and his other friends speak again and again of his eternal smile, his golden smile, and in a period one of the most delightful features of which was a brotherhood among poets, and a readiness among them, so many of whom were also critics, to extend a warm welcome to talent in the young, no more sympathetic soul gladdened his fellows than Théodore de Banville. To him it was that John Payne dedicated his translation of Villon, as 'to one of the sweetest souls that ever sanctified humanity.' There are some fine, but unnamed, stanzas of his of which Baudelaire said that they are 'stanzas worthy of Ronsard for their audacity, their elasticity, and their amplitude; their very commencement is full of grandiloquence, and proclaims a more than human exaltation of pride and joy':

> Vous en qui je salue une nouvelle aurore,
>   Vous tous qui m'aimerez,
> Jeunes hommes des temps qui ne sont pas encore,
>   O bataillons sacrés!

The spirit that animated such a trumpet-blast as this makes one understand how it was that the wild young prodigy, Arthur Rimbaud, eating his heart out at Charleville, addressed to Banville some of his precocious efforts, and in the covering letter, dated 24th May 1870, poured out his fifteen-year-old enthusiasm and eager aspirations.

The best known of Banville's poems is that he addresses to the home of his childhood, *A la Font-Georges*. Of all such tributes paid by poets, and they are numerous enough, this of Banville perhaps stands out pre-eminent. Hear how it begins:

> O champs pleins de silence,
> Où mon heureuse enfance
> Avait des jours encor
>   Tous filés d'or!

> O ma vieille Font-Georges,
> Vers qui les rouges-gorges
> Et le doux rossignol
>   Prenaient leur vol!

As our contribution towards the rendering in English of his radiant poetry we offer versions of two poems of his which cling to the memory of any one who reads them, so delicate and yet so penetrating is their charm. The first is the poem addressed to one of his young friends, Adolphe Gaïffe, which might appropriately be called *The Creed of Youth*.

(119)

THE CREED OF YOUTH

Young man from melancholy free,
Blond as the sun in Italy,
Let thy fair folly treasured be.

'Tis wisdom's self! To relish wine,
Love beauty and the spring divine,
Fulfils thy need. All else resign.

Smile, even when thy luck takes wing,
And when, once more, returns the spring,
Her blossoms in the goblet fling.

And of thy body in the tomb
What memory 's left? There love found room
And lit, a brief May-time, life's gloom.

'Cause and effect' thy time employ,
The wise men tell us, to annoy.
Words, idle words!   Life's rose enjoy.

The next is a lovely piece, dreamy in sentiment, and rendered
in a metre that rises and falls like a lullaby—which has not saved
it from being the subject of stern analysis by Professor Grammont
in his *Le Vers français*:

(120)

LOVE AND SLEEP

Come, let us love and sleep,
To others' thoughts and feelings dead!
And neither ocean-wave, nor tempest from the steep,
While warm our love we keep,
Will make thee bow thy golden head;
For Love is stronger far
Than Death and Godhead are!

The sun will close his eye,
That so thy beauty shine more white.
The roaring wind that bends to earth the forest high
Dares not, in passing by,
To wanton with thy tresses light
So long as on my breast
Thou lay'st thy head to rest.

And when our two hearts go
To Heaven's high home of happiness
Where, watered by our tears, celestial lilies blow,
Then, swept by passion's glow,
Lip close to lip like flowers we'll press,
And strive with one long kiss
To drain Death's cup in bliss.

Of Banville's mastery of metre two examples in the original
French will be enough.   To those who suggest that Alexandrines
cannot sing, here are lines that provide adequate reply:

Nous n'irons plus aux bois, les lauriers sont coupés,
Les amours des bassins, les Naïades en groupe
Voient reluire au soleil en cristaux découpés
Les flots silencieux qui coulaient de leur coupe.

And here are verses which show that in a short metre, where French verse excels, Banville is perhaps only surpassed among modern French poets by Verlaine at his best:

Pourquoi, courtisane,
Vendre ton amour,
La fleur diaphane,

La fleur diaphane,
Qui fleurit le jour
Et que la main fane,

La rose d'amour?

Pourquoi, blond poète,
Ouvrir au passant
Ta douleur muette,

Ta douleur muette,
Lys éblouissant
Que la foule jette

Et brise en passant?

We have said that it was Banville's success in reviving old French metres, such as the triolet, that fired English poets to follow him, and among them Robert Bridges.   In his article on the triolet in the *Encyclopaedia Britannica*, Ed. XI, Edmund Gosse quotes Robert Bridges as the first author, in 1873, of a modern English triolet.   We have quoted on page 130 the triolet by Ranchin, rightly called the King of Triolets, but that of the late poet laureate is so good, as a complete poem in tiny compass, that we make bold to quote it here, a sad sequel to Ranchin's gay lines:

When first we met we did not guess
That Love would prove so hard a master;
Of more than common friendliness
When first we met we did not guess.
Who could foretell the sore distress,
This irretrievable disaster,
When first we met?—We did not guess
That Love would prove so hard a master.

* H

It will serve as an introduction to the study of the sinister figure of Baudelaire, which comes near the beginning of the next chapter, if we quote, and bear in mind in thinking of Baudelaire the poet, a very remarkable passage from Baudelaire the critic's notice of Banville, where he hits off with a detachment as uncanny as his insight the contrast between his friend's temperament and poetry and his own: 'It was Beethoven that began to stir the worlds of melancholy that mass like clouds in the heaven of man's inner consciousness . . . Byron in poetry, and Poe in poetry and the analytical prose-tale . . . have admirably expressed the blasphemous element in passion; they have projected splendid, dazzling rays on the latent Lucifer who is installed in every human heart. And it seems that this infernal part of man, which man takes pleasure in explaining to himself, grows daily, as if the devil amused himself in swelling it by artificial means, as chicken-farmers do, patiently cramming the human race in their proper poultry yards to prepare for himself a more succulent repast. But Théodore de Banville refuses to dwell on these swamps of blood, these bottomless pits of mud. . . . In his verses, all, even pleasure itself, has an air of gaiety and innocence. . . . In an atmosphere charged with Satanism and Romanticism, in the midst of a concert of imprecations, he has the courage to hymn the goodness of the gods, and to remain a perfect classic— in the most noble and truly historic meaning of the word.'

CHAPTER VIII

NEW DEPARTURES

BAUDELAIRE, THE PARNASSIANS, SYMBOLISM

THE second half of the nineteenth century was marked by new departures. It seemed as if the younger poets who reached maturity towards the middle of the century or soon after it were taking stock of the position, and resolved either to consolidate the ground won by the impetuous onset of the first heroes of the war of liberation, or to break out in fresh adventures of their own. Lamartine was out of fashion; Victor Hugo an Olympian exile throned on his eyrie in the Channel, an object of veneration, an institution not to be assailed by sacrilegious hands, but to be regarded as one standing apart; Musset's Byronic attitude had become repugnant to a new and self-reliant generation. Alfred de Vigny and Théophile Gautier were the models to be admired, both of them distinguished by dignified restraint and the latter by what seemed absolute perfection of form, both free from mere rhetoric and a too facile sentimentality. It was Gautier on his objective side that triumphed first, and Leconte de Lisle that was to lead the first new movement, though later on in the century it was the mystic element in Vigny that was to suggest a new departure, and Mallarmé who was to be its prophet.

But before we speak of the Parnassians, or say a word of the Symbolists, we have to consider a greater than Leconte de Lisle, a greater than Mallarmé, one who, like Villon, stood in isolation and, for all his tremendous influence, founded no school, Charles Baudelaire. His personality calls for fuller notice than we have been able to devote to others than Villon, because his poetry was his life, and it is because the horror of his poetry was the horror of his life, displayed in verse as splendid as any ever written, that it is meaningless to speak of one without the other. His morbid fancies, his exotic sensuality, his pitiful compassion not merely

203

for himself, but for other victims of vices and miseries like his own, and even the element of Satanism that possessed him were the result of a nervous disposition of quite abnormal sensitivity. And yet the genius of poetry breathed on him throughout his sentient existence, and enabled him, not without the most painful effort on his part, to bequeath, not indeed a long poem, but a long series of short masterpieces, bizarre many of them and macabre, so that even putrefaction becomes the subject of a flawless poem—masterpieces so fine that the world at large, and not only the esoteric circles of decadence, cannot fail to recognize them as reaching the very height of art.

A remarkable feature of his poetry, and by no means a superficial one, cannot be dismissed without comment. Mr. Robert Lynd once termed Wordsworth a noseless poet, and certainly there is little enough appeal in his poetry to the sense of smell. But Baudelaire reeks of perfume, not the scent of fresh flowers or ambrosial air, but of musk, ambergris, nard, opium, incense, and the acrid smells of benzine and stale tobacco. Tobacco is no easy word to introduce into poetry. Baudelaire's skill, however, triumphs, and whereas in one of his *Petits Poèmes en prose* he says of his lover's hair, *Dans l'ardent foyer de ta chevelure je respire l'odeur de tabac mêlé à l'opium et au sucre*, he rises in the *Fleurs du Mal* to this:

> Bizarre déité, brune comme les nuits,
> Au parfum mélangé de musc et de havane.

Critic after critic, and his intimate friends, Gautier and Banville, have laid stress on the part played in his poetry by the sense of smell. Gautier says: 'His nose, fine and delicate, a little rounded at the tip, with quivering nostrils, seems to sense subconsciously vague odours from afar.' Banville speaks of 'his nose, graceful in shape, ironic in expression, prominent in plan, and whose tip, a little rounded and projecting, makes one think at once of the poet's famous saying: "My soul flutters over perfumes, as other men's over music."' The full import of this dominance of the sense of smell is given by one of the most psychological of novelists and critics, Paul Bourget: 'The sensations he preferred were those of smell, because they rouse more than others that mysterious element of obscure and melancholy sensuality which is part of our being.'

Charles Baudelaire [1] was born in Paris in 1821, the son of a
mother aged twenty-six and a father aged sixty. The father, a
retired official, had inherited a competence from his first wife,
and the family was then in easy circumstances. When the boy
was six years old his father died, and then came the child's
happiest year, for he had to himself the mother he adored. Too
soon, in 1828, came the shock of her second marriage, to a soldier
of suitable age, thirty-nine, Lieutenant-Colonel Aupick, who had
already had a distinguished career, and was to become a general
and rise high in the diplomatic service. In 1848 indeed, and on
the nomination of the poet Lamartine, then Foreign Secretary,
he became Ambassador to the Sublime Porte, and a few years
later was transferred to Madrid. The sensitive child regarded
his mother's second marriage as an act of infidelity, and he hated
his stepfather, who, though undoubtedly a martinet, and quite
ignorant of the nervous, irritable, introspective, self-indulgent
type of boy he had to handle, was an honourable and upright
man, anxious to do his best for him according to his lights.

It was not only the general who found his stepson difficult.
At sixteen years of age he was sent to his last place of education,
the famous Collège Louis-le-Grand, and two years later was
expelled from it in disgrace, despite the brilliance in Latin verse
that he showed. For the next year or two he lived as loosely
as he could, while still an inmate of his mother's house, and it
may be that at this early period he contracted the disease that,
after running its slow, secret, intermittent course for over twenty
years, destroyed his brain before his body, and killed him at the
age of forty-five. Presently serious trouble arose at home. At
an official dinner in his stepfather's house Baudelaire let fall
some unbecoming remark, the general sharply reproved him,
and when the young man made as though to strike him, soundly
cuffed him, and reduced him to hysterics. A family council,
that useful French institution, was held, and it was decided to
send him off on a long sea-voyage to India. He was placed
under the care of a merchant-captain, a fine type of sailor-
man who, naturally enough, proved no more acceptable to the
degenerate youth in his charge than did the rest of the ship's

---

[1] The following sketch was written before the publication of Miss Starkie's
Baudelaire, to which readers may be referred who desire to consult an
exhaustive study.

company. He got as far as Mauritius and Réunion, but would go no farther, and induced his captain to tranship him to a vessel returning to France. Thus, after an absence of nine months he returned to Paris in February 1842, bringing with him, if not a more docile disposition, a store of exotic impressions to enrich his poetry.

In a few months Baudelaire reached his majority, and there was a division of property between a much older stepbrother and himself. He was at last free to set up an establishment of his own and to devote himself to literature. But he proved a slow, fastidious, and desultory worker, and it was not long before he entered on a liaison with an actress playing an insignificant part at some small theatre, an actress half of negro blood, and to this black Venus, as he thought her, he was tied all through his wretched life, displaying a patience with her, and a tender care of her quite exemplary. His money soon began to slip between his fingers, and within two years his stepfather and mother again had recourse to the sensible provision of French law, and another family council was summoned. About half his patrimony was left, and this was placed in trust, the income being doled out to him in monthly payments. Still the prodigal son continued in his ways, and debts accumulated. His mistress drank, and Baudelaire himself tried to drown his cares in wine, brandy, English beer and porter and, finally, opium, which he took in the form of laudanum. He still saw his mother, almost furtively, from time to time; she never abandoned him, though it is clear from his letters to her that at times she could not refrain from reproaches, notwithstanding which he sponged on her mercilessly. When her husband died she retired to live in reduced circumstances at Honfleur, and there she gladly provided a welcome refuge for her son from time to time.

The marvel is that, leading the disordered life he did, he managed to do any work at all; but genius is a plant that cannot be wholly repressed, and he must during his lucid, comparatively care-free, periods have had an incredible power of concentration lasting for days at a time. He became early a figure of note in the brilliant literary Bohemia of his day, for in daring and originality he was intellectually the superior of all he met, and his private means, so long as they lasted, enabled him to play the dandified figure dear to one of his temperament. What first

gave him fame outside his immediate circle was his criticisms
of the pictures in the Salons of 1845 and 1846, distinguished by
flashes of insight which make him a real pioneer in the appreciation of new tendencies in art. Manet in particular became
one of his intimates, and at the first glance he recognized the
genius of Méryon. But his range extended beyond painting, for
he was one of the first to embrace the cause of Wagner's music,
and he was foremost in the fight against the chauvinism which
led his countrymen to ban the musical genius of the age because
he was a foreigner. Certainly Baudelaire had few prejudices.
About the same time he became acquainted with, and was
captivated by, the works of Edgar Allan Poe, in whom he thought
he recognized a spiritual brother. From his mother, who,
though purely French, was born in London, and had spent her
early childhood in England, he learnt English, and so for more
than ten years after his discovery of Poe he engaged himself in
the task of translating all his prose works and succeeded in
producing one of the finest of all translations that exist.

A few poems from time to time circulated among his friends,
or appeared in obscure and short-lived periodicals, and in 1855
the *Revue des Deux Mondes* published, nervously and half-apolo-
getically, eighteen of his poems under the title (not of Baudelaire's
invention) *Fleurs du Mal*. A collected edition of his poems had
been announced for ten years, but it was not until 1857 that it
appeared under the provocative title just mentioned. The
consummate art of its contents appealed only to a small audience,
and the book became a byword for unwholesomeness. Hugo,
the Olympian, wrote to him: 'Vous dotez le ciel de l'art d'un
rayon macabre, vous créez un frisson nouveau.' But poet and
printer were successfully prosecuted for an offence against public
morals, and six of the poems were ordered to be suppressed.

Baudelaire was now indeed famous, but neither materially nor
morally did the conditions of his life improve, and he was riddled
with debts. The misery displayed in his begging letters to his
mother and his trustee is pitiful in the extreme; money he wants,
money he must have, to free him from the anxieties that render
him incapable of work. In a letter to his mother dated 31st
December 1853 he writes: 'Laissez-moi me débrouiller et
travailler cinq ou six jours. . . . Il faut à tout prix un travail
violent, comme une espèce de cautérisation sur les vieilles plaies.'

In 1864, when he was forty-three years old, he sought a refuge from his embarrassments in flight to Brussels. M. Jacques Crépet, the devoted editor of the final edition of his poems, thus describes him at that moment: 'He seemed an old man, and was the living image of despair in revolt.' Witness the terrible face that looks out at one from the frontispiece to Crépet's volume!

In Brussels he spent two miserable years, then paralysis struck him, and in an asylum in Paris he died on the 31st August 1867. He had, before he left Paris in 1864, premonitions of his end. In his intimate journal occurs this entry: 'J'ai cultivé mon hystérie avec jouissance et terreur. Maintenant, j'ai toujours le vertige, et aujourd'hui, 23 janvier 1862, j'ai subi un singulier avertissement, j'ai senti passer sur moi le vent de l'aile de l'imbécillité.' Certainly if any man while yet alive made full payment for his sins, and sins is the word he would himself have chosen, that man was Baudelaire. There is a terrible line of his that sums up the feelings of remorse and despair that came over him at times:

Ne cherchez plus mon cœur; les bêtes l'ont mangé.

Seek now no more my heart; the dogs have eaten it.

It must not be forgotten that Baudelaire had a heart, had a soul and conscience, had a core of religion within him that found expression in moments of extreme misery. Perhaps the most poignant of all the poignant letters he wrote to his mother is one, written probably in October 1860, in which he says: 'Je suis horriblement malheureux et si tu crois qu'une prière puisse avoir de l'efficacité (je parle sans plaisanterie), prie pour moi, et vigoureusement, j'en ai besoin.' And as early as June 1845 he wrote a letter to a correspondent unnamed of which the following somewhat disjointed fragment is printed in the collection of his letters published in 1906: '. . . je me tue, parce que je suis inutile aux autres et dangereux à moi-meme. Je me tue, parce que je me crois immortel et que *j'espère*. . . . Montrez-lui mon épouvantable exemple et comment le désordre d'esprit et de vie mène à un désespoir sombre et à un anéantissement complet. —*Raison et utilité*, je vous en supplie. . . .'

He could distinguish between good and evil, but it was the perverse side of him, the Satanic element as he himself would have called it, that continually prevailed, and could cunningly persuade him that in giving the world an artistic presentation of evil he was performing some sort of moral service. One can even imagine him singing with tears Racine's great hymn. Thus in a letter from Brussels, dated 1864, to his trustee, M. Ancelle, he says of his *Fleurs du Mal*: 'Ce maudit livre (*dont je suis très fier*) est donc bien obscur, bien inintelligible! Je porterai longtemps la peine d'avoir osé peindre le mal avec quelque talent.' And again, in 1866: 'Faut-il vous dire, à vous qui ne l'avez pas plus deviné que les autres, que dans ce livre *atroce* j'ai mis *tout mon cœur, toute ma tendresse, toute ma religion* (travestie), *toute ma haine* ? Il est vrai que j'écrirai le contraire, que je jurerai mes grands dieux que c'est un livre *d'art pur*, de *singerie*, de *jonglerie*, et je mentirai comme un arracheur de dents.' Finally, let us not forget that in his *Journaux intimes* the last entries are full of injunctions to prayer, and prayer to God. 'L'homme qui fait sa prière, le soir,' he says, 'est un capitaine qui pose des sentinelles. Il peut dormir.'

Baudelaire merits the attention we have given to him, for as a psychological study he is very remarkable, and this quite apart from the fact that in sheer power, in perfection of form, in the impeccable use of words inevitably right, even when strange, in the immense influence he has exerted on art, literature, and life since his day, he stands out as one of the greatest poets of the century in any language. There are reverberations to be got from the hard, metallic, sonorous quality of some of his verses, the muffled tones and luxurious melancholy of others, where thought or feeling are invariably phrased with epigrammatic force, such as are to be had from none other. 'Every poem,' said Gautier, 'is reduced by the genius of concentration to a drop of essence enclosed in a flask of crystal with a thousand facets . . . that one must drink or breathe with precaution, like all liqueurs of an exquisite intensity.' And Lytton Strachey, while admitting that 'his vision is black and terrible,' and that most of his pages are no fit reading for the young and ignorant, claims that there are to be found 'in this lurid poetry elements of profundity and power which are rare indeed, [and] . . . a passionate imagination which clothes the thought with splendour, and lifts the strange words of this unhappy mortal into the deathless regions of the sublime.'

We offer a few versions of his poems in the hope that they will convey to those who do not know them some intimation of their power, and will not altogether shock by their inadequacy those who do know them. The first two were addressed to a well-known beauty of the time who lived in luxury and entertained lavishly the notable artists and poets who paid their court to her. The last verse of the second poem is a good example of the paradoxical ingenuity of thought and phrase of which Baudelaire was a master, and which made the Symbolists claim him as one of the sources of their inspiration:

(121)

Hymn

To her most fair, her I adore,
   Who fills my heart with radiancy,
My angel, idol evermore,
   All hail in immortality!

She fills my being like the tide
   That brings a salt breath from the sea,
And gives my soul unsatisfied
   The savour of eternity.

A fragrant sachet, fading not,
   That scents a nook for love's delight,
A perfumed altar-lamp forgot,
   That burns in secret through the night.

How, love for ever pure and clean,
   Express all I should say of thee?
A grain of musk that lurks unseen,
   Deep in the eternal part of me.

To her most kind, her I adore,
   Who gives me joy and sanity,
My angel, idol evermore,
   All hail in immortality!

(122)

A Perfect Whole

The devil in my chamber high,
  This morning came to visit me,
And, hoping so to catch me out,
  Spake thus: 'I fain would ask of thee:

'Mid all the beauties manifold
  That go to fill thy Circe's cup,
Mid all the objects black and rose
  That build her charming body up,

'Which is the sweetest?' O my soul,
  Thus answer thou the accursed one:
'Since she is all one scented flower
  I yield the preference to none.

'Where all is ravishing, who knows
  What detail can seduce the sight?
She dazzles me as doth the dawn,
  Gives consolation like the night.

'So exquisite the harmony
  That regulates her body fair,
In vain analysis would note
  What numerous accords are there.

'O mystic metamorphosis,
  Where all my senses one appear!
Like perfume is her voice to me,
  And music in her breath I hear.'

Next comes a sonnet that gives some indication of the remorse
and disgust of self that at times overtook the poet:

(123)

Spiritual Dawn

After debauch, when rises white and red
The dawn attended by remorse of soul,
Through retribution's mystical control
An angel stirs within each brutish head.

The spirit's heaven, glimpsed in sheer azure height,
On fallen man, rapt in his painful dream,
Opens and whirls him down an eddying stream.
So, goddess dear, thou essence pure and bright,

Mid the stale reek left by dull nights of shame
Thoughts of thee fairer, rosier once, more sweet,
In ceaseless flight my quickened vision greet.

The sun makes murky now the candles' flame;
And so thy ghost, victorious still, is one,
O splendid spirit, with the immortal sun.

The following sonnet is from a section of his poems called *Tableaux parisiens*. Every sentiment indulged in by Baudelaire is fierce, and this sonnet, like other poems in the section, shows how fierce could be his pity:

(124)

The Blind

Regard them, O my soul, dreadful they are;
Dummies that move; somehow ridiculous;
Awful; sleep-walker-like; mysterious;
Darting glazed eye-balls whitherwards afar?

Their eyes, wherefrom the spark divine has fled,
Ever in distant gaze to heaven ascend;
One never sees them towards the pavement bend
Foreheads weighed down by thought heavy as lead.

And so they wander through the boundless dark,
Own brother to eternal silence. Hark!
O city, savagely to lust inclined,

While round us people laugh, and sing, and bay,
I stumble too, but ask, more dull than they:
What seek they there in heaven, these many blind?

Finally, here are the last two stanzas of *Le Voyage*, the poem
that closes *Les Fleurs du Mal*:

(125)

THE VOYAGE

'Tis time, old captain, Death; the anchor let us weigh!
We 're weary of this earth, let us hoist sail in flight!
What though dark sky and sea make black as ink the day,
Our hearts which thou dost know are full of radiant light.

Give, then, to comfort us, draughts from thy poisoned well!
We would, so fierce the flame that sets our brain on fire,
Plunge deep within the gulf—what matter, heaven or hell?—
Deep down in the Unknown to find some new Desire.

We have treated Baudelaire, and rightly we hope, as the
founder of no school, but as the source of a wide influence from
which few subsequent poets of whatever school wholly escaped.
We come now to the leader of the Parnassians, Leconte de Lisle,
a creole born in the island of Réunion in 1818. He was educated partly in his birthplace, partly at Rennes in Brittany. His
father, an army surgeon, destined him for a commercial career,
and he was sent to travel in the East Indies. But in 1847 he
abandoned all thoughts of an active life, and settled down in
Paris to devote himself to literature. His dream was to describe
in a series of short poems, elaborated to a finish which rivals the
art of Gautier or Baudelaire, the life and thought, the illusions,
hard experience and misery, the atmosphere and the natural
setting, not only of mankind in different ages and climes, but
also of the great birds and beasts, the condor, the jaguar, and the
elephant, that fired his imagination. And he succeeded. Each
picture or episode, complete in itself, is a finished work of art,
realistic not merely in externals, but conveying as well the
impression a thing seen or a sound heard must leave on the
sentient mind, even when painter or poet adds no rhetorical
flourish of his own.

Sonority and sculpturesque diction were his in the highest
degree; some say with Banville, he wrought in gold, others say
in marble. He was an heroic figure, according to Anatole
France, a magnificent human animal, according to Maurice
Barrès. Impassivity all attribute to him, and it is because of this

impassivity, because of the absence of any exposure of inordinate desires, or denunciation of the philosophic pessimism possessing him, that his appeal has not the throbbing intensity that makes Baudelaire's irresistible. His erudition was enormous, and he poured it out not only in his *Poèmes antiques*, his *Poèmes barbares*, and his *Poèmes tragiques*, but also in volume after volume of translations into French prose from the great Greek and Latin authors. Leconte de Lisle was clearly marked out to be a leader in some new departure. Poverty had made his life a hard struggle, but in 1872 he was appointed sub-librarian to the Senate, which gave him a competence and an official residence, where he exercised until his death in 1894 a benevolent despotism over many of the younger poets, even some of those with leanings towards Symbolism, who came to do him honour.

The school of poets, of which he became the recognized leader, are known as the Parnassians, a name derived from a collection of poems published in 1866 under the title *Le Parnasse contemporain*. Practically all the poets of any celebrity then writing contributed to it, with the exception of Victor Hugo, whose seat was, of course, not on Parnassus, but on Olympus. The contributors indeed form such a concert of musical, high-sounding names as would be difficult to match: Gautier, Banville, Leconte de Lisle, Baudelaire, Sully Prudhomme, José-Maria de Heredia, Paul Verlaine, Stéphane Mallarmé, Villiers de l'Isle-Adam. Not all of these are to be accounted Parnassians, for the names of some are to be linked rather with the later development that followed the Parnassian, viz. that of the Symbolists. We may reckon as two outstanding Parnassians in the train of Leconte de Lisle Sully Prudhomme and Heredia, and on them we shall have a word to say when we have finished with their leader. The first example we offer of his work is a version of one of his poems with the untranslatable title of *Les Hurleurs*, a study of animal despair, and a poem greatly admired by Baudelaire:

(126)

Dumb Despair

The sun had plunged his torch within its watery grave,
And neath the fog-bound hills asleep the city lay;
Over the giant rocks, besprent with foam and spray,
The sombre, rumbling sea poured lofty wave on wave.

The darkness multiplied the endless sound of woe;
No star shone forth to light the blank immensity.
Only the pallid moon, in rifts of clouded sky,
Swung like a lonely lamp to shed a dismal glow.

Dumb world, branded and signed with anger's blazonry,
Shard of a shattered globe hurled whither chance may call,
From off her frozen orb silently she let fall
A cold sepulchral gleam across the polar sea.

Roofed by the stifling sky, Africa northward swept
Past sight, and sheltered her beneath the thick brown haze;
Her drooping lions starved on steaming, sandy ways,
Her herds of elephants, couched by the marshes, slept.

But on the barren shore reeking with odours foul,
Where fallen horse and ox had left their rotting bones,
Hordes of lean scattered hounds, nosing the filthy stones,
Whined in their misery, and raised gaunt heads to howl.

Their tails curled underneath bellies that pant and strain,
With staring eyes they stood, twitching on fevered feet,
Or hugged the ground; all howled, motionless in the heat,
Until their bodies shook with sudden thrills of pain.

The salt sea-foam upon their backs had matted tight
Long hairs that left exposed their knotty vertebrae,
And when the wash of waves leapt on them from the sea
Beneath their blood-red lips their chattering teeth gleamed
        white.

Under the wandering moon with rays of livid light,
What unknown agony, by the dark waters' side,
Made some lost soul cry out that your foul forms would hide?
Why did ye moan so loud, O spectres of affright?

I know not; but, ye dogs that howled along the shore,
After so many suns that will not rise again,
Deep in my troubled past I hear that desperate strain,
The cry of savage grief for your wild hearts too sore.

A gloomy poem this, but there was a deep strain of pessimism in Leconte de Lisle, which finds its extreme expression in his *Requies*.   A man, having reached the height of his earthly journey, looks back at the enchanted country of his happy youth and early manhood, that he will see no more, and weeps bitterly.   Thus the poem ends:

Le temps n'a pas tenu ses promesses divines;
Tes yeux ne verront point reverdir tes ruines;
Livre leur cendre morte au souffle de l'oubli.

Endors-toi sans tarder en ton repos suprême;
Et souviens-toi, vivant dans l'ombre enseveli,
Qu'il n'est plus en ce monde un seul être qui t'aime.

   .   .   .   .   .

Rentre au tombeau muet où l'homme enfin s'abrite,
Et là, sans nul souci de la terre et du ciel,
Repose, ô malheureux, pour le temps eternel!

Time hath not kept for thee his promises divine;
Thou wilt not see fresh green about thy ruins twine;
Let the dead dust be borne on chill oblivion's breath.

Seek thou supreme repose, hasten, and have no fear;
But bear this well in mind, living in shades of death,
There 's no one left on earth who holds thy memory dear.

   .   .   .   .   .

Enter the silent tomb, for us the final home
And there with never a thought of earth or of the sky
Lie still, O hapless one, and for eternity!

Another gloomy poem of Leconte de Lisle's, but with a fine romantic appeal, is *Le Cœur de Hialmar*. This poem of his has not been singled out as it ought to have been, for in the whole range of the poetry of his time there is nothing finer. The poem tells how on a battle-field covered with the bodies of stricken Norsemen their leader, Hialmar, wounded to death, comes to himself under a clear night-sky, chilled by an icy wind. He calls for one of his carles who may yet have breath in him: but there is none to reply. Then from the sable flock of birds of prey that hover around he summons a raven, and this is the message he delivers to that grim messenger:

Viens par ici, Corbeau, mon brave mangeur d'hommes!
Ouvre-moi la poitrine avec ton bec de fer.
Tu nous retrouveras demain tels que nous sommes.
Porte mon cœur tout chaud à la fille d'Ylmer.

Dans Upsal, où les Jarls boivent la bonne bière,
Et chantent, en heurtant les cruches d'or, en chœur,
A tire d'aile vole, ô rôdeur de bruyère!
Cherche ma fiancée et porte-lui mon cœur.

.   .   .   .   .

Va, sombre messager, dis-lui bien que je l'aime,
Et que voici mon cœur.   Elle reconnaîtra
Qu'il est rouge et solide, et non tremblant et blême;
Et la fille d'Ylmer, Corbeau, te sourira!

Les Elfes, another of his shorter poems with a romantic appeal, is well known, for it, again, is one of the finest poems of its kind in the range of French poetry, and is of the kindred of Keats's *La Belle Dame sans Merci* and *The Erl-King*. It is quite untranslatable with its refrain:

Couronnés de thym et de marjolaine,
Les Elfes joyeux dansent sur la plaine.

But here is one of the rare flowers of a simpler kind to be found in his work, a poem written on the cliff-top:

(127)

THREE STRANDS OF GOLD

Down there, like a swallow I 'd fain be gone
Seawards, and farther than eye can behold!
But vain is my wish, for my cruel one
Has bound my heart fast with three strands of gold.

The first is her eyes, the second her smile,
The third, to be brief, her mouth like a flower;

But too great my love; I 'm martyred the while:
Three strands of gold keep my heart in her power!

Ah! could I at last but loosen my chain!
Farewell to my tears; to leap I 'd be bold.
But no, no! better to die in my pain,
Than tear you apart, my three strands of gold!

We cannot leave Leconte de Lisle without mention of one of his greatest achievements, viz. his superb adaptation of the Aeschylean trilogy, *Les Érinnyes,* which has made more than one triumphant appearance on the stage of the Odéon.

Sully Prudhomme was born in Paris in 1839, and came of good commercial stock. He tried both engineering and law, but found neither congenial, and, having private means, devoted himself to literature and the study of philosophy. Few poets have held the rank he does as a philosopher: he made a profound study of Pascal, translated admirably the first book of Lucretius, and wrote two important philosophical poems of his own, *La Justice* and *Le Bonheur.* Ill-health dogged his last years, and it is probable that he never recovered entirely from a serious illness brought upon him by his exertions and privations in the defence of Paris during the terrible winter of 1870. It is to his credit that towards the close of his life he played a courageous part as one of the champions of Captain Dreyfus.

His title to fame rests on the consummate art and fastidious diction of the many lovely lyrics he wrote during the earlier years of his poetic career. His lyrics are as graceful as any of his time, and, though impersonal for the most part, as befits a true Parnassian, they have a rare subtlety as may be expected of a philosopher. Here is a version of a lyric entitled *Carelessly Buried*; the last two lines of the second verse show the accomplished metaphysician:

(128)

CARELESSLY BURIED

When she is dead you loved so dear,
  Short the farewell there 's time to say;
They close her eyes, they lift the bier,
  And she is lost to you for aye.

But her I loved I still can see,
   And catch, though mine no more, her smile;
More living than a shadow she,
   Nearer than memory all the while.

And through my life she dies to me
   In never-ending, sad good-byes;
O dead one, buried carelessly,
   They quite forgot to close thine eyes.

All, however, of his shorter poems are not as simple as this.
Here is one with a veritable Freudian flavour:

(129)

Last Solitude

In this great masquerade through which we live our lives
We speak not as we please, nor walk as we would walk;
Made to reveal our thoughts, speech wraps them up in talk;
Our faces are but masks a cunning brain contrives.

But when the body fails, unfaithful servant he,
Disguising now no more the soul far scattered hence,
In sinister repose collapsing suddenly,
What was accomplice once turns now king's evidence.

Then the dark swarm appears, brood of subconscious
    thought,
That force of human will so far has driven back,
And travels on in front, like a cloud thick and black
That holds the true motive of all on earth one sought.

The heart shows on the face; traits of anxiety
No more can artful smiles confusedly eclipse:
One's gaze no more can force eyes to convey a lie,
And what one has not said is written on one's lips.

'Tis now confession's hour. A corpse the truth must tell,
Wearing the last imprint left by the breath in flight;
And man, himself again in his own self's despite,
Turns stranger to the friends who thought they knew him
    well.

The laughter of the gay relaxes to a moan,
And gravest ones at times make laughter visible;
We all die as we are, sincere somehow unknown:
It is Death's truthfulness that makes it terrible.

We have suggested that most of his graceful lyrics were written early in his career, but a lyrical vein did persist, for in one of his latest volumes appears a lyric worthy of his prime. This, which is entitled an *Idyll without Words*, tells how a nymph, gazing at her reflection as she stoops to drink, is seen by Hylas, hiding on the bank. Hylas plucks a rose, kisses it, presses it near his heart, and throws it on the flowing stream. The sweet-scented messenger of love floats down, and only stays its course when it reaches the nymph's moistened lips. Thus the poem begins:

Naïs, vierge blonde à l'œil noir,
Au bord du fleuve agenouillée,
Y mire sa bouche mouillée
Par le mobile et frais miroir.

Naïs, blonde nymph with eye of black,
Kneeling beside the river's brink,
Sees there her lips, which, as they drink,
Cool moving waters mirror back.

And thus it ends:

Ah! souris ou du moins pardonne,
Vierge, à ce timide baiser,
Tu ne peux pas le refuser:
C'est une fleur qui te le donne.

Ah, maiden, smile! or graciously
Grant this shy kiss thy pardon, pray:
Take it, thou canst not turn away;
It is a flower that gives it thee.

José-Maria de Heredia, born in 1842 at Santiago de Cuba, was, like Leconte de Lisle, a creole, from the West instead of the East Indies. He was of good Spanish stock on his father's side; his mother was French. Much of his boyhood was spent in France, but at sixteen years of age he returned to Cuba and spent a year at the University of Havana. He then returned to France to study at the École des Chartes. He soon fell under the influence of Leconte de Lisle, of whom he was proud to call himself the 'loved disciple.' He contributed to the *Parnasse contemporain* in 1866, and to its later issues, but it was not until 1893 that he published the collection of 118 sonnets, under the title of *Les Trophées*, which practically represents his life's work in poetry, for though he lived on until 1905, he wrote little more. *Les Trophées* is one of the greatest sonnet sequences in any language. His friend, François Coppée, called it a *Légende des Siècles* in sonnets for, passing in review Greece and Sicily, Rome and the Barbarians, the Middle Ages and the Renaissance, the East and the Tropics, he flashes on us, like a miniaturist working in verse, a brilliant series of word-pictures that make the life and art and atmosphere of each successive phase of culture live before our eyes.

Such labour in art recalls the patient craftsmanship of the early medieval period in the West, and of all ages in the Far East. And the result was well worth the pains expended on the work, for *Les Trophées* is a monument that will endure. The art of compression, without overcrowding, cannot, one feels, be carried further if clearness of statement is to be considered as a virtue; nor within so small a compass can more sonorous music, and greater variety of rhythm and cadence, be achieved. It is often claimed that the last line of every sonnet should clinch it to perfection. All Heredia's do that, but some do more, and while clinching all that has gone before throw open suddenly a vista of what more is to come. Of this no more striking example is to be found than at the end of the second of the two sonnets which follow.

The first describes the flight of Perseus and Andromeda on Pegasus, the winged courser of fable:

(130)

PERSEUS AND ANDROMEDA

The great winged courser rears in silent flight,
Puffing his smoky breath through nostrils wide;
And borne aloft on rustling plumes they glide
Through starry aether and the sapphire night.

They go. Down plunges Afric's wind-lasht bight,
Then Asia . . . desert-land . . . the mists that hide
Lebanon . . . and, behold, the foam-flecked tide,
Mysterious sea, where Helle sank to sight.

The giant wings, each like a mighty sail,
From star to star whirled by the swelling gale,
Make a warm cradle where those lovers twine.

They watch their shadows palpitate on high,
And, past the Waterer and the Ram, divine
Their Constellations dawn on dark blue sky.

The second tells of Antony and Cleopatra:

(131)

ANTONY AND CLEOPATRA

They watched, they twain, where high the terrace stands,
Egypt beneath a brazen sky opprest,
And, cleaving the black Delta, east and west
Nile roll his waters, spoil of rich, fat lands.

The Roman felt within his corslet's bands,
Soldier and slave nursing a child to rest,
The pulsing beat on his triumphant breast
Of passionate limbs clasped in his strenuous hands.

Her pale face yearning through her hair's dark frame,
Whose perfume made him drunken with desire,
She sought him with her lips, and glances bright.

Bent o'er her, the Great Captain all aflame
Saw in her eyes, star-lit with points of fire,
A wide wide sea with galleys in full flight.

A Parnassian of less rank as a poet than the three we have
dealt with deserves mention because of the prominent place he
held in the literary world of the latter part of the nineteenth
century. This was François Coppée, born in Paris in 1842.
He attained immense popularity as a writer of clear, simple, and
musical verse marked by a vein of sentimentality. Favourite

themes of his were the joy of youthful love and the lives of the poor and humble; he became known indeed as *le poète des humbles*. But, author of *Le Luthier de Crémone*, he was also a playwright of distinction, and a successful writer of short stories and of dramatic criticism.

We may turn now to consider the second of the new departures that marked the second half of the nineteenth century. In the *Parnasse contemporain*, as we have already stated, are to be found examples of the work of some of the younger poets who were not satisfied with the definiteness of subject, precision of statement, and classic perfection of form that were the aims of the Parnassians. Sensitive to the haunting charm of mysticism and illusion, of suggestion and allusion as opposed to precise statement, they sought to capture for French poetry some of the inarticulate charm of music, and to enrich the form and content of French literature, too long dominated as they thought by Latin realism, with qualities to be found in English and German poetry, also in German philosophy, and notably in the Wagnerian synthesis of thought, emotion, art, and music. These qualities, it was claimed, are not to be regarded as wholly alien, since the Teutonic and Celtic stocks are among those that make up the mixed ancestry of the French.

But two considerations have to be borne in mind. First, a strict classification of the later poets of the nineteenth century as between Parnassians and Symbolists is only too likely to prove either arbitrary or fanciful. For they were naturally influenced by what attracted them in both developments, so that they may be claimed for either, or partly for the one and partly for the other. Secondly, there are two phases of Symbolism, the first content with the haunting charm of mystery and suggestion in place of precise statement, the effort to reproduce in poetry the actual tone, as it were, of music, and the search for the common element in the joys of the five senses, sight, hearing, smell, taste, and touch; the second, which goes far beyond the first, seeks to discover what Rimbaud in a brilliant phrase hit off as 'the alchemy of the word,' to find a form of expression that is significant without conveying what is ordinarily understood as a meaning, just as certain modernist artists and art-critics claim to be able to recognize 'significant form,' and to soar to a cool and rarefied atmosphere as remote from the life of the ordinary man as the higher mathematics or regions of metaphysical speculation.

Of the first phase the great exemplar is Paul Verlaine, of the second Stéphane Mallarmé. We propose in this chapter to speak of Mallarmé, reserving Verlaine and subsequent poets for the next. In discussing Symbolism and Mallarmé in particular it behoves an Englishman to walk delicately, even if he has Mr. Arthur Symons as his guide. However well versed an Englishman may be in the French literature of the past, handling as it were a library of standard authors, it is impossible for him unless he is actually living like a native in the centre of a new movement abroad to feel any confidence in his judgment on what new author he can safely add to the standard authors already on his shelves. He has neither the knowledge nor the peculiar tact or taste that is drawn from the atmosphere, or comes by inheritance, to serve him. To those who desire to pursue a study of the development of Symbolism under the guidance of a French scholar and critic of immense erudition and, though leaning himself to Symbolism and dominated by Baudelaire, scrupulously fair, may be recommended John Charpentier's *L'Évolution de la Poésie lyrique*, published in 1930. After reading such a book the student will carry away a clear idea of the valuation set by a cultured Frenchman on the French poets of the last hundred years, and thus be in a position to check some of the impressions left after a perusal of the present work.

Charpentier gives, as indeed do others, the genealogy of the Symbolists as follows: accepting Vigny and Baudelaire as ancestors, and Nerval, Gautier, and Banville as godfathers, we may attach them directly to Verlaine, Mallarmé, and Rimbaud, though we must recall that nearly all of them draw the purest element in their inspiration from popular poetry however artless it be. The last clause is a hard saying for an Englishman to appreciate in the absence of more documentation under this head than the author affords. But then he goes on, as if by an afterthought, to invoke the name of Villiers de l'Isle-Adam, a Breton like Chateaubriand, to show how far foreign influences, particularly German, which Charpentier is disposed to belittle as compared with English, contributed to the full development of the Symbolist school. We may well bring Villiers under review before Mallarmé.

Villiers de l'Isle-Adam was born at Saint-Brieuc in 1838, and died in Paris in 1889. He was descended from one of the heroes of the Crusades, a Grand Master of the Knights of Malta. His idealism, coupled with his intense pride of race, encountered a rude shock when faced with the hard materialism of the world; for grinding poverty was his constant attendant in life. Nevertheless his pride was so fantastic as to make him the Don Quixote of the literary Paris of his time, and if he sought expression for his idealism in a few poems and plays he spent his energies as much in the effort to arraign in fierce satire the age in which he lived, its bourgeoisie, its science, its money-making, and what is called 'progress,' all of which he hated. His powerful and independent intellect made him a philosopher as well as an artist; he absorbed the philosophy of Hegel, and not only admired Wagner and his music, but made personal contact with him. He was thus well fitted to be one of the prophets of Symbolism, and the following version of one of his poems, published in 1866 in the *Parnasse contemporain*, certainly indicates the trend in his mind towards Symbolism in its first phase:

(132)

To One Who will not Speak

I 've lost them all, forest and plain,
Fresh April days that once could please.
—Give me thy lips! Their breath again
Will waft a whisper of the trees.

And I have lost the sullen sea,
Billows that echo, waves that weep.
—Say to me aught that pleaseth thee!
'Twill bring low murmurs from the deep.

Restless, with no kind shadow's veil,
Head bowed, beneath the sun my flight!
—O hide me in thy bosom pale!
'Twill bring the calm that comes with night.

But it is on his prose rather than on his verse that his reputation rests. Many of the short stories to be found in his *Contes cruels* show the influence of both Hoffmann, the most famous of German

I

Romantic story-tellers, and of Poe, and though not equal to the very best of either, have merit enough of their own still to live. One of his plays, entitled *La Révolte*, and commended by Wagner, out of politeness we suspect, has been claimed as a forerunner of Ibsen's *Doll's House*, but without any sufficient ground; for it is merely a short and crude satire on the subject of a banker who kills all the idealism in his wife by making a book-keeper of her.

It is *Axël*, the longest and most important of his plays, on which he worked through much of his life, and which was only published after his death, that gives him the high position assigned to him by many in the ranks of Symbolism. The plot of the play is as wildly romantic as anything to be found in the first half of last century, and the mingling of Hegelian philosophy and medieval mysticism that permeates it, with here and there the intrusion of touches of stark realism, make the whole play, and above all its soliloquies, tiring to read. Nevertheless it has to be read if one seeks to form some idea of the full purport of Symbolism, and of the sources from which it may be that such a playwright as Maeterlinck, for instance, derived some of his inspiration.

The real father of Symbolism in its second phase, the master from whom derive the Symbolists of the present century, with the illustrious names of Paul Valéry and Paul Claudel at their head, who are outside the scope of this work, was Mallarmé. When we approach a study of him we find ourselves in a cool atmosphere, academic in its freedom from the reek and the racket, the sensual indulgence, sick headache, disease, and remorse which punctuated the delights of life in the literary and artistic Bohemia of the nineteenth century.

Stéphane Mallarmé, who came of an old civil service family, was born in Paris in 1842. Completing his education at the Lycée de Sens he betook himself to London in order to perfect himself in English, for which his early reading of Poe had given him something like a passion. In later years, indeed, he translated most of Poe's poems into exquisite French prose, as Baudelaire had done before him with his tales. On his return to France he entered on his life's work as professor of English at a series of colleges and *lycées* in different cities, and from 1873 onwards in Paris. Like Lamartine, Vigny, and Laforgue, he married an English wife, and his literary outlook and actual work were greatly influenced by his familiarity with the vague but luminous charm of such a poet as Shelley, as also with contemporaries in both painting and art, notably Tennyson and Rossetti, and the whole circle of the Pre-Raphaelites followed by Burne-Jones and Whistler.

These English influences are not to be exaggerated, for he owed much to Gautier, Baudelaire, and, be it not forgotten, to Banville also, whose poetry he frankly adored. But he himself went far beyond Shelley's 'Where music and moonlight and feeling are one,' or Baudelaire's 'Les parfums, les couleurs et les sons se répondent.' Severely intellectual, he sought in his maturer years to give pure intellectual thought even more prominent expression than music or feeling. No master has yet arisen who has found it possible to represent in language the dry light of modern philosophic thought, some of whose high priests have been driven to take refuge in mathematical signs and formulae. While some of Mallarmé's earlier poems, written under the direct influence of Baudelaire, are quite straightforward and understandable, as, e.g. the fine description of the old man in some sort of Poor Law infirmary in a poem entitled *Les Fenêtres*, and published in the *Parnasse contemporain*, his later poems call for much hard study before their meaning, or the mental impression they seek to convey, can be appreciated. Nor is the task lightened by his taking to the omission of punctuation in the printing of his poems.

Evidently he wrote with great difficulty, obsessed continually by the horror of putting down anything commonplace. His output of verse was small, but what he wrote attracted the young intellects of Paris during the last decades of the nineteenth century, and the charm of his personality and an entrancing gift of conversation kept his hospitable rooms full one night a week with poets, painters, and musicians, Englishmen among them, seeking a new direction at the end of what they possibly considered a worn-out age. In England he is best known as the author of *L'Après-midi d'un Faune*, which inspired the Symbolist composer, Debussy. This poem and *Hérodiade*, a fragment full of lyric grace, which he was endeavouring to complete at the time of his death, are his most considerable pieces.

It cannot be denied that at the end of his career he passed, so far as regards even readers of more than average intelligence, not only through the mysterious to the obscure, but also through the obscure to the unintelligible. So sympathetic a critic as Remy de Gourmont,[1] whom Arthur Symons has happily termed 'that delicate amateur of the curiosities of beauty,' had to say of him: 'Having voluntarily killed in himself the spontaneity of an impressionable being, little by little the gifts of the artist replaced in him the gifts of the poet; he loved words for their possible meaning rather than for their actual meaning, and he combined them in mosaics of an exquisite simplicity.' By 'simplicity' clearly the critic means here nothing but a formal simplicity, and it is the difficulty of avoiding complication that makes it well-nigh impossible to translate into English any of Mallarmé's characteristic verse. There is always the danger of producing a version which, if it is not a mere paraphrase, is more precise and definite than the poet himself intended, and removes as it were the glaze that gives the picture its tone.

The present writer has failed unaided to accomplish the task, and he is deeply indebted to Mr. Arthur Ellis for permission to work on three of the close renderings from his *Stéphane Mallarmé in English Verse*, published by Jonathan Cape, and enriched by a critical study of the poet by Professor Turquet-Milnes, which is as well worth pondering over as her earlier book on the influence of Baudelaire. The examples we give are to be regarded as our joint work. No one need be ashamed of confessing to a difficulty in understanding Mallarmé. Indeed, a man must be suspected of being either a rogue or a prig who claims that he finds him easy. Frenchmen of eminence have struggled with him, e.g. Jules Lemaître, who makes, with many apologies, an attempt in the fifth volume of his *Les Contemporains* to make plain sense of Mallarmé's sonnet on Edgar Allan Poe. The classic example of such attempts is that of the Belgian poet and critic, Albert Mockel, from whom presently we shall draw freely, as others have done.

To begin with we give a specimen of Mallarmé's lighter verse in the form of a rondel, for it has to be borne in mind that, however enigmatic in content, his verse is always exquisitely classic in form; he never runs to seed in free verse. We print Mr. Ellis's version, as Mallarmé did his original, without punctuation:

---

[1] This distinguished scholar and critic, and poet withal, has given in the two series of his *Livre des Masques* the most brilliant, original, penetrating, and yet brief analyses of the authors of his time that can be found.

(133)

RONDEL

An if thou wilt so love we will
But with thy lips and ne'er it tell
This rose's petals never spill
Save but to weave more silent spell

As from a smile for all song's skill
From song such radiance never fell
An if thou wilt so love we will
But with thy lips and ne'er it tell

Amid the ringlets mute and still
A king in purple's pomp as well
As sylph one kiss aflame would quell
The lip its winglet-tip until
An if thou wilt so love we will

Next we give our version of Mallarmé's sonnet on Wagner, which we have selected in illustration of the importance of Wagner's influence as musician, poet, and philosopher on French thought and poetry during the last half of the nineteenth century, notably on his devotees, Baudelaire, Villiers, Verlaine, and Mallarmé himself, all of them, consciously or unconsciously, associated with the Symbolist movement:

(134)

HOMAGE

This silence now is death's fast gathering gloom, whose pall
Blots out the furnished scene with silken fold on fold,
And as the pillar sinks that should the scene uphold
The scene and all thereon to dark extinction fall.

Triumphant play of words that held us once in thrall,
Dead hieroglyphs, wherein they feel, the herd unsoul'd,
With pulse of wing the thrill they 've known so well of old,—
As in some empty chest let us entomb them all!

From out the glorious stress of powers contending flung,
And primal clash of splendour, lo there hath upsprung
Within those courts ordained to be their imaged shrine,

Where soaring trumps of gold on pictured vellum fade,
Wagner, the god, his throne with light divine arrayed,
That even the ink finds speech in breath's sobs sibylline.

The remarkable version of the very difficult last line is due to
Mr. Ellis, but the present writer ventures to offer an alternative
interpretation of that terrible crux, the twelfth line, which runs:

Trompettes tout haut d'or pâmé sur les vélins

It is quite possible according to Mallarmé's syntax, that *d'or*
has nothing to do with *trompettes*, and there may be two clauses
in the line, so that the line may read thus:

Where trumpets blare, and, dimmed, the gilded missals fade

Far-fetched, you may say, but is it too far-fetched for Mallarmé?
And what a picture it gives of the pagan, Teutonic splendour for
which the Nibelungen Ring stands!

Now we come to perhaps the most famous of his poems,
The Swan, which may be regarded as a key-poem, a close
examination of which will show what Symbolism meant to
Mallarmé, and what his disciples have made a positive cult of.
Before we print our version, it is fair to point out that the central
image of the swan in exile did not arise spontaneously in Mallarmé's brain. It has been suggested that the first suggestion
of this elaborate composition was derived from two lines in one
of Gautier's *Fantaisies d'Hiver*:

Dans le bassin des Tuileries
Le cygne est pris en nageant. . . .

From what we know of the Muse's methods of approach to
Mallarmé, this is very likely; but what may be taken as quite
certain is that he must have known well and brooded over
Baudelaire's *Le Cygne*, until he was possessed with the image
there given of the lost swan, and realized how much more he could
himself make of it. However, here is our version of the sonnet:

(135)
The Swan

The virginal to-day, brimming with life and light,
Will 't break for us at last with wing's impassioned blow
Oblivion's rime-bound lake that 's haunted far below
With limpid, glacial tides of yet arrested flight!

A swan remembers still 'tis he of old, as white,
As proud as erst he was, but yields to bleak despair,
For that he did not hail his home of otherwhere
When glittered first the dawn of sterile winter's blight.

With outstretched neck he 'll shake from him the white
        dismay
Space on the bird inflicts who dares space to gainsay,
But not the loathed soil that fetters fast his wing.

A phantom to this haunt by his sheer splendour driven,
To that cold dream of scorn O see him stiffening
Which vests in banishment inane the Swan of heaven.

To realize the full content of this most remarkable poem, single
lines of which thrill one with their beauty, let us turn to the
analysis of it furnished by M. Albert Mockel in his illuminating
Stéphane Mallarmé, un Héros, published in 1899.   He says: 'There
I see appear the image of a swan caught in a frozen lake, that of
a swan struggling to set itself free, that (by allusion) of the bird
that devours space, and that of the white desert of snow.   There
I see the Platonic conception of a soul that has fallen from its
ideal, and aspires thereto as to the fatherland of its birth—the
conception too that genius must be isolated for the very reason
that it implies aristocracy.   The poem suggests to us also the
misery of the poet in exile here — but now he would have
been a prophet—the poet who outlives his time.   And the stoical
resolve: to conquer misfortune by disdain, while holding high
one's head.   In short, we can make of it moral adaptations divers
enough—the following, e.g., which was, I think, in the author's
mind.   The superior man, if he succumbs to the routine of daily
life, is the victim of his own indifference in the past: *pour n'avoir
pas chanté la région où vivre*, because he has not shaken off in
time the prejudices which now strangle him, captive despite his
indignation.'   And Mockel goes on to say: 'From his position
at the centre of these ideas and of these images, the poet envisages
them as a whole; he sees them all at once, yes, and in every
detail.   And when he speaks, it is not to *expose* them to us,
discursively; rather he *recalls* them to us, as if he were spelling

out to us the confidences of an emotion that we have already divined.' No better statement of Mallarmé's attitude has ever been given.

So much for Albert Mockel, an early devotee of the master. During the last few years M. Soula, of the University of Toulouse, where he professes not poetry but physiology, has addressed himself, with a skill and psychological insight that one cannot but admire, to the elucidation of several of Mallarmé's poems which even his admirers have found difficult to paraphrase, and which indeed have been termed his *œuvres hermétiques*. With these he has generally been extraordinarily successful, but in the case of the most difficult of all, the famous *Un Coup de Dés jamais n'abolira le Hasard*, many will be left, despite the professor's exhaustive efforts, with the impression of little more than a typographical curiosity remote from anything which has hitherto passed for poetry, and as hard for most of us to understand as Einstein's Relativity. But some general observations of M. Soula's are worth quoting: 'The sense of poetry in the child creates a language free of any obligation to logic, having no meaning. The sense of poetry in Mallarmé, though subject to the laws of a written theme, aims in no wise at conveying a meaning, at any rate makes no expository concession to the meaning that it might have, if it had one.' He proceeds to claim for the poetry both of the child and of Mallarmé a magical something that transcends sense. This is true, and the quest of this magical something will always have a fascination for poets and critics of an order by no means to be ignored.

That Mallarmé was a great master is attested by the fact that in this twentieth century two poets of such distinction as Paul Valéry and Paul Claudel are proud to call themselves his disciples, though the latter has frankly owned how great is the debt he owes also to that inspired boy, Rimbaud. Mallarmé's goal was the Absolute, but in his pursuit of it he was brought up against a wall through which he could not see. 'When death,' says Charpentier, 'by a spasm of the larynx choked Mallarmé, it did but interrupt a forlorn and desolate silence. Let us not forget the poet's confession to Louis le Cardonnel [1]: "My art is an impasse."' To him may be applied, in all reverence, the

[1] Poet and priest.

fourth and the last stanzas of what is perhaps the finest poem
Gautier ever wrote, *L'Aveugle* :

> Dieu sait quelles chimères noires
> Hantent cet opaque cerveau !
> Et quels illisibles grimoires
> L'idée écrit en ce caveau !
>
> Mais peut-être aux heures funèbres
> Quand la mort souffle le flambeau,
> L'âme habituée aux ténèbres
> Y verra clair dans le tombeau !

CHAPTER IX

VERLAINE AND RIMBAUD, CORBIÈRE

PAUL VERLAINE,[1] the son of a captain of engineers, was born at Metz in 1844. Educated in Paris, he soon renounced the study of law, which was the career chosen for him by his father, and after a few months as clerk in an insurance office he secured through the influence of his father's friends a post in the civil service, where he remained for eight years. He was early conscious of his powers as a poet, and in 1866 appeared his first volume of poems, the *Poèmes saturniens*. From the first he showed a light, feminine touch, a feeling for music, and a freedom of rhythm hitherto rare in French verse which distinguished him from his fellows; and the intimate revelation of his own delicate feelings and impressions, by suggestion rather than conscious effort at self-expression, pointed to the role which he was to play, without any conscious effort on his part, in the development of the first phase of Symbolism.

Unfortunately for him the exciting café-life of the Bohemia of his time broke down what little moral restraint there was in his nature, and he became more and more the slave of absinthe. His marriage in 1870 pulled him up for a short time. But the Franco-German war upset all ordered existence, and after it, as a sympathizer to some extent with the Commune, he played a cowardly and ineffective part. Then, in the person of Arthur Rimbaud, fate met him, and carried him off from his wife. Rimbaud is one of the most remarkable figures in all literary history, and his literary life, short though it was, is so inextricably mixed up with Verlaine's, that we shall take leave to intertwine our accounts of both of them. No more than in the cases of Villon and Baudelaire can we understand or appreciate their poetry, and the wonder of it, unless we know what manner of men they were.

[1] See, among many French lives, M. F. Porché's *Verlaine tel qu'il fut*. Mr. Harold Nicolson's *Paul Verlaine* is far the best account of him in English, and deals fully also with Rimbaud.

Born at Charleville in the Ardennes in 1854, Rimbaud [1] as a child showed extraordinary precocity, not only as a poet, but also as a thinker in fierce revolt against the suppression of individualism which a stern, unbending mother was quite unable to repress. Like Baudelaire he distinguished himself at the age of 14–15 by the excellence of his Latin verse; several of his prize compositions survive, and are of what we should call 'real scholarship standard.' One prank of his at school deserves mention. He served up as his own a translation of the first twenty-six lines of Lucretius, which was adjudged to be worth printing in the Official Bulletin of Douai. But what the young rogue presented was a copy of the first lines of Sully Prudhomme's recently published translation of the first book of Lucretius, here and there touched up and positively improved by himself.

It is doubtful whether even the case of our own Chatterton affords an example of such maturity, such virility at an early age as are to be found in the far from scanty remains left by Rimbaud when he abandoned literature for ever at the age of nineteen. During the Franco-German war, when he was aged sixteen, he wandered afoot through the enemy-infested country between Charleville and Paris and Charleville and Brussels, hiding in thickets and ditches when danger threatened. Here is a version of one of his sonnets written during these wanderings:

(136)

MY VAGABONDAGE

I walked with hands thrust through my pockets' gaping
    seams,
And for an overcoat the ghost of one I wore;
I walked beneath the sky, O Muse, thy servitor;
Ah me! what dreams of love I dreamed, what splendid
    dreams!

My only pair of trews were nearly torn in two.
A little Jack-o'-dreams, I counted, wandering there,
My tale of rhymes beneath the sign of the Great Bear;
My stars in heaven above, they made a soft *frou-frou*.

---

[1] See M. J.-M. Carré's *La Vie aventureuse de J.-A. Rimbaud,* and also his *Lettres de la Vie littéraire d'Arthur Rimbaud.*

And I could hear them well, sitting beside the way,
Those good September nights, while on my brow the spray
Of dew fell down like drops wrung from the vine's strong
    fruit;

While, as I rhymed amid shadows that made one start,
I thought I touched a lyre, when, close beside my heart,
My fingers pluckt a worn elastic-sided boot.

This sonnet was one of the poems chosen by Charles Bonnier to represent the poet in his *Lignée des Poètes français*. But the English version fails to give adequately the Symbolist quality of the second line:

> Mon paletot aussi devenait idéal,

which, with the eighth:

> Mes étoiles au ciel avaient un doux frou-frou,

might have been written either by Mallarmé or Laforgue. Others besides Rimbaud may have thought they sensed the faint pulsing of the stars among the strange noises of a still summer night.

And here is another sonnet, in which with the hand of a master he reveals to us one of the poignant scenes on which his eyes must have lighted again and again in those same wanderings:

(137)

THE SLEEPER IN THE VALE

It is a nest of green, a singing river by,
That fondly flicks the grass with tattered lights that gleam
Silvery; where the sun shines from the hill-top high.
It is a little vale, with bubbling beam on beam.

And there a soldier-boy, mouth open and head bare,
Bathing his languid neck among cool cresses blue,
Sleeps; on the grass outstretched, happed by the humid air,
Pale on his bed of green, where daylight drips like dew.

His feet among the flowers, he sleeps. Wearing a smile
Such as a sick child's face may wear, he dreams awhile.
Nurse him and keep him warm, nature; how cold he is!

His nostrils quiver not, no scents can mar their rest;
He sleeps there in the sun, his hand upon his breast,
At peace.   Two deep red wounds on the right side are his.

Finally here is the version of a poem in which a passionate youth gives expression to some mystical yearning that comes over him when the thought of eternity strikes his teeming brain:

(138)

Eternity

She is found again:
   What?   Eternity!
'Tis the sun that 's gone
   And with it the sea.

Come, sentinel soul,
   Confess the desire
Of night so empty
   And day all afire.

From what men wish for,
   Ambitions all share,
You set yourself free:
   To fly away . . . where?

No more to hope for;
   No *orietur*.
Learning by suffering . . .
   The penalty 's sure.

Soft silken ashes
   Your ardour when past;
Vanishes duty
   Though none calls: 'At last!'

She is found again:
   What?   Eternity!
'Tis the sun that 's gone
   And with it the sea.

Rimbaud was fortunate in winning the enthusiastic admiration of one of his schoolmasters, and of other friends; so that, for all his contempt for Charleville, he did not languish for want of encouragement. In 1871 he sent some of his verses to Verlaine, who hailed him as a genius and invited him to Paris. Thus in the autumn of 1871 the rough, dirty, shock-headed, raw-boned, rude, aggressive youth of seventeen suddenly presented himself at the house of Verlaine's father-in-law, where the poet was at the time uneasily domiciled. Neither Verlaine's family, nor his friends among poets, however Bohemian, could at first stand the dirt and truculence of a boy whose genius they were not as quick as Verlaine to recognize. Remy de Gourmont's account of him is far from kind. Nevertheless, he must soon have won a place for himself. Banville, the good soul, and his mother befriended him; Madame de Banville, indeed, and Verlaine's wife undertook the cleaning of his head—to be rewarded by a poem, *Chercheuses des Poux*, describing the process, so marvellously elevated into the realm of poetry, that even Gourmont confessed he could tolerate it.

There is a well-known portrait-group by Fantin-Latour, where among a group of well-known literary men of the day Rimbaud, a mere youth with a strong not unhandsome head, sits, distrait, at table next to Verlaine, then of a comfortable *bourgeois* appearance, and not the grotesquely ugly amalgam of bald-headed satyr and faun that he became in later years. Rimbaud's *Bateau ivre*, the most considerable of his poems, and by universal consent a veritable masterpiece in the rough, swept Verlaine off his feet; he positively fell in love with his young friend, and finally, in July 1872, he eloped with him to Brussels and London. Naturally enough Verlaine's wife never forgave him, but he had, like Baudelaire, and unlike Rimbaud, an indulgent mother to sponge upon. For a year they lived together, most of the time in London. Here, dated as from Soho, is a version of one of Verlaine's poems of this time, suggested by the dancing groups that used to surround the barrel-organs in the side-streets of the poorer quarters:

(139)

STREETS

Let 's dance a jig!
Full well I loved her pretty eyes,
More brilliant than the starry skies;
I loved them for their rogueries.
Let 's dance a jig!

And little ways, indeed, she had
To drive poor lovers raving mad;
And how, instead, she made them glad!
    Let 's dance a jig!

But 'twas a kiss I loved the best,
The kiss on flower-like lips hard prest
When she had swooned upon my breast.
    Let 's dance a jig!

I call to mind, I call to mind
The hours we spent in converse kind,
What better solace could I find?
    Let 's dance a jig!

They must have worked hard, both endeavouring to make money by giving lessons; Verlaine certainly drank hard. Quarrels between the two poets were not infrequent. Rimbaud grew tired of the older man, alternately irritable and maudlin in his cups. At the end of June 1873 a violent scene took place between them. Verlaine, who had been marketing for the odd *ménage*, brought in some stale fish, and Rimbaud poured over him a flood of sarcasm and abuse. Mad with rage he flung one of the stale herrings in Rimbaud's face and bolted, leaving the latter almost penniless. Now, for the moment, he had had enough of his young friend. In the evening he sailed for Antwerp, and summoned his mother and his wife. His obedient mother answered the appeal, but not his wife. A few days later he telegraphed to Rimbaud to rejoin him at Brussels. He came, but only to demand money to enable him to return to France alone. After a hot discussion Verlaine, beside himself with drink and excitement, took out a revolver he had just bought, and shot Rimbaud in the left wrist. The wound was dressed at a hospital near by, and the wretched mother, who had been present throughout the scene, pressed on Rimbaud the money to see him home to Charleville. On the way to the station Verlaine again threatened the lad, who ran off pursued by Verlaine, brandishing the revolver and screaming. The end of it was Verlaine's sentence to two years' imprisonment.

In prison, while awaiting trial, he wrote an untranslatable poem, quite short, one of the rarest he ever wrote, so musical is

it, so human, so simple and straightforward, and very English
in its rhythm.   He begins by describing what he can see and
hear through the window of his cell, a calm blue sky, against it
gently swaying the topmost branch of a tree, the sweet tones of a
bell from the church tower which he can just glimpse, the plaintive song of some bird perched on the tree.   Then in the last
two verses his heart pours itself out:

> Mon Dieu, mon Dieu, la vie est là,
>   Simple et tranquille.
> Cette paisible rumeur-là
>   Vient de la ville.
>
> — Qu'as-tu fait, ô toi que voilà
>   Pleurant sans cesse,
> Dis, qu'as-tu fait, toi que voilà,
>   De ta jeunesse?

That touch at the end of the first verse, the invasion of his
prison cell by the peaceful murmur of life outside, and the note of
remorse in the last verse, these give us the inimitable Verlaine,
the touch of nature that makes the whole world kin, the under-
tone of poignancy that will endear him for ever to all who love
poetry.   Heine, or, for the matter of that, the Shropshire Lad,
never struck a note so poignant, because so simple and
direct.

During his incarceration at Mons, Verlaine found, for a time,
religion.   The peace and the ordered life there were good for
him, and he had a wise friend in the chaplain.   And yet, while
in a mood conforming to his faith he wrote a series of exquisite
religious poems in prison, in another mood he wrote poems of an
entirely different complexion; so unstable was his character, so
fickle the play of his emotions.   On his release he had difficulty
in finding a publisher, and many of his old associates not un-
naturally fought shy of him.   It was not until five years had
passed that his religious poems were published under the title of
Sagesse.   This was in 1881, when he was thirty-six years old.
Still hoping for a reconciliation with his wife he sent her the
volume, containing a most plaintive and musical appeal to her,
which runs pretty well as follows:

(140)

A Plaintive Song

Hear the soft voice that sings of loss;
  'Tis for your pleasure she makes moan.
  Discreet and delicate in tone,
A runnel quivering over moss.

The voice was known to you (and dear?)
  But for the moment wears a veil,
  Like a lone widow proud though pale,
And proud as hers the words you hear.

And in the long folds of the veil,
  That wavers in the autumn breeze,
  The wondering heart can lose, and seize,
The truth that, star-like, cannot fail.

She says, the voice so well you know,
  That kindliness makes up our life,
  And, as for hate and jealous strife,
In face of death away they go.

She tells too of simplicity,
  And modest hopes that win increase,
  Of golden weddings, and the peace
That cometh by no victory.

Welcome the still persistent voice,
  Pleading an artless lover's case;
  Oh, surely will the soul find grace
That bids a suffering soul rejoice!

A pilgrim soul in sorrow sings,
  Upbraiding not for all her pain;
  Then, since the moral is so plain,
Take the sage counsel that she brings.

It seems to be the idea of some of the poet's devotees that she
ought to have sacrificed herself if sacrifice was called for. But

she, whom he had married as an ingenuous child, was now a grown woman not of a sort to be victimized by him for life, or to sink with him into the abyss. She knew her man, she knew the satyr that was in him, and, to her credit be it said, she was obdurate, and remained obdurate to the end of his life, even divorcing him and carrying off their son. To her courage we owe that wonderful poem of his, which shows how passionately in some fugitive, regenerate mood he still yearned for her:

(141)

A WIDOWER SPEAKS

A group stands out upon the sea.
  What sea? The ocean of my tears!
My eyes the wind stings bitterly
  On this dread night of gloom and fears
Are like two stars fixed on the sea.

I see a woman young, still young,
  Beside the sturdy child she bore,
Tost in a boat wild waves among,
  No mast or sail, no labouring oar . . .
A little boy, a woman young.

Down the wild waves storm-tost they go;
  The child clings to his mother's side;
Where borne, by whom, she doth not know,
  Knows nought, but fondly trusts the tide
And the wild waves down which they go.

Oh, hope in God, poor woman wild,
  Trust in our Father, little one!
The ravin of the waves up-piled
  Heaven tells my heart will soon be done:
'Twill cease, my child, poor woman wild.

Peace to the group upon the sea,
  The restful sea of wholesome tears!
My happy eyes where stars shine free
  On this calm night with no more fears
Are two good angels on the sea.

In 1875, soon after his release from prison, and again in 1877, Verlaine had returned to England, on each occasion to take up duty as French master, first in Lincolnshire, and then in Bournemouth. Two years as teacher in a Roman Catholic school in the Ardennes followed, and on his dismissal from it he was thrown again on the resources of his mother, resources which he had already done so much to dissipate. In Paris he secured some poorly paid work in journalism, enough apparently to keep himself in absinthe. But soon an article he wrote for the organ of a group of younger poets on Rimbaud, revealing his genius to their receptive minds, and another he wrote on himself under the title of *Le Pauvre Lélian*, made him famous, and enabled him to lord it over the crowds that frequented the Café François Premier. Then suddenly, at the age of forty, he abandoned his brightening prospects for a farming venture in the Ardennes country known to him, so, as it would appear, to escape a moral collapse.

His personality and his manners did not endear him to his neighbours. Ugly rumours spread of ill-treatment of his mother. In the spring of 1885 he was charged with assaulting her, and, despite her efforts to secure his acquittal, he was sentenced to a month's imprisonment and a heavy fine, which the unfortunate, distracted mother had herself to pay. With what little money remained to them mother and son returned to Paris. Hardly had Verlaine arrived there when he was attacked by arthritis. He entered a public hospital, and only left it to become a cripple for life. His mother, to whom he had become reconciled, died in January 1886. The proceeds of a small legacy from her, and another from an old aunt, were almost entirely absorbed by the cost of his mother's funeral, and debts claimed by his wife's solicitors.

Ten years of a lamentable existence remained to him, now in hospital, now in some miserable lodging, but happy when enthroned in one café or another of the Latin Quarter, where he was one of the recognized Parisian shows. Everything he wrote fetched some small sum; a publisher was ready to take whatever reached him; scraps and impromptus in prose or verse dashed off on a café table, or in his lodging at the demand of one of his drab, competing mistresses, fetched a few francs each. Respectable interludes in his later years were lecture tours in

Holland, Belgium, and England, when his friends and admirers met him with honour, and dismissed him with money in his pocket. At the very last the *Figaro* opened a subscription for him, and the Government made him a small grant. Thus he was able to keep up a sort of hiccuping gaiety almost to his end, and death when it came to him came grimly enough, but not so grimly as to Baudelaire. He was honoured by what amounted to a public funeral, attended by thousands, with a number of the most conspicuous literary figures in Paris at their head.

Such was the man to whom, as poet, we owe some of the most musical verse ever written in France, and musical in a new way, for more than any of his predecessors he enfranchised French poetry from rules that seemed inevitable so long as logical statement, clear, precise expression, and a strict metrical regularity were regarded as essential to it. He was thus able to enlarge the scope of rhythm, even to introduce rhythms hitherto more familiar to us than to his countrymen, with the result that he captivated English lovers of French poetry, and gave to the new school of Symbolism, which owed him so much in its first phase, a vogue which it could not without him have acquired. Both Verlaine and Gautier wrote poems in expression of their poetic faith. Both poems are admirable works of art, but how different the general message each enshrines! Here are two verses of Verlaine's:

> De la musique avant toute chose,
> Et pour cela préfère l'impair
> Plus vague et plus soluble dans l'air,
> Sans rien en lui qui pèse ou qui pose.
>
> Car nous voulons la Nuance encore,
> Pas la Couleur, rien que la nuance!
> Oh! la nuance seule fiance
> Le rêve au rêve et la flûte au cor!

And here are the first and last verses of Gautier's profession:

> Oui, l'œuvre sort plus belle
> D'une forme au travail
>   Rebelle,
> Vers, marbre, onyx, émail.

> Sculpte, lime, cisèle;
> Que ton rêve flottant
> Se scelle
> Dans le bloc résistant.

But Gautier would have endorsed Verlaine's stern injunction expressed in an emphatic line:

> Prends l'éloquence et tords-lui son cou!

The kindest and truest verdict on Verlaine is that of his countryman, Anatole France: 'Il ne faut pas juger ce poète comme on juge un homme raisonnable. Il a des idées que nous n'avons pas, parce qu'il est à la fois beaucoup plus et beaucoup moins que nous. Il est inconscient, et c'est un poète comme il ne s'en rencontre pas un par siècle. . . . Il est fou, dites-vous; je le crois bien. Et si je doutais qu'il le fût, je déchirerais les pages que je viens d'écrire. Certes, il est fou. Mais prenez garde que ce pauvre insensé a créé un art nouveau et qu'il y a quelque chance qu'on dise un jour de lui ce qu'on dit aujourd'hui de François Villon, auquel il faut bien le comparer: c'était le meilleur poète de son temps.'

But what of Rimbaud? What became of him, that still more astonishing figure? Soon after the tragedy at Brussels he abandoned, at the age of nineteen, literature for ever. And yet in the last few months of literary life that remained to him he wrote a book in what Verlaine called his 'diamond prose,' interspersed with a few poems. A fantastic legend grew up around this book, *A Season in Hell*, because Rimbaud was believed to have destroyed all but two or three copies of it, though, in due course, this was found not to be so. This *Saison en Enfer* is one of the most terrible books ever written; it might have been etched in acid. He pours out his hatred of beauty and morals, his contempt for religion, philosophy, and literature. He places himself outside the pale either of good or evil, reverts, in a word, to his conception of primitive man. As one of the great Symbolists of to-day, Claudel, a sworn admirer of Rimbaud, has said: 'He was a mystic in the savage state.' Savage indeed! A terrible scene in this psychological nightmare of his is one where he pictures himself as *l'Époux infernal* receiving 'the confession of a companion in Hell,' the *vierge folle*, Verlaine. Verlaine it is, singed and scorched as it might be by the Devil himself.

In fierce contempt for himself and his literary triumphs, including his famous sonnet giving the colour and character of all the vowels, which made him the idol of young Symbolists, he speaks thus of his *alchimie du verbe*, alchemy of the word: 'For myself! The history of one of my follies. . . . I invented the colour of the vowels!—A, black; E, white; I, red; O, blue; U, green!—I regulated the shape and the movement of every consonant and, by rhythms that came by instinct, I flattered myself that I had invented a poetic language accessible, one day or another, to all the senses. . . . I put in writing silence and night; I set down the inexpressible. I fixed vertigo fast.' Like Lucifer, Rimbaud will not bow his head, and, if he casts aside all the trammels of civilization that have hitherto bound him, literature among the meanest of them, he will justify his absolutism by a life of violence.

The shock of Verlaine's revolver-shot must have been even more terrible in its moral than in its physical result thus to affect its victim. He was left with a hatred, contempt, and physical loathing for one we may call either his companion or accomplice as we please, a contempt for the circle of poets, poetasters, and their hangers-on whose paltry trade, as it now seemed to him, it had been his boyish ambition to pursue, and a contempt for himself for having indulged what he now regarded as an ignoble ambition. Withal there may have contributed feelings of disappointment and mortification. and even a consciousness that the thread of poetic inspiration had snapped in him never to be re-joined, to drive him not to suicide, but to quite another great adventure in life. Genius was in him, and it must out.

For five years, from 1873 to 1878, he led an astonishing life of vagrancy and desperate hard work, now with his brains, now with his hands. His wanderings led him at one time or another to Belgium, Holland, Germany, Denmark, Sweden, Austria, and Italy; he studied languages and the practical sciences; he worked as a dock-labourer; he joined a circus; he enlisted in the Carlist forces for Spain, but deserted as soon as he got an advance of pay; he enlisted in the Dutch East India force, but again deserted as soon as he reached Java, where he roamed through the jungle for weeks. Ultimately he found a job as interpreter upon an English ship bound for Liverpool, and so, like the proverbial bad penny, was able to turn up again, as after so many of his shorter wanderings, at home.

In 1880, however, he left Europe for good. For a month or two he found work in Cyprus, as overseer during the building of the High Commissioner's summer villa. Then he visited Egypt and various ports on the Red Sea, and at Aden entered the service of a French mercantile firm, by which he was presently sent to break new ground in Abyssinia. There he showed great courage and resource not only as a trader but also as an explorer in most difficult and dangerous country. By 1881 he had got in touch with Menelik, and by his dominant personality and gift for acquiring languages and dialects won the fear and respect of the natives. He established his headquarters at Harrar in the southern highlands, and soon began to make money by the exchange of sugar, rice, cotton, silks, knick-knacks, guns and ammunition for coffee, gums, frankincense, ivory, and gold brought to him from the south.

By February 1891 his prosperity was at its height, and he was on the way to amass a fortune. Then came the cruel end, like Verlaine's, but even more cruel. A painful tumour attacked his right knee; he was carried down in agony on the rough journey to the coast, shipped to Aden, and thence to Marseilles where, on arrival, his leg was at once amputated. He was conveyed to his mother's farm at Charleville; but his condition grew worse, and in August another agonizing but useless journey to Marseilles was forced on him. There, in hospital, he died in November 1891 at the age of thirty-seven. His end was even more charged with torture than those of Baudelaire and Verlaine, but in his, unlike theirs, there was an element of the heroic. For he was more than a pen-man; there was in him some of the spirit of the old Spanish conquistador.

A remarkable poet, born in 1845, a year after Verlaine, was Tristan Corbière, native of Morlaix, the son of a Breton sailor, who became a well-known writer of sea-stories. He deserves to be regarded as one of the outstanding poets of his time, not only for his actual merits, but also because he anticipated in freedom of thought and expression, in poignancy of feeling and contempt of the poetry of his time, and indeed of most things human and divine, including himself, the young Rimbaud, who, early notorious, was to become a real portent. As a boy Corbière inherited his father's passionate love of the sea, and in his delicate youth he was encouraged to seek health and hardihood in daring adventures afloat. He was a fine, handsome fellow, a love of art and poetry developed in him, and the lure of Paris drew him to the capital. He published in 1873, the year of his arrival in Paris, a volume of poems entitled *Les Amours jaunes*, but hardly a copy was sold; he remained almost unknown, and two years of semi-starvation and wild night-life finished him. In 1875 he crept back to Morlaix to die.

His fame was not made until 1884, when someone drew Verlaine's attention to the *Amours jaunes*; he recognized at once their remarkable quality, and enshrined Corbière as the first figure in his *Poètes maudits*. There was nothing impeccable, says Verlaine, about his rhyme or his prosody, but he asks: what are the impeccables? 'Wood, wood, and wood again. Corbière was made, like a common man, of flesh and bone. His verse lives and laughs, weeps but little, is full of irony, but fuller still of *blague*. Bitter, besides, and salt as his beloved ocean, no soothing nurse as sometimes happens with his turbulent friend, but tossing like it rays of sun, of moon, and stars in the phosphorescence of a billow and the angry waves.'

The epitaph he wrote for himself is one of the outstanding efforts of its kind, sardonic to the highest degree. But the longest and the greatest of his poems is *La Rapsode foraine et le Pardon de Sainte-Anne*, inspired by homely memories of his native Brittany, stark in its material setting, coarse here and there, steeped in the Breton atmosphere, devotion, superstition, and misery. It reminds one, curiously, of Heine's *Wallfahrt nach Kevlaar*; so like is it, and yet so unlike, that one who knows both can hardly think of one without thinking of the other. Corbière's is the stronger poem and, indeed, we make bold, though not *français de race*, to suggest that no stronger poem than his *Pardon* has been written in France since its publication in 1873 in the *Amours jaunes*.

Strength no one can deny him, and here and there in his writings comes a touch of linguistic alchemy; but now and again a coarse, even gross intrusion has shocked French critics, more indulgent to others not less guilty. Laforgue indignantly, and rightly, repudiated the suggestion that he was a disciple of Corbière, but the charge made him less than just in what he said of the other's art: 'Nothing of poetry, nothing of verse, scarcely anything of literature.' Remy de Gourmont, though alive to his faults, is generous in his estimate of his genius. And Verlaine's enthusiastic account of him was the one that caught the ear of the young poets of the eighties of last century, and made him a power among them. Of his unique gift of telling phrase, where the nail is hit fairly on the head, take this single couplet from his *Un Riche en Bretagne*:

> Lui, n'est pas pauvre: il est Un Pauvre, et s'en contente,
> C'est un petit rentier, moins l'ennui de la rente.

Some idea of his daring and originality may be gleaned from the following version, omitting one coarse stanza, of his fine poem, *La Fin*, which was probably inspired by Hugo's *Oceano Nox*, and in which is, as Verlaine said, all the sea:

(142)

THE END

Ah, well! these sailor-men, deck-hands and captains all,
In their great ocean's depths swallowed for evermore,
Who started free of care for some far port of call,
Are dead—just as they stood when they put forth from
    shore. . . .

Ay, that is but their job; there in their boots they died!
Alive in their oil-skins, kept warm by rum inside. . . .
—*Dead*. . . . Thank you! For sea-legs, the Noseless One
    has none;
Let her lie down by you: for she's your own good wife. . . .
—*They!* cut off bodily by wave as by a knife!
    Or in some squall fordone. . . .

A squall. . . . Can this be death? The while with lowered
    sails
We battle with the flood! That we call *labouring*. . . .
A leaden blow from the sea, then the tall masts like flails
Flogging the billows flat,—that we call *foundering*.

—Foundering,—stress the word. Your *death* is something
    pale,
A trifle there on board, under the pounding gale. . . .

A trifle there, before the sailor's majesty,
At bay with bitter smile.—Come then, yield pride of place!
That phantom old and thin, Death, shows an altered face:
      The Sea! . . .

Drowned?—Ah, not so! To drown is a fresh-water death.
—Sunk, body, soul, and gear! An oath on their last breath,
Even the cabin-boy's, defiance in his eye!
Spitting a half-chewed quid upon the foaming must,
Drinking the last long draught of salt without disgust. . . .
    —As when they drained the rum-cask dry.—

    .   .   .   .   .

No churchyard rats they fear, no six-foot grave have they:
Their enemy's the shark! And the brave sailor's soul
In no potato-plot oozes in slow decay,
    But breathes where billows roll. . . .

    .   .   .   .   .

Hark, hark! What torment there, what bellowing in the
    skies! . . .
Their anniversary, how often it comes round!
O poet, keep for thee thy lamentable cries;
—For them storm's trumpet-blasts their *De Profundis* sound.

. . . Let them roll on for aye through spaces infinite!
    Roll on livid and bare,
No nails, no coffin-planks, no lid, no candles lit. . . .
—So let them then roll on, landsmen at last got *there*! . . .

With the burden of this poem compare the following striking passage from the Saga of Aloysius Horn. Says the old adventurer, speaking of death: 'Such a child of Nature as he must surely prefer the country. Aye; I'd rather fall in with him on the sea itself than between four walls, even if it were the Pope's antechamber. 'Twould be a natural spot to every man that is not *homo stultus*. Some getaway for the soul is necessary, and that can only be found in the open, whether air *or* water. There's no denying that Death does his best for the sailors. There's less than half of them die in their beds. The undertakers'll never encourage a man to go to sea. The sea's the sailor's home, and it's there he'll be found on the ultimate day.'

When we are confronted with the *poètes maudits*, Baudelaire, Verlaine, Rimbaud, and Corbière, we find ourselves far from the austere Miltonic view of poetry and the poet: 'He who would not be frustrate of his hope to write well hereafter in laudable things ought himself to be a true poem.' And we miss in them that love of Nature, that close companionship with her, which has done so much to keep English poetry clean. But taking them as they are, who can deny their quality as poets? If we rate none of these moderns as high as Villon, we may well recall what Belloc eloquently said of him, and recognize the truth of it as applied to others: 'Of his greatness nothing can be said; it is like the greatness of all the chief poets, a thing too individual to seize in words. It is superior and external to the man. Genius of that astounding kind has all the qualities of an extraneous thing. A man is not answerable for it. It is nothing to his salvation; it is little even to his general character. It has been known to come and go, to be put on and off like a garment, to be lent by Heaven and taken away, a capricious gift.'

CHAPTER X

We have dealt with all who may be called the epoch-making poets of the nineteenth century, but there still remains a number of delightful poets whom it is impossible to omit from a review of French poetry during the latter portion of the period, all of them emancipated from the first frenzy of Romanticism, most of them from the objectivism of the Parnassians, though not all from the stateliness of their diction, and most of them, again, touched by the influence of Symbolism. We may take first Auguste Angellier, born at Dunkirk in 1848, educated at Boulogne and in Paris, a poet greatly admired by many in France who keep clear of schools of poetry, do not trouble themselves over fashion in verse, and are content to understand without effort what they read. He made himself a great English scholar, held many high professorial chairs in English, and has placed us under a special debt for the elaborate study he published of the life and works of Robert Burns.

It is difficult to recall any English work on a French author so monumental as this of Angellier on Burns. Very attractive and extraordinarily skilful are the numerous translations in that rhythmic, poetical prose of which the French have peculiarly the gift, whereby he introduces to his countrymen the unique qualities which give Burns his greatness and his charm; even the very idiom of the Scottish dialect seems to be at times wafted across the Channel. And his appreciation of the differences between the attitude to nature of Burns and the chief English poets of last century makes his work a masterpiece of critical exposition. Indeed, the whole of it is punctuated with critical *aperçus* of the highest quality. He was no precocious genius such as Rimbaud, Corbière, and Laforgue, for he published no volume of verse before 1896. He shows no trace of the influence either of Baudelaire or the Symbolists, but there is a quality in his sonnets, his lyrics, and his most important work, *Dans la Lumière*

252

antique, with its grave thoughts on love and life and nature, which appeals to English readers whose tastes have been formed by following the main currents of English and French verse.

In Albert Samain we have a rarer, a more exquisite poet, born in 1858 at Lille of a family of tradespeople. His early life was a hard struggle, for he had to fend for his education as best he could while helping to keep his family, but in 1883 he earned enough to live, and leisure for poetry, as a clerk in the civil service. In 1893 he published his charming volume, *Au Jardin de l'Infante*, and he was at once hailed as a new poet. Unfortunately early privations had been too much for him, his health broke down, and he died of consumption in the summer of 1900. His *Chariot d'Or*, his next volume of poems, was published posthumously, and a sylvan tragedy he wrote, *Polyphème*, was successfully produced, also after his death. He was a delicate and beautiful poet, tinged with Symbolism, but such Symbolism as is spontaneously English, and he struck a quiet, plaintive note that haunts the ear. Familiar is that glorious line of his which begins his poem *L'Infante*:

Mon âme est une infante en robe de parade.

Of these two poets, Angellier and Samain, we must content ourselves with offering one short poem by each. The first is the rendering of one of Angellier's short lyrics:

(143)

THE OLD BRIDGE

On the old bridge with mosses green,
And scarred with lichen's ruddy stain,
Two lovers, whispering softly, lean:
    It was we twain!

He, turning tenderly to her,
Spoke of the love and loyalty
That set his faithful heart astir:
    And it was I!

She pale, uncertain standing near,
Caught trembling, not with fear, his vow,
But seemed a far-off voice to hear:
    And it was thou!

On the old bridge, unchanged e'en now,
Two lovers keep their tryst again;
He tells, and she believes, his vow:
No more we twain!

And the following is a version of one of Samain's characteristic
notes of brooding melancholy:

(144)

AUTUMN

Down the park avenues, long vistas veiled in mist,
Where, as they bid adieu, tall trees with rustling whist
Let fall their leaves of gold amid the solitude,
Beneath a sky grown pale as if from lassitude,
We 'll walk, if so thou wilt, till eve with footsteps slow,
To nurse in our wan hearts the summer ere it go.
We 'll pace the alley-ways, haunt of the quiet Muse;
And that strange acrid scent that comes from plants we bruise,
The silence and the charm, so full of languid grace,
That lovely autumn gives, autumn the sad of face,
And springs from pleasances, and woods and waters still,
And from bare garden-plots, with marble nymphs a-chill,
Will softly steep our souls, while yet there 's light above,
Like an old handkerchief still redolent of love.

A very remarkable poet, born in 1856, was Jean Moréas. He
was a Greek by birth, son of a distinguished Athenian lawyer,
and his real name was no less a one than Papadiamantopoulos.
From early childhood he had steeped himself in French poetry;
he was given a cosmopolitan education, travelled much, and in
1872, when he was sixteen years old, visited Paris, and only left
it with the determination to return. His father had destined
him for the magistracy, and he did presently go back to Paris to
pursue in desultory fashion the study of the law; but to write
poetry, and French poetry, was his fixed resolve. In early
manhood he definitely settled in Paris, changed his name to the
picturesque one by which he is now known, and became as
near a Frenchman as an alien could.

His earliest volume was published in 1884, and shows markedly
the influence of both Baudelaire and Verlaine, though his

meticulous study of the French language from the Pleiad downwards enabled him to assimilate a vocabulary and a range of expression so varied as to enable him to strike a new and original note. Two years later he joined the Symbolists, who were then asserting themselves, and published in the *Figaro* in 1886 a manifesto in defence of the aesthetic of the new school, the most powerful and the most definite that had yet appeared. The very definiteness of this manifesto proved its Achilles' heel. He met with criticism severe enough from some of the great ones of the day, and Anatole France happily termed him 'the Ronsard of Symbolism.' But he found an enthusiastic band of supporters, and his handsome head was able to lord it at the Café d'Harcourt, as did Verlaine at the Café François Premier.

Gradually, however, he tired of what seemed to him the ineffectiveness of the devotees of Symbolism in the use of language to convey their message, if so definite a term may be permitted, and he withdrew from them to establish his own *École romane*. The substantial idea that led on to his final development, when he cut himself adrift from all coteries and cliques, had doubtless lain dormant all his life in one whose blood was Greek. 'My instinct,' he says, 'was not slow to warn me that one must get back to the true classicism, and so to a versification traditionally the most severe.' The ultimate outcome was a series of short poems called *Les Stances*, written in verse austere but perfect in form, choice in word and phrase, ample in harmony and lofty in thought. Here we may give versions of two of these *Stances*, prefixing to them a version of an earlier poem written while he was still under the influence of Symbolism, and indulging himself in a modified form of free verse:

(145)

INVESTITURE

We 'll skirt the railings of the park,
The hour when the Great Bear declines;
And, as I 'll have it, you shall wear
Among the tresses of your hair
The lily-flower called asphodel.

Your eyes will gaze into my eyes,
The hour when the Great Bear declines:

And in my eyes you 'll see the hue
Worn by the flower called asphodel.

Your eyes will gaze into my eyes,
And all your being thrill again,
As thrilled of old the mythic rock,
So goes the tale, beneath a shock,
Touched by the flower called asphodel.

(146)

THE ROSES THAT I LOVED

The roses that I loved fade day by day;
    Pale, yellow buds show not through all the year;
Zephyrs have breathed too long; the cruel sway
    Of northern blasts congeals the waters drear.

Why shouldst thou, Joy, swell out in tones so grand?
    Dost thou not know how foolish it must be
To come, uncalled, and pluck beneath my hand
    A vibrant chord vowed to Melancholy?

(147)

I HAUNT THE TOMBS

I haunt the tombs, heard only of the dead,
    Unto the end myself mine enemy.
Thankless my pride; for crows my grain is spread;
    I dig and sow, but fill no granary.

I shall not grieve.   Let the chill north wind blow,
    And shame and scorn and malice work their will;
I touch thee, O Apollo's lyre, and lo,
    Thy tones again, more cunning, purer still!

Remy de Gourmont is no warmer in his praise of Moréas
than was Anatole France.   But another critic of note in his day,
Émile Faguet, said of his last development: 'This is one of the
most extraordinary manifestations of "the poetic soul" that we
have seen for years and years,' and we have Francis Jammes's

testimony for the fact that Charles Guérin could not speak of him without emotion. He died at the height of his fame in 1910, a rare example of a writer of one race, without tie of language, ancestry, or family with another, becoming accepted in that other as one of its classic authors. Two Americans, Stuart Merrill and Vielé-Griffin, delightful poets both of them, were admitted to circles of the elect in Moréas's lifetime, but we have to quote the case of Joseph Conrad in England to find an exact parallel to Jean Moréas.

We pass to a very different poet, Jules Laforgue, a Frenchman of the French, born at Montevideo in 1860. His father, born at Tarbes, was a teacher who had emigrated to pursue his calling abroad; on his mother's side he was of Breton origin. When eight years old the boy was brought to France, and sent to school at Tarbes, though he completed his education in Paris. On leaving the Lycée Fontanes, at the age of nineteen, he got in touch at once with various literary coteries, and secured the insertion of his verses in more than one periodical of the time. Among the odd jobs that came his way and earned him a pittance was that of research work in the libraries for M. Charles Ephrussi, director of the *Gazette des Beaux Arts*. A letter of his, dated 1881, to his sister at Tarbes, gives a most touching picture of his poverty at this time. The bulk of the letter is printed in the *Poètes d'aujourd'hui*, and it should be read; for the affection it breathes, the suffering it reveals, the fine feeling running through it all, with now and then a wry smile irradiating the gloom, make the man live for us as a charming personality whom one cannot but love and admire.

Soon his prospects brightened. Through the influence of M. Ephrussi and Paul Bourget, who took a kindly interest in the struggling young poet, he obtained the post of reader to the Empress Augusta, wife of the Emperor William. At Berlin he lived for nearly five years, writing verses, visiting museums and galleries, and falling in love with a graceful English girl. He returned to Paris in 1886, married his Miss Lee at the end of the year, and the young couple set up house with high hopes of happiness and success. But the seeds of consumption were in him, and in July 1887 he was finally struck down by the disease and died within a month. His devoted young wife contracted the disease in nursing him, and in eight months' time she too was dead.

K

Though he died so young Laforgue left enough verse to stamp him as one of the most highly gifted of all the poets of his time. There may be traces of the influence of Baudelaire, Verlaine, Corbière, or Rimbaud in his work, but they do not hit the eye. There is certainly some of the verbal alchemy that Rimbaud played with and that Mallarmé took up as a serious pursuit. But he had greater variety than any of those whom we have named, and was far too gifted, too rich in veins of his own to be dependent upon others. His trend was to Symbolism, and he was in the way to bring to it qualities of intellect equal to those of any of its masters and, one of the rarest of all gifts, a combination of cold irony and warm humanity which would have made of it a more compelling force than it has been.

No one can read that astonishing but not easy volume of his prose, *Les Moralités légendaires*, fantastic variations on such themes as Hamlet, Salome, Lohengrin, Pan and Syrinx, without feeling that Remy de Gourmont's almost dazzling estimate of him is justified. Of the *Moralités* he says: 'Here is literature entirely remade and unexpected, disconcerting and giving the curious and, above all, rare sensation that one has never read anything like it; a bunch of grapes with all its bloom on it in the morning light, but with strange reflexes and an appearance as if every single grape had been frozen within by a breath of ironic wind come from beyond the pole.' Like Keats, Laforgue has left the insoluble problem of what one so richly dowered might have become, had he but lived.

We can hardly hope to give in English a fair representation of the work of one so individual, so serious, so whimsical, and so certain of himself in either mood. Here, however, are attempts to render two of his best-known poems:

(148)

ANOTHER BOOK!

Another book; oh, home I 'd be
Far from this vulgar, cockney herd,
Far from hand-shake and dun's sharp word,
Far from all phraseology!

Another of my pierrots dead;
A chronic orphan, so he died;

He had a heart well dandified,
The loony with his funny head.

The gods are gone, but bores endure;
Ah, things grow worse from day to day;
I 've done my time, I slink away
Towards the Inclusive Sinecure.

(149)

CERTAIN ENNUIS

A sunset of Cosmogonies!
Ah! Life, how day-to-day and slow. . . .
That I was dull—a genius, no!
Is truest of my memories. . . .

But there are things I would disclose,
To startle us upon our way,
And, once for all, the truth display
That shows the self through every pose.

We fain would drain the Silence dry,
Set exiled conversation free;
But no, these ladies can't agree
On questions of priority.

They sulk there, looking capable;
While men, outside, explain they 're sure
By what confused aesthetic lure
These creatures are adorable.

Just now, one of them called to me;
A ring of hers she bade me trace
Lost (where, ah, where in some vague place?)
A souvenir of Love, said she!

These creatures are adorable!

But how is it possible to translate such a poem as the one he himself entitles *L'Impossible,* whose first verse runs something like this:

> Yes, I may die to-night! Sun, wind, and pouring rain
> Will scatter everywhere marrow, sinews, and heart.
> The last word said, I 'll dream no more, nor wake again.
> Among the stars? Ah, no: there I 'll have had no part.

his *Song of the Little Consumptive,* beginning thus:

> C'est d'un' maladie de cœur
> Qu'est mort', m'a dit l'docteur,
> Tir-lan-laire!
> Ma pauv' mère;
> Et que j'irai là-bas,
> Fair' dodo z'avec elle.
> J'entends mon cœur qui bat,
> C'est maman qui m'appelle!

or his *Complaint of Forgetfulness of the Dead,* whose first verse follows?

COMPLAINTE
DE L'OUBLI DES MORTS

> Mesdames et Messieurs,
> Vous dont la mère est morte,
> C'est le bon fossoyeux
> Qui gratte à votre porte.
> Les morts
> C'est sous terre;
> Ça n'en sort
> Guère.

And there are others more difficult, but of a difficulty other than what confronts one in dealing with Symbolism of the second phase. Who can fail to detect in the two latter poems from which we quote the accent of the folk, the native, non-classical note struck by Béranger?

More orthodox than Laforgue, and less original, is Henri de Régnier, born in 1864, described by the editors of the *Poètes d'aujourd'hui* as 'the first and most celebrated' of the poets of his time. But he has had a long life, and it is probable that, in advanced literary circles at least, his pre-eminence has passed to Paul Valéry or Paul Claudel—though this eclipse, like most others indeed, may be temporary. With Henri de Régnier we are definitely out of Bohemia, and enter the circle of the rich and well-born, out of which came so many French poets of the past.

Born at Honfleur, he came on his father's side of an old and distinguished Picard family, and on his mother's side of equally distinguished Burgundian stock. He was educated in Paris, qualified as a barrister, and passed an examination for the Foreign Office. He was thus spared the miseries and privations through which so many of the most distinguished French poets of last century had to make their painful way, e.g. Nerval, Villiers, Verlaine (by his own fault), Rimbaud, Corbière, Samain, and Laforgue. Hence too the absence of complexes that troubled several of them: the spirit of fierce revolt, the itch to shock their more respectable neighbours, a passionate self-indulgence amid the sensual delights offered them so freely in Paris, then the earthly paradise of the civilized world, all of which did at the same time force them to work, when they did work, at white heat, and stimulate every precious grain of genius that was in them.

In the early years of a serene career Régnier was apparently uncertain whether his line was to be that of novelist or poet. Happily he chose the latter, though in the course of a long literary life he interspersed his successive volumes of poetry with several novels and collections of sketches and tales. He was soon admitted to the then circle of the elect, the Parnassians, and had close relations with Leconte de Lisle, Sully Prudhomme, and Heredia, one of whose daughters he married; later he was attracted by Mallarmé, and moved rather to his side. He was among those young enthusiasts who did much to help Verlaine, and to cheer with their homage the failing, fading figure of Villiers.

Though he is ranked by some as a Symbolist, he has little of the Mallarmesque about him; he has none of the intellectual asceticism or chill perfection, and none of the occasional indulgence in verbal alchemy that marks the intellectual who aims at passing into the second phase of Symbolism. He is never unintelligible, but clearer even than Verlaine, and when he breaks into free verse it is fine rhythmical stuff with the beat of the Alexandrine running through it. He is a great and a sumptuous artist in verse, and his stately grandiloquence entitles us to suggest that if he is to be called a Symbolist at all, and if Moréas was, as Anatole France said, the Ronsard of Symbolism, Régnier is its Parnassian. There is subtlety in him withal; and we offer as an example of his art the following version of a dignified, highly decorated piece of his:

(150)

INVOCATION

That night should give delight, the roses all in bloom
  From perfumed garden-plot right to the grey house-wall
Should breathe through casements wide soft odours in the
      room,
  Where we in scented dusk sit dumb an interval.

That night should be superb, the dreaming countryside
  Should lie all hushed and dim beneath a starry sky,
And we should hear, we twain, the thoughts in us we hide
  By voices that speak not repeated silently.

That night should be superb, delightful, and divine,
  The silence and the flowers are not enough by far,
Nor garden at nightfall, round which the roses twine,
  Nor yet the sleeping earth whose peace no footsteps mar.

For thou, fair Love, alone, if moved benignantly,
  On hearts by passion bound canst shed a kindly gleam
And to these perfect hours impart in secrecy
  Beauty that graver yet, profounder, is supreme.

We come now to the last two of the French poets whose work this book will attempt to illustrate, Charles Guérin and Francis Jammes. Charles Guérin, born in 1873, came of a prosperous industrial family at Lunéville in Lorraine, and was educated at Nancy. He visited Paris from time to time, and travelled a good deal, but for most of his short life (he died in 1907) was faithful

to his native province, and it is fortunate that one so delicate, so
sensitive, was never sucked into the whirlpool of the capital.
His volume of poems, *Le Cœur solitaire*, published in 1898, gave
him instantly a great reputation, and he was welcomed as a
contributor to the *Revue des Deux Mondes*. He attached himself
to no particular school, but reveals a talent which, though in
the main tradition of French poetry, and reminding one now
and again both of Sully Prudhomme and Samain, was yet a
personal one, for he allowed himself considerable freedom in
rhyme and rhythm, quite ruthlessly at times ignoring the caesura,
and he blended thought and emotion in a fashion quite his own.
One notable gift of his was the writing of unforgettable first
lines, e.g. :

Je voudrais être un homme ; or rien dans mes poèmes
Ne répond au sanglot de la détresse humaine.

O mon ami, mon vieil ami, mon seul ami !

Nuit d'ombre, nuit tragique, ô nuit désespérée !

O Jammes, ta maison ressemble à ton visage.

Entrerai-je, ce soir, Seigneur, dans ta maison ?

Bien que mort à la foi qui m'assurait de Dieu.

The most famous of his early poems is his tribute to the
poet of the Pyrenean foothills, that charming, simple character,
Francis Jammes. Tributes from one poet to another are common
enough, but none has ever been written in which the personality
of the subject has been so intimately, so tenderly, so affectionately,
and so admiringly revealed. Nay, more is given : the atmosphere
he breathes, the house he lives in, his garden, the sights and
sounds of the countryside around him, and the poignant happiness of friend at one with friend. Always given to self-analysis,
self-criticism, confession of his weaknesses, his sins, and his
doubts, and prayer for forgiveness, Guérin passed through a
religious crisis which left him not unscathed. His self-analysis
became more severe, he catechized his doubts, but yet failed to

attain peace. In his last volume, *L'Homme intérieur*, will be found this terrible outburst of despair:

(151)

Ah, What a Dreadful Noise is Life

Ah, what a dreadful noise is life!
　To sleep were better, underground
Where jostling the grave-digger's pick
　The pebbles yield a griding sound.

The sun has earned my utter hate;
　It satiates me still to see
His shining face, day in, day out,
　Of my despair make mockery.

Ah, could I then, at last, recline
　On the one bed no others crowd,
And in the dark, attentive hear,
　The busy worms unsew my shroud!

When heart and brain, my conscious self,
　The path of dissolution tread,
Midmost the eternal silence, I
　Would be but one among the dead!

There, too, will be found this plaintive expression of his sense of loss when there flashes on him the realization of a simplicity that once was his, and is gone beyond recovery:

(152)

My Verse of Old

Men say that in my verse of old
　There ran a vein of poetry,
An all-ingenuous child that seemed
　An azure streamlet lisping by.

I let her steal from out my heart
　And follow nature's kindly lead;
She only had her dewy prime
　And careless ease her cause to plead.

> I took no trouble then at all,
>   Strove not towards perfect form to soar;
> Why could I not remain, as then,
>   A simple poet, and no more?

Francis Jammes, for whom Charles Guérin had so whole-hearted an admiration, is almost unique among French poets, and his simplicity, his neglect of form, and downright carelessness at times in rhyme, metre, and rhythm, are not without attraction to English readers accustomed to the freedom of their own language. He was born of good *bourgeois* stock at Tournay in the Hautes-Pyrénées in 1868, and was educated at Pau and Bordeaux. On his father's death he settled with his mother at Orthez, and there has dwelt ever since.

For some years he earned his living as clerk in a notary's office, but from early youth lived his real life in his poems. The little pamphlets, locally printed, in which his first essays appeared, created much puzzlement and equal curiosity when they were first circulated in Paris. It was not easy to decide whether he was to be taken seriously. His originality and *naïveté* gradually gained him appreciative friends, and when his first collected volume, *De l'Angelus de l'Aube à l'Angelus du Soir*, was published in 1898, his future as an accepted poet was assured, and he has drawn to him more real affection and devoted admiration for his personality, as well as for his work, than perhaps any other poet of his time. In what contrast to the manifestoes and the café clamour of Paris in the nineteenth century is the humble preface to this collection of his poems written between 1888 and 1898:

'My God, you have called me among men. Here am I. I suffer and I love. I have spoken with the voice which you have given me. I have written with the words which you have taught my father and my mother, who have handed them on to me. I pass on the roadway like a loaded ass which children mock, and which hangs its head. I will go where you would have me go, and when you would. The Angelus is ringing.

'FRANCIS JAMMES.'

A new note this in French poetry! His joy in the simple things, and the life of the countryside, his deep sympathy with

* K

the humble and poor, his delicate spiritual sense and unfailing charity, are but the outpourings of his spirit. In his love for domestic animals and the creatures of the farm there is an intimacy of feeling which can only be found elsewhere, perhaps, in Robert Burns; and Thomas Hardy's poem, *The Oxen*, might have been written by him.

His most imposing poem is *Les Géorgiques chrétiens*, a rural epic in seven cantos, written in rudely rhymed, detached Alexandrine couplets, which, it must be confessed, becomes monotonous at times, and in which he introduces somewhat awkwardly digressions, such as a disquisition on his *Art poétique*. But there are delightful Virgilian touches in it, and the figure of Burns again suggests itself, the Burns of the *Cotter's Saturday Night*. As is only natural with one whose art is akin to improvisation he may in a long life have written too much (his work includes excellent prose as well as verse), and probably his first volume, *De l'Angelus de l'Aube à l'Angelus du Soir*, contains the fairest representation of his manner, thought, and proper charm. He has always stoutly asserted his independence, but one of his contemporaries has imposed himself on him to a certain degree. Much as Jammes loved and admired the work of Moréas, Régnier, Samain, Vielé-Griffin, for Mallarmé his feeling was nothing short of reverence. Thus here and there a breath of Symbolism, and even, occasionally, a gust of it, sweeps through a poem, as in that on a *Poet's Life and Death*, which closes his first volume.

Early in the nineties of last century Francis Jammes must have encountered Hubert Crackanthorpe, that talented young Englishman, who died too soon, but whom none who ever met him in his short life will have forgotten. He dedicated one of his poems to him. Another English contact he had. The late poet laureate, Robert Bridges, knew at least his work, for he dedicated a sonnet to him, sufficiently remarkable as a tribute from one of the most sophisticated of poets to perhaps the least sophisticated of our time. The octet of the sonnet runs as follows:

'Tis April again in my garden, again the grey stone-wall
   Is prankt with yellow alyssum and lilac aubrey cresses;
   Half-hidden the mavis caroleth in the tassely birchen
      tresses
And awhile on the sunny air a cuckoo tuneth his call:

Now cometh to mind a singer whom country joys enthral,
  Francis Jammes, so grippeth him Nature in her caresses
  She hath steeped his throat in the honey'd air of her
    wildernesses
With beauty that countervails the Lutetian therewithal.

As examples of his work we offer, first, the version of a lyric
written in 1882:

(153)

I Know how Poor thy Lot . . .

I know how poor thy lot:
Thou dressest modestly.
Sweet one, I offer thee
My grief: 'tis all I 've got.

Thou 'rt fairer to my sight
Than others, and more sweet
Thy breath: when our hands meet
I 'm lost in wild delight.

Thy poverty is why
Thou art so good and kind;
Kisses and roses twined
Thou biddest me supply.

For thou art child-like yet:
And books have taught thee this,
And tales of faerie bliss,
One needs a hedge quickset,

Roses and mulberries,
Wild flowers in the fields,
While every poet yields
Hymns to the branching trees.

I know how poor thy lot:
Thou dressest modestly.
Sweet one, I offer thee
My grief: 'tis all I 've got.

Next we take a poem that is as characteristic of Jammes as
anything he ever wrote, a poem that thrills one to read, it is so
quaint, so original, so finely touched with sentiment. The

rhyming of the poem is so irregular that we have ventured, in order to give as literal a rendering of it as possible, to present it in blank verse:

(154)

PRAYER THAT ONE MAY GO TO PARADISE WITH THE ASSES

When I must go to you, my God, permit
That this be when the countryside *en fête*
Is full of dust. I would, as here below,
So there in Paradise, with stars at noon,
Select a road to walk on that I like.
I 'll take my staff, and on the broad highway
I 'll go, and to my friends, the asses, say:
I 'm Francis Jammes, and bound for Paradise,
For in the Good God's counrty is no hell.
I 'll bid them: Come, sweet friends of the blue sky,
You poor, dear beasts who with a flick of ear
Shake off the flat horse-flies, and blows, and bees. . . .

Let me appear before you mid these beasts
I love so much because they hang the head
Meekly, and, stopping, join their little feet
So daintily, you can but pity them.
I 'll come, and lead thousands of long grey ears,
Asses that bore great baskets on their flanks,
And those that drew the travelling showmen's carts,
Or vans of feather-dusters and tin cans,
Or held round water-vessels on their backs,
She-asses, big like wine-skins, stumbling on,
And those on which good folk put little drawers
By reason of the blue and festering sores
The stubborn flies make, settling circle-wise.
My God, grant that with them I come to you;
Grant that in peace angels may lead us on
To bosky streams where cherries dangle down
Smooth as the laughing cheeks of little girls,
And grant that, bending in this home of souls
Over your sacred pools, I 'm like the ass
Who mirrors his meek, humble poverty
In the limpidity of love eterne.

Finally we give a version of his short prayer for a dying child, a subject that has drawn the best from many a great poet; but none has ever written lines more poignant, more highly charged with all that gives a poem the note of passionate prayer:

(155)

PRAYER THAT A CHILD DIE NOT

O God, preserve for them this little child,
As Thou dost shield a plant in tempest wild.
Why is it, when Thou hear'st the mother weep,
Thou dost not let him straightway fall on sleep,
Even here and now, as something that must be?
But let him live! When comes Thy Feast-day he
    Will fling Thee roses next gay summer-tide.

Thou art too kind. My God, 'tis not Thy touch
That rosy cheeks with death's blue stain will smutch,
Unless Thou hast fair places where to set,
Within the light, mothers and children met?
And why not here? Ah, since the hour is nigh,
Remember, God, this dying infant by,
    Thou livest always at Thy Mother's side.

A review of French poetry up to the end of the nineteenth century might well end with this note on the work of a poet so grateful to old-fashioned English feeling as Francis Jammes. No Belgian poets of last century have been represented in the collection, distinguished as many of them have been, Verhaeren, Maeterlinck, Grégoire le Roy and others. And yet the writer must, for personal reasons, beg leave to add by way of epilogue the version of one Belgian poem of exquisite simplicity and comforting appeal. He had a dear friend who, while still young, was struck down by a mortal disease. He showed a courage that was sublime. One day the writer, with his thoughts full of his friend's case, came across Grégoire le Roy's *La Dernière Visiteuse*. He set to work at once in the effort to make an English rendering of it; and the work gave him consolation, for he could not but feel that to one who had lived a life so benign death, when it came, must come as a friend.

(156)

The Last Visitor

As came the well-beloved she 'll come to me;
She will not knock, to pay a formal call;
She 'll make no noise, nor any stir at all;
In short, she 'll come like one I 'm used to see.

And, just as if the dear one knew my case,
She will not start to meet my gaze distraught,
Face worn and pale, but full of tender thought
Beside my bed, silent, she 'll take her place.

And I, who long have known that she would come
One day, and grown accustomed, shall not be
Afraid to see her come, but cheerfully
Will let her hold in hers my fingers numb.

Then she will speak, sweetly and very low,
Of things long past, of a dear countryside,
A house that walls and trees mysterious hide,
And tragic love whose memory haunts me so.

And mother-like, as my own mother did,
When of the blessed Lord she 's talked awhile,
'Wilt thou not sleep?' she 'll ask with loving smile,
And I, content, will close each dreaming lid.

APPENDIX

French Text of Authors and Anonymous Poems quoted.

(1)

CANTILÈNE DE SAINTE EULALIE

Text as in Studer and Walters's *Historical French Reader*.

Buona pulcella fut Eulalia,
Bel auret corps, bellezour anima.
Voldrent la veintre li Deo inimi,
Voldrent la faire diaule servir.
Elle non eskoltet les mals conselliers,
Qu'elle Deo raneiet, chi maent sus en ciel,
Ne por or ned argent ne paramenz,
Por manatce regiel ne preiement.
Niule cose non la pouret omque pleier,
La polle sempre non amast lo Deo menestier.
E por o fut presentede Maximiien,
Chi rex eret a cels dis soure pagiens.
Il li enortet, dont lei nonque chielt,
Qued elle fuiet lo nom christiien.
Ell' ent adunet lo suon element;
Melz sostendreiet les empedementz
Qu'elle perdesse sa virginitét:
Por os furet morte a grand honestét.
Enz enl fou la getterent, com arde tost.
Elle colpes non auret, por o nos coist.
A czo nos voldret concreidre li rex pagiens;
Ade un spede li roveret tolir lo chief.
La domnizelle celle kose non contredist;
Volt lo seule lazsier, si ruovet Krist.
In figure de colomb volat a ciel.
Tuit oram que por nos degnet preier,
Qued awisset de nos Christus mercit
Post la mort, et a lui nos laist venir
Par sowe clementia.

AUTEUR INCONNU.

271

(2)

MORT DE ROLAND
Bédier's version of the Oxford text.

CLXXI

Ço sent Rollant la veüe ad perdue,
Met sei sur piez, quanqu'il poet s'esvertuet;
En sun visage sa culur ad perdue.
Dedevant lui ad une perre brune.
.X. colps i fiert par doel e par rancune.
Cruist li acers, ne freint ne ne s'esgruignet.
'E!' dist li quens, 'seinte Marie, aiue!
E! Durendal, bone, si mare fustes!
Quant jo me perd, de vos n'en ai mais cure.
Tantes batailles en camp en ai vencues
E tantes teres larges escumbatues,
Que Carles tient, ki la barbe ad canue!
Ne vos ait hume ki pur altre fuiet!
Mult bon vassal vos ad lung tens tenue.
Jamais n'ert tel en France la solue.'

CLXXIV

Ço sent Rollant que la mort le tresprent,
Devers la teste sur le quer li descent.
Desuz un pin i est alet curant,
Sur l'erbe verte s'i est culchet adenz,
Desuz lui met s'espee e l'olifan,
Turnat sa teste vers la paiene gent:
Pur ço l'at fait que il voelt veirement
Que Carles diet e trestute sa gent,
Li gentilz quens, qu'il fut mort cunquerant.
Cleimet sa culpe e menut e suvent,
Pur ses pecchez Deu en puroffrid lo guant.

CLXXVI

Li quens Rollant se jut desuz un pin,
Envers Espaigne en ad turnet sun vis.
De plusurs choses a remembrer li prist,

De tantes teres cum li bers cunquist,
De dulce France, des humes de sun lign,
De Carlemagne, sun seignor, kil nurrit;
Ne poet muer n'en plurt e ne suspirt.
Mais lui meïsme ne volt mettre en ubli,
Cleimet sa culpe, si priet Deu mercit:
'Veire Patene, ki unkes ne mentis,
Seint Lazaron de mort resurrexis
E Daniel des leons guaresis,
Guaris de mei l'anme de tuz perilz,
Pur les pecchez que en ma vie fis!'
Sun destre guant a Deu en puroffrit.
Seint Gabriel de sa main l'ad pris.
Desur sun braz teneit le chef enclin;
Juntes ses mains est alet a sa fin.
Deus tramist sun angle Cherubin
E seint Michel del Peril;
Ensembl' od els sent Gabriel i vint.
L'anme del cunte portent en pareïs.

AUTEUR INCONNU.

(3)

MORT D'AUDE

CCLXVIII

Li empereres est repairet d'Espaigne
E vient a Ais, al meillor sied de France;
Muntet el palais, est venut en la sale.
As li Alde venue, une bele damisele.
Ço dist al rei: 'O est Rollant le catanie,
Ki me jurat cume sa per a prendre?'
Carles en ad e dulor e pesance,
Pluret des oilz, tiret sa barbe blance:
'Soer, cher' amie, d'hume mort me demandes.
Jo t'en durai mult esforcet eschange:
Ço est Loewis, mielz ne sai a parler;
Il est mes filz e si tendrat mes marches.'
Alde respunt: 'Cest mot mei est estrange.

Ne place Deu ne ses seinz ne ses angles
Après Rollant que jo vive remaigne!'
Pert la culor, chet as piez Carlemagne,
Sempres est morte.   Deus ait mercit de l'anme!
Franceis barons en plurent e si la pleignent.

CCLXIX

Alde la bel' est a sa fin alee.
Quidet li reis que el se seit pasmee;
Pited en ad, sin pluret l'emperere;
Prent la as mains, si l'en ad relevee.
Desur les espalles ad la teste clinee.
Quant Carles veit que morte l'ad truvee,
Quatre cuntesses sempres i ad mandees:
A un muster de nuneins est portee;
La noit la guaitent entresqu'a l'ajurnee.
Lunc un alter belement l'enterrerent.
Mult grant honur i ad li reis dunee.

AUTEUR INCONNU.

(4)

CHANSON

Text as in Studer and Walters's *Historical French Reader*.

Par amors ferai chançon
Pour la tres bele loër:
Tout me sui mis a bandon
En li servir et amer.
Mult m'a fet maus endurer,
Sin atent le guerredon,
N'onques n'en oi se mal non.
He las! si l'ai ge tant amee:
  Dame, il fust mes bien seson
  Que vostre amor me fust donee.

Onques riens mes cuers n'ama
Fors la bele pour qui chant,
Ne ja mes riens n'amera,
Ce sai je bien, autretant.

Ma douce dame vaillant,
Bien sai, quant il vous plera,
En pou d'eure me sera
Ma grant paine guerredonnee.
   Dame, qui je aim pieça,
   Et quant m'iert vostre amor donee?

Dame ou touz biens sont assis,
Une riens dire vos vueil:
Se vous estes de haut pris,
Por Dieu! gardez vous d'orgueil,
Et soiez de bel acueil
Et as grans et as petiz;
Vos ne serez pas touz dis
Ensi requise et demandee.
   Dame, ou j'ai tout mon cuer mis,
   Et quant m'iert vostre amor donee?

Se vous vivez longuement,
Dame, il ert oncore un tens
Ou viellece vous atent.
Lors diroiz a toutes genz:
'Lasse, je fui de mal sens
Que n'amai en mon jouvent
Ou requise iere souvent;
Or sui de chascun refusee.'
   Dame, que j'aim loiaument,
   Et quant m'iert vostre amor donee?

Chançon, va tost sanz delai
A la tres bele au vis cler,
Et si li di de par moi
Que je muir por bien amer,
Car je ne puis plus durer
A la dolor que je trai;
Ne ja respas n'en avrai,
Puis que ma mort tant li agree.
   Dame, que j'aim de cuer vrai,
   Et quant m'iert vostre amor donee?

RICHART DE SEMILLI.

(5)

CAROLE

Bartsch, *Chrestomathie provençale.*

A l'entrada del tems clar, eya,
Per joja recomençar, eya,
E per jelos irritar, eya,
Vol la regina mostrar
Qu'el' es si amoroza.
Alavi', alavia, jelos,
Laissaz nos, laissaz nos
Ballar entre nos, entre nos.

El' a fait per tot mandar, eya,
Non sia jusqu'à la mar, eya,
Piucela ni bachalar, eya,
Que tuit non venguan dançar
En la dansa jojoza.

Lo reis i ven d'autra part, eya,
Per la dansa destorbar, eya,
Que el es en cremetar, eya,
Que om no li vɔill' emblar
La regin' aurilloza.

Mais per nient lo vol far, eya,
Qu'ela n'a sonh de viellart, eya,
Mais d'un leugier bachalar, eya,
Qui ben sapcha solaçar
La domna savoroza.

Qui donc la vezes dançar, eya,
E son gent cors deportar, eya,
Ben pogra dir de vertat, eya,
Qu'el mont non aja sa par
La regina jojoza.
Alavi', alavia, jelos,
Laissaz nos, laissaz nos
Ballar entre nos, entre nos.

AUTEUR INCONNU.

(6)

REVERDIE

Bartsch, *Altfranzösische Romanzen und Pastourellen.*

En mai au douz tens nouvel,
Que raverdissent prael,
Oi soz un arbroisel
Chanter le rosignolet.
  Saderala don!
  Tant fet bon
  Dormir lez le buissonet.

Si com g'estoie pensis,
Lez le buissonet m'assis:
Un petit m'i endormi
Au douz chant de l'oiselet.
  Saderala don!
  Tant fet bon
  Dormir lez le buissonet.

Au resveillier que je fis
A l'oisel criai merci
Q'il me doint joie de li:
S'en serai plus jolivet.
  Saderala don!
  Tant fet bon
  Dormir lez le buissonet.

Et quant je fui sus levez,
Si conmenz a citoler
Et fis l'oiselet chanter
Devant moi el praelet.
  Saderala don!
  Tant fet bon
  Dormir lez le buissonet.

Li rosignolez disoit:
Par un pou qu'il n'enrajoit

Du grant duel que il avoit,
Que vilains l'avoit oi.
     Saderala don!
     Tant fet bon
     Dormir lez le buissonet.

AUTEUR INCONNU.

(7)

ALBA

Bartsch, *Chrestomathie provençale*.

En un vergier sotz folha d'albespi
Tenc la dompna son amic costa si,
Tro la gaita crida que l'alba vi.
Oi deus, oi deus, de l'alba! tan tost ve.

'Plagues a deu ja la noitz non falhis,
Nil meus amics lonh de mi nos partis,
Ni la gaita jorn ni alba no vis!
Oi deus, oi deus, de l'alba! tan tost ve.

'Bels dous amics, baizem nos eu e vos
Aval els pratz on chantols auzellos;
Tot o fassam en despeit del gilos:
Oi deus, oi deus, de l'alba! tan tost ve.

'Bels dous amics, fassam un joc novel,
Ins el jardi on chanton li auzel,
Tro la gaita toque son caramel.
Oi deus, oi deus, de l'alba! tan tost ve.

'Per la douss' aura qu'es venguda de lai,
Del meu amic bel e cortes e gai,
Del seu alen ai begut un dous rai:
Oi deus, oi deus, de l'alba! tan tost ve.'

La dompna es agradans e plazens,
Per sa beutat la gardon mantas gens,
Et a son cor en amor lejalmens.
Oi deus, oi deus, de l'alba! tan tost ve.

AUTEUR INCONNU.

(8)

BELE EREMBOR

Oxford Book of French Verse.

Quant vient en mai que l'on dit as lons jors,
Que Franc de France repairent de roi cort,
Reynauz repaire devant el premier front,
Si s'en passa lez lo meis Erembor,
Ainz n'en dengna le chief drecier amont.
      E! Reynaut amis!

Bele Erembors à la fenestre au jor
Sor ses genolz tient paile de color.
Voit Frans de France qui repairent de cort
E voit Reynaut devant el premier front.
En haut parole, si a dit sa raison:
      'E! Reynaut amis!

'Amis Reynaut, j'ai jà véu cel jor
Se passisoiz selon mon pere tor,
Dolans fussiez se ne parlasse à vos.
— Jel mesfaïstes, fille d'empereor.
Autrui amastes, si obliastes nos.'
      — E! Reynaut amis!

'Sire Reynaut, je m'en escondirai;
A cent puceles sor sainz vos jurerai,
A trente dames que avuec moi menrai,
C'oncques nul home fors vostre cors n'amai.
Prennez l'emmende, et je vous baiserai.
      E! Reynaut amis!'

Li cuens Reynauz en monta lo degré.
Gros par espaules, greles par lo baudré,
Blonde ot lo poil menu recercelé,
En nule terre n'ot si biau bacheler.
Voit l'Erembors, si comence à plorer.
      E! Reynaut amis!

Li cuens Reynauz est montez en la tor,
Si s'est asis en un lit point à flors,

. . . .

Dejoste lui se siet bele Erembors;
Lors recomencent lor premieres amors.
E! Reynaut amis!

AUTEUR INCONNU.

(9)

BELE DOETTE

Bartsch, *Altfranzösische Romanzen und Pastourellen.*

Bele Doette as fenestres se siet,
Lit en un livre, mais au cuer ne l'en tient:
De son ami Doon li ressovient,
Q'en autres terres est alez tornoier
    E or en ai dol.

Uns escuiers as degrez de la sale
Est dessenduz, s'est destrosse sa male.
Bele Doette les degrez en avale,
Ne cuide pas oir novele male.
    E or en ai dol.

Bele Doette tantost li demanda
'Ou est mes sires que ne vi tel pieca?'
Cil ot tel duel que de pitie plora.
Bele Doette maintenant se pasma.
    E or en ai dol.

Bele Doette s'est en estant drecie,
Voit l'escuier, vers lui s'est adrecie;
En son cuer est dolante et correcie
Por son seignor dont ele ne voit mie.
    E or en ai dol.

Bele Doette li prist a demander
'Ou est mes sires cui je doi tant amer?'
'En non deu, dame, nel vos quier mais celer:
Morz est mes sires, ocis fu au joster.'
    E or en ai dol.

Bele Doette a pris son duel a faire.
'Tant mar i fustes, cuens Do, frans debonaire.
Por vostre amor vestirai je la haire,
Ne sor mon cors n'avra pelice vaire.
    E or en aidol:
Por vos devenrai nonne en l'eglyse saint Pol.

Por vos ferai une abbaie tele,
Qant iert li jors que la feste iert nomeie,
Se nus i vient qui ait s'amor fauseie,
Ia del mostier ne savera l'entreie.
    E or en ai dol:
Por vos devenrai nonne a l'eglise saint Pol.

Bele Doette prist s'abaiie a faire,
Qui mout est grande et ades sera maire:
Toz cels et celes vodra dedanz atraire
Qui por amor sevent peine et mal traire.
    E or en ai dol:
Por vos devenrai nonne a l'eglise saint Pol.

Auteur inconnu.

(10)

PASTOURELLE

Oxford Book of French Verse.

De Saint-Quentin a Cambrai
Chevalchoie l'autre jour.
Lés un buisson esgardai,
Touse i vi de bel atour:
    La colour
Ot fresche com rose en mai.
    De cuer gai
Chantant la trovai
Ceste chansonnette:
'En non Deu, j'ai bel ami
    Cointe et joli,
Tant soie je brunete.

Vers la pastoure tornai,
Quant la vi en son destour,
Hautement la saluai,
Et dis 'Deus vos doinst bon jour
     Et honour!
Celle ke ci trové ai,
     Sans delai
Ses amis serai.'
Dont dist la doucete:
'En non Deu, j'ai bel ami
     Cointe et joli,
Tant soie je brunete.'

Delés li seoir alai,
Et li priai de s'amour.
Celle dist: 'Je n'amerai
Vos ne autrui par nul tour,
     Sens pastour
Robin, ke fiancié l'ai.
     Joie en ai,
Si en chanterai
Ceste chansonnete:
'En non Deu, j'ai bel ami,
     Cointe et joli,
Tant soie je brunete.'

                        AUTEUR INCONNU.

(11)

AUCASSIN ET NICOLETTE

Text mainly as in Mario Roques's edition, with Gaston Paris's suggested filling
of gap in star-song, lines 6–9.

Nicole est en prison mise
En une canbre vautie
Ki faite est par grant devisse,
Panturee a miramie.
A la fenestre marbrine
La s'apoia la mescine:
Ele avoit blonde la crigne,

Et bien faite la sorcille,
La face clere et traitice;
Ainc plus bele ne veïstes.
Esgarda par le gaudine
Et vit la rose espanie
Et les oisax qui se crient,
Dont se clama orphenine:
'Ai mi! lasse moi, caitive!
Por coi sui en prison misse?
Aucassins, damoisiax sire,
Ja sui jou li vostre amie
Et vos ne me haés mie;
Por vos sui en prison misse
En ceste canbre vautie
U je trai molt male vie;
Mais, par Diu le fil Marie,
Longement n'i serai mie,
    Se jel puis fare.'

AUTEUR INCONNU.

(12)

'Estoilete, je te voi,
Que la lune trait a soi;
Nicolete est aveuc toi,
M'amïete o le blont poil.
Je quid Dix le veut avoir
Por la lumiere de soir
Que par li plus bele soit.
Bele amie, or ne te voi.
Pleüst ore au sovrain roi,
Que que fust du recaoir,
Que fuisse lassus o toi:
Je te baiseroie estroit.
Se j'estoie fix a roi,
S'afferriés vos bien a moi,
    Suer douce amie.'

AUTEUR INCONNU.

(13)

Quant or entent Aucassins
De s'amie o le cler vis
Qu'ele est venue el païs,
Or fu liés, ainc ne fu si.
Aveuc la dame s'est mis,
Dusqu'a l'ostel ne prist fin ;
En le cambre se sont mis,
La u Nicholete sist.
Quant ele voit son ami,
Or fu lie, ainc ne fu si ;
Contre lui en piés sali.
Quant or le voit Aucassins,
Andex ses bras li tendi,
Doucement le recoulli,
Les eus li baisse et le vis.
La nuit le laissent ensi,
Tresqu'au demain par matin
Que l'espousa Aucassins :
Dame de Biaucaire en fist ;
Puis vesquirent il mains dis
Et menerent lor delis.
Or a sa joie Aucassins
Et Nicholete autresi :
No cantefable prent fin,
    N'en sai plus dire.

AUTEUR INCONNU.

(14)

COMPLAINTE

Text as given by J. Bédier : line 4 of verse iii is a happy invention of G. Paris
to fill a gap.

Sire cuens, j'ai vïelé
Devant vous en vostre ostel,
Si ne m'avez riens doné
Ne mes gages aquité :
    C'est vilanie !

Foi que doi sainte Marie,
Ensi ne vous sieurré mie.
M'aumosniere est mal garnie
Et ma boursse mal farsie.

Sire cuens, car conmandez
De moi vostre volenté.
Sire, s'il vous vient a gré,
Un biau don car me donez
        Par courtoisie !
Talent ai, n'en doutez mie,
De raler a ma mesnie :
Quant g'i vois boursse esgarnie,
Ma fame ne me rit mie.

Ainz me dit : 'Sire Engelé,
En quel terre avez esté,
Qui n'avez riens conquesté ?
Trop vos estes deporté
        Aval la ville.
Vez com vostre male plie !
Ele est bien de vent farsie !
Honiz soit qui a envie
D'estre en vostre compaignie !'

Quant je vieng a mon ostel
Et ma fame a regardé
Derrier moi le sac enflé,
Et je qui sui bien paré
        De robe grise,
Sachiez qu'ele a tost jus mise
La conoille sanz faintise ;
Ele me rit par franchise,
Ses deus braz au col me plie.

Ma fame va destrousser
Ma male sanz demorer ;
Mon garçon va abuvrer
Mon cheval et conreer ;

Ma pucele va tuer
Deus chapons pour deporter
  A la jansse alie;
Ma fille m'aporte un pigne
En sa main par cortoisie.
Lors sui de mon ostel sire
A mult grant joie sanz ire
Plus que nuls ne porroit dire.

COLIN MUSET (XIIIème siècle).

(15)

DES BÉGUINES

Text as in Jubinal's edition, 1839.

En riens que Béguine die
N'entendeiz tuit se bien non;
Tot est de religion
Quanque hon trueve en sa vie:
Sa parole est prophécie;
S'ele rit, c'est compaignie;
S'el' pleure, dévocion;
S'ele dort, ele est ravie;
S'el' songe, c'est vision;
S'ele ment, non créeiz mie.

Se Béguine se marie,
C'est sa conversacions:
Ces veulz, sa prophécions
N'est pas à toute sa vie.
Cest an pleure et cest an prie,
Et cest an panrra baron.
Or est Marthe, or est Marie;
Or se garde, or se marie,
Mais n'en dites se bien non:
Li Rois no sofferroit mie.

RUTEBEUF (XIIIème siècle).

(16)

C'EST DE LA POVRETEI RUTEBEUF

Text as in Jubinal's edition, 1839.

Je ne sai par où je coumance
Tant ai de matyère abondance
Por parleir de ma povretei.
Por Dieu vos pri, frans Rois de France,
Que me doneiz queilque chevance :
Si fereiz trop grant charitei.
J'ai vescu de l'autrui chatei
Que hon m'a créu et prestei ;
Or me faut chacuns de créance,
C'om me seit povre et endetei :
Vos r'aveiz hors dou reigne estei
Où toute avoie m'atendance.

Entre chier tens et ma mainie,
Qui n'est malade ne fainie,
Ne m'ont laissié deniers ne gage.
Gent truis d'escondire arainie
Et de doneir mal enseignie :
Dou sien gardeir est chacuns sages.
Mors me r'a fait de granz damages,
Et vos, boens Rois, en ii voiages
M'aveiz bone gent esloignié,
Et li lointainz pélerinages
De Tunes qui est leuz sauvages,
Et la male gent renoié.

Granz Rois, c'il avient qu'à vos faille,
A touz ai-ge failli sanz faille :
Vivres me faut et est failliz.
N'uns ne me tent, n'uns ne me baille
Je touz de froit, de fain baaille,
Dont je suis mors et maubailliz.
Je suis sanz coutes et sans liz ;
N'a si povre juqu'à Senliz.

Sire, si ne sai quel part aille :
Mes costeiz connoit le pailliz,
Et liz de paille n'est pas liz,
Et en mon lit n'a fors la paille.

Sire, je vos fais asavoir
Je n'ai de quoi do pain avoir :
A Paris sui entre touz biens,
Et n'i a nul qui i soit miens.
Pou i voi et si i preig pou ;
Il m'i souvient plus de saint Pou
Qu'il ne fait de nul autre apôtre.
Bien sai *Pater*, ne sai qu'est *notre*,
Que li chiers tenz m'a tot ostei,
Qu'il m'a si vuidié mon hostei
Que li *Credo* m'est dévéeiz,
Et je n'ai plus que vos véeiz.

RUTEBEUF.

(17)

BLANCHE COM LYS

Blanche com lys, plus que rose vermeille,
Resplendissant com rubis d'Oriant,
En remirant vo biauté non pareille,
Blanche com lys, plus que rose vermeille,
Suy si ravis que mes cuers toudis veille
Afin que serve à loy de fin amant,
Blanche com lys, plus que rose vermeille,
Resplendissant com rubis d'Oriant.

GUILLAUME DE MACHAULT (*c.* 1290–1377).

(18)

MON COER S'ESBAT

Mon coer s'esbat en oudourant la rose
Et s'esjoïst en regardant ma dame :
Trop mieulz me vault l'une que l'autre chose,
Mon coer s'esbat en oudourant la rose.

L'oudour m'est bon, mès dou regart je n'ose
Juer trop fort, je le vous jur par m'ame;
Mon coer s'esbat en oudourant la rose
Et s'esjoïst en regardant ma dame.

JEAN FROISSART (1337–c. 1410).

(19)

REVIENS, AMY

Reviens, amy, trop longue est ta demeure;
Elle me fait avoir peine et doulour.
Mon esperit te demande à toute heure.
Reviens, amy; trop longue est ta demeure;

Car il n'est nul, fors toi, qui me sequeure,
Ne secourra, jusques à ton retour.
Reviens, amy, trop longue est ta demeure;
Elle me fait avoir peine et doulour.

JEAN FROISSART.

(20)

ON DOIT ALLER GUERROIER EN ESTÉ

On doit aller guerroier en esté
Et ou printemps, que l'erbette point drue,
Que li chaut vient et yver se remue:
Les chevaulx ont lors tous biens a plenté,
Et le logeis de mal en bien se mue.
L'en doit aler guerroier en esté
Et ou printemps, que l'erbette point drue:
Neige et gresil sont en terre bouté,
On oit chanter chascun parmi la rue;
Arme toy lors, tiens toy l'iver en mue.
L'en doit aler guerroier en esté,
Et ou printemps, que l'erbette point drue,
Que li chaut vient et yver se remue.

EUSTACE DESCHAMPS (c. 1340–1410).

L

(21)

RONDEL

Venez a mon jubilé :
J'ay passé la cinquantaine :

Tout mon bon temps est alé :
Venez a mon jubilé.

Mon corps est tout affolé.
Adieu ! de moy vous souviengne !
Venez a mon jubilé :
J'ay passé la cinquantaine.

EUSTACE DESCHAMPS.

(22)

RIANS VAIRS YEUX

Rians vairs yeulx, qui mon cuer avez pris
Par vos regars pleins de laz amoureux,
A vous me rens, si me tiens eüreux
D'estre par vous si doulcement surpris.

On ne pourroit sommer le très grant pris
De vos grans biens qui tant sont savoureux,
Rians vairs yeulx, qui mon cuer avez pris.

Tant estes doulz, plaisant et bien apris,
Qu'ou monde n'a homme si doulereux
Que, s'un regart en avoit doulcereux,
Que tantost n'eust par vous confort repris,
Rians vairs yeulx, qui mon cuer avez pris.

CHRISTINE DE PISAN (c. 1363–c. 1430).

(23)

SE SOUVENT VAIS AU MOUSTIER

Se souvent vais au moustier
C'est tout pour veoir la belle
Fresche com rose nouvelle.

D'en parler n'est nul mestier,
Pour quoy fait on tel nouvelle
Se souvent vais au moustier?

Il n'est voye ne sentier
Ou je voise que pour elle;
Folz est qui fol m'en appelle
Se souvent vais au moustier.

CHRISTINE DE PISAN.

(24)

DURE CHOSE EST A SOUSTENIR

Dure chose est a soustenir
Quant cuer pleure et la bouche chante.

Et de faire dueil se tenir,
Dure chose est a soustenir.

Faire le fault qui soustenir
Veult honneur qui mesdisans hante,
Dure chose est a soustenir.

CHRISTINE DE PISAN.

(25)

O FOLZ DES FOLZ

O folz des folz, et les folz mortelz hommes,
Qui vous fiez tant és biens de fortune!
En celle terre, és pays où nous sommes,
Y avez vous de chose propre aucune?
Vous n'y avez chose vostre nes-une
Fors les beaulx dons de grace et de nature.
Se Fortune donc, par case d'adventure,
Vous toult les biens que vostre vous tenez,
Tort ne vous fait, ainçois vous fait droicture,
Car vous n'aviez riens quand vous fustes nez.

Ne laissez plus le dormir à grans sommes
En vostre lict, par nuit obscure et brune,
Pour acquester richesses a grans sommes,
Ne convoitez choses dessoubs la lune,
Ne de Paris jusques à Pampelune,
Fors ce qui fault, sans plus, à creature
Pour recouvrer sa simple nourriture;
Suffise vous d'estre bien renommez,
Et d'emporter bon loz en sepulture:
Car vous n'aviez riens quand vous fustes nez.

Les joyeulx fruicts des arbres, et les pommes,
Au temps que fut toute chose commune,
Le beau miel, les glandes et les gommes
Souffisoient bien à chascun et chascune.
Et pour ce fut sans noise et sans rancune.
Soyez contens des chaulx et des froidures,
Et me prenez Fortune doulce et seure.
Pour vos pertes, griesve dueil n'en menez,
Fors à raison, à point, et à mesure,
Car vous n'aviez riens quand vous fustes nez.

Se fortune vous fait aucune injure,
C'est de son droit, jà ne l'en reprenez,
Et perdissiez jusques à la vesture:
Car vous n'aviez riens quand vous fustes nez.

Alain Chartier (c. 1386–1449).

(26)

COMPLAINTE NORMANDE

Text as in Gaston Paris's *Chansons du P. XVᵉᵐᵉ siècle*, 1873.

Hellas! Olivier Bachelin,
Orron nous plus de voz nouvelles?
Vous ont les Anglois mis a fin?

Vous soulliés gaiment chanter
Et demener jouyeuse vie,

Et la blanche livrée porter
Par le pais de Normandie.

Jusqu'a saint Gille en Coutantin
En une compaignie tresbelle
Oncques ne vy tel pellerin.

Les Anglois ont fait desraison
Aux compaignons du val de Vire:
Vous n'orez plus dire chançon
A ceulx qui souloyent bien dire.

Nous prirons Dieu de bon cueur fin
Et la doulce vierge Marie
Qu'il doynt aux Anglois male fin.

AUTEUR INCONNU.

(27)

COMPLAINTE POPULAIRE

'Gentilz gallans de France,
Qui en la guerre allez,
Je vous prie qu'il vous plaise
Mon amy saluer.'

'Comment le saluroye
Quant point ne le congnois?'
'Il est bon a congnoistre,
Il est de blanc armé;

'Il porte la croix blanche,
Les esperons dorez,
Et au bout de sa lance
Ung fer d'argent doré.'

'Ne plorez plus, la belle,
Car il est trespassé:
Il est mort en Bretaigne,
Les Bretons l'ont tué.

'J'ay veu faire sa fousse
L'orée d'ung vert pré,
Et veu chanter sa messe
A quatre cordelliers.'

AUTEUR INCONNU.

(28)

DES LETTRES

Text as in Gaston Paris's *Chansons du XVème siècle.*

Et j'ay eu des lettres vrayment
Que mon amy m'envoye ;
Hellas ! je les garderay tant !
J'en ay eu si grant joye !

Car sur ma foy je l'ayme tant
Que pour chose que j'aie
Jamès n'auré le cueur contant
Tant qu'avecques luy soye.

Tout aultre plaisir n'est que vent,
Quelque chose qu'on veoye,
Que d'estre o son amy souvent.
Est-il point de tel joie ?

AUTEUR INCONNU.

(29)

LE TEMPS A LAISSIÉ SON MANTEAU

Le temps a laissié son manteau
De vent, de froidure et de pluye,
Et s'est vestu de brouderie,
De soleil luyant, cler et beau.
  Il n'y a beste, ne oyseau,
Qu'en son jargon ne chant ou crie :
Le temps a laissié son manteau
De vent, de froidure et de pluye.

Riviere, fontaine et ruisseau
Portent, en livrée jolie,
Gouttes d'argent et d'orfaverie,
Chascun s'abille de nouveau.
Le temps a laissié son manteau.

CHARLES D'ORLÉANS (1391–1465).

(30)

DIEU, QU'IL LA FAIT BON REGARDER

Dieu, qu'il la fait bon regarder,
La gracieuse, bonne et belle!
Pour les grans biens qui sont en elle,
Chascun est prest de la louer.
    Qui se pourroit d'elle lasser!
Tousjours sa beaulté renouvelle.
Dieu, qu'il la fait bon regarder,
La gracieuse, bonne et belle!
    Par deçà, ne delà la mer,
Ne sçay Dame ne Demoiselle
Qui soit en tous biens parfais telle;
C'est un songe que d'y penser.
Dieu, qu'il la fait bon regarder!

CHARLES D'ORLÉANS.

(31)

'GRANT TESTAMENT', XXXV

Povre je suis de ma jeunesse,
De povre et de petite extrace;
Mon pere n'ot oncq grant richesse,
Ne son ayeul, nommé Orace;
Povreté tous nous suit et trace.
Sur les tombeaulx de mes ancestres,
Les ames desquelz Dieu embrasse,
On n'y voit couronnes ne ceptres.

FRANÇOIS VILLON (1431–?).

(32)

'GRANT TESTAMENT,' XXVI—XXIX

Hé! Dieu, se j'eusse estudié
Ou temps de ma jeunesse folle,
Et à bonnes meurs dedié,
J'eusse maison et couche molle.
Mais quoy? je fuyoie l'escolle,
Comme fait le mauvais enfant.
En escripvant ceste parolle,
A peu que le cuer ne me fent.

Le dit du Saige trop le feiz
Favorable, bien n'en puis mais,
Qui dit: 'Esjoÿs toy, mon filz,
En ton adolescence'; mais
Ailleurs sert bien d'ung autre mes,
Car 'Jeunesse et adolescence,'
C'est son parler, ne moins ne mais,
'Ne sont qu'abus et ignorance.'

Mes jours s'en sont allez errant
Comme, dit Job, d'une touaille
Font les filetz, quant tisserant
En son poing tient ardente paille:
Lors, s'il y a nul bout qui saille,
Soudainement il le ravit.
Si ne crains plus que rien m'assaille,
Car à la mort tout s'assouvit.

Où sont les gracieux gallans
Que je suivoye ou temps jadis,
Si bien chantans, si bien parlans,
Si plaisans en faiz et en dis?
Les aucuns sont mors et roidis,
D'eulx n'est il plus riens maintenant:
Repos aient en paradis,
Et Dieu saulve le demourant!

VILLON.

(33)

BALLADE

DES DAMES DU TEMPS JADIS

Dictes moy où, n'en quel pays,
Est Flora, la belle Rommaine;
Archipiada, ne Thaïs,
Qui fut sa cousine germaine;
Echo, parlant quand bruyt on maine
Dessus riviere ou sus estan,
Qui beaulté ot trop plus qu'humaine?
Mais où sont les neiges d'antan!

Où est la très sage Helloïs,
Pour qui fut chastré et puis moyne
Pierre Esbaillart à Saint-Denis?
Pour son amour ot cest essoyne.
Semblablement, où est la royne
Qui commanda que Buridan
Fust gecté en ung sac en Saine?
Mais où sont les neiges d'antan!

La royne Blanche comme lis,
Qui chantoit à voix de seraine;
Berte au grant pié, Bietris, Allis;
Haremburgis qui tint le Maine,
Et Jehanne, la bonne Lorraine,
Qu'Englois brulerent à Rouan;
Où sont elles, Vierge souvraine? . . .
Mais où sont les neiges d'antan!

ENVOI

Prince, n'enquerez de sepmaine
Où elles sont, ne de cest an,
Que ce reffrain ne vous remaine:
Mais où sont les neiges d'antan!

VILLON.

*L

(34)

'GRANT TESTAMENT,' LXXV—LXXIX

Premier, je donne ma povre ame
A la benoiste Trinité,
Et la commande à Nostre Dame,
Chambre de la divinité;
Priant toute la charité
Des dignes neuf Ordres des cieulx,
Que par eulx soit ce don porté
Devant le Trosne precieux.

Item, mon corps je donne et laisse
A nostre grant mere la terre;
Les vers n'y trouveront grant gresse:
Trop luy a fait fain dure guerre.
Or luy soit delivré grant erre:
De terre vint, en terre tourne.
Toute chose, se par trop n'erre,
Voulentiers en son lieu retourne.

Item, et à mon plus que pere
Maistre Guillaume de Villon
Qui esté m'a plus doulx que mere;
Enfant eslevé de maillon,
Degeté m'a de maint boullon,
Et de cestuy pas ne s'esioye,
Si luy requiers à genoullon,
Qu'il n'en laisse toute la joye.

Je luy donne ma librairie,
Et le *Rommant du Pet au Deable*
Lequel Maistre Guy Tabarie
Grossa qui est homs veritable.
Par cayers est soubz une table.
Combien qu'il soit rudement fait,
La matiere est tres notable
Qu'elle amende tout le mesfait.

Item, donne à ma povre mère
Pour saluer nostre Maistresse,
Qui pour moy ot douleur amere,
Dieu le scet, et mainte tristesse;
Autre chastel n'ay, ne fortresse,
Où me retraye corps et ame,
Quand sur moy court malle destresse,
Ne ma mere, la povre femme.

VILLON.

(35)

BALLADE

Que Villon feit à la requeste de sa mere pour prier Nostre-Dame.

Dame des cieulx, regente terrienne,
Emperiere des infernaux paluz,
Recevez moy, vostre humble chrestienne,
Que comprinse soye entre vos esleuz,
Ce non obstant qu'oncques rien ne valuz.
Les biens de vous, ma dame et ma maistresse,
Sont trop plus grans que ne suis pecheresse,
Sans lesquelz biens ame ne peut merir
N'avoir les cieulx, je n'en suis jungleresse.
En ceste foi je vueil vivre et mourir.

A vostre Filz dictes que je suis sienne;
De luy soyent mes pechiez aboluz:
Pardonne moy comme à l'Egipcienne,
Ou comme il feist au clerc Théophilus,
Lequel par vous fut quitte et absoluz,
Combien qu'il eust au deable fait promesse.
Preservez moy, que ne face jamais ce,
Vierge portant, sans rompure encourir
Le sacrement qu'on celebre à la messe.
En ceste foy je vueil vivre et mourir.

Femme je suis povrette et ancienne,
Qui riens ne sçay; oncques lettre ne leuz;
Au moustier voy dont suis paroissienne

Paradis paint, où sont harpes et luz,
Et ung enfer où dampnez sont boulluz :
L'ung me fait paour, l'autre joye et liesse.
La joye avoir me fay, haulte Deesse,
A qui pecheurs doivent tous recourir,
Comblez de foy, sans fainte ne paresse.
En ceste foy je vueil vivre et mourir.

ENVOI

Vous portastes, digne Vierge, princesse,
Iesus regnant, qui n'a ne fin ne cesse.
Le Tout-Puissant, prenant nostre foiblesse,
Laissa les cieulx et nous vint secourir,
Offrit à mort sa tres chiere jeunesse.
Nostre Seigneur tel est, tel le confesse,
   En ceste foy je vueil vivre et mourir.

VILLON.

(36)

BALLADE DES PENDUS

Freres humains, qui après nous vivez,
N'ayez les cuers contre nous endurcis,
Car, se pitié de nous povres avez,
Dieu en aura plus tost de vous mercis.
Vous nous voiez cy atachez cinq, six ;
Quant de la chair, que trop avons nourrie,
Elle est pieça devorée et pourrie,
Et nous, les os, devenons cendre et pouldre.
De nostre mal personne ne s'en rie,
Mais priez Dieu que tous nous vueille absouldre !

Se freres vous clamons, pas n'en devez
Avoir desdaing, quoy que fusmes occis
Par justice.   Toutesfois, vous sçavez
Que tous hommes n'ont pas bon sens assis ;
Excusez nous — puis que sommes transsis —
Envers le filz de la Vierge Marie,

Que sa grace ne soit pour nous tarie,
Nous preservant de l'infernale fouldre.
Nous sommes mors, ame ne nous harie;
Mais priez Dieu que tous nous vueille absouldre!

La pluye nous a buez et lavez,
Et le soleil desechez et noircis;
Pies, corbeaulx, nous ont les yeux cavez,
Et arraché la barbe et les sourcilz.
Jamais, nul temps, nous ne sommes assis;
Puis çà, puis là, comme le vent varie,
A son plaisir sans cesser nous charie,
Plus becquetez d'oiseaulx que dez à couldre.
Ne soiez donc de nostre confrairie,
Mais priez Dieu que tous nous vueille absouldre!

ENVOI

Prince Jhesus, qui sur tous a maistrie,
Garde qu'Enfer n'ait de nous seigneurie:
A luy n'ayons que faire ne que souldre.
Hommes, icy n'a point de mocquerie,
Mais priez Dieu que tous nous vueille absouldre!

VILLON.

(37)

RONDEAU

Mort, j'appelle de ta rigueur,
Qui m'a ma maistresse ravie,
Et n'es pas encore assouvie,
Si tu ne me tiens en langueur.
Onc puis n'eus force ne vigueur;
Mais que te nuysoit elle en vie,
        Mort?
Deux estions et n'avions qu'ung cuer;
S'il est mort, force est que devie,
Voire, ou que je vive sans vie,
Comme les images, par cuer,
        Mort!

VILLON.

(38)

CHANSON

Au retour de dure prison,
Où j'ai laissié presque la vie,
Se Fortune a sur moy envie,
Jugiez s'elle fait mesprison !
Il me semble que, par raison,
Elle deust bien estre assouvie
     Au retour.
Se si plaine est de desraison
Que vueille que du tout devie,
Plaise à Dieu que l'ame ravie
En soit lassus en sa maison,
     Au retour !

VILLON.

(39)

EPITAPHE

CY GIST ET DORT EN CE SOLLIER,
QU'AMOURS OCCIST DE SON RAILLON,
UNG POVRE PETIT ESCOLLIER,
QUI FUST NOMMÉ FRANÇOYS VILLON.
ONCQUES DE TERRE N'OT SILLON.
IL DONNA TOUT, CHASCUN LE SCET :
TABLES, TRESTEAULX, PAIN, CORBEILLON.
AMANS, DICTES-EN CE VERSET.

RONDEAU

Repos eternel, donne à cil,
Sire, et clarté perpetuelle,
Qui vaillant plat ni escuelle
N'eut oncques, n'ung brain de percil.
Il fut rez, chief, barbe et sourcil,
Comme ung navet qu'on ret ou pelle.
    Repos eternel donne à cil.

Rigueur le transmit en exil,
Et luy frappa au cul la pelle,
Non obstant qu'il dit: 'J'en appelle!'
Qui n'est pas terme trop subtil.
　　Repos eternel donne à cil.

VILLON.

(40)
CHANSON

Qui veult avoir liesse
Seulement d'un regard
Vienne veoir ma maistresse
Que Dieu maintienne et gard:
Elle a si bonne grace,
Que celluy qui la veoit
Mille douleurs efface,
Et plus s'il en avoit.

Les vertus de la belle
Me font esmerveiller;
La souvenance d'elle
Faict mon cueur esveiller;
Sa beauté tant exquise
Me faict la mort sentir;
Mais sa grace requise
M'en peult bien garantir.

CLÉMENT MAROT (1495–1544).

(41)
DE SOY MESME

Plus ne suis ce que j'ay esté,
Et ne le sçaurois jamais estre;
Mon beau printemps et mon esté
Ont fait le sault par la fenestre.
Amour, tu as esté mon maistre:
Je t'ai servi sur tous les dieux.
O si je pouvais deux fois naistre,
Comme je te servirois mieulx.

MAROT.

(42)

LE LIEUTENANT CRIMINEL ET SAMBLANÇAY

Lors que Maillart, juge d'Enfer, menoit
A Monfaulcon Samblançay l'ame rendre,
A vostre advis, lequel des deux tenoit
Meilleur maintien?   Pour le vous faire entendre,
Maillart sembloit homme qui mort va prendre,
Et Samblançay fut si ferme vieillart,
Que l'on cuydoit, pour vray, qu'il menast pendre
A Monfaulcon le lieutenant Maillart.

MAROT.

(43)

SONNET

Tout aussitot que je commence à prendre
Dens le mol lit le repos desiré,
Mon triste esprit hors de moy retiré
S'en va vers toy incontinent se rendre.

Lors m'est avis que, dedens mon sein tendre,
Je tiens le bien où j'ay tant aspiré,
Et pour lequel j'ay si haut souspiré,
Que de sanglots ay souvent cuidé fendre.

O dous sommeil, ô nuit à moy heureuse!
Plaisant repos, plein de tranquilité,
Continuez toutes les nuits mon songe;

Et si jamais ma povre ame amoureuse
Ne doit avoir de bien en verité,
Faites au moins qu'elle en ait en mensonge.

LOUISE LABÉ (1526–66).

(44)

SONNET

Tant que mes yeus pourront larmes espandre,
A l'heur passé avec toy regretter;
Et qu'aus sanglots et soupirs resister
Pourra ma voix, et un peu faire entendre;

Tant que ma main pourra les cordes tendre
Du mignart lut, pour tes graces chanter;
Tant que l'esprit se voudra contenter
De ne vouloir rien fors que toy comprendre;

Je ne souhaitte encore point mourir:
Mais, quand mes yeus je sentiray tarir,
Ma voix cassée, et ma main impuissante,

Et mon esprit, en ce mortel sejour,
Ne pouvant plus montrer signe d'amante;
Priray la Mort noircir mon plus cler jour.

Louise Labé.

(45)

QUAND VOUS SEREZ BIEN VIEILLE

Quand vous serez bien vieille, au soir, à la chandelle,
Assise auprès du feu, devidant et filant,
Direz chantant mes vers, en vous esmerveillant:
Ronsard me celebroit du temps que j'estois belle.

Lors vous n'aurez servante oyant telle nouvelle,
Desja sous le labeur à demy sommeillant,
Qui au bruit de mon nom ne s'aille resveillant,
Benissant vostre nom de louange immortelle.

Je seray sous la terre, et, fantosme sans os,
Par les ombres myrteux je prendray mon repos:
Vous serez au fouyer une vieille accroupie,

Regrettant mon amour et vostre fier desdain.
Vivez, si m'en croyez, n'attendez à demain:
Cueillez dès aujourd'huy les roses de la vie.

Pierre de Ronsard (1524–85).

(46)

MIGNONNE

Mignonne, allons voir si la rose
Qui ce matin avoit desclose
Sa robe de pourpre au soleil,
A point perdu ceste vesprée
Les plis de sa robe pourprée,
Et son teint au vostre pareil.

Las! voyez comme en peu d'espace,
Mignonne, elle a dessus la place
Las! las! ses beautez laissé cheoir!
O vrayment marastre Nature,
Puis qu'une telle fleur ne dure
Que du matin jusques au soir!

Donc, si vous me croyez, mignonne,
Tandis que vostre âge fleuronne
En sa plus verte nouveauté,
Cueillez, cueillez vostre jeunesse :
Comme à ceste fleur la vieillesse
Fera ternir vostre beauté.

RONSARD.

(47)

LA ROSE DE MAY

Comme on void sur la branche au mois de may la rose
En sa belle jeunesse, en sa premiere fleur,
Rendre le ciel jaloux de sa vive couleur,
Quand l'aube de ses pleurs au poinct du jour l'arrose :

La grace dans sa feuille, et l'amour se repose,
Embasmant les jardins et les arbres d'odeur :
Mais battue ou de pluye ou d'excessive ardeur,
Languissante elle meurt feuille à feuille déclose.

Ainsi en ta premiere et jeune nouveauté,
Quand la terre et le ciel honoroient ta beauté,
La Parque t'a tuée, et cendre tu reposes.

Pour obseques reçoy mes larmes et mes pleurs,
Ce vase plein de laict, ce pannier plein de fleurs,
Afin que vif et mort ton corps ne soit que roses.

RONSARD.

(48)

LA MATINALE ROSE

Qui a peu voir la matinale rose
D'une liqueur celeste emmiellée,
Quand la rougeur de blanc entremeslée
Sur le naïf de sa branche repose :

Il aura veu incliner toute chose
A sa faveur : le pié ne l'a foulée,
La main encor' ne l'a point violée,
Et le troupeau aprocher d'elle n'ose.

Mais si elle est de sa tige arrachée,
De son beau teint la frescheur dessechée
Perd la faveur des hommes et des Dieux.

Hélas ! on veult la mienne devorer :
Et je ne puis que, de loing, l'adorer
Par humbles vers (sans fruit) ingenieux.

JOACHIM DU BELLAY (1525–60).

(49)

D'UN VANNEUR DE BLÉ AUX VENTS

A vous troppe legere,
Qui d'aele passagere
Par le monde volez,
Et d'un sifflant murmure

L'ombrageuse verdure
Doulcement esbranlez,

J'offre ces violettes,
Ces lis et ces fleurettes,
Et ces roses icy,
Ces vermeillettes roses,
Tout freschement écloses,
Et ces œilletz aussi.

De vostre doulce halaine
Éventez ceste plaine,
Éventez ce sejour :
Ce pendant que j'ahanne
A mon blé, que je vanne
A la chaleur du jour.

Du Bellay.

(50)

ROME EN ROME

Nouveau venu, qui cherches Rome en Rome,
Et rien de Rome en Rome n'apperçois,
Ces vieux palais, ces vieux arcz que tu vois,
Et ces vieux murs, c'est ce que Rome on nomme.

Voy quel orgueil, quelle ruine : et comme
Celle qui mist le monde sous ses loix,
Pour donter tout, se donta quelquefois,
Et devint proye au temps, qui tout consomme.

Rome de Rome est le seul monument,
Et Rome Rome a vaincu seulement.
Le Tybre seul, qui vers la mer s'enfuit,

Reste de Rome. O mondaine inconstance !
Ce qui est ferme, est par le temps destruit,
Et ce qui fuit, au temps fait resistance.

Du Bellay.

(51)

LA BERECYNTHIENNE

Telle que dans son char la Berecynthienne
Couronnee de tours, et joyeuse d'avoir
Enfanté tant de Dieux, telle se faisoit voir
En ses jours plus heureux ceste ville ancienne:

Ceste ville qui fut plus que la Phrygienne
Foisonnante en enfans, et de qui le pouvoir
Fut le pouvoir du monde, et ne se peult revoir
Pareille à sa grandeur, grandeur sinon la sienne.

Rome seule pouvoit à Rome ressembler,
Rome seule pouvoit Rome faire trembler:
Aussi n'avoit permis l'ordonnance fatale,

Qu'autre pouvoir humain, tant fust audacieux,
Se vantast d'égaler celle qui fit égale
Sa puissance à la terre, et son courage aux cieux.

Du Bellay

(52)

LE CHESNE

Qui a veu quelquefois un grand chesne asseiché,
Qui pour son ornement quelque trophee porte,
Lever encor' au ciel sa vieille teste morte,
Dont le pied fermement n'est en terre fiché,

Mais qui dessus le champ plus qu'à demy panché
Monstre ses bras tout nuds et sa racine torte,
Et sans fueille umbrageux, de son poix se supporte
Sur son tronc noüailleux en cent lieux esbranché:

Et bien qu'au premier vent il doive sa ruine,
Et maint jeune à l'entour ait ferme la racine,
Du devot populaire estre seul reveré:

Qui tel chesne a peu voir, qu'il imagine encores
Comme entre les citez , qui plus florissent ores
Ce vieil honneur poudreux est le plus honnoré !

Du Bellay.

(53)

MAY

M. A. Gouverneur's edition, 1863.

Pendant que ce mois renouvelle
D'une course perpétuelle
La vieillesse et le tour des ans :
Pendant que la tendre jeunesse
Du ciel remet en allegresse
Les hommes, la terre, et le temps :

Pendant que l'humeur printaniere
Enfle la mammelle fruitiere
De la terre, en ces plus beaux jours,
Et que sa face sursemee
De fleurs, et d'odeurs embasmee
Se pare de nouveaux attours :

Pendant que les Arondelettes
De leurs gorges mignardelettes
Rappellent le plus beau de l'an,
Et que pour leurs petits façonnent
Une cuvette, qu'ils massonnent
De leur petit bec artizan :

En ce mois Venus la sucree,
Amour, et la troupe sacree
Des Graces, des Ris, et des Jeux,
Vont r'allumant dedans nos veines
L'ardeur des amoureuses peines,
Qui glissent en nous par les yeux.

Pendant que la vigne tendrette
D'une entreprise plus secrette

Forme le raisin verdissant,
Et de ses petits bras embrasse
L'orme voisin, qu'elle entrelasse
De pampre mollement glissant :

Et que les brebis camusettes
Tondent les herbes nouvelettes,
Et le chevreau à petits bons
Eschauffe sa corne et sautelle
Devant sa mere, qui broutelle
Sur le roch les tendres jettons :

Pendant que la vois argentine
Du Rossignol, dessus l'espine
Degoise cent fredons mignars :
Et que l'Avette mesnagere
D'une aile tremblante et legere
Volle en ses pavillons bruyars :

Pendant que la terre arrosee
D'une fraische et douce rosee
Commence à brouter et germer :
Pendant que les vents des Zephyres
Flattent le voile des navires
Frisant la plaine de la mer :

Ce pendant que les tourterelles,
Les pigeons et les colombelles
Font l'amour en ce mois si beau,
Et que leurs bouchettes bessonnes
A tours et reprises mignonnes
Frayent pres le coulant d'une eau :

Et que la tresse blondissante
De Cerés, sous le vent glissante,
Se frize en menus crespillons,
Comme la vague redoublee
Pli sur pli s'avance escoulee
Au galop dessus les sablons :

Bref, pendant que la terre, et l'onde,
Et le flambeau de ce bas monde,
Se resjouissent à leur tour,
Pendant que les oiseaux se jouent
Dedans l'air, et les poissons nouent
Sous l'eau pour les feux de l'Amour :

Qu'il te souvienne que les roses
Du matin jusqu'au soir écloses,
Perdent la couleur et l'odeur,
Et que le temps pille et despouille
Du printemps la douce despouille,
Les fueilles, le fruit, et la fleur.

Souvienne toy que la vieillesse
D'une courbe et lente foiblesse
Nous fera chanceller le pas,
Que le poil grison et la ride,
Les yeux cavez et la peau vuide
Nous traineront tous au trespas.

REMI BELLEAU (1528–77).

(54)

ONQ UNE SI BELLE ROSE . . .

. . . Onq une si belle rose
Aus rayons d'un beau soleil
Ne fut si fresche declose ;
Œillet ne fleurit pareil
A ce vif sanguin vermeil
De ta bouche, qui éteint
Des fleurs tout le plus beau teint.

On ne suce point encore
Une si douce liqueur,
Par les doits rosins d'Aurore
Mise sur la tendre fleur,

Durant la verte vigueur
Du beau printemps odoureux,
Comme est ce miel savoureux.

J'ay sucé la fleur doucéte
Du buissonnier chevre-fueil,
Et de la soigneuse avéte
Le laborieux recueil;
Mais ton baizer nompareil
Le chevre-fueil flétrira
Et le miel afadira. . . .

J.–A. DE BAÏF (1532–89).

(55)

ÉPITAPHE DE RABELAIS

O Pluton, Rabelais reçoy,
Afin que toy qui es le roy
De ceux qui ne rient jamais
Tu ais un rieur desormais.

DE BAÏF.

(56)

SI JE ME SIEZ A L'OMBRE . . .

Si je me siez à l'ombre, aussi soudainement
Amour, laissant son arc, s'assied et se repose;
Si je pense à des vers, je le voy qui compose;
Si je plains mes douleurs, il se plaint hautement.

Si je me plains au mal, il accroist mon tourment;
Si je respans des pleurs, son visage il arrose;
Si je monstre ma playe, en ma poitrine enclose,
Il défait son bandeau, l'essuyant doucement.

Si je vais par les bois, aux bois il m'accompagne;
Si je me suis cruel, dans mon sang il se bagne;
Si je vais à la guerre, il devient mon soldart.

Si je passe la mer, il conduit ma nacelle;
Bref, jamais l'importun de moy ne se départ,
Pour rendre mon désir et ma peine éternelle.

PHILIPPE DESPORTES (1546–1606).

(57)

IDYLLE

Entre les fleurs, entre les lis,
Doucement dormoit ma Philis,
Et tout autour de son visage
Les petits Amours, comme enfans,
Jouoient, folastroient, triomphans,
Voyant des cieux la belle image.

J'admirois toutes ces beautez
Égalles à mes loyautez,
Quand l'esprit me dit en l'oreille:
Fol, que fais-tu? Le temps perdu
Souvent est chèrement vendu;
S'on le recouvre, c'est merveille.

Alors, je m'abbaissai tout bas,
Sans bruit je marchai pas à pas,
Et baisai ses lèvres pourprines:
Savourant un tel bien, je dis
Que tel est dans le paradis
Le plaisir des asmes divines.

VAUQUELIN DE LA FRESNAYE (1536–1606).

(58)

ÉPITAPHE DE REGNIER

J'ay vécu sans nul pensement,
Me laissant aller doucement
A la bonne loy naturelle,
Et si m'étonne fort pourquoy
La mort osa songer à moy,
Qui ne songeay jamais à elle.

MATHURIN REGNIER (1575–1606).

(59)

SUR LA MORT DE SON FILS

Que mon fils ait perdu sa dépouille mortelle,
Ce fils qui fut si brave, et que j'aimai si fort,
Je ne l'impute point à l'injure du sort,
Puisque finir à l'homme est chose naturelle.

Mais que de deux marauds la surprise infidèle
Ait terminé ses jours d'une tragique mort,
En cela ma douleur n'a point de réconfort,
Et tous mes sentiments sont d'accord avec elle.

O mon Dieu, mon Sauveur, puisque, par la raison,
Le trouble de mon âme étant sans guérison,
Le vœu de la vengeance est un vœu légitime,

Fais que de ton appui je sois fortifié;
Ta justice t'en prie, et les auteurs du crime
Sont fils de ces bourreaux qui t'ont crucifié.

FRANÇOIS DE MALHERBE (1555–1628).

(60)

SUR LA MORT DE MLLE DE CONTY

N'égalons point cette petite
Aux déesses que nous récite
L'histoire des siècles passés :
Tout cela n'est qu'une chimère ;
Il faut dire, pour dire assez,
Elle est belle comme sa mère.

MALHERBE.

(61)

SONNET

Il faut finir mes jours en l'amour d'Uranie ;
L'absence ni le temps ne m'en sauraient guérir,
Et je ne vois plus rien qui me pût secourir,
Ni qui sût rappeler ma liberté bannie.

Dès longtemps je connais sa rigueur infinie;
Mais pensant aux beautés, pour qui je dois périr,
Je bénis mon martyre, et content de mourir,
Je n'ose murmurer contre sa tyrannie.

Quelquefois ma raison par de faibles discours
M'incite à la révolte et me promet secours;
Mais lorsqu'à mon besoin je me veux servir d'elle,

Après beaucoup de peine et d'efforts impuissants,
Elle dit qu'Uranie est seule aimable et belle,
Et m'y rengage plus que ne font tous mes sens.

VINCENT VOITURE (1598–1648).

(62)

RONDEAU

Ma foi, c'est fait de moi; car Isabeau
M'a conjuré de lui faire un rondeau,
Cela me met en une peine extrême.
Quoi! treize vers, huit en eau, cinq en ème!
Je lui ferais aussitôt un bateau.

En voilà cinq pourtant en un monceau,
Faisons-en huit, en invoquant Brodeau,
Et puis mettons par quelque stratagème:
    Ma foi, c'est fait!

Si je pouvais encor de mon cerveau
Tirer cinq vers, l'ouvrage serait beau.
Mais cependant je suis dedans l'onzième,
Et ci je crois que je fais le douzième,
En voilà treize ajustés au niveau:
    Ma foi, c'est fait!

VOITURE.

(63)

ÉPITAPHE

Ci-gît Paul qui baissait les yeux
A la rencontre des gens sobres,
Et qui priait toujours les cieux
Que l'année eût plusieurs Octobres.
Ce grand pilier de cabaret
Avecque un hareng soret
Humait des bouteilles sans nombre;
Passant qui t'es ici porté,
Sache qu'il voudrait que son ombre
Eût de quoi boire à ta santé.

FRANÇOIS MAYNARD (1582–1642).

(64)

LE CID—ACTE I. Sc. v

O rage! ô désespoir! ô vieillesse ennemie!
N'ai-je donc tant vécu que pour cette infamie?
Et ne suis-je blanchi dans les travaux guerriers
Que pour voir en un jour flétrir tant de lauriers?
Mon bras, qu'avec respect toute l'Espagne admire,
Mon bras, qui tant de fois a sauvé cet empire,
Tant de fois affermi le trône de son roi,
Trahi donc ma querelle, et ne fait rien pour moi?
O cruel souvenir de ma gloire passée!
Œuvre de tant de jours en un jour effacée!
Nouvelle dignité fatale à mon bonheur!
Précipice élevé d'où tombe mon honneur!
Faut-il de votre éclat voir triompher le comte,
Et mourir sans vengeance, ou vivre dans le honte?

PIERRE CORNEILLE (1606–84).

(65)

HORACE—ACTE III. Sc. v

Je veux bien l'avouer, ces nouvelles m'étonnent;
Et je m'imaginais dans la divinité
Beaucoup moins d'injustice et bien plus de bonté.

Ne nous consolez point; contre tant d'infortune
La pitié parle en vain, la raison importune.
Nous avons en nos mains la fin de nos douleurs,
Et qui veut bien mourir peut braver les malheurs.
Nous pourrions aisément faire en votre présence
De notre désespoir une fausse constance,
Mais quand on peut sans honte être sans fermeté,
L'affecter au dehors, c'est une lâcheté;
L'usage d'un tel art, nous le laissons aux hommes,
Et ne voulons passer que pour ce que nous sommes.
Nous ne demandons point qu'un courage si fort
S'abaisse à notre exemple à se plaindre du sort.
Recevez sans frémir ces mortelles alarmes;
Voyez couler nos pleurs sans y mêler vos larmes;
Enfin, pour toute grâce, en de tels déplaisirs,
Gardez votre constance, et souffrez nos soupirs.

CORNEILLE.

(66)

HORACE—ACTE IV. SC. V

HORACE

Ma sœur, voici le bras qui venge nos deux frères,
Le bras qui rompt le cours de nos destins contraires,
Qui nous rend maîtres d'Albe; enfin voici le bras
Qui seul fait aujourd'hui le sort de deux États;
Vois ces marques d'honneur, ces témoins de ma gloire,
Et rends ce que tu dois à l'heur de ma victoire.

CAMILLE

Recevez donc mes pleurs, c'est ce que je lui dois.

HORACE

Rome n'en veut point voir après de tels exploits,
Et nos deux frères morts dans le malheur des armes
Sont trop payés de sang pour exiger des larmes:
Quand la perte est vengée, on n'a plus rien perdu.

CAMILLE

Puisqu'ils sont satisfaits par le sang épandu,
Je cesserai pour eux de paraître affligée,
Et j'oublierai leur mort que vous avez vengée;
Mais qui me vengera de celle d'un amant,
Pour me faire oublier sa perte en un moment?

HORACE

Que dis-tu, malheureuse?

CAMILLE

O mon cher Curiace!

HORACE

O d'une indigne sœur insupportable audace!
D'un ennemi public dont je reviens vainqueur
Le nom est dans ta bouche et l'amour dans ton cœur!
Ton ardeur criminelle à la vengeance aspire!
Ta bouche la demande, et ton cœur la respire!
Suis moins ta passion, règle mieux tes désirs,
Ne me fais plus rougir d'entendre tes soupirs;
Tes flammes désormais doivent être étouffées;
Bannis-les de ton âme, et songe à mes trophées.
Qu'ils soient dorénavant ton unique entretien.

CAMILLE

Donne-moi donc, barbare, un cœur comme le tien;
Et si tu veux enfin que je t'ouvre mon âme,
Rends-moi mon Curiace ou laisse agir ma flamme:
Ma joie et mes douleurs dépendaient de son sort;
Je l'adorais vivant, et je le pleure mort.
  Ne cherche plus ta sœur où tu l'avais laissée;
Tu ne revois en moi qu'une amante offensée,
Qui, comme une furie, attachée à tes pas,
Te veut incessamment reprocher son trépas.
Tigre altéré de sang, qui me défends les larmes,
Qui veux que dans sa mort je trouve encor des charmes,

Et que, jusques au ciel élevant tes exploits,
Moi-même je le tue une seconde fois !
Puissent tant de malheurs accompagner ta vie
Que tu tombes au point de me porter envie ;
Et toi bientôt souiller par quelque lâcheté
Cette gloire si chère à ta brutalité !

HORACE

O ciel ! qui vit jamais une pareille rage !
Crois-tu donc que je sois insensible à l'outrage,
Que je souffre en mon sang ce mortel déshonneur ?
Aime, aime cette mort qui fait notre bonheur,
Et préfère du moins au souvenir d'un homme
Ce que doit ta naissance aux intérêts de Rome.

CAMILLE

Rome, l'unique objet de mon ressentiment !
Rome, à qui vient ton bras d'immoler mon amant !
Rome qui t'a vu naître, et que ton cœur adore !
Rome enfin que je hais parce qu'elle t'honore !
Puissent tous ses voisins ensemble conjurés
Saper ses fondements encor mal assurés !
Et si ce n'est assez de toute l'Italie,
Que l'Orient contre elle à l'Occident s'allie ;
Que cent peuples unis des bouts de l'univers
Passent pour la détruire et les monts et les mers !
Qu'elle-même sur soi renverse ses murailles,
Et de ses propres mains déchire ses entrailles !
Que le courroux du ciel, allumé par mes vœux,
Fasse pleuvoir sur elle un déluge de feux !
Puissé-je de mes yeux y voir tomber ce foudre,
Voir ses maisons en cendre, et tes lauriers en poudre
Voir le dernier Romain à son dernier soupir,
Moi seule en être cause, et mourir de plaisir.

HORACE [*mettant la main à l'épee et poursuivant sa sœur qui s'enfuit*]

C'est trop, ma patience à la raison fait place ;
Va dedans les enfers plaindre ton Curiace !

CAMILLE [*blessée derrière le théâtre*]

Ah! traître!

HORACE [*revenant sur le théâtre*]

Ainsi reçoive un châtiment soudain
Quiconque ose pleurer un ennemi romain!

CORNEILLE.

(67)

PHÈDRE—ACTE IV. SC. VI

PHÈDRE

Que fais-je? Où ma raison se va-t-elle égarer?
Moi jalouse! et Thésée est celui que j'implore!
Mon époux est vivant, et moi je brûle encore!
Pour qui? Quel est le cœur où prétendent mes vœux?
Chaque mot sur mon front fait dresser mes cheveux.
Mes crimes désormais ont comblé la mesure.
Je respire à la fois l'inceste et l'imposture.
Mes homicides mains, promptes à me venger,
Dans le sang innocent brûlent de se plonger.
Misérable! et je vis? et je soutiens la vue
De ce sacré soleil dont je suis descendue?
J'ai pour aïeul le père et le maître des dieux;
Le ciel, tout l'univers est plein de mes aïeux.
Où me cacher? Fuyons dans la nuit infernale.
Mais que dis-je? mon père y tient l'urne fatale;
Le sort, dit-on, l'a mise en ses sévères mains:
Minos juge aux enfers tous les pâles humains.
Ah! combien frémira son ombre épouvantée,
Lorsqu'il verra sa fille à ses yeux présentée,
Contrainte d'avouer tant de forfaits divers,
Et des crimes peut-être inconnus aux enfers!
Que diras-tu, mon père, à ce spectacle horrible?
Je crois voir de ta main tomber l'urne terrible;
Je crois te voir, cherchant un supplice nouveau,
Toi-même de ton sang devenir le bourreau.

M

Pardonne.   Un dieu cruel a perdu ta famille;
Reconnais sa vengeance aux fureurs de ta fille.
Hélas! du crime affreux dont la honte me suit
Jamais mon triste cœur n'a recueilli le fruit.
Jusqu'au dernier soupir de malheurs poursuivie,
Je rends dans les tourments une pénible vie.

JEAN RACINE (1639–99).

(68)
PHÈDRE—ACTE V. SC. VII
THÉSÉE

Hé bien! vous triomphez, et mon fils est sans vie.
Ah! que j'ai lieu de craindre! et qu'un cruel soupçon,
L'excusant dans mon cœur, m'alarme avec raison!
Mais, madame, il est mort, prenez votre victime:
Jouissez de sa perte, injuste ou légitime.
Je consens que mes yeux soient toujours abusés.
Je le crois criminel, puisque vous l'accusez.
Son trépas à mes pleurs offre assez de matières,
Sans que j'aille chercher d'odieuses lumières,
Qui ne pouvant le rendre à ma juste douleur,
Peut-être ne feraient qu'accroître mon malheur.
Laissez-moi, loin de vous et loin de ce rivage,
De mon fils déchiré fuir la sanglante image.
Confus, persécuté d'un mortel souvenir,
De l'univers entier je voudrais me bannir.
Tout semble s'élever contre mon injustice.
L'éclat de mon nom même augmente mon supplice.
Moins connu des mortels, je me cacherais mieux.
Je hais jusques aux soins dont m'honorent les dieux
Et je m'en vais pleurer leurs faveurs meurtrières
Sans plus les fatiguer d'inutiles prières.
Quoi qu'ils fissent pour moi, leur funeste bonté
Ne me saurait payer de ce qu'ils m'ont ôté.

PHÈDRE

Non, Thésée, il faut rompre un injuste silence
Il faut à votre fils rendre son innocence,
Il n'était point coupable.

Thésée

Ah ! père infortuné !
Et c'est sur votre foi que je l'ai condamné !
Cruelle, pensez-vous être assez excusée. . . .

Phèdre

Les moments me sont chers, écoutez-moi, Thésée.
C'est moi qui sur ce fils chaste et respectueux
Osai jeter un œil profane, incestueux.
Le ciel mit dans mon sein une flamme funeste ;
La détestable Œnone a conduit tout le reste.
Elle a craint qu'Hippolyte, instruit de ma fureur,
Ne découvrît un feu qui lui faisait horreur.
La perfide, abusant de ma faiblesse extrême,
S'est hâtée à vos yeux de l'accuser lui-même.
Elle s'en est punie, et, fuyant mon courroux,
A cherché dans les flots un supplice trop doux.
Le fer aurait déjà tranché ma destinée ;
Mais je laissais gémir la vertu soupçonnée.
J'ai voulu, devant vous exposant mes remords,
Par un chemin plus lent descendre chez les morts.
J'ai pris, j'ai fait couler dans mes brûlantes veines
Un poison que Médée apporta dans Athènes.
Déjà jusqu'à mon cœur le venin parvenu
Dans ce cœur expirant jette un froid inconnu ;
Déjà je ne vois plus qu'à travers un nuage
Et le ciel et l'époux que ma présence outrage ;
Et la mort, à mes yeux dérobant la clarté,
Rend au jour, qu'ils souillaient, toute sa pureté.

Panope

Elle expire, seigneur !

Thésée

D'une action si noire
Que ne peut avec elle expirer la mémoire !
Allons, de mon erreur, hélas ! trop éclaircis,
Mêler nos pleurs au sang de mon malheureux fils.

Allons de ce cher fils embrasser ce qui reste,
Expier la fureur d'un vœu que je déteste.
Rendons-lui les honneurs qu'il a trop mérités;
Et pour mieux apaiser ses mânes irrités,
Que, malgré les complots d'une injuste famille,
Son amante aujourd'hui me tienne lieu de fille.

RACINE.

(69)
ÉPITAPHE D'ÉLISABETH RANQUET

Ne verse point de pleurs sur cette sépulture,
Passant: ce lit funèbre est un lit précieux,
Où gît d'un corps tout pur la cendre toute pure;
Mais le zèle du cœur vit encore en ces lieux.

Avant que de payer le droit à la nature,
Son âme, s'élevant au delà de ses yeux,
Avait au Créateur uni la créature;
Et marchant sur la terre elle était dans les cieux.

Les pauvres bien mieux qu'elle ont senti sa richesse:
L'humilité, la peine étaient son allégresse;
Et son dernier soupir fut un soupir d'amour.

Passant, qu'à son exemple un beau feu te transporte,
Et loin de la pleurer d'avoir perdu le jour,
Crois qu'on ne meurt jamais quand on meurt de la
sorte.

PIERRE CORNEILLE.

(70)
HYMNE

Mon Dieu, quelle guerre cruelle,
Je trouve deux hommes en moi:
L'un veut que, plein d'amour pour toi,
Mon cœur te soit toujours fidèle;
L'autre, à tes volontés rebelle,
Me révolte contre ta loi.

L'un, tout esprit et tout céleste,
Veut qu'au ciel sans cesse attaché,
Et des biens éternels touché,
Je compte pour rien tout le reste ;
Et l'autre par son poids funeste,
Me tient vers la terre penché.

Hélas ! en guerre avec moi-même,
Où pourrai-je trouver la paix ?
Je veux, et n'accomplis jamais ;
Je veux : mais (ô misère extrême !)
Je ne fais pas le bien que j'aime,
Et je fais le mal que je hais.

O grâce ! ô rayon salutaire !
Viens me mettre avec moi d'accord,
Et domptant par un doux effort
Cet homme qui t'est si contraire,
Fais ton esclave volontaire
De cet esclave de la mort.

                                    RACINE.

(71)
LE MULET SE VANTANT DE SA GÉNÉALOGIE

Le mulet d'un prélat se piquait de noblesse,
        Et ne parlait incessamment
        Que de sa mère la jument,
        Dont il contait mainte prouesse.
Elle avait fait ceci ; puis avait été là.
        Son fils prétendait pour cela
        Qu'on le dût mettre dans l'histoire.
Il eût cru s'abaisser servant un médecin.
Étant devenu vieux, on le mit au moulin :
Son père l'âne alors lui revint en mémoire.

        Quand le malheur ne serait bon
        Qu'à mettre un sot à la raison,
        Toujours serait-ce à juste cause
        Qu'on le dit bon à quelque chose.
            JEAN DE LA FONTAINE (1621–95).

(72)

LE LOUP ET LE CHIEN

Un loup n'avait que les os et la peau,
 Tant les chiens faisaient bonne garde.
Ce loup rencontre un dogue aussi puissant que beau,
Gras, poli, qui s'était fourvoyé par mégarde.
  L'attaquer, le mettre en quartiers,
  Sire loup l'eût fait volontiers;
  Mais il fallait livre bataille;
  Et le mâtin était de taille
  A se défendre hardiment.
  Le loup donc l'aborde humblement;
 Entre en propos, et lui fait compliment
  Sur son embonpoint, qu'il admire.
  Il ne tiendra qu'à vous, beau sire,
D'être aussi gras que moi, lui repartit le chien.
  Quittez les bois, vous ferez bien:
  Vos pareils y sont misérables;
  Cancres, hères, et pauvres diables,
Dont la condition est de mourir de faim.
 Car, quoi! rien d'assuré! point de franche lippée!
  Tout à la pointe de l'épée!
 Suivez-moi, vous aurez un bien meilleur destin.
  Le loup reprit: Que me faudra-t-il faire?
 Presque rien, dit le chien: donner la chasse aux gens
  Portants bâtons, et mendiants;
 Flatter ceux du logis, à son maître complaire:
  Moyennant quoi votre salaire
 Sera force reliefs de toutes les façons,
  Os de poulets, os de pigeons;
  Sans parler de mainte caresse.
 Le loup déjà se forge une félicité
  Qui le fait pleurer de tendresse.
 Chemin faisant, il vit le coup du chien pelé.
 Qu'est-ce là? lui dit-il. — Rien — Quoi! rien! — Peu
  de chose.
 Mais encor? Le collier dont je suis attaché
 De ce que vous voyez est peut-être la cause. —

Attaché! dit le loup: vous ne courez donc pas
 Où vous voulez? — Pas toujours: mais qu'im-
 porte? —
Il importe si bien, que de tous vos repas
 Je ne veux en aucune sorte,
Et ne voudrais pas même à ce prix un trésor.
Cela dit, maître loup s'enfuit, et court encor.

La Fontaine.

(73)
UN FOU ET UN SAGE

Certain fou poursuivait à coups de pierre un sage.
Le sage se retourne, et lui dit: Mon ami,
C'est fort bien fait à toi, reçois cet écu-ci.
Tu fatigues assez pour gagner davantage;
Toute peine, dit-on, est digne de loyer:
Vois cet homme qui passe, il a de quoi payer;
Adresse-lui tes dons, ils auront leur salaire.
Amorcé par le gain, notre fou s'en va faire
 Même insulte à l'autre bourgeois.
On ne le paya pas en argent cette fois.
Maint estafier accourt: on vous happe notre homme,
 On vous l'échine, on vous l'assomme.

Auprès des rois il est de pareils fous:
A vos dépens ils font rire le maître.
Pour réprimer leur babil, irez-vous
Les maltraiter? Vous n'êtes pas peut-être
Assez puissant. Il faut les engager
A s'adresser à qui peut se venger.

La Fontaine.

(74)
LE SAVETIER ET LE FINANCIER

Un savetier chantait du matin jusqu'au soir:
 C'était merveilles de le voir,
Merveilles de l'ouïr; il faisait des passages,
 Plus content qu'aucun des sept sages.

Son voisin, au contraire, étant tout cousu d'or,
        Chantait peu, dormait moins encor:
        C'était un homme de finance.
Si sur le point du jour parfois il sommeillait,
Le savetier alors en chantant l'éveillait;
Et le financier se plaignait
        Que les soins de la Providence
N'eussent pas au marché fait vendre le dormir
        Comme le manger et le boire.
        En son hôtel il fait venir
Le chanteur, et lui dit: Or çà, sire Grégoire,
Que gagnez-vous par an? — Par an! ma foi, monsieur,
        Dit avec un ton de rieur
Le gaillard savetier, ce n'est point ma manière
De compter de la sorte; et je n'entasse guère
    Un jour sur l'autre: il suffit qu'à la fin
        J'attrape le bout de l'année;
        Chaque jour amène son pain.
    — Eh bien! que gagnez-vous, dites-moi, par journée?
    — Tantôt plus, tantôt moins: le mal est que toujours
(Et sans cela nos gains seraient assez honnêtes),
Le mal est que dans l'an s'entremêlent des jours
        Qu'il faut chômer; on nous ruine en fêtes;
L'une fait tort à l'autre; et monsieur le curé
De quelque nouveau saint charge toujours son prône.
Le financier, riant de sa naïveté,
Lui dit: Je vous veux mettre aujourd'hui sur le
        trône.
Prenez ces cent écus; gardez-les avec soin,
        Pour vous en servir au besoin.
Le savetier crut voir tout l'argent que la terre
        Avait, depuis plus de cent ans,
        Produit pour l'usage des gens.
Il retourne chez lui: dans sa cave il enserre
        L'argent, et sa joie à la fois.
Plus de chant: il perdit la voix
Du moment qu'il gagna ce qui cause nos peines.
        Le sommeil quitta son logis:
        Il eut pour hôtes les soucis,
        Les soupçons, les alarmes vaines.

Tout le jour il avait l'œil au guet ; et la nuit,
    Si quelque chat faisait du bruit,
Le chat prenait l'argent.   A la fin le pauvre homme
S'en courut chez celui qu'il ne réveillait plus :
Rendez-moi, lui dit-il, mes chansons et mon somme,
    Et reprenez vos cent écus.

LA FONTAINE.

(75)

INVOCATION

O douce Volupté, sans qui, dès notre enfance,
Le vivre et le mourir nous deviendraient égaux ;
Aimant universel de tous les animaux,
Que tu sais attirer avecque violence !
    Par toi tout se meut ici-bas.
    C'est pour toi, c'est pour tes appas,
    Que nous courons après la peine :
    Il n'est soldat, ni capitaine,
Ni ministre d'État, ni prince, ni sujet,
    Qui ne t'ait pour unique objet.
Nous autres nourrissons, si pour fruit de nos veilles,
Un bruit délicieux ne charmait nos oreilles,
Si nous ne nous sentions chatouillés de ce son,
    Ferions-nous un mot de chanson?
Ce qu'on appelle gloire en termes magnifiques,
Ce qui servait de prix dans les jeux olympiques,
N'est que toi proprement, divine Volupté,
Et le plaisir des sens n'est-il de rien compté?
    Pour quoi sont faits les dons de Flore,
    Le Soleil couchant et l'Aurore,
    Pomone et ses mets délicats,
    Bacchus, l'âme des bons repas,
    Les forêts, les eaux, les prairies,
    Mères des douces rêveries?
Pour quoi tant de beaux arts, qui tous sont tes enfants?
Mais pour quoi les Chloris aux appas triomphants,
    Que pour maintenir ton commerce?

* M

J'entends innocemment : sur son propre désir
   Quelque rigueur que l'on exerce,
   Encor y prend-on du plaisir.

Volupté, Volupté, qui fus jadis maîtresse
   Du plus bel esprit de la Grèce,
Ne me dédaigne pas, viens-t'en loger chez moi ;
   Tu n'y seras pas sans emploi :
J'aime le jeu, l'amour, les livres, la musique,
La ville et la campagne, enfin tout ; il n'est rien
   Qui ne me soit souverain bien,
Jusqu'au sombre plaisir d'un cœur mélancolique.
Viens donc ; et de ce bien, ô douce Volupté,
Veux-tu savoir au vrai la mesure certaine ?
Il m'en faut tout au moins un siècle bien compté ;
   Car trente ans, ce n'est pas la peine.
                       LA FONTAINE.

(76)

ÉPITAPHE

   Celui qui ci maintenant dort
   Fit plus de pitié que d'envie,
   Et souffrit mille fois la mort
   Avant que de perdre la vie.
   Passant, ne fais ici de bruit,
   Prends garde qu'aucun ne l'éveille ;
   Car voici la première nuit
   Que le pauvre Scarron sommeille.
             PAUL SCARRON (1610–60).

(77)

SUR MÉNAGE

   Laissons en paix Monsieur Ménage ;
   C'était un très bon personnage
   Pour n'être pas de ses amis :

Souffrez qu'à son tour il repose
Lui dont les vers et dont la prose
Nous ont si souvent endormi.

LA MONNOYE (1641–1728).

(78)

LE ROI DES TRIOLETS

Le premier jour du mois de mai
Fut le plus heureux de ma vie :
Le beau dessein que je formais,
Le premier jour du mois de mai !
Je vous vis et je vous aimais.
Si ce dessein vous plut, Sylvie,
Le premier jour du mois de mai
Fut le plus heureux de ma vie.

JACQUES RANCHIN (c. 1690).

(79)

INSCRIPTION POUR UNE STATUE DE L'AMOUR

Qui que tu sois, voici ton maître ;
Il l'est, le fut, ou le doit être.

F.-M. AROUET DE VOLTAIRE (1694–1778).

(80)

DÉVISE POUR MADAME DU CHÂTELET

Du repos, des riens, de l'étude,
Peu de livres, point d'ennuyeux,
Un ami dans la solitude ;
Voilà mon sort, il est heureux.

VOLTAIRE.

(81)

SUR UN CHRIST HABILLÉ EN JÉSUITE

Admirez l'artifice extrême
De ces moines industrieux;
Ils vous ont habillé comme eux,
Mon Dieu, de peur qu'on ne vous aime.

VOLTAIRE.

(82)

SUR SON PORTRAIT ENTRE CEUX DE LA BEAUMELLE ET DE FRÉRON

Le Jay vient de mettre Voltaire
Entre La Beaumelle et Fréron;
Ce serait vraiment un Calvaire,
S'il s'y trouvait un bon larron.

VOLTAIRE.

(83)

FRÉRON PIQUÉ D'UN SERPENT

L'autre jour, au fond d'un vallon,
Un serpent piqua Jean Fréron.
Que pensez-vous qu'il arriva?
Ce fut le serpent qui creva.

VOLTAIRE.

(84)

JÉRÉMIE TRADUIT PAR LEFRANC

Savez-vous pourquoi Jérémie
A tant pleuré pendant sa vie?
C'est qu'en prophète il prévoyait
Qu'un jour Lefranc le traduirait.

VOLTAIRE.

(85)

ÉPITAPHE

Ci-gît dont la suprême loi
Fut de ne vivre que pour soi.
Passant, garde-toi de le suivre;
Car on pourrait dire de toi:
'Ci-gît qui ne dut jamais vivre.'

VOLTAIRE.

(86)

À MADAME LULLIN

Hé quoi! vous êtes étonnée
Qu'au bout de quatre-vingts hivers
Ma muse faible et surannée
Puisse encore fredonner des vers?

Quelquefois un peu de verdure
Rit sous les glaçons de nos champs;
Elle console la nature,
Mais elle sèche en peu de temps.

Un oiseau peut se faire entendre
Après la saison des beaux jours;
Mais sa voix n'a plus rien de tendre;
Il ne chante plus ses amours.

Ainsi je touche encor ma lyre,
Qui n'obéit plus à mes doigts;
Ainsi j'essaye encor ma voix
Au moment même qu'elle expire.

'Je veux dans mes derniers adieux,
Disait Tibulle à son amante,
Attacher mes yeux sur tes yeux,
Te presser de ma main mourante.'

Mais quand on sent qu'on va passer,
Quand l'âme fuit avec la vie,
A-t-on des yeux pour voir Délie,
Et des mains pour la caresser?

Dans ce moment chacun oublie
Tout ce qu'il a fait en santé,
Quel mortel s'est jamais flatté
D'un rendez-vous à l'agonie?

Délie elle-même à son tour
S'en va dans la nuit éternelle,
En oubliant qu'elle fut belle,
Et qu'elle a vécu pour l'amour.

Nous naissons, nous vivons, bergère,
Nous mourons sans savoir comment :
Chacun est parti du néant :
Où va-t-il? . . . Dieu le sait, ma chère.

VOLTAIRE.

(87)

LE DÉSASTRE DE LISBONNE

O malheureux mortels! ô terre déplorable!
O de tous les mortels assemblage effroyable!
D'inutiles douleurs éternel entretien!
Philosophes trompés qui criez : 'Tout est bien,'
Accourez, contemplez ces ruines affreuses,
Ces débris, ces lambeaux, ces cendres malheureuses,
Ces femmes, ces enfants l'un sur l'autre entassés,
Sous ces marbres rompus ces membres dispersés ;
Cent mille infortunés que la terre dévore,
Qui, sanglants, déchirés, et palpitants encore,
Enterrés sous leurs toits, terminent sans secours
Dans l'horreur des tourments leurs lamentables jours!
Aux cris demi-formés de leurs voix expirantes,
Au spectacle effrayant de leurs cendres fumantes,
Direz-vous : 'C'est l'effet des éternelles lois,

Qui d'un Dieu libre et bon necessitent le choix'?
Direz-vous, en voyant cet amas de victimes:
'Dieu s'est vengé; leur mort est le prix de leurs crimes'?
Quel crime, quelle faute ont commis ces enfants
Sur le sein maternel écrasés et sanglants?
Lisbonne, qui n'est plus, eut-elle plus de vices
Que Londres, que Paris, plongés dans les délices?
Lisbonne est abimée, et l'on danse à Paris.
Tranquilles spectateurs, intrépides esprits,
De vos frères mourants contemplant les naufrages,
Vous recherchez en paix les causes des orages:
Mais du sort ennemi quand vous sentez les coups
Devenus plus humains, vous pleurez comme nous.
Croyez-moi, quand la terre entr'ouvre ses abîmes,
Ma plainte est innocente, et mes cris légitimes.
Partout environnés des cruantés du sort,
Des fureurs des méchants, des pièges de la mort,
De tous les éléments éprouvant les atteintes,
Compagnons de nos maux, permettez-nous les plaintes. . . .
    Ainsi du monde entier tous les membres gémissent:
Nés tous pour les tourments, l'un par l'autre ils périssent:
Et vous composerez, dans ce chaos fatal,
Des malheurs de chaque être un bonheur général!
Quel bonheur! ô mortel et faible et misérable,
Vous criez: 'Tout est bien,' d'une voix lamentable,
L'univers vous dément, et votre propre cœur
Cent fois de votre esprit a réfuté l'erreur.
Éléments, animaux, humains, tout est en guerre.
Il le faut avouer, le *mal* est sur la terre:
Son principe secret ne nous est point connu.
De l'auteur de tout bien le mal est-il venu? . . .
    Mais comment concevoir un Dieu, la bonté même,
Qui prodigua ses biens à ses enfants qu'il aime,
Et qui versa sur eux les maux à pleines mains?
Quel œil peut pénétrer dans ses profonds desseins?
De l'Être tout parfait le mal ne pouvait naître;
Il ne vient point d'autrui, puisque Dieu seul est maître;
Il existe pourtant.   O tristes vérités!
O mélange étonnant de contrariétés! . . .

                                    VOLTAIRE.

(88)

LE PHÉNIX

Le Phénix, venant d'Arabie,
Dans nos bois parut un beau jour:
Grand bruit chez les oiseaux, leur troupe réunie
Vole pour lui faire sa cour.
Chacun l'observe, l'examine:
Son plumage, sa voix, son chant mélodieux,
Tout est beauté, grâce divine,
Tout charme l'oreille et les yeux.
Pour la première fois on vit céder l'envie
Au besoin de louer et d'aimer son vainqueur.
Le rossignol disait: 'Jamais tant de douceur
N'enchanta mon âme ravie.
— Jamais, disait le paon, de plus belles couleurs
N'ont eu cet éclat que j'admire:
Il éblouit mes yeux et toujours les attire.'
Les autres répétaient ces éloges flatteurs,
Vantaient le privilège unique
De ce roi des oiseaux, de cet enfant du ciel,
Qui, vieux, sur un bûcher de cèdre aromatique
Se consume lui-même et renaît immortel.
Pendant tous ces discours, la seule tourterelle,
Sans rien dire, fit un soupir.
Son époux, la poussant de l'aile,
Lui demande d'où peut venir
Sa rêverie et sa tristesse:
'De cet heureux oiseau désires-tu le sort?
— Moi! mon ami, je le plains fort:
Il est le seul de son espèce.'

JEAN-PIERRE CLARIS DE FLORIAN (1755–94).

(89)

SUR LA MORT D'UNE JEUNE FILLE

Son âge échappait à l'enfance;
Riante comme l'innocence,
Elle avait les traits de l'Amour.

Quelques mois, quelques jours encore,
Dans ce cœur pur et sans détour
Le sentiment allait éclore.
Mais le Ciel avait au trépas
Condamné ses jeunes appas.
Au Ciel elle a rendu sa vie,
Et doucement s'est endormie
Sans murmurer contre ses lois.
Ainsi le sourire s'efface ;
Ainsi meurt, sans laisser de trace,
Le chant d'un oiseau dans les bois.

ÉVARISTE DE PARNY (1754–1801).

(90)

LES DEUX RUISSEAUX

Daphnis, privé de son amante,
Conta cette fable touchante
A ceux qui blâmaient ses douleurs :
Deux ruisseaux confondaient leur onde,
Et, sur un pré semé de fleurs,
Coulaient dans une paix profonde.
Dès leur source, aux mêmes déserts,
La même pente les rassemble,
Et leurs vœux sont d'aller ensemble
S'abîmer dans le sein des mers.
Faut-il que le destin barbare
S'oppose aux plus tendres amours ?
Ces ruisseaux trouvent dans leur cours
Un roc affreux qui les sépare.
L'un d'eux, dans son triste abandon,
Se déchaînait contre sa rive,
Et tous les échos du vallon
Répondaient à sa voix plaintive.
Un passant lui dit brusquement :
— Pourquoi sur cette molle arène,
Ne pas murmurer doucement ?
Ton bruit m'importune et me gêne.

— N'entends-tu pas, dit le ruisseau,
A l'autre bord de ce coteau,
Gémir la moitié de moi-même?
Poursuis ta route, ô voyageur,
Et demande aux dieux que ton cœur
Ne perde jamais ce qu'il aime!

NICOLAS-GERMAIN LÉONARD (1744–93).

(91)

ADIEUX A LA VIE

J'ai révélé mon cœur au Dieu de l'innocence;
   Il a vu mes pleurs pénitents;
Il guérit mes remords, il m'arme de constance:
   Les malheureux sont ses enfants.

Mes ennemis, riant, ont dit dans leur colère:
   'Qu'il meure, et sa gloire avec lui!'
Mais à mon cœur calmé le Seigneur dit en père:
   'Leur haine sera ton appui.

'A tes plus chers amis ils ont prêté leur rage.
   Tout trompe ta simplicité:
Celui que tu nourris court vendre ton image,
   Noire de sa méchanceté.

'Mais Dieu t'entend gémir, Dieu vers qui te ramène
   Un vrai remords né des douleurs,
Dieu qui pardonne enfin à la nature humaine
   D'être faible dans les malheurs.

'J'éveillerai pour toi la pitié, la justice
   De l'incorruptible avenir;
Eux-même épureront, par leur long artifice,
   Ton honneur qu'ils pensent ternir.'

Soyez béni, mon Dieu, vous qui daignez me rendre
   L'innocence et son noble orgueil,
Vous qui, pour protéger le repos de ma cendre,
   Veillerez près de mon cercueil!

Au banquet de la vie, infortuné convive,
    J'apparus un jour, et je meurs;
Je meurs, et sur ma tombe, où lentement j'arrive,
    Nul ne viendra verser des pleurs.

Salut, champs que j'aimais! et vous, douce verdure!
    Et vous, riant exil des bois!
Ciel, pavillon de l'homme, admirable nature,
    Salut pour la dernière fois!

Ah! puissent voir longtemps votre beauté sacrée
    Tant d'amis sourds à mes adieux!
Qu'ils meurent pleins de jours, que leur mort soit
        pleurée,
    Qu'un ami leur ferme les yeux!

                NICOLAS-LAURENT-JOSEPH GILBERT (1751–80).

(92)
LA FLÛTE

Toujours ce souvenir m'attendrit et me touche,
Quand lui-même, appliquant la flûte sur ma bouche,
Riant et m'asseyant sur lui, près de son cœur,
M'appelait son rival et déjà son vainqueur.
Il façonnait ma lèvre inhabile et peu sûre
A souffler une haleine harmonieuse et pure;
Et ses savantes mains prenaient mes jeunes doigts,
Les levaient, les baissaient, recommençaient vingt fois,
Leur enseignant ainsi, quoique faibles encore,
A fermer tour à tour les trous du buis sonore.

                    ANDRÉ CHÉNIER (1762–94).

(93)
CLYTIE

Mes Mânes à Clytie: 'Adieu, Clytie, adieu.
Est-ce toi dont les pas ont visité ce lieu?
Parle, est-ce toi, Clytie, ou dois-je attendre encore?
Ah! si tu ne viens pas seule ici, chaque aurore,

Rêver au peu de jours où j'ai vécu pour toi,
Voir cette ombre qui t'aime et parler avec moi,
D'Élysée à mon cœur la paix devient amère,
Et la terre à mes os ne sera plus légère.
Chaque fois qu'en ces lieux un air frais du matin
Vient caresser ta bouche et voler sur ton sein,
Pleure, pleure, c'est moi; pleure, fille adorée;
C'est mon âme qui fuit sa demeure sacrée,
Et sur ta bouche encore aime à se reposer.
Pleure, ouvre-lui tes bras et rends-lui son baiser.'

CHÉNIER.

(94)

SUR LA MORT D'UN ENFANT

L'innocente victime, au terrestre séjour,
N'a vu que le printemps qui lui donna le jour.
Rien n'est resté de lui qu'un nom, un vain nuage,
Un souvenir, un songe, une invisible image.
Adieu, fragile enfant échappé de nos bras;
Adieu, dans la maison d'où l'on ne revient pas.
Nous ne te verrons plus, quand, de moissons couverte,
La campagne d'été rend la ville déserte;
Dans l'enclos paternel nous ne te verrons plus,
De tes pieds, de tes mains, de tes flancs demi-nus,
Presser l'herbe et les fleurs dont les nymphes de Seine
Couronnent tous les ans les coteaux de Lucienne;
L'axe de l'humble char à tes jeux destiné,
Par de fidèles mains avec toi promené,
Ne sillonnera plus les prés et le rivage.
Tes regards, ton murmure, obscur et doux langage,
N'inquiéteront plus nos soins officieux;
Nous ne recevrons plus avec des cris joyeux
Les efforts impuissants de ta bouche vermeille
A bégayer les sons offerts à ton oreille.
Adieu, dans la demeure où nous nous suivrons tous,
Où ta mère déjà tourne ses yeux jaloux.

CHÉNIER.

(95)

SAINT-LAZARE

Comme un dernier rayon, comme un dernier zéphyre,
　　Animent la fin d'un beau jour,
Au pied de l'échafaud j'essaye encor ma lyre ;
　　Peut-être est-ce bientôt mon tour ;
Peut-être, avant que l'heure en cercle promenée
　　Ait posé sur l'émail brillant,
Dans les soixante pas où sa route est bornée,
　　Son pied sonore et vigilant,
Le sommeil du tombeau pressera ma paupière !
　　Avant que de ses deux moitiés
Ce vers que je commence ait atteint la dernière,
　　Peut-être en ces murs effrayés
Le messager de mort, noir recruteur des ombres,
　　Escorté d'infâmes soldats,
Remplissant de mon nom ces longs corridors sombres,
　　Où, seul, dans la foule à grands pas
J'erre, aiguisant ces dards persécuteurs du crime,
　　Du juste trop faibles soutiens,
Sur mes lèvres soudain va suspendre la rime ;
　　Et, chargeant mes bras de liens,
Me traîner, amassant en foule à mon passage
　　Mes tristes compagnons reclus,
Qui me connaissaient tous avant l'affreux message,
　　Mais qui ne me connaissent plus.

　.　　　.　　　.　　　.　　　.

Eh bien ! j'ai trop vécu.　Quelle franchise auguste,
　　De mâle constance et d'honneur
Quels exemples sacrés, doux à l'âme du juste,
　　Pour lui quelle ombre de bonheur,
Quelle Thémis terrible aux têtes criminelles,
　　Quels pleurs d'une noble pitié,
Des antiques bienfaits quels souvenirs fidèles,
　　Quels beaux échanges d'amitié,
Font digne de regrets l'habitacle des hommes?
　　La Peur blême et louche est leur dieu.

Le désespoir !... la feinte ! Ah ! lâches que nous sommes,
    Tous, oui, tous.   Adieu, terre, adieu.
Vienne, vienne la mort !   Que la mort me délivre !
    Ainsi donc, mon cœur abattu
Cède au poids de ses maux ?   Non, non, puissé-je vivre !
    Ma vie importe à la vertu :
Car l'honnête homme enfin, victime de l'outrage,
    Dans les cachots, près du cercueil,
Relève plus altiers son front et son langage
    Brillants d'un généreux orgueil.
S'il est écrit aux cieux que jamais une épée
    N'étincellera dans mes mains,
Dans l'encre et l'amertume une autre arme trempée
    Peut encor servir les humains.
Justice, vérité, si ma bouche sincère,
    Si mes pensers les plus secrets
Ne froncèrent jamais votre sourcil sévère,
    Et si les infâmes progrès,
Si la risée atroce ou (plus atroce injure !)
    L'encens de hideux scélérats
Ont pénétré vos cœurs d'une longue blessure,
    Sauvez-moi ; conservez un bras
Qui lance votre foudre, un ami qui vous venge.
    Mourir sans vider mon carquois !
Sans percer, sans fouler, sans pétrir dans leur fange,
    Ces bourreaux barbouilleurs de lois,
Ces vers cadavéreux de la France asservie,
    Égorgée. . . . O mon cher trésor !
O ma plume ! fiel ! bile ! horreur, dieux de ma vie !
    Par vous seuls je respire encor,
Comme la poix brûlante agitée en ses veines
    Ressuscite un flambeau mourant.
Je souffre, mais je vis.   Par vous, loin de mes peines,
    D'espérance un vaste torrent
Me transporte.   Sans vous, comme un poison livide,
    L'invincible dent du chagrin,
Mes amis opprimés, du menteur homicide
    Les succès, le sceptre d'airain,
Des bons proscrits par lui la mort ou la ruine,
    L'opprobre de subir sa loi,

Tout eût tari ma vie, ou contre ma poitrine
   Dirigé mon poignard.   Mais quoi?
Nul ne resterait donc pour attendrir l'histoire
   Sur tant de justes massacrés ;
Pour consoler leurs fils, leurs veuves, leur mémoire ;
   Pour que des brigands abhorrés
Frémissent aux portraits, noirs de leur ressemblance,
   Pour descendre jusqu'aux enfers
Chercher le triple fouet, le fouet de la vengeance,
   Déjà levé sur ces pervers ;
Pour cracher sur leur nom, pour chanter leur supplice !
   Allons, étouffe tes clameurs ;
Souffre, ô cœur gros de haine, affamé de justice,
   Toi, Vertu, pleurs si je meurs.

CHÉNIER.

(96)

LA JEUNE FILLE

Elle était bien jolie, au matin, sans atours,
De son jardin naissant visitant les merveilles,
Dans leur nid d'ambroisie épiant ses abeilles,
Et du parterre en fleurs suivant les longs détours.

Elle était bien jolie, au bal de la soirée,
Quand l'éclat des flambeaux illuminait son front,
Et que de bleus saphirs ou de roses parée
De la danse folâtre elle menait le rond.

Elle était bien jolie, à l'abri de son voile
Qu'elle livrait, flottant, au souffle de la nuit,
Quand pour la voir de loin, nous étions là sans bruit,
Heureux de la connaître au reflet d'une étoile.

Elle était bien jolie ; et de pensers touchants
D'un espoir vague et doux chaque jour embellie,
L'amour lui manquait seul pour être plus jolie ! . . .
Paix ! . . . voilà son convoi qui passe dans les champs ! . . .

CHARLES NODIER (1780–1844).

(97)

L'OREILLER D'UNE PETITE FILLE

Cher petit oreiller, doux et chaud sous ma tête,
Plein de plume choisie, et blanc! et fait pour moi!
Quand on a peur du vent, des loups, de la tempête,
Cher petit oreiller, que je dors bien sur toi!

Beaucoup, beaucoup d'enfants pauvres et nus, sans mère,
Sans maison, n'ont jamais d'oreiller pour dormir;
Ils ont toujours sommeil. O destinée amère!
Maman! douce maman! cela me fait gémir.

Et quand j'ai prié Dieu pour tous ces petits anges
Qui n'ont pas d'oreiller, moi, j'embrasse le mien.
Seule, dans mon doux nid qu'à tes pieds tu m'arranges,
Je te bénis, ma mère, et je touche le tien.

Je ne m'éveillerai qu'à la lueur première
De l'aube; au rideau bleu c'est si gai de la voir!
Je vais dire tout bas ma plus tendre prière:
Donne encore un baiser, douce maman! Bonsoir!

.   .   .   .   .

Dieu des enfants! le cœur d'une petite fille,
Plein de prière (écoute!), est ici sous mes mains;
On me parle toujours d'orphelins sans famille:
Dans l'avenir, mon Dieu, ne fais plus d'orphelins!

Laisse descendre au soir un ange qui pardonne,
Pour répondre à des voix que l'on entend gémir.
Mets, sous l'enfant perdu que la mère abandonne,
Un petit oreiller qui le fera dormir!

MARCELINE DESBORDES-VALMORE (1786–1859).

(98)

ROMANCE

S'il avait su quelle âme il a blessée,
Larmes du cœur, s'il avait pu vous voir,
Ah! si ce cœur, trop plein de sa pensée,
De l'exprimer eût gardé le pouvoir,

Changer ainsi n'eût pas été possible;
Fier de nourrir l'espoir qu'il a déçu,
A tant d'amour il eût été sensible,
  S'il avait su.

S'il avait su tout ce qu'on peut attendre
D'une âme simple, ardente et sans détour,
Il eût voulu la mienne pour l'entendre.
Comme il l'inspire, il eût connu l'amour.
Mes yeux baissés recélaient cette flamme;
Dans leur pudeur n'a-t-il rien aperçu?
Un tel secret valait toute son âme,
  S'il avait su.

Si j'avais su, moi-même, à quel empire
On s'abandonne en regardant ses yeux,
Sans le chercher comme l'air qu'on respire,
J'aurai porté mes jours sous d'autres cieux.
Il est trop tard pour renouer ma vie;
Ma vie était un doux espoir déçu:
Diras-tu pas, toi qui me l'as ravie,
  Si j'avais su?

    MARCELINE DESBORDES-VALMORE.

(99)

SOUVENIR

Quand il pâlit un soir, et que sa voix tremblante
S'éteignit tout à coup dans un mot commencé;
Quand ses yeux, soulevant leur paupière brûlante,
Me blessèrent d'un mal dont je le crus blessé;
Quand ses traits plus touchants, éclairés d'une flamme
  Qui ne s'éteint jamais,
S'imprimèrent vivants dans le fond de mon âme;
  Il n'aimait pas, j'aimais!

    MARCELINE DESBORDES-VALMORE.

(100)

LE PAPILLON

Naître avec le printemps, mourir avec les roses;
Sur l'aile du zéphyr nager dans un ciel pur;
Balancé sur le sein des fleurs à peine écloses,
S'enivrer de parfums, de lumière et d'azur;
Secouant, jeune encor, la poudre de ses ailes,
S'envoler comme un souffle aux voûtes éternelles,
Voilà du papillon le destin enchanté.
Il ressemble au désir, qui jamais ne se pose,
Et sans se satisfaire, effleurant toute chose,
Retourne enfin au ciel chercher la volupté!

ALPHONSE DE LAMARTINE (1790–1869).

(101)

LES PROPHÈTES

Il est, parmi les fils les plus doux de la femme,
Des hommes dont les sens obscurcissent moins l'âme,
Dont le cœur est mobile et profond comme l'eau,
Dont le moindre contact fait frissonner la peau,
Dont la pensée, en proie à de sacrés délires,
S'ébranle au doigt divin, chante comme des lyres,
Mélodieux échos semés dans l'univers
Pour comprendre sa langue et noter ses concerts:
C'est dans leur transparente et limpide pensée
Que l'image infinie est le mieux retracée
Et que la vaste idée où l'Éternel se peint
D'ineffables couleurs s'illumine et se teint!
Ceux-là, fuyant la foule et cherchant les retraites,
Ont avec le désert des amitiés secrètes;
Sur les grèves des flots en égarant leurs pas,
Ils entendent des voix que nous n'entendons pas:

.   .   .   .   .   .

Écoutez-les prier, car ils sont vos prophètes.

LAMARTINE.

(102)

CANTATE POUR LES ENFANTS D'UNE MAISON DE CHARITÉ

. . . Les docteurs de la loi, les chefs de la prière,
    Étaient assis dans leur orgueil;
Sous leurs sourcils pensifs ils cachaient leur paupière,
Ou lançaient sur la foule un superbe coup d'œil;
Leur voix interrogeait la timide jeunesse;
Les rides de leur fronts témoignaient leur sagesse,
Respirant du Sina l'antique majesté;
De leurs cheveux blanchis, de leur barbe touffue,
On croyait voir glisser sur leur poitrine nue
    La lumière et la charité,
    Comme des neiges des montagnes
Descendent, ô Sâron, sur tes humble campagnes
    Le jour et la fertilité!

Un enfant devant eux s'avança, plein de grâce;
La foule, en l'admirant, devant ses pas s'ouvrait,
    Puis se refermait sur sa trace;
Il semblait éclairer l'espace
D'un jour surnaturel que lui seul ignorait.

    Des ombres de sa chevelure
    Son front sortait, comme un rayon
    Échappé de la nue obscure
    Éclaire un sévère horizon.

    Ce front pur et mélancolique
    S'avançait sur l'œil inspiré,
    Tel qu'un majestueux portique
    S'avance sur un seuil sacré!

    L'éclair céleste de son âme
    S'adoucissait dans son œil pur,
    Comme une étoile dont la flamme
    Sort plus douce des flots d'azur.

Il parla : les sages doutèrent
De leur orgueilleuse raison,
Et les colonnes l'écoutèrent,
Les colonnes de Salomon !

LAMARTINE.

(103)

ELOA

Toute parée, aux yeux du Ciel qui la contemple,
Elle marche vers Dieu comme une épouse au temple,
Son beau front est serein et pur comme un beau lis,
Et d'un voile d'azur il soulève les plis ;
Ses cheveux, partagés comme des gerbes blondes,
Dans les vapeurs de l'air perdent leurs molles ondes,
Comme on voit la comète errante dans les cieux
Fondre au sein de la nuit ses rayons glorieux ;
Une rose aux lueurs de l'aube matinale
N'a pas de son teint frais la rougeur virginale ;
Et la lune, des bois éclairant l'épaisseur,
D'un de ses doux regards n'atteint pas la douceur.
Ses ailes sont d'argent ; sous une pâle robe,
Son pied blanc tour à tour se montre et se dérobe,
Et son sein agité, mais à peine aperçu,
Soulève les contours du céleste tissu.
C'est une femme aussi, c'est une ange charmante ;
Car ce peuple d'esprits, cette famille aimante,
Qui, pour nous, près de nous, prie et veille toujours,
Unit sa pure essence en de saintes amours :
L'archange Raphaël, lorsqu'il vint sur la terre,
Sous le berceau d'Éden conta ce doux mystère.
Mais nulle de ces sœurs que Dieu créa pour eux
N'apporta plus de joie au ciel des Bienheureux.

ALFRED DE VIGNY (1797-1863).

(104)

LA MORT DU LOUP

Hélas ! ai-je pensé, malgré ce grand nom d'Hommes,
Que j'ai honte de nous, débiles que nous sommes !
Comment on doit quitter la vie et tous ses maux,
C'est vous qui le savez, sublimes animaux !

A voir ce que l'on fut sur terre et ce qu'on laisse,
Seul le silence est grand; tout le reste est faiblesse.
— Ah! je t'ai bien compris, sauvage voyageur,
Et ton dernier regard m'est allé jusqu'au cœur!
Il disait: 'Si tu peux, fais que ton âme arrive,
A force de rester studieuse et pensive,
Jusqu'à ce haut degré de stoïque fierté
Où, naissant dans les bois, j'ai tout d'abord monté.
Gémir, pleurer, prier, est également lâche.
Fais énergiquement ta longue et lourde tâche
Dans la voie où le sort a voulu t'appeler,
Puis, après, comme moi, souffre et meurs sans parler.'

VIGNY.

(105)

NOUVELLE CHANSON SUR UN VIEIL AIR

S'il est un charmant gazon
  Que le ciel arrose,
Où brille en toute saison
  Quelque fleur éclose,
Où l'on cueille à pleine main
Lis, chèvrefeuille et jasmin,
J'en veux faire le chemin
  Où ton pied se pose!

S'il est un sein bien aimant
  Dont l'honneur dispose!
Dont le ferme dévoûment
  N'ait rien de morose,
Si toujours ce noble sein
Bat pour un digne dessein!
J'en veux faire le coussin
  Où ton front se pose!

S'il est un rêve d'amour,
  Parfumé de rose,
Où l'on trouve chaque jour
  Quelque douce chose,

Un rêve que Dieu bénit,
Où l'âme à l'âme s'unit,
Oh! j'en veux faire le nid
Où ton cœur se pose!

VICTOR HUGO (1802–85)
(*Chants du Crépuscule*).

(106)

AUBADE

L'aube naît et ta porte est close!
Ma belle, pourquoi sommeiller?
A l'heure où s'éveille la rose
Ne vas-tu pas te réveiller?

> O ma charmante,
> Écoute ici
> L'amant qui chante
> Et pleure aussi!

Tout frappe à ta porte bénie;
L'aurore dit: Je suis le jour!
L'oiseau dit: Je suis l'harmonie!
Et mon cœur dit: Je suis l'amour!

> O ma charmante,
> Écoute ici
> L'amant qui chante
> Et pleure aussi!

Je t'adore ange et t'aime femme,
Dieu qui par toi m'a complété
A fait mon amour pour ton âme
Et mon regard pour ta beauté!

> O ma charmante,
> Écoute ici
> L'amant qui chante
> Et pleure aussi!

HUGO
(*Chants du Crépuscule*).

(107)

L'ENFANCE

L'enfant chantait; la mère au lit, exténuée,
Agonisait, beau front dans l'ombre se penchant;
La mort au-dessus d'elle errait dans la nuée;
Et j'écoutais ce râle, et j'entendais ce chant.

L'enfant avait cinq ans, et près de la fenêtre
Ses rires et ses jeux faisaient un charmant bruit;
Et la mère, à côté de ce pauvre doux être
Qui chantait tout le jour, toussait toute la nuit.

La mère alla dormir sous les dalles du cloître;
Et le petit enfant se remit à chanter. —
La douleur est un fruit; Dieu ne le fait pas croître
Sur la branche trop faible encor pour le porter.

HUGO
(*Les Contemplations—Autrefois*).

(108)

LE MATIN

Le voile du matin sur les monts se déploie.
Vois, un rayon naissant blanchit la vieille tour;
Et déjà dans les cieux s'unit avec amour,
   Ainsi que la gloire à la joie,
Le premier chant des bois aux premiers feux du jour.

Oui, souris à l'éclat dont le ciel se décore!
Tu verras, si demain le cercueil me dévore,
Un soleil aussi beau luire à ton désespoir,
Et les mêmes oiseaux chanter la même aurore,
   Sur mon tombeau muet et noir!

Mais dans l'autre horizon l'âme alors est ravie.
L'avenir sans fin s'ouvre à l'être illimité.
   Au matin de l'éternité,
   On se réveille de la vie,
Comme d'une nuit sombre ou d'un rêve agité.

HUGO
(*Odes et Ballades*)

(109)

HYMNE

Ceux qui pieusement sont morts pour la patrie
Ont droit qu'à leur cercueil la foule vienne et prie.
Entre les plus beaux noms leur nom est le plus beau.
Toute gloire près d'eux passe et tombe éphémère;
 Et, comme ferait une mère,
La voix d'un peuple entier les berce en leur tombeau.
 Gloire à notre France éternelle!
 Gloire à ceux qui sont morts pour elle!
 Aux martyrs, aux vaillants, aux forts!
 A ceux qu'enflamme leur example,
 Qui veulent place dans le temple,
 Et qui mourront comme ils sont morts!

C'est pour ces morts, dont l'ombre est ici bienvenue,
Que le haut Panthéon élève dans la nue,
Au-dessus de Paris, la ville aux mille tours,
La reine de nos Tyrs et de nos Babylones,
 Cette couronne de colonnes
Que le soleil levant redore tous les jours!
 Gloire à notre France éternelle!
 Gloire à ceux qui sont morts pour elle!
 Aux martyrs, aux vaillants, aux forts!
 A ceux qu'enflamme leur exemple
 Qui veulent place dans le temple,
 Et qui mourront comme ils sont morts!

Ainsi, quand de tels morts sont couchés dans la tombe,
En vain l'oubli, nuit sombre où va tout ce qui tombe,
Passe sur leur sépulchre où nous nous inclinons.
Chaque jour, pour eux seuls se levant plus fidèle,
 La gloire, aube toujours nouvelle,
Fait luire leur mémoire et redore leurs noms!
 Gloire à notre France éternelle!
 Gloire à ceux qui sont morts pour elle!

Aux martyrs, aux vaillants, aux forts!
A ceux qu'enflamme leur exemple,
Qui veulent place dans le temple,
Et qui mourront comme ils sont morts!

HUGO
(*Chants du Crépuscule*).

Note: Inserted by the desire of M. Delagrave, who controls the copyright
of Victor Hugo's works: 'Ceux de nos lecteurs qui désireraient un choix plus
abondant d'extraits de Victor Hugo peuvent se reporter aux trois volumes
parus dans la Collection Pallas (Éd. Delagrave), ou au recueil de M. Maurice
Levaillant: *L'Œuvre de Victor Hugo* (Éd. Delagrave).'

(110)

UNE ALLÉE DU LUXEMBOURG

Elle a passé, la jeune fille,
Vive et preste comme un oiseau:
A la main une fleur qui brille,
A la bouche un refrain nouveau.

C'est peut-être la seule au monde
Dont le cœur au mien répondrait;
Qui venant dans ma nuit profonde
D'un seul regard l'éclairerait! . . .

Mais non, — ma jeunesse est finie . . .
Adieu, doux rayon qui m'a lui, —
Parfum, jeune fille, harmonie . . .
Le bonheur passait — il a fui!

GÉRARD DE NERVAL (1808–55).

(111)

DANS LES BOIS

Au printemps, l'oiseau naît et chante:
N'avez-vous jamais ouï sa voix? . . .
Elle est pure, simple et touchante
La voix de l'oiseau — dans les bois!

L'été, l'oiseau cherche l'oiselle;
Il aime, et n'aime qu'une fois!
Qu'il est doux, paisible et fidèle
Le nid de l'oiseau — dans les bois!

N

Puis, quand vient l'automne brumeuse
Il se tait . . . avant les temps froids.
Hélas! qu'elle doit être heureuse
La mort de l'oiseau — dans les bois!

NERVAL.

(112)
ARTÉMIS

La treizième revient. . . . C'est encor la première;
Et c'est toujours la seule, — ou c'est le seul moment :
Car es-tu reine, ô toi! la première ou dernière?
Es-tu roi, toi le seul ou le dernier amant? . . .

Aimez qui vous aima du berceau dans la bière;
Celle que j'aimai seul m'aime encor tendrement :
C'est la mort — ou la morte. . . . O délice! ô tourment!
La rose qu'elle tient, c'est la *rose trémière*.

Sainte napolitaine aux mains pleines de feux,
Rose au cœur violet, fleur de sainte Gudule :
As-tu trouvé ta croix dans le désert des cieux?

Roses blanches, tombez! vous insultez nos dieux :
Tombez, fantômes blancs, de votre ciel qui brûle;
— La sainte de l'abîme est plus sainte à mes yeux.

NERVAL.

(113)
ÉLÉGIE [1]

Mes chers amis, quand je mourrai,
Plantez un saule au cimetière.
J'aime son feuillage éploré,
La pâleur m'en est douce et chère,
Et son ombre sera légère
A la terre où je dormirai.

ALFRED DE MUSSET (1810–57).

---

[1] A Latin version by H. Broadbent, Exeter College, *Nova Anthol. Oxon.*:

> O socii cari, cum venerit hora suprema,
> Sit salicem in tumulo ponere cura meo:
> Frons lacrimosa placet, pallor dulcissimus ille est:
> Proteget et somni non gravis umbra locum.

(114)

CHANSON DE FORTUNIO

Si vous croyez que je vais dire
    Qui j'ose aimer,
Je ne saurais, pour un empire,
    Vous la nommer.

Nous allons chanter à la ronde,
    Si vous voulez,
Que je l'adore et qu'elle est blonde
    Comme les blés.

Je fais ce que sa fantaisie
    Veut m'ordonner,
Et je puis, s'il lui faut ma vie,
    La lui donner.

Du mal qu'une amour ignorée
    Nous fait souffrir,
J'en porte l'âme déchirée
    Jusqu'à mourir.

Mais j'aime trop pour que je die
    Qui j'ose aimer,
Et je veux mourir pour ma mie
    Sans la nommer.

MUSSET.

(115)

TRISTESSE

J'ai perdu ma force et ma vie,
Et mes amis et ma gaîté;
J'ai perdu jusqu'à la fierté
Qui faisait croire à mon génie.

Quand j'ai connu la Vérité,
J'ai cru que c'était une amie;

Quand je l'ai comprise et sentie,
J'en étais déjà dégoûté.

Et pourtant elle est éternelle,
Et ceux qui se sont passés d'elle
Ici-bas ont tout ignoré.

Dieu parle, il faut qu'on lui réponde.
Le seul bien qui me reste au monde
Est d'avoir quelquefois pleuré.

MUSSET.

(116)

LES PAPILLONS

Les papillons couleur de neige
Volent par essaims sur la mer;
Beaux papillons blancs, quand pourrai-je
Prendre le bleu chemin de l'air?

Savez-vous, ô belle des belles,
Ma bayadère aux yeux de jais,
S'ils me pouvaient prêter leurs ailes,
Dites, savez-vous où j'irais?

Sans prendre un seul baiser aux roses
A travers vallons et forêts,
J'irais à vos lèvres mi-closes,
Fleur de mon âme, et j'y mourrais.

THÉOPHILE GAUTIER (1811–72).

(117)

LE SPECTRE DE LA ROSE

Soulève ta paupière close
Qu'effleure un songe virginal;
Je suis le spectre d'une rose
Que tu portais hier au bal.

Tu me pris encore emperlée
Des pleurs d'argent de l'arrosoir,
Et parmi la fête étoilée
Tu me promenas tout le soir.

O toi qui de ma mort fus cause,
Sans que tu puisses le chasser,
Toute la nuit mon spectre rose
A ton chevet viendra danser.
Mais ne crains rien, je ne réclame
Ni messe ni *De profundis*;
Ce léger parfum est mon âme,
Et j'arrive du paradis.

Mon destin fut digne d'envie :
Pour avoir un trépas si beau,
Plus d'un aurait donné sa vie,
Car j'ai ta gorge pour tombeau.
Et sur l'albâtre où je repose
Un poète avec un baiser
Écrivit : Ci-gît une rose
Que tous les rois vont jalouser.

GAUTIER.

(118)

LE MONDE EST MÉCHANT

Le monde est méchant, ma petite :
Avec son sourire moqueur
Il dit qu'à ton côté palpite
Une montre en place de cœur.
— Pourtant ton sein ému s'élève
Et s'abaisse comme la mer,
Aux bouillonnements de la sève
Circulant sous ta jeune chair.

Le monde est méchant, ma petite :
Il dit que tes yeux vifs sont morts,
Et se meuvent dans leur orbite
A temps égaux et par ressorts.

— Pourtant une larme irisée
Tremble à tes cils, mouvant rideau,
Comme une perle de rosée
Qui n'est pas prise au verre d'eau.

Le monde est méchant, ma petite :
Il dit que tu n'as pas d'esprit,
Et que les vers qu'on te récite
Sont pour toi comme du sanscrit.
— Pourtant, sur ta bouche vermeille,
Fleur s'ouvrant et se refermant,
Le rire, intelligente abeille,
Se pose à chaque trait charmant.

C'est que tu m'aimes, ma petite,
Et que tu hais tous ces gens-là.
Quitte-moi; — comme ils diront vite:
Quel cœur et quel esprit elle a !

GAUTIER.

(119)

A ADOLPHE GAÏFFE

Jeune homme sans mélancolie,
Blond comme un soleil d'Italie,
Garde bien ta belle folie.

C'est la sagesse ! Aimer le vin,
La beauté, le printemps divin,
Cela suffit. Le reste est vain.

Souris, même au destin sévère !
Et quand revient la primevère,
Jettes-en les fleurs dans ton verre.

Au corps sous la tombe enfermé
Que reste-t-il? D'avoir aimé
Pendant deux ou trois mois de mai.

'Cherchez les effets et les causes,'
Nous disent les rêveurs moroses.
Des mots! des mots! cueillons les roses.

THÉODORE DE BANVILLE (1823–91).

(120)

AIMONS-NOUS ET DORMONS

Aimons-nous et dormons
Sans songer au reste du monde!
Ni le flot de la mer, ni l'ouragan des monts,
Tant que nous nous aimons
Ne courbera ta tête blonde,
Car l'amour est plus fort
Que les Dieux et la Mort!

Le soleil s'éteindrait
Pour laisser ta blancheur plus pure.
Le vent, qui jusqu'à terre incline la forêt,
En passant n'oserait
Jouer avec ta chevelure
Tant que tu cacheras
Ta tête entre mes bras!

Et lorsque nos deux cœurs
S'en iront aux sphères heureuses
Où les célestes lys écloront sous nos pleurs,
Alors, comme deux fleurs,
Joignons nos lèvres amoureuses,
Et tâchons d'épuiser
La Mort dans un baiser!

BANVILLE.

(121)

HYMNE

A la très-chère, à la très-belle
Qui remplit mon cœur de clarté,
A l'ange, à l'idole immortelle,
Salut en immortalité!

Elle se répand dans ma vie
Comme un air imprégné de sel,
Et dans mon âme inassouvie
Verse le goût de l'éternel.

Sachet toujours frais qui parfume
L'atmosphère d'un cher réduit,
Encensoir oublié qui fume
En secret à travers la nuit.

Comment, amour incorruptible,
T'exprimer avec vérité?
Grain de musc qui gis, invisible,
Au fond de mon éternité?

A la très-bonne, à la très-belle
Qui fait ma joie et ma santé,
A l'ange, à l'idole immortelle,
Salut en immortalité!

CHARLES BAUDELAIRE (1821–67).

(122)

TOUT ENTIÈRE

Le Démon, dans ma chambre haute,
Ce matin est venu me voir,
Et, tâchant à me prendre en faute,
Me dit: 'Je voudrais bien savoir,

'Parmi toutes les belles choses
Dont est fait son enchantement,
Parmi les objets noirs ou roses
Qui composent son corps charmant,

'Quel et le plus doux?' — O mon âme!
Tu répondis à l'Abhorré:
'Puisque en Elle tout est dictame,
Rien ne peut être préféré.

'Lorsque tout me ravit, j'ignore
Si quelque chose me séduit.
Elle éblouit comme l'Aurore
Et console comme la Nuit.

'Et l'harmonie est trop exquise,
Qui gouverne tout son beau corps,
Pour que l'impuissante analyse
En note les nombreux accords.

'O métamorphose mystique
De tous mes sens fondus en un !
Son haleine fait la musique,
Comme sa voix fait le parfum.'

BAUDELAIRE.

(123)
L'AUBE SPIRITUELLE

Quand chez les débauchés l'aube blanche et vermeille
Entre en société de l'Idéal rongeur,
Par l'opération d'un mystère vengeur
Dans la brute assoupie un Ange se réveille.

Des Cieux Spirituels l'inaccessible azur,
Pour l'homme terrassé qui rêve encore et souffre,
S'ouvre et s'enfonce avec l'attirance du gouffre.
Ainsi, chère Déesse, Être lucide et pur,

Sur les débris fumeux des stupides orgies
Ton souvenir plus clair, plus rose, plus charmant,
A mes yeux agrandis voltige incessamment.

Le soleil a noirci la flamme des bougies ;
Ainsi, toujours vainqueur, ton fantôme est pareil,
Ame resplendissante, à l'immortel Soleil !

BAUDELAIRE.

* N

(124)
LES AVEUGLES

Contemple-les, mon âme; ils sont vraiment affreux!
Pareils aux mannequins; vaguement ridicules;
Terribles, singuliers comme les somnambules;
Dardant on ne sait où leur globes ténébreux.

Leurs yeux, d'où la divine étincelle est partie,
Comme s'ils regardaient au loin, restent levés
Au ciel; on ne les voit jamais vers les pavés
Pencher rêveusement leur tête appesantie.

Ils traversent ainsi le noir illimité,
Ce frère du silence éternel. O cité!
Pendant qu'autour de nous tu chantes, ris et beugles,

Éprise du plaisir jusqu'à l'atrocité,
Vois, je me traîne aussi! mais, plus qu'eux hébété,
Je dis: Que cherchent-ils au Ciel, tous ces aveugles?

BAUDELAIRE.

(125)
LE VOYAGE [1]

. . . O Mort, vieux capitaine, il est temps! levons l'ancre!
Ce pays nous ennuie, ô Mort! Appareillons!
Si le ciel et la mer sont noirs comme de l'encre,
Nos cœurs que tu connais sont remplis de rayons!

Verse nous ton poison pour qu'il nous réconforte!
Nous voulons, tant ce feu nous brûle le cerveau,
Plonger au fond du gouffre, Enfer ou Ciel, qu'importe?
Au fond de l'Inconnu pour trouver du *nouveau!*

BAUDELAIRE.

[1] Latin version by H. Broadbent, Exeter College, *Nova Anthol. Oxon.*:

> Mors age, dux longaeva, ratem quin solvimus? hujus
> Pertaesum est—cessas pandere vela?—plagae.
> Si color est caelo, si fluctibus, atramenti,
> Pectora quae nosti lumine plena vides.
> Funde tuum fessos doctum recreare venenum:
> Hac domitos flamma gurgitis ima trahunt,
> Seu latet Elysium seu Tartarus, ima petemus;
> Quid sit in ignotis stat reperire novi.

(126)

LES HURLEURS

Le soleil dans les flots avait noyé ses flammes,
La ville s'endormait au pied des monts brumeux ;
Sur de grands rocs lavés d'un nuage écumeux
La mer sombre en grondant versait ses hautes lames.

La nuit multipliait ce long gémissement.
Nul astre ne luisait dans l'immensité nue ;
Seule, la lune pâle, en écartant la nue,
Comme une morne lampe oscillait tristement.

Monde muet, marqué d'un signe de colère,
Débris d'un globe mort au hasard dispersé,
Elle laissait tomber de son orbe glacé
Un reflet sépulcral sur l'océan polaire.

Sans borne, assise au Nord, sous les cieux étouffants,
L'Afrique, s'abritant d'ombre épaisse et de brume,
Affamait ses lions dans le sable qui fume,
Et couchait près des lacs ses troupeaux d'éléphants.

Mais sur la plage aride, aux odeurs insalubres,
Parmi les ossements de bœufs et de chevaux,
De maigres chiens, épars, allongeant leurs museaux,
Se lamentaient, poussant des hurlements lugubres.

La queue en cercle sous leurs ventres palpitants,
L'œil dilaté, tremblant sur leurs pattes fébriles,
Accroupis çà et là, tous hurlaient, immobiles,
Et d'un frisson rapide agités par instants.

L'écume de la mer collait sur leurs échines
De longs poils qui laissaient les vertèbres saillir ;
Et quand les flots par bonds les venaient assaillir,
Leurs dents blanches claquaient sous leurs rouges babines.

Devant la lune errante aux livides clartés,
Quelle angoisse inconnue, au bord des noires ondes,
Faisait pleurer une âme en vos formes immondes?
Pourquoi gémissiez-vous, spectres épouvantés?

Je ne sais; mais, ô chiens qui hurliez sur les plages,
Après tant de soleils qui ne reviendront plus,
J'entends toujours, au fond de mon passé confus,
Le cri désespéré de vos douleurs sauvages.

LECONTE DE LISLE (1818–94).

(127)

TRE FILA D'ORO

Là-bas, sur la mer, comme l'hirondelle,
Je voudrais m'enfuir, et plus loin encor!
Mais j'ai beau vouloir, puisque la cruelle
A liè mon cœur avec trois fils d'or.

L'un est son regard, l'autre son sourire,
La troisième, enfin, est sa lèvre en fleur;
Mais je l'aime trop, c'est un vrai martyre:
Avec trois fils d'or elle a pris mon cœur.

Oh! si je pouvais dénouer ma chaîne!
Adieu, pleurs, tourments; je prendrais l'essor.
Mais non, non! mieux vaut mourir à la peine
Que de vous briser, ô mes trois fils d'or!

LECONTE DE LISLE.

(128)

MAL ENSEVELIE

Quand votre bien-aimée est morte,
Les adieux vous sont rendus courts;
Sa paupière est close, on l'emporte,
Elle a disparu pour toujours.

Mais je la vois ma bien-aimée,
Qui sourit sans m'appartenir,
Comme une ombre plus animée,
Plus présente qu'un souvenir !

Et je la perds toute ma vie
En d'inépuisables adieux,
O morte mal ensevelie,
Ils ne t'ont pas fermé les yeux.

                    SULLY PRUDHOMME (1839–1908).

(129)

DERNIÈRE SOLITUDE

Dans cette mascarade immense des vivants
Nul ne parle à son gré ni ne marche à sa guise ;
Faite pour révéler, la parole déguise,
Et la face n'est plus qu'un masque aux traits savants.

Mais vient l'heure où le corps, infidèle ministre,
Ne prête plus son geste à l'âme éparse au loin
Et, tombant tout à coup dans un repos sinistre,
Cesse d'être complice, et demeure témoin.

Alors l'obscur essaim des arrière-pensées,
Qu'avait su refouler la force du vouloir,
Se lève et plane au front comme un nuage noir
Où gît le vrai motif des œuvres commencées ;

Le cœur monte au visage, où les plis anxieux
Ne se confondent plus aux lignes du sourire ;
Le regard ne peut plus faire mentir les yeux,
Et ce qu'on n'a pas dit vient aux lèvres s'écrire.

C'est l'heure des aveux.   Le cadavre ingénu
Garde du souffle absent une empreinte suprême,
Et l'homme, malgré lui redevenant lui-même,
Devient un étranger pour ceux qui l'ont connu.

Le rire des plus gais se détend et s'attriste,
Les plus graves parfois prennent des traits riants;
Chacun meurt comme il est, sincère à l'improviste:
C'est la candeur des morts qui les rend effrayants.

SULLY PRUDHOMME.

(130)

LE RAVISSEMENT D'ANDROMÈDE

D'un vol silencieux, le grand Cheval ailé
Soufflant de ses naseaux élargis l'air qui fume,
Les emporte avec un frémissement de plume
A travers la nuit bleue et l'éther étoilé.

Ils vont.　L'Afrique plonge au gouffre flagellé,
Puis l'Asie...un désert...le Liban ceint de brume...
Et voici qu'apparaît, toute blanche d'écume,
La mer mystérieuse où vint sombrer Hellé.

Et le vent gonfle ainsi que deux immenses voiles
Les ailes qui, volant d'étoiles en étoiles,
Aux amants enlacés font un tiède berceau;

Tandis que, l'œil au ciel où palpite leur ombre,
Ils voient, irradiant du Bélier au Verseau,
Leurs Constellations poindre dans l'azur sombre.

J.-M. DE HEREDIA (1842–1906).

(131)

ANTOINE ET CLÉOPATRE

Tous deux il regardaient, de la haute terrasse,
L'Égypte s'endormir sous un ciel étouffant,
Et le fleuve, à travers le Delta noir qu'il fend,
Vers Bubaste ou Saïs roule son onde grasse.

Et le Romain sentait sous la lourde cuirasse,
Soldat captif berçant le sommeil d'un enfant,
Ployer et défaillir sur son cœur triomphant
Le corps voluptueux que son étreinte embrasse.

Tournant sa tête pâle entre ses cheveux bruns
Vers celui qu'enivraient d'invincibles parfums,
Elle tendit sa bouche et ses prunelles claires;

Et sur elle courbé, l'ardent Imperator
Vit dans ses larges yeux étoilés de points d'or
Toute une mer immense où fuyaient des galères.

HEREDIA.

(132)

A UNE ENFANT TACITURNE

J'ai perdu la forêt, la plaine,
Et les frais avrils d'autrefois.
Donne tes lèvres, leur haleine
Ce sera le souffle des bois!

J'ai perdu l'Océan morose,
Son deuil, ses vagues, ses échos,
Dis-moi n'importe quelle chose,
Ce sera la rumeur des flots!

Sans repos, sans ombre amicale,
Front lourd, sous le soleil, je fuis;
Oh! cache-moi dans ton sein pâle,
Ce sera le calme des nuits!

VILLIERS DE l'ISLE-ADAM (1838–89).

(133)

RONDEL

Si tu veux nous nous aimerons
Avec tes lèvres sans le dire
Cette rose ne l'interromps
Qu'à verser un silence pire

Jamais des chants ne lancent prompts
Le scintillement du sourire
Si tu veux nous nous aimerons
Avec tes lèvres sans le dire

Muet muet entre les ronds
Sylphe dans la pourpre d'empire
Un baiser flambant se déchire
Jusqu'aux pointes des ailerons
Si tu veux nous nous aimerons

STÉPHANE MALLARMÉ (1842–98).[1]

(134)
HOMMAGE

Le silence déjà funèbre d'une moire
Dispose plus qu'un pli seul sur le mobilier
Que doit un tassement du principal pilier
Précipiter avec le manque de mémoire.

Notre si vieil ébat triomphal du grimoire
Hiéroglyphes dont s'exalte le millier
A propager de l'aile un frisson familier!
Enfouissez-le moi plutôt dans une armoire.

Du souriant fracas originel haï
Entre elles de clartés maîtresses a jailli
Jusque vers un parvis né pour leur simulacre,

Trompettes tout haut d'or pâmé sur les vélins,
Le dieu Richard Wagner irradiant un sacre
Mal tu par l'encre même en sanglots sibyllins.

MALLARMÉ.

(135)
LE CYGNE

Le vierge, le vivace et le bel aujourd'hui
Va-t-il nous déchirer avec un coup d'aile ivre
Ce lac dur oublié que hante sous le givre
Le transparent glacier des vols qui n'ont pas fui!

[1] Stéphane Mallarmé – Poésies – Éditions de la N.R.F. – droits reservés –.

Un cygne d'autrefois se souvient que c'est lui
Magnifique mais qui sans espoir se délivre
Pour n'avoir pas chanté la région où vivre
Quand du stérile hiver a resplendi l'ennui.

Tout son col secouera cette blanche agonie
Par l'espace infligée à l'oiseau qui le nie,
Mais non l'horreur du sol où le plumage est pris.

Fantôme qu'à ce lieu son pur éclat assigne,
Il s'immobilise au songe froid de mépris
Que vêt parmi l'exil inutile le Cygne.

MALLARMÉ.

(136)

MA BOHÊME

Je m'en allais, les poings dans mes poches crevées;
Mon paletot aussi devenait idéal;
J'allais sous le ciel, Muse! et j'étais ton féal;
Oh! là! là! que d'amours splendides j'ai rêvées!

Mon unique culotte avait un large trou.
— Petit Poucet rêveur, j'égrenais dans ma course
Des rimes. Mon auberge était à la Grande-Ourse;
— Mes étoiles au ciel avaient un doux frou-frou.

Et je les écoutais, assis au bord des routes,
Ces bons soirs de septembre où je sentais des gouttes
De rosée à mon front, comme un vin de vigueur;

Où, rimant au milieu des ombres fantastiques,
Comme des lyres, je tirais les élastiques
De mes souliers blessés, un pied près de mon cœur!

ARTHUR RIMBAUD (1854–91).

(137)

LE DORMEUR DU VAL

C'est un trou de verdure, où chante une rivière
Accrochant follement aux herbes des haillons
D'argent, où le soleil, de la montagne fière,
Luit. C'est un petit val qui mousse de rayons.

Un soldat jeune, bouche ouverte, tête nue,
Et la nuque baignant dans le frais cresson bleu,
Dort; il est étendu dans l'herbe, sous la nue,
Pâle dans son lit vert où la lumière pleut.

Les pieds dans les glaïeuls, il dort. Souriant comme
Sourirait un enfant malade, il fait un somme.
Nature, berce-le chaudement: il a froid!

Les parfums ne font pas frissonner sa narine;
Il dort dans le soleil, la main sur sa poitrine,
Tranquille.   Il a deux trous rouges au côté droit.

RIMBAUD.

(138)
ÉTERNITÉ

Elle est retrouvée
 Quoi? l'éternité.
C'est la mer allée
 Avec le soleil.

Âme sentinelle,
 Murmurons l'aveu,
De la nuit si nulle
 Et du jour en feu.

Des humains suffrages,
 Des communs élans,
Donc tu te dégages:
 Tu voles selon . . .

Jamais l'espérance;
 Pas d'*orietur*.
Science avec patience . . .
 Le supplice est sûr.

De votre ardeur seule,
 Braises de satin,

Le devoir s'exhale
   Sans qu'on dise : enfin.

Elle est retrouvée.
   Quoi ? L'éternité.
C'est la mer allée
   Avec le soleil.

RIMBAUD.

(139)

STREETS

   Dansons la gigue !
J'aimais surtout ses jolis yeux,
Plus clairs que l'étoile des cieux,
J'aimais ses yeux malicieux.
   Dansons la gigue !

Elle avait des façons vraiment
De désoler un pauvre amant,
Que c'en était vraiment charmant !
   Dansons la gigue !

Mais je trouve encore meilleur
Le baiser de sa bouche en fleur,
Depuis qu'elle est morte à mon cœur.
   Dansons la gigue !

Je me souviens, je me souviens
Des heures et des entretiens,
Et c'est le meilleur de mes biens.
   Dansons la gigue !

PAUL VERLAINE (1844–96).

(140)

CHANSON DOUCE

Écoutez la chanson bien douce
Qui ne pleure que pour vous plaire.
Elle est discrète, elle est légère :
Un frisson d'eau sur de la mousse !

La voix vous fut connue (et chère?),
Mais à présent elle est voilée
Comme une veuve désolée,
Pourtant comme elle encore fière,

Et dans les longs plis de son voile
Qui palpite aux brises d'automne
Cache et montre au cœur qui s'étonne
La vérité comme une étoile.

Elle dit, la voix reconnue,
Que la bonté c'est notre vie,
Que de la haine et de l'envie
Rien ne reste, la mort venue.

Elle parle aussi de la gloire
D'être simple sans plus attendre,
Et de noces d'or et du tendre
Bonheur d'une paix sans victoire.

Accueillez la voix qui persiste
Dans son naïf épithalame.
Allez, rien n'est meilleur à l'âme
Que de faire une âme moins triste !

Elle est 'en peine' et 'de passage,'
L'âme qui souffre sans colère,
Et comme sa morale est claire ! . . .
Écoutez la chanson bien sage.

VERLAINE.

(141)

UN VEUF PARLE

Je vois un groupe sur la mer.
Quelle mer? Celle de mes larmes.
Mes yeux mouillés du vent amer
Dan cette nuit d'ombre et d'alarmes
Sont deux étoiles sur la mer.

C'est une toute jeune femme
Et son enfant déjà tout grand
Dans une barque où nul ne rame,
Sans mât ni voile, en plein courant . . .
Un jeune garçon, une femme!

En plein courant dans l'ouragan!
L'enfant se cramponne à sa mère
Qui ne sait plus où, non plus qu'en . . .
Ni plus rien, et qui, folle, espère
En le courant, en l'ouragan.

Espérez en Dieu, pauvre folle,
Crois en notre Père, petit.
La tempête qui vous désole,
Mon cœur de là-haut vous prédit
Qu'elle va cesser, petit, folle!

Et paix au groupe sur la mer,
Sur cette mer de bonnes larmes!
Mes yeux joyeux dans le ciel clair,
Par cette nuit sans plus d'alarmes,
Sont deux bons anges sur la mer.

VERLAINE.

(142)

LA FIN

Eh bien, tous ces marins, — matelots, capitaines,
Dans leur grand océan à jamais engloutis,
Partis insoucieux pour leurs courses lointaines,
Sont morts, — absolument comme ils étaient partis . . .

Allons! c'est leur métier, ils sont morts dans leurs bottes!
Leur *boujaron* au cœur, tout vifs dans leurs capotes . . .
— Morts. . . . Merci: la *Camarde* a pas le pied marin;
Qu'elle couche avec vous: c'est votre bonne femme . . .
— Eux, allons donc: Entiers! enlevés par la lame!
    Ou perdus dans un grain . . .

Un grain . . . est-ce la mort, ça? la basse voilure
Battant à travers l'eau! — Ça se dit *encombrer* . . .
Un coup de mer plombé, puis la haute mâture
Fouettant les flots ras, — et ça se dit *sombrer.*

— Sombrer, — sondez ce mot. Votre *mort* est bien pâle
Et pas grand'chose à bord, sous la lourde rafale . . .
Pas grand'chose devant le grand sourire amer
Du matelot qui lutte — Allons donc, de la place! —
Vieux fantôme éventé, la Mort change de face :
      La Mer! . . .

Noyés? — Eh! allons donc! Les *noyés* sont d'eau douce.
— Coulés! corps et biens! Et, jusqu'au petit mousse,
Le défi dans les yeux, dans les dents le juron!
A l'écume crachant une chique râlée,
Buvant sans hauts-de-cœur *la grand'tasse salée* . . .
      — Comme ils ont bu leur boujaron. —

   .   .   .   .   .

Pas de fond de six pieds, ni rats de cimetière :
Eux, ils vont aux requins! L'âme d'un matelot,
Au lieu de suinter dans vos pommes de terre,
      Respire à chaque flot . . .

   .   .   .   .   .

Écoutez, écoutez la tourmente qui beugle! . . .
C'est leur anniversaire. Il revient bien souvent.
O poète, gardez pour vous vos chants d'aveugle ;
— Eux, le *De profundis* que leur corne le vent.

. . . Qu'ils roulent infinis dans les espaces vierges!
      Qu'ils roulent verts et nus,
Sans clous et sans sapin, sans couvercle, sans cierges . . .
— Laissez-les donc rouler, *terriens* parvenus!

            TRISTAN CORBIÈRE (1845–75).

(143)
LE VIEUX PONT

Sur le vieux pont verdi de mousse
Et tout rongé de lichens roux,
Deux amants parlaient à voix douce :
    Et c'était nous !

Lui, penché tendrement vers elle,
Lui disait l'amour et la foi
Qu'il portait en son cœur fidèle ;
    Et c'était moi !

Elle semblait, pâle, incertaine,
Tremblante et pourtant sans effroi,
Écouter une voix lointaine ;
    Et c'était toi !

Sur le vieux pont toujours le même,
Deux amants ont pris rendez-vous :
Il lui dit, elle croit, qu'il l'aime ;
    Ce n'est plus nous !

Auguste Angellier (1848–1911).

Reprinted by permission of the publishers, the Librairie Hachette and the Faculty of Literature at Lille University.

(144)
AUTOMNE

Dans le parc aux lointains voilés de brume, sous
Les grands arbres d'où tombe avec un bruit très doux
L'adieu des feuilles d'or parmi la solitude,
Sous le ciel pâlissant comme de lassitude,
Nous irons, si tu veux, jusqu'au soir, à pas lents,
Bercer l'été qui meurt dans nos cœurs indolents.
Nous marcherons parmi les muettes allées ;
Et cet amer parfum qu'ont les herbes foulées,
Et ce silence, et ce grand charme langoureux
Que verse en nous l'automne exquis et douloureux

Et qui sort des jardins, des bois, des eaux, des arbres
Et des parterres nus où grelottent les marbres,
Baignera doucement notre âme tout un jour,
Comme un mouchoir ancien qui sent encor l'amour.

ALBERT SAMAIN (1858–1900).

(145)

L'INVESTITURE

Nous longerons la grille du parc,
A l'heure où la Grande-Ourse décline;
Et tu porteras — car je le veux —
Parmi les bandeaux de tes cheveux
La fleur nommée asphodèle.

Tes yeux regarderont mes yeux;
A l'heure où la Grande-Ourse décline —
Et mes yeux auront la couleur
De la fleur nommée asphodèle.

Tes yeux regarderont mes yeux,
Et vacillera tout ton être,
Comme la mythique rocher
Vacillait, dit-on, au toucher
De la fleur nommée asphodèle.

JEAN MORÉAS (1856–1910).

(146)

LES ROSES QUE J'AIMAIS . . .

Les roses que j'aimais s'effeuillent chaque jour,
Toute saison n'est pas au blondes pousses neuves;
Le zéphir a soufflé trop longtemps; c'est le tour
Du cruel Aquilon qui condense les fleuves.

Vous faut-il, Allégresse, enfler ainsi la voix
Et ne savez-vous point que c'est grande folie,
Quand vous venez sans cause agacer sous mes doigts
Une corde vouée à la Mélancolie?

MORÉAS.

(147)

LES MORTS M'ÉCOUTENT SEULS . . .

Les morts m'écoutent seuls, j'habite les tombeaux.
Jusqu'au bout je serai l'ennemi de moi-même.
Ma gloire est aux ingrats, mon grain est aux corbeaux,
Sans récolter jamais je laboure et je sème.

Je ne me plaindrai pas.   Qu'importe l'Aquilon,
L'opprobre et le mépris, la face de l'injure !
Puisque quand je te touche, ô lyre d'Apollon,
Tu sonnes chaque fois plus savante et plus pure?

MORÉAS.

(148)

ENCORE UN LIVRE . . .

Encore un livre; ô nostalgies.
Loin de ces très goujates gens,
Loin des saluts et des argents,
Loin de nos phraséologies !

Encore un de mes pierrots morts;
Mort d'un chronique orphelinisme;
C'était un cœur plein de dandysme
Lunaire, en un drôle de corps.

Les dieux s'en vont; plus que des hures;
Ah ! ça devient tous les jours pis;
J'ai fait mon temps, je déguerpis
Vers l'Inclusive Sinécure.

JULES LAFORGUE (1860–87).

(149)

COMPLAINTE SUR CERTAINS ENNUIS

Un couchant des Cosmogonies !
Ah ! que le Vie est quotidienne . . .
Et, de plus vrai qu'on se souvienne,
Comme on fut piètre et sans génie . . .

On voudrait s'avouer des choses,
Dont on s'étonnerait en route,
Qui feraient une fois pour toutes !
Qu'on s'entendrait à travers poses.

On voudrait saigner le Silence,
Secouer l'exil des causeries ;
Et non ! ces dames sont aigries
Par des questions de préséance.

Elles boudent là, l'air capable.
Et sous le ciel, plus d'un s'explique,
Par quel gâchis suresthétique
Ces êtres-là sont adorables.

Justement une nous appelle,
Pour l'aider à chercher sa bague
Perdue (où, dans ce terrain vague ?) :
Un souvenir d'Amour, dit-elle !

Ces êtres-là sont adorables !

LAFORGUE.

(150)

INVOCATION

Pour que la nuit soit douce, il faudra que les roses,
Du jardin parfumé jusques à la maison,
Par la fenêtre ouverte à leurs odeurs écloses,
Parfument mollement l'ombre où nous nous taisons.

Pour que la nuit soit belle, il faudra le silence
De la campagne obscure et du ciel étoilé.
Et que chacun de nous entende ce qu'il pense
Redit par une voix qui n'aura pas parlé.

Pour que la nuit soit belle et douce et soit divine,
Le silence et les fleurs ne lui suffiront pas,
Ni le jardin nocturne et ses roses voisines,
Ni la terre qui dort, sans rumeurs et sans pas.

Car vous seul, bel Amour, vous pouvez, si vous êtes
Favorable à nos cœurs qu'unit la volupté,
Ajouter en secret à ces heures parfaites
Une grave, profonde et suprême beauté.

HENRI DE RÉGNIER (1864–   ).

(151)

AH! CE BRUIT AFFREUX DE LA VIE . . .

Ah! ce bruit affreux de la vie!
Et que dormir serait meilleur
Dans la terre où le caillou crie
Sous la bêche du fossoyeur!

Le soleil a toute ma haine;
Je suis rassasié de voir
Sa lumière quotidienne
Se rire de mon désespoir.

Ah! pouvoir donc enfin m'étendre
Dans le seul lit où l'on soit seul,
Et dans l'ombre attentive entendre
Les vers découdre mon linceul!

Et, quand en moi l'être qui pense
Sera dissous lui-même, alors,
Au cœur de l'éternel silence
N'être qu'un mort entre les morts!

CHARLES GUÉRIN (1873–1907).

(152)

ON TROUVE DANS MES ANCIENS VERS . . .

On trouve dans mes anciens vers
Une veine de poésie,
Tout ingénue avec des airs
De ruisseau bleu qui balbutie.

Je lui laissais hors de mon cœur
Suivre sa pente naturelle;
Elle n'avait que sa fraîcheur
Et sa négligence pour elle.

J'étais libre alors du souci
D'atteindre à la forme parfaite:
Pourquoi ne suis-je pas ainsi
Resté naïvement poète?

GUÉRIN.

(153)

JE SAIS QUE TU ES PAUVRE . . .

Je sais que tu es pauvre:
Tes robes sont modestes.
Mine douce, il me reste
Ma douleur: je te l'offre.

Mais tu es plus jolie
Que les autres, ta bouche
Sent bon — quand tu me touches
La main, j'ai la folie.

Tu es pauvre, et à cause
De cela tu es bonne;
Tu veux que je te donne
Des baisers et des roses.

Car tu es jeune fille,
Les livres t'ont fait croire
Et les belles histoires,
Qu'il fallait des charmilles,

Des roses et des mûres,
Et des fleurs des prairies,
Que dans la poésie
On parlait de ramures.

Je sais que tu es pauvre :
Tes robes sont modestes.
Mine douce, il me reste
Ma douleur : je te l'offre.

FRANCIS JAMMES (1868–   ).

(154)

POUR ALLER AU PARADIS AVEC LES ÂNES

Lorsqu'il faudra aller vers Vous, ô mon Dieu, faites
Que ce soit par un jour où la campagne en fête
Poudroiera.   Je désire, ainsi que je fis ici-bas,
Choisir un chemin pour aller, comme il me plaira,
Au Paradis, où sont en plein jour les étoiles.
Je prendrai mon bâton et sur la grande route
J'irai, et je dirai anx ânes, mes amis :
Je suis Francis Jammes et je vais au Paradis,
Car il n'y a pas d'enfer au pays du Bon-Dieu.
Je leur dirai : Venez, doux amis du ciel bleu,
Pauvres bêtes chéries qui, d'un brusque mouvement d'oreille,
Chassez les mouches plates, les coups et les abeilles . . .

Que je Vous apparaisse au milieu de ces bêtes
Que j'aime tant parce qu'elles baissent la tête
Doucement, et s'arrêtent en joignant leurs petits pieds
D'une façon bien douce et qui vous fait pitié.
J'arriverai suivi de leurs milliers d'oreilles,
Suivi de ceux qui portèrent au flanc des corbeilles,
De ceux traînant des voitures de saltimbanques
Ou des voitures de plumeaux et de fer-blanc,
De ceux qui ont au dos des bidons bossués,
Des ânesses pleines comme des outres, aux pas cassés,
De ceux à qui l'on met de petits pantalons
A cause des plaies bleues et suintantes que font
Les mouches entêtées qui s'y groupent en ronds.
Mon Dieu, faites qu'avec ces ânes je Vous vienne,
Faites que, dans la paix, des anges nous conduisent
Vers des ruisseaux touffus où tremblent des cerises

Lisses comme la chair qui rit des jeunes filles,
Et faites que, penché dans ce séjour des âmes,
Sur vos divines eaux, je sois pareil aux ânes
Qui mireront leur humble et douce pauvreté
A la limpidité de l'amour éternel.

JAMMES.

(155)

PRIÈRE POUR QU'UN ENFANT NE MEURE PAS

Mon Dieu, conservez-leur ce tout petit enfant,
Comme vous conservez une herbe dans le vent.
Qu'est-ce que ça vous fait, puisque la mère pleure,
De ne pas le faire mourir là, tout à l'heure,
Comme une chose que l'on ne peut éviter?
Si vous le laissez vivre, il s'en ira jeter
Des roses, l'an prochain, dans la Fête-Dieu claire!

Mais vous êtes trop bon. Ce n'est pas vous, mon Dieu,
Qui, sur les joues en roses, posez la mort bleue,
A moins que vous n'ayez de beaux endroits où mettre
Auprès de leurs mamans leurs fils à la fenêtre?
Mais pourquoi pas ici? Ah! Puisque l'heure sonne,
Rappelez-vous, mon Dieu, devant l'enfant qui meurt,
Que vous vivez toujours auprès de votre Mère.

JAMMES.

(156)

LA DERNIÈRE VISITEUSE

Elle entrera chez moi, comme ma bien-aimée,
Sans frapper à la porte et familièrement,
Ne faisant ni de bruit, ni de dérangement,
Enfin comme entrerait la femme accoutumée.

D'ailleurs, comme déjà la chère le savait,
Elle n'aura pas peur en voyant mon visage
Si pâle et si défait, et bien douce et bien sage,
S'assoiera sans parler à mon triste chevet.

Et moi, qui dès longtemps suis fait à la pensée
D'être un jour visité par elle, je serai
Sans émoi de la voir, et je la laisserai,
Sans dégoût, dans sa main prendre ma main glacée.

Lors elle parlera, doucement et très bas,
Des choses du passé, d'une province chère,
D'une maison bien close et pleine de mystère,
Et de tristes amours que je n'oublierai pas.

Et, maternellement, comme l'eût fait ma mère,
Après m'avoir parlè quelque temps du bon Dieu,
La chère me dira : 'Veux-tu dormir un peu?'
Et, content de rêver, je clorai ma paupière.

GRÉGOIRE LE ROY (1862–).

INDEX OF FIRST LINES OF TRANSLATIONS

o

INDEX OF AUTHORS AND TITLES OF
ANONYMOUS POEMS IN APPENDIX

GENERAL INDEX